The editors and authors of this volume wish to acknowledge the generous support of the Spencer Foundation and the Annenberg Institute for School Reform. Grants from these organizations made possible the conference at which these chapters were first presented.

CLIO

AT THE TABLE

HISTORY OF
SCHOOLS &
SCHOOLING

Alan R. Sadovnik and Susan F. Semel
General Editors

Vol. 52

PETER LANG
New York • Washington, D.C./Baltimore • Bern
Frankfurt am Main • Berlin • Brussels • Vienna • Oxford

CLIO

AT THE TABLE

Using History to Inform
and Improve Education Policy

Edited by
Kenneth K. Wong & Robert Rothman

PETER LANG
New York • Washington, D.C./Baltimore • Bern
Frankfurt am Main • Berlin • Brussels • Vienna • Oxford

Library of Congress Cataloging-in-Publication Data

Clio at the table: using history to inform and improve education policy /
edited by Kenneth Wong, Robert Rothman.
p. cm. — (History of schools and schooling; vol. 52)
Includes bibliographical references and index.
1. Urban schools—United States. 2. Education and state—United States.
3. School improvement programs—United States.
4. Educational change—United States. 5. Education—History—20th century.
I. Wong, Kenneth K. II. Rothman, Robert.
LC5131.C556   379.73—dc22   2008040422
ISBN 978-1-4331-0409-1 (hardcover)
ISBN 978-1-4331-0410-7 (paperback)
ISSN 1089-0678

Bibliographic information published by **Die Deutsche Bibliothek**.
Die Deutsche Bibliothek lists this publication in the "Deutsche
Nationalbibliografie"; detailed bibliographic data is available
on the Internet at http://dnb.ddb.de/.

Cover design by Clear Point Designs

The paper in this book meets the guidelines for permanence and durability
of the Committee on Production Guidelines for Book Longevity
of the Council of Library Resources.

© 2009 Peter Lang Publishing, Inc., New York
29 Broadway, 18th floor, New York, NY 10006
www.peterlang.com

Printed in the United States of America

Table OF Contents

Bringing Clio TO THE Table

KENNETH K. WONG AND ROBERT ROTHMAN

Policymakers and history have long had an uneasy relationship. On the one hand, policymakers often misapply historical analogies to argue for contemporary policies. On the other hand, policymakers sometimes ignore history altogether and propose ideas that a study of history might suggest are inappropriate.

There are many examples of efforts by policymakers to invoke historical analogies to support the particular policies they advocate. Consider debates about national security. Those who back military efforts to stop potential foes from aggression frequently raise the cry of "Munich," referring to the British Prime Minister Neville Chamberlain's 1938 agreement that failed to stop Hitler's march across Europe. By analogy, policymakers contend that any agreement with a potential aggressor would be similarly futile.

At the same time, opponents of military action often cry "Vietnam" to warn against armed involvement with uncertain ends. By using this analogy, policymakers warn that military action might lead to a protracted, costly war that jeopardizes public support.

Historians often wince at these analogies and point out, usually futilely, that those who invoke them are often selective in the historical facts they muster, and that the current situations to which they apply the analogies are rarely comparable to the historical periods to which they refer. Nevertheless, the analogies at least bring history into the debate.

Not so in the cases when policymakers propose ideas without regard to the historical record. In their eagerness to try something new, policymakers frequently come up with plans that might have been tried before. For example, in 1991 President George H.W. Bush proposed establishing "New American Schools" that would implement innovative designs in 535 communities around the nation. As some educators noted at the time, President Nixon had implemented a similar plan, known as "experimental schools," twenty years before, and that idea had left little lasting impact.[1]

Despite the sometimes tense connections between policy and history, there are many ways in which the two can work together effectively. A study of history can offer some important perspectives to educators and policymakers engaged in debates over education policy in the early twenty-first century.

For one thing, history shows that many of today's debates are hardly new, and have raged for decades, if not centuries. In the mid-nineteenth century, for example, educators in Washington, DC, fought fiercely over what to teach and how to teach it, in language that has many echoes in today's "reading wars." How our counterparts dealt with such questions in the 1800s can help inform how we address them today.

In addition, a study of history can also imbue educators and policymakers with a dose of humility. Perhaps more than most endeavors, education has long been the subject of millennial hopes and aspirations, most of which fell far short of their initial goals (the title of David Tyack and Larry Cuban's classic work, *Tinkering Toward Utopia*, neatly sums up the record). Not only have reforms been aimed at improving education, they have often been designed explicitly to transform American society, whether by turning millions of immigrants into patriotic Americans and industrious laborers or quelling urban unrest by strengthening youths' civic values. By showing the gaps between the ambitious goals of reformers and the changes that they managed to accomplish, a study of history might help persuade latter-day reformers to seek more realistic aims.

History can also help lower the volume on contemporary debates by illuminating the provenance of contemporary ideas and suggesting to today's educators that their foes might represent a significant historical tradition. For example, one of the most heated issues over the past few years has been the federal role in education. This is an issue that has been fought in some form since the inception of the Republic, and partisans of both local control and federal involvement would do well to understand the arguments and traditions of each over the past 220 years.

CLIO AT THE TABLE

To examine the role history could play in policymaking, the Brown University Education Department held a conference in June 2007, which brought together some leading education historians to examine issues that are relevant to contemporary debates over education policy. The conference was held to honor one of the nation's preeminent education historians, Carl Kaestle, who was retiring at the end of that month, and it focused on issues that are prominent in his work: urban education, equity, federalism, and the federal role in education.

The title of the conference, "Clio at the Table," was meant to invoke the Greek muse of history and suggest ways that she could join policymaking discussions. But it also refers to comments made by some of the conference participants about the role that history can and ought to play in such circumstances.

HOW THIS BOOK IS ORGANIZED

This book emerged from the conference. Like the meeting, it is organized around the key themes.

Part I examines urban school systems and their purposes. Looking at three different periods in American history, it considers issues that are at the top of the agenda in 2008, including teaching for democracy, closing the achievement gap between white and black students, and equity in a system characterized by racial separation.

Chapter 1, "Educating Citizens: Social Problems Meet Progressive Education in Detroit, 1930–1952," by Jeffrey Mirel and Anne-Lise Halvorsen, analyzes the Detroit Citizenship Education Study, a five-year effort, begun in 1945, to promote civic education through the use of Progressive approaches. The chapter explores why it is difficult for Progressive approaches to develop student learning of discipline-based content, and the influence of political and social conditions on education reform.

John Rury looks at black student attainment in Chapter 2, "Attainment amidst Adversity: Black High Schools in Metropolitan North, 1940–1980." Contrary to the conventional view of black education as one of crisis, Rury shows that black students in urban metropolitan areas in the north demonstrated remarkable success between 1940 and 1980. Particularly after 1960, the black high school graduation rate in the metropolitan north increased rapidly, and at a faster rate than that for Whites. This chapter examines some of the possible reasons for the improvement, and some reasons the improvement came to a halt in 1980.

Chapter 3, "When Wisdom Was Better than Rubies: The Public Schools of Washington, D.C. in the Nineteenth Century," by William J. Reese, examines how the major issues that confronted educators throughout the United States—whether education was for everyone, or just the poor; whether white and black children should attend school together or separately; how should schools be funded; and whether new child-centered, Progressive techniques should be used in schools—played out in the development of the school system in the nation's capital in the last half of the nineteenth century.

Part II, School Districts and States in Education Reform, considers the evolving role of districts and state departments of education, and the implications for shared governance.

Chapter 4, "Democracy Undone: Reforming and Reinventing the American School District, 1945–2005", by David Gamson, examines how school districts evolved over the last half of the twentieth century, through federal and state mandates and social transformations, and how reformers have repeatedly, and unsuccessfully, sought to get rid of districts.

Kathryn A. McDermott examines the recent evolution of the state role in education in Chapter 5, "The State Role in the Standards-Based Reform Movement, 1980–2007." McDermott analyzes the evolution of state sanctions against underperforming schools and districts in the late 1980s and 1990s, emphasizing the strongest forms of accountability sanctions: state power to intervene in schools' staffing or shut them down entirely, and state receivership or direct operation of school districts. The chapter suggests that these policies represented a substantial shift in the state role in education.

In Chapter 6, "Learning from Head Start: Preschool Advocates and the Lessons of History," Elizabeth Rose looks at the growing state-level interest in preschool education. She examines the history of Head Start and shows that contemporary advocates of universal preschool education have misread that history and ignored lessons that might inform the current debate.

Part III, Equity and the Role of the Federal Government, looks at the evolution of federal involvement over the past 40 years. Originally conceived as a way of promoting equity by providing aid to underserved students, the federal role has been transformed to focus on a broader set of issues, with consequences for underserved groups.

Chapter 7, "Education Interest Groups and Policy Agendas in the 109th and 110th Congresses: Applying an Advocacy Coalition Framework," by Elizabeth DeBray-Pelot, provides one explanation for the evolution. She examines the coalitions of advocacy groups, specifically think tanks and civil-rights organizations, that formed to press for revisions to the testing and accountability provisions of the No Child Left Behind Act during the period 2005–2007, and compares them with previous coalitions that formed around earlier legislation.

In Chapter 8, "Equal, Adequate, Appropriate: Defining Educational Opportunity in the United States, 1950–1990," Adam Nelson looks specifically at one type of aid—at the provision of special education services—in one city—Boston—to consider how the meaning of "equity" has evolved over time.

Gail Sunderman examines the evolution in the federal role by focusing on policies under two Republican presidents. In Chapter 9, "Examining the Federal Role in Education: From Reagan's Excellence Movement to Bush and No Child Left Behind," Sunderman contrasts the conception of the federal role in education of the Reagan Administration, which sought to shift the focus from equity to excellence and limit federal involvement, with that of the George W. Bush Administration, which greatly expanded the federal role in an effort to meet political and policy goals.

Part IV, Standards, Literacy, and Policy, looks more closely at the standards movement and the federal role in recent years.

In Chapter 10, "Standards-based Reform: Lessons from the Past, Directions for the Future," Margaret Goertz examines the recent history of standards-based reform to consider the prospects for national standards.

Chapter 11, "No Child Left Behind and Highly- Qualified High School History Teachers: Some Historical and Policy Perspectives," by Maris Vinovskis, examines research on student learning and the qualifications of U.S. history teachers to consider whether the "highly qualified teacher" provision of the No Child Left Behind Act are improving instruction in history.

Part V, The Uses and Misuses of History, reflects on the role of history and historians in the policymaking arena.

In Chapter 12, "Conflicting Questions: Why Historians and Policymakers Miscommunicate on Urban Education," Jack Dougherty examines research and policy discussions about metropolitan Hartford to show how historians and policymakers ask conflicting questions based on conflicting orientations about the past, present, and future; conflicting purposes of historical interpretation; and conflicting views of historical understanding versus political action.

In Chapter 13, "Lessons from the Past: A Plea and a Caution for Policy-Relevant History," Tracy L. Steffes argues that historians ought to become more engaged in policy-relevant debates, yet warns that they should not abandon the principles of their discipline in doing so.

In Chapter 14, "Clio at the Table: The Uses of History in Making Policy," Carl F. Kaestle reflects on the preceding chapters to show how historical analyses can bring differing perspectives to the policy table.

LOOKING FORWARD, LOOKING BACKWARD

What is the prospect for Clio at the policymaking table? In many respects, policymakers in education often adopt the two unfortunate uses of history in their debates—both to selectively appropriate historical analogies and events that support their point of view, and to ignore history in order to come up with something new. Historians can provide useful correctives to these positions, but it is not always clear whether they will be heard.

At the same time, though, historians can play important roles by documenting the dramatic transformations that are underway in education policy. Education policy in many ways is like Faulkner's South, in which "the past isn't dead; it's not even past." After all, a significant federal involvement is only 40 years old, and it is continually evolving. Many of the chapters in this book, while retrospective, end up speculating about possible future trends, because the historical trends they chronicle are still advancing.

In addition, history itself—the study of education policy—will continue to evolve. Just as historians continue to write books about the Founders, based on new information and new interpretations, education policy will continue to be subject to examination. A future edition of this volume, even one that examines the same issues and events, will likely look quite different from this one. Keeping Clio at the table will help ensure that this evolving perspective informs policymaking.

NOTE

1. Robert Rothman, "New Schools: Can They Make a Revolution?" *Education Week*, May 8, 1991; http://www.edweek.org/ew/articles/1991/05/08/10270012.h10.html?qs=New%20American%20 schools, accessed May 21, 2008.

I. URBAN SCHOOL SYSTEMS AND THEIR PURPOSES

CHAPTER ONE

Educating Citizens

Social Problems Meet Progressive Education IN Detroit, 1930–52

ANNE-LISE HALVORSEN AND JEFFREY E. MIREL

In January 1951, Stanley Dimond, who had recently joined the faculty of the School of Education at the University of Michigan, published an article that was highly critical of current efforts to teach citizenship in K-12 schooling.[1] Supporting his argument, Dimond quoted from General Omar Bradley, one of the heroes of World War II, who lamented that American soldiers were, for the most part, were politically illiterate. "[W]herever our armies were stationed," Bradley observed, "the people were bewildered by Americans who appeared indifferent to the political and philosophical origins and nature of the most powerful and progressive nation in the world." He continued,

> When driven into a corner intellectually, our soldiers were forced to fall back on our wage scales, our automobiles, our refrigerators—and eventually and triumphantly to the American bathroom—for their defense. Here is an indictment not only of American education but of the irresponsible indifference of citizens who have permitted this vacuum to remain.[2]

Dimond agreed with Bradley's observations, stating that many of the supposed truths of teaching citizenship had become little more than clichés parroted by teachers who had no sense of how to make them meaningful to young people.[3]

Since the Great Depression, educators and other civic leaders had been concerned about the dismal state of civic knowledge among young Americans.

During the 1930s and 1940s, these leaders grew increasingly alarmed about the potential allure totalitarian ideologies had for large numbers of disillusioned and angry young people. As the country entered World War II and then the Cold War, these concerns intensified and educational leaders sought to create programs and curricular materials that would affirm basic democratic values and help unite the nation around its core political beliefs.[4]

Stanley Dimond was at the center of these efforts. Prior to coming to the University of Michigan, Dimond was the director of social studies in the Detroit Public Schools (DPS). His most nationally renowned achievement in that position was directing a large and astonishingly well-funded investigation of civic education, the Detroit Citizenship Education Study (DCES). Begun in 1945, the DCES was supported by five-year grant of $425,000 (worth almost $4.5 million today) from the Volker Fund of Kansas City, Missouri. The purpose of the grant was to "underwrite a research study and experiment in citizenship education" in selected Detroit schools.[5] Specifically, the DCES focused on "ways of increasing the understanding, interest, competence and participation of boys and girls in the activities of good citizens, so that they will try to be active citizens throughout their lives."[6] DCES researchers studied educational practices on both the elementary and secondary levels and from their research suggested ways for vitalizing and improving civic education programs in Detroit and the nation.

This essay analyzes the DCES and the researchers' conclusions that were published at the end of the study. The DCES researchers had high hopes that their findings and recommendations would solve the problems of young Americans' civic ignorance—perhaps even insuring that future citizens would not suffer from the political illiteracy of Americans that General Bradley had decried. Unfortunately, despite these lofty goals, the DCES educators produced a curriculum that emphasized "getting along with others" more than it did knowledge of the "political and philosophical origins and nature" of American democracy.[7] Through its analysis of the DCES, this essay thus focuses on several key questions in curriculum history: Why has it been so difficult for educators to translate progressive educational ideas into programs and practices that facilitate student learning of discipline-based subjects such as civic and history? Are some aspects of school programs (e.g., the extra-curriculum) more amenable to progressive educational practices than others? Is such translation easier and more effective on the elementary than the secondary level? These questions address larger issues in education about the tensions between disciplinary (learning in history and civics) and progressive education (learning that is more relevant and applicable to children's lives); specifically about the changing notions of citizenship, and the influence of political and societal conditions on curriculum reform. We begin by describing the sociopolitical context prior to and within which the study was born and conducted.

A CRISIS IN CIVIC EDUCATION, 1931—39

Throughout the industrialized world, the Great Depression of the 1930s produced an unprecedented youth crisis. The economic collapse caused massive unemployment, particularly for young people, shattering youthful dreams even before these dreams had fully taken shape. In the United States alone, a 1937 survey found nearly 4 million 16–24-year-olds out of work.[8] American political and educational leaders feared that these millions of angry and disillusioned young people would be easy prey for demagogues bent on subverting American democracy. As early as 1932, prominent political leaders such as Newton D. Baker, mayor of Cleveland, Ohio, issued dire warnings about radicalized youth. Writing in *The New York Times* about growing armies of young "nomads" who roamed the country in searching of work, Baker declared:

> If there is any doubt in our minds of the seriousness the present transient problem brings with it, we have only to turn to Russia for a somewhat similar tragedy for which that government paid dearly. The question which every American community faces today and which demands an immediate answer is, can we afford to permit permanent injury to the character of this generation of youth?[9]

As young Germans flocked to the Nazi banner and such homegrown bigots as Detroit-based Father Charles Coughlin attracted ever-larger American audiences, U.S. leaders grew increasingly fearful, particularly about the future of the country's youth. Indeed, by the mid-1930s, a wide array of radical organizations ranging from the Communists on the left to the Fascist Silver Shirts on the right vied for the hearts and minds of American youth.[10]

The best picture we have of the condition of youth in America at this time, Howard Bell's 1938 study *Youth Tell Their Story*, corroborated these fears. After surveying a representative sample of about 13,500 young people between the ages of 16 and 25, Bell found, for example, that nearly a third expressed considerable cynicism about electoral democracy. Even more troubling is that, Bell argued that most of the young people in his survey strongly desired the government to play a larger role in solving national problems but that " ... this enthusiasm for the extension of the sphere of government has been accompanied by a somewhat lukewarm faith in some of the basic methods and procedures of democracy."[11] Many American civic and educational leaders believed that this combination— the desire for greater governmental action *and* lack of faith in democracy—made young people potentially susceptible to authoritarian or totalitarian ideologies.

While national political leaders created the Civilian Conservation Corps (CCC) in 1933 and the National Youth Administration (NYA) in 1935 to address these developments, for the most part Americans looked to the public schools as the primary institution for dealing with youth problems.[12] As Homer Rainey, president of the American Youth Commission explained in a letter to a member of the Detroit Board of Education, "It is becoming increasingly evident, as nation after nation succumbs to dictatorship, that our own democracy will survive and prosper only if the schools put forth their utmost efforts in the development of a new and vital program of education in democracy."[13]

As the threat of world war grew in the late 1930s, leading American educators issued a series of manifestos related to that issue.[14] Typical were the publications of the Educational Policies Commission (EPC) of the National Education Association, the single most important group of educational leaders in the nation.[15] The EPC book, *The Education of Free Men in American Democracy*, provided the most eloquent and substantive discussion of civic education of all the EPC publications. Written in 1941 by George S. Counts, professor of education at Teachers College, Columbia University, *The Education of Free Men in American Democracy* begins with an impassioned plea for educators to recognize that the "current threat to democracy is genuine and ominous."[16] Counts argued that this threat was as much intellectual as military and economic, thus putting educators on the front lines in the battle for the hearts and minds of the young. If proponents of democracy were to win this struggle, he declared, educators needed to create a program that would clearly articulate democratic ideals:

> The first necessity in the development of such a program is the achievement of a clear understanding of the nature of democracy and a clear perception of the values at stake … Only when this has been done can education for democracy, as part of an inclusive program of action, take on meaning, pattern, and direction. [17]

The remainder of the book laid out a thoughtful and comprehensive vision of civic education. Counts argued that all students needed a firm grounding in the philosophical underpinnings of democratic thought and a detailed understanding of the essential differences between democracy and totalitarianism, all of which would be based on substantial knowledge of such disciplines as economics, sociology, and international relations. Above all, Counts argued, students needed an in-depth understanding of history, particularly "*the long struggle to liberate the human mind and to civilize the human heart*" (emphasis in the original). Such understanding demanded that students feel "at home in the great liberal and humanistic heritage, in the thought and achievements of the thinkers, artists, prophets, and scientists of all ages and countries." Moreover, he argued that teaching history had to include both the successes and failures of democratic states and it must examine "the forces and trends tending to obstruct and divert the march of their democracy."[18]

For Counts, civic education had to be intellectually rich and based in disciplinary knowledge. The problem with this perspective was that it clashed with what was fast becoming one of the fundamental pedagogical beliefs of the era, namely that most students on both the elementary and secondary levels were unwilling or unable to master traditional disciplinary subject matter. In fact, for most of the twentieth century, increasing numbers of American educators firmly believed that the majority of students were neither interested in nor capable of mastering "the great liberal and humanistic heritage."[19] The clash between the academically rich vision presented by Counts and the ideas of educators who believed that most American students could not handle an academically oriented program unquestionably influenced the development of civic education.

THE YOUTH PROBLEM AND CIVIC EDUCATION
IN DETROIT, 1931–40

Detroit is an excellent site for examining how American educators responded to the challenge of providing effective civic education in the late 1930s and 1940s. During this era, it was the fifth largest city in the United States and one of the great industrial centers in the world. Early in the twentieth century, large numbers of European immigrants flocked to the city lured by plentiful jobs in the automobile industry. By the 1920s these immigrants had changed the demographic character of the city from a bastion of northern European Protestantism to an ethnically and religiously diverse metropolis with large Greek, Italian, Jewish, and Polish communities. In the early 1940s, a massive migration of African Americans in search of jobs in the war industries broadened the diversity of the city even more. Conflict among these different groups was common in the first part of the twentieth century. In the 1920s, for example, Ku Klux Klan (KKK) support helped elect an anti-Catholic mayor. But in the 1930s, controversies about ethnicity, race, and religion reached new levels of intensity. Throughout the 1930s, Father Coughlin declaimed his popular anti-Semitic, pro-fascist radio broadcasts from a Detroit suburb. At the same time, the Black Legion, a violent KKK splinter group, enlisted sizable numbers of young men into its ranks.[20]

Class conflict was equally common. In the 1920s and 1930s, Detroit was home to one of the most powerful antiunion efforts in the country. It was also home to active Communist and Socialist Party locals as well as numerous small radical left-wing groups. These organizations often attracted attention far beyond their numbers. In 1932, for example, the city witnessed a massive Communist-led march (estimated as large as 60,000 people) protesting against a police killing of four men during a demonstration against Ford Motor Company. In the late

1930s, as Detroit made a rapid shift from being one of the most antiunion to the one of the most unionized cities in the nation, the city became the scene of intense labor violence, violence frequently attributed to Communist or Fascist agitation.[21]

Young Detroiters were caught up in these events. Huge numbers of them had been thrown out of work during the Depression. Jobless and aimless, they loomed as a potential threat to the established order. In the mid-1930s, civic leaders commissioned two surveys to get an in-depth view of the condition of youth in the city. In 1934, Rachel Stutsman, a local psychologist, conducted the more important of the two studies, a survey of 500 Detroiters between the ages of 16 and 24.[22] In her interviews with these young people, Stutsman found that their lives had been devastated by the Depression. Over 47 percent were out of work and a large proportion of those who were working were underemployed or employed at "dead end" jobs. Like Howard Bell, Stutsman found evidence that these conditions could lead young Detroiters to seek radical solutions to the nation's problems. Stutsman argued that most of these young people retained what she believed was a naive faith that the government would rescue them from the Depression. She feared that such naiveté would lead many of them to radical political movements. As one interviewee declared, "I would like to see Roosevelt dictator." [23]

Given these sentiments, it is hardly surprising that Stutsman called for more effective civic education. Specifically, she urged schools to offer such courses as "Problems in American Life" that would allow young people to understand and debate economic and political questions and encourage them to participate in politics.[24]

In the late 1930s and early 1940s, as the country prepared for and then entered World War II, some of the problems besetting young people, notably chronic unemployment, dissipated amid the enormous demand for workers in defense industries. But, if the war solved one youth problem, it contributed substantially to two others, namely a sharp rise in race related conflicts and an equally dramatic increase in juvenile delinquency. As large numbers of African Americans moved to Detroit to work in defense plants, racial tensions in the city worsened. In February 1942, violence between blacks and whites broke out as black families attempted to move into a public housing project in a sparsely populated white neighborhood. Sixteen months later, a far bloodier race riot erupted at Belle Isle Park and quickly spread to other parts of the city. Ultimately, 25 blacks and 9 whites were killed and millions of dollars in property was damaged or destroyed. Most of the perpetrators of the violence both black and white were young men.[25]

The race riot not only intensified fears about black-white relations in Detroit, but also deepened concerns about juvenile delinquency. As early as 1938, the second youth study published by the Detroit Board of Education that argued "delinquencies are numerous—an unmistakable sign of serious economic and social maladjustment." Ray Johns, the author of the study, pointed to a rising number of young men being arrested for crimes such as burglary and auto theft and a growing number of young women being jailed for prostitution.[26] During the war things got worse as truancy rates rose, crimes committed by children under the age of ten jumped dramatically, incidents of vandalism committed by young people soared, parents reported growing numbers of "ungovernable" children, and the public officials labeled a sizable number of young women as delinquent primarily for "sexual misconduct."[27]

The educators of the DCES believed that their work would help mitigate all of these youth problems. The social studies program of the DPS was already regarded as one of the finest in the country. Indeed, two of the leaders of the program, C. C. Barnes and Dimond, were nationally renowned figures in the area of civic education.[28] The huge infusion of funds put Detroit in the very center of efforts to transform and improve citizenship education in the country.

In their planning for the study, DCES leaders identified four key problem areas for special attention. The first was what these leaders described as the lack of intelligent participation in citizenship activities as represented by the poor voter turnout in elections (e.g., only 53 percent of registered voters participated in the 1944 presidential election and just 51 percent voted in 1948). Second was juvenile delinquency, which had increased sharply during the war years. DCES leaders noted, for example, that 31 percent of prisoners in the federal prisons were between the ages of 18 to 24 years, a fact that the DCES researchers interpreted as signifying the "unique failure of citizenship education programs" in schools. The third problem area was general social unrest and conflict, exemplified by the race riots, plus labor-management strife, and even growing family problems such as divorce. Lastly, the Detroit educators believed that democracy was under threat from totalitarian ideologies and young people did not appear to understand the nature of this threat.[29] The researchers argued that poor citizenship education programs in most American schools—programs that were unsystematic and uncoordinated—had contributed to all these problems. They were confident that their study would find ways to improve citizenship education both in Detroit and the nation.

BACKGROUND OF THE DCES

At the time, the DCES was the most ambitious and best funded study of citizenship education in American educational history. Its purpose was to evaluate current trends and practices in its schools' citizenship programs, to determine where they were falling short, to make recommendations for improvement, and finally to implement the needed changes into school practice. It drew upon the participation of social studies experts, classroom teachers, students, parents, and community members.[30]

In order to study and learn how to improve upon current programs, researchers selected eight schools from a larger list of volunteering schools to participate—four elementary schools; two intermediate (junior high) schools; and two high schools. The schools represented a "fairly typical" cross-section of the city in terms of race, religion, and socioeconomic status—"bright children and dull children; Negro and white; Catholic, Protestant, and Jew; rich and poor; sons and daughters of labor union members, or workers not in labor unions, of businessmen, and of professional men." Over 12,000 students and 300 teachers participated in the study each year.[31]

Before embarking on the study, the researchers worked diligently on a definition of citizenship that would guide their work. They sought to move beyond the "narrow" definition of citizenship as legal status in the country (i.e., voting, holding political office) and move toward a broader meaning that addressed the skills and values necessary for living in a democratic society. Thus, they defined citizenship as: "The relations of the individual to his government, and, in addition, his relation to other members and groups in a democratic society."[32] Specifically, a good citizen "(1) gives allegiance to the ideals of democracy; (2) recognizes and endeavors to help in the solution of the social problems of the times; (3) is aware of the importance of meeting basic human needs and is concerned with the extension of the essentials of life to more individuals; (4) practices the kinds of human relationships that are consistent with a democratic society; and (5) possesses and uses knowledge, skills, and abilities to facilitate the process of democratic living."[33] With this broad definition, the researchers claimed that citizenship studies were not solely the bailiwick of social studies classes but belonged in all subject areas, extracurricular activities, and community programs.[34]

As scholar Julie Reuben argues, this new conception of citizenship (which actually had roots in the course in community civics recommended by the NEA Social Studies Committee, part of the Commission on the Reorganization of Secondary Education 1918 Report, the *Cardinal Principles of Secondary Education*) differed drastically from how earlier educators had conceived of citizenship education, particularly in the traditional course's "apolitical definition of citizenship." Whereas the traditional civics course was mainly geared toward high school students and focused on the principles and systems of government (generally at the national level), the community civics course also reached students below high school and was designed to foster action rather than knowledge, and focused on local government so children could gain familiarity with the workings of their community.[35] Students learned about democracy "in action" rather than by studying the historical and theoretical principles that undergirded a democratic system. Given concerns about problems facing young people, particularly their social and emotional adjustment, Detroit educators gravitated toward this new conception of citizenship that they felt had direct bearing on young peoples' lives as citizens of their local community.

What is also striking in the DCES's new definition of citizenship is the relatively small emphasis placed upon "knowledge"—it is mentioned, but just as one of five aspects. Moreover, its placement as last might further suggest its lack of importance. Citizenship on their terms was learning about the community and its services and other "practical problems of city government"; for example, "everyday problems which we as citizens face, such as transportation facilities, parks and playgrounds, taxation, traffic congestion and housing conditions, community health. ... "[36] The emphasis was on helping children become productive and resourceful citizens who could solve local problems. This conception of citizenship was a radical change from that of the early twentieth century that had its basis in the study such important people in American history as George Washington and Abraham Lincoln, and such documents as the Declaration of Independence and the U.S. Constitution.[37] The momentum of change was decidedly toward a "real-world" focus—on the application of democratic principles in practice. Moreover, for the first time, citizenship education also included a focus on students' "mental health." This emphasis on emotional well-being signaled yet another dramatic difference from earlier notions of citizenship.

Following their establishing a definition of citizenship, the researchers began their work studying citizenship in schools. The DCES had two related parts. The first part sought to evaluate the effectiveness of different methods for teaching citizenship. DCES researchers identified five distinct approaches to citizenship education, which they called the cultural-concept approach (i.e., "Democracy is learned as a byproduct of growing up in a particular culture"); the emotional-appeals approach (i.e., "Democracy is taught through emotional appeals" such as flag ceremonies, and singing the national anthem); the intellectual-understanding approach (i.e., "Democracy is learned by an intellectual process"—the only specifically discipline-based approach); the democratic-participation approach (i.e., "Democracy is learned through participation in activities where one can act democratically" such as in student government); and the mental health approach (i.e., "Democracy is acquired most readily by those who have good mental health").[38]

The second part of the study involved data gathering about and analysis of these various approaches to citizenship education and to new initiatives promoted by the DCES. The investigators spent extensive amounts of time visiting schools, participating in discussions with administrators and teachers, and observing classes. They administered a broad range of standardized tests. On the elementary level, researchers collected data on pupils' social relationships and psychological well-being. On the high school level, the DCES researchers tested students in such areas as their psychological health, general reading skills, ability to interpret reading material in social studies, as well as their knowledge of current events, American history, government, and economics.[39]

The researchers decided the first step in data collection they should take was to secure data that would serve as baseline information on students, teachers, and schools. They administered to students tests in reading, work-study skills, personal problems, social studies abilities, and attitudes toward school in all eight schools. Teachers completed questionnaires about homeroom practices, out-of-class activities, pupil failures in each grade, and teachers' beliefs about ways to improve citizenship. Finally, principals also completed questionnaires about school activities (i.e., clubs, honor societies, service organizations, faculty zcommittees, and schedules) and about school conditions (number of broken windowpanes of the school and broken street lights nearby; voting record of adults in the participating neighborhood; and number of complaints to the Police Department against boys from each neighborhood).[40] This latter focus recalls Stutsman's and John's concerns about juvenile delinquency.

Although the researchers produced numerous publications on their study's conclusions, they were less transparent about their research design. Or, perhaps, they did not have a fully developed design. They stated they employed a "cooperative-curriculum procedures" approach as the major approach (which was used in the Progressive Education Association's Eight Year Study). This approach involves all participants of the educative process—teachers, principals, pupils, and parents—and requires them to start with a "real-world" school situation, grapple with it, and then devise ways for faculty to attempt solutions of these school problems while involving a "total-school" approach.[41]

What occurred during the five years of the study? Generally, it appeared that teachers and the research staff spent a good deal of time in workshops and meetings for the project, developing curricula and citizenship "resource kits" that were then implemented in classrooms. These citizenship programs seemed to be school-specific (i.e., teachers at each school developed their own curricula), suggesting the importance and workability of solving problems locally. Researchers then collected data on student learning and behavior. This emphasis on the "local" over the "national" reflected the new conception of citizenship that was developing, whereby students' knowledge of and participation in their immediate communities took on greater importance over the study of national history, civics, and geography. These choices shaped all aspects of the DCES project.

THE DCES AT THE ELEMENTARY LEVEL

At the elementary level, the DCES influenced citizenship education and social studies classes in several ways. Virtually all of their findings rested on the idea that citizenship education for young children should be as relevant as possible to the pupil's daily lives. This meant that programs developed for the elementary students should be based on current events rather than history; actual experiences rather than abstract ideas; active participation in roles related to citizenship rather than the "passive" study of civics; and focused on developing good "emotional adjustment," which the DCES researchers felt was the most important foundation for good citizenship.

After giving elementary pupils a battery of tests, DCES researchers found that children's knowledge of democracy was confined to a small number of key phrases and ideas that the students had memorized by rote, rather than on a substantive understanding of the principles of democracy. Yet that lack of understanding was not what troubled the researchers; instead they were concerned about the fact that children seemed quite unclear about their responsibilities as citizens of their family, school, and community. The DCES researchers believed children needed to better understand the concept of democracy, but they defined this process mainly in terms of elementary pupils' becoming more involved in student government and on safety patrols, as well as in such activities as serving as cafeteria helpers, library assistants, hall monitors, and teacher assistants—roles that supposedly would teach children about democracy. The researchers argued that these opportunities provided real "practice" in being democratic citizens.[42]

Somewhat related to the first finding was the second, which concerned the importance of increasing attention toward students' development to think critically, gather and weigh evidence, and analyze propaganda (the researchers often used the phrases "critical thinking" and "problem solving" interchangeably). The study found that students were uninformed about current events and contemporary social issues. For example, they argued that students should understand the newspaper and be able to recognize propaganda when they saw it. The researchers also believed social studies teachers should introduce discussions of controversial social issues in their classrooms, although they found that many teachers were reluctant to do so. The researchers argued that it was particularly important for children to develop these critical thinking skills through these activities, explaining that without a citizenry equipped with such skills, democracy was threatened. They even cited how people without critical thinking skills were vulnerable to totalitarianism ideas: "Hitler demonstrated that the agencies of mass communication can destroy the critical faculties of a citizenry in a few years."[43] As such, the researchers empha-sized the importance of teachers demonstrating a process of problem solving to their students, using such real and relevant contemporary problems as conflicts among classmates in the classroom, cafeteria, or playground.

The third finding reemphasized the importance of "firsthand experiences" with social, civic, and economic institutions of one's local community. According to the study, these "direct experiences" in practicing democratic principles provided better citizen preparation than a textbook study of democracy could. In 1949 the DCES researchers questioned students in sixth, ninth, and twelfth grades about their patterns of "directly experiencing" aspects of their community: how often and with whom (e.g., a school group, a club, parents).[44] The study found that while families provided the most direct experiences for learning about citizenship, the researchers maintained that teachers could and should use the many opportunities available within Detroit to offer students other direct experiences. For example, they noted that schools could arrange visits to museums, libraries, factories, government offices, and recreational facilities. Unfortunately, how teachers could make these field trips into teachable experiences about citizenship and/or democracy received less attention from the DCES researchers than the activities themselves.

While the DCES educators were not terribly forthcoming about *how* to make these direct experiences useful for citizenship education, they were quite clear about *why* these activities were better for developing good citizens than what they perceived as traditional elementary social studies content. One of the most striking aspects of the DCES recommendations for the elementary grades was the researchers' belief that younger children (ages six to eight) were *fearful*, and that these fears were aggravated by the key elements of the traditional elementary social studies curriculum. The DCES researchers were particularly concerned about children learning stories that featured mythological characters, witches, monsters, or heroes who used violence to triumph over their enemies. Consequently, the authors of the study argued that, as part of the shift to more direct experiences, pupils should read stories about children like themselves, watch funny movies with children and animals as the central characters, and engage in learning experiences from things that touch their lives—stories about what happened at home or going to stores, or adventures featuring pets. The DCES researchers argued that the traditional elementary curriculum that centered on teaching fables, myths, fairy tales, and legends, all of which typically contained violence and evil characters, was simply inappropriate for modern day citizenship education.[45]

Another major finding focused on the need for students to become more effective problem solvers by teaching them to apply the scientific method (that is, logical steps) in dealing with social problems. In 1948, the DCES study even published a separate *Problem Solving* pamphlet that discussed "problems" in the various social contexts of individual relations, small groups, larger groups, neighborhoods, local communities, and the world.[46] The pamphlet was essentially a step-by-step guide for dealing with conflicts (i.e., defining the problem, working on the problem, drawing a conclusion, and carrying out the conclusion). Each step had ministeps that outlined objects and provided cautions about what pitfalls to avoid. The guide was clear, concise, and logical, and probably fairly easy for teachers to implement for classroom conflicts. Moreover, it reflected pedagogical approaches that were active and child-centered. Yet, curiously, the conflict-resolution guide was not grounded in any larger civic ideals; there was no connection to democratic processes or to the judicial or legislative system—the actual public contexts where these future citizens could expect to face such problems. For example, the notion of due process—clearly relevant to dealing with problems fairly in the classroom and elsewhere—was not mentioned. In short, the pamphlet totally lacked grounding in substantive disciplinary content. Rather it reflected a curriculum whose main purpose seemed to be convincing children to get along with one another.

The last and most important finding stated that "emotional adjustment" was the key factor, or "missing ingredient," in determining good citizenship. Indeed, this was the principal conclusion of the entire study (and was also the subject of a book published by the researchers).[47] While the researchers also identified such behaviors as participation in public affairs, obedience to the law, and knowledge of American history and government as key requisites of good citizenship, they stressed that the individual's relationship to others in society was particularly important. Healthy emotional adjustment was the key factor in developing good relationships and thus good citizenship. Again, while we believe that these are certainly important character traits for the country's future citizens, what is striking is the lack of emphasis on disciplinary content knowledge or skills. In fact, researchers faulted teachers who placed too much emphasis on the cultivation of knowledge and not enough on the emotional adjustment of children.[48] The researchers flatly stated that the belief that "academic subjects are the most important aspect of a school ... is false."[49]

In making their case about the importance of mental adjustment for pupils at the elementary level, researchers claimed to identify two types of "disturbed" children: those rejected by others and social isolates.[50] What did an emotionally well-adjusted student look like? Using the fictitious examples of Mary and John, the researchers stated that children could also be identified as poor or good citizens. Whereas Mary disliked her playmates, did not want to go to school, and generally "did the wrong thing," John enjoyed school and his classmates and felt comfortable expressing his ideas. The researchers attributed both children's behaviors to their level of emotional adjustment and concluded that helping children overcome emotional disturbances had positive effects for the individuals themselves as well as for the classroom and the school as a whole. Thus, indicators of good citizenship were social and behavioral in nature, strongly reflecting a focus on emotional health. Such indicators included having friends, earning good grades, respecting authority, and having good parental relationships. The study found that teachers played an important role in setting misguided children on better life paths by showing children love, attention, and compassion.[51]

If the missing ingredient were emotional adjustment, how did the DCES determine the ways teachers should go about emotionally adjusting children? The researchers explained that teachers needed to recognize differences among students' growth patterns and social class backgrounds and that they needed to provide for eight basic needs (love, affection, self-respect, economic security, among others). For example, due to the DCES recommendations, the DPS introduced courses in "Home and Family Living" and "Social Living" elementary level. The DCES researchers praised these courses because they enabled pupils to "talk out their tensions" with other members of the group—providing "good therapy values."[52]

Specifically, the researchers determined that some of children's "fundamental needs" included needing to (1) feel successful in something; (2) accept other people as individuals and to be accepted by them; (3) develop a feeling of his own worth.[53] Therefore, teachers needed to attend carefully to creating conditions in the classroom (i.e., rules and procedures) that met those needs.[54] Doing so would produce emotionally adjusted, happy children who would be capable of and willing to preserve democratic principles rather than fall prey to totalitarian ideas.

What implications did these findings have for elementary education? DCES researchers urged that citizenship studies become more affective than academic in character. For example, one publication from the study focused on the developmental growth of children and how that related to children's roles as citizens. The study showed how the act of sharing held different meanings for a 5-year-old and a 17-year-old—the younger child shared toys, while the older child shared ideas. The level of "concern" also distinguished the younger from the older child—a young child showed simple concern by using a handkerchief, while an older child was concerned with protecting society from tuberculosis.[55] This differentiation in children's behaviors and motives resulted in varying academic expectations for children, depending on their age or stage of development. Yet both reflected an emphasis on practice, rather than cultivation of knowledge, skills, or values.

The DCES researchers acknowledged that the social studies teachers had a unique responsibility in citizenship education, since in their subject "the very nature of the content has for its main objectives the development of better human relations." [56] However, the researchers strongly emphasized that citizenship development was a *total*-school experience. They stated, "Citizenship education is not something added to a curriculum, something to exhort children to do. It is not confined to a unit, a course, or a subject matter area. It is not a fixed, crystallized program, but a continuing, dynamic function of the total school. It is part and parcel of the daily living in the school." [57] These researchers definitively concluded that it was not knowledge itself, but the practice of citizenship skills that provided the foundation for good citizenship. The report stated:

> A study of current citizenship programs, however, furnishes little evidence to support the idea that civic knowledge and information about citizenship responsibilities are sufficient to produce responsible citizens. There is apparent agreement that hand in hand with the study of the responsibilities and privileges of citizens in a democracy must go the opportunity for young people to learn these through practice. [58]

In effect, the more emphasis the DCES leaders placed on implementing these principles in practice, the less educators stressed academic content. The researchers essentially made the similar recommendations on the high school level, with even more pronounced and detrimental effects on substantive academic learning.

THE DCES ON THE HIGH SCHOOL LEVEL

The DCES recommendations were equally as consequential on the secondary level. By watering down the curriculum and spreading citizenship education across both other courses and extracurricular classes, Detroit's junior- and senior-high-school-aged students were deprived of the very content and knowledge necessary to have a thorough understanding of democracy at a particularly influential and important time in their lives. Nevertheless, in taking this approach, the DCES researchers believed they were directly addressing the youth problems that surfaced during the Depression and war (e.g., the concerns about radicalism and juvenile delinquency). Yet, their good intentions were routinely undone in large part because they were also following a pedagogical pattern established in the 1930s and 1940s, which assumed that the majority of high school students were either unable or unwilling to master discipline-based subjects. [59] Thus, as with their recommendations on the elementary level, the DCES researchers promoted courses and approaches that were designed to be more engaging, but less intellectually demanding, than those in "traditional" civics and history instruction. Ironically, the DCES researchers' own data provided evidence that a more academic approach actually improved student knowledge about democracy, but the study found virtually *no* evidence that a more relevant, student-centered approach bolstered students' knowledge or changed their attitudes about citizenship.

One thing the DCES study clearly demonstrated was that, like many high school students in the United States, Detroit students tested by the DCES had only modest knowledge about current events, economics, American history, and government. Indeed, the "Knowledge and Skills" chapter in the final report that summarized findings on students' knowledge in these areas presented a depressing empirical picture. Typical were the results of standardized, multiple-choice tests on knowledge of "current affairs" that DCES researchers gave in 1945, 1947, and 1949 to ninth-and twelfth-grade students. Twelfth-graders in the 1945 cohort were the most successful on these exams and their scores were decent at best. Out of 60 possible right answers to questions such as "Who is the prime minister of Great Britain?" the median score for girls was about 37 right answers and for boys, 43. In 1949, the scores fell to a lamentable 25 and 30, respectively. After surveying these data, Stanley Dimond concluded that "knowledge of current affairs possessed by the pupils tested by the Study was meager." Scores on a standardized economics test were even worse (the median score for students in the top performing high school was only 24 correct answers out of 88 questions). It is worth noting that at this time passing an economics course was a graduation requirement in Detroit.[60]

The test results on knowledge of American history were equally troubling, although Dimond dismissed the problems with an intellectual sleight of hand. Each June, DCES researchers administered a standardized test on American history to graduating seniors of the two high schools in the study. Dimond reported the results only for 1949. The median scores for the two high schools were, respectively, 42 and 43 correct answers out of 98 questions. Instead of drawing the obvious conclusion that these results were horrendous, Dimond argued that since the test was norm referenced, these students actually were "doing well in the field of American history." Dimond argued that a "comparison with national norms shows that a score of 42 is at the 55th percentile, based on the testing of 25,000 students in 110 schools" across the country.[61] Dimond did not address an equally valid interpretation of the national data, which was that American high school students were woefully deficient in knowledge of their nation's history.

Given the clever way that Dimond avoided addressing the apparent lack of knowledge Detroit high school students had about American history and government, it is perhaps not surprising that Dimond was unenthusiastic about the DCES finding that courses specifically designed to address students' ignorance in these areas produced impressive results. DCES researchers described these courses as examples of what they termed "the intellectual-understanding approach" to citizenship education. In the summary of DCES findings, Dimond simply stated, "The high school democracy experiment ... does show that all classes using the intellectual approach gained in democratic attitudes. ..." Specifically, the median score on pre- and posttests of democratic attitudes of students who studied units on democracy for two hours a day for 14 weeks jumped from 77 to 90 correct answers. From these results, Dimond concluded, "Student attitudes and understanding can be changed by the use of intellectual processes." [62]

Given their findings, one might suspect that Dimond and the other DCES researchers would have recommended at least a bit more attention to a discipline-based approach for improving citizenship education in Detroit. Such an approach might have been akin to what Counts had urged in 1941, namely a strong emphasis on teaching more history, economics, and government as a means for better understanding the dangerous world young people were facing. Instead, the DCES researchers veered off in a totally different direction. As they did in elementary program, the researchers argued that "good emotional adjustment," not "intellectual-understanding," was the most important foundation for good citizenship and that schools should organize their programs in ways that ensured such adjustment in all their students.

How the DCES arrived at this conclusion is one the most intriguing aspects of the study. Two key assumptions, which were rooted in the Depression and war-era youth problems and educational responses to these problems, seemed to undergird this conclusion. First, DCES researchers believed that "maladjusted" young people could easily become "useful dupes for those concerned with totalitarian ends." Dimond noted, for example, that some of Hitler's early supporters were "frustrated youth," and that "there is some support for the belief that certain individuals become Communists because of personal maladjustment." [63] The second assumption was that since many if not most high school students were unwilling or unable to handle traditional academic courses, requiring such courses would exacerbate the "maladjustment" of these students. As Dimond explained, "Children are often expected or required to learn things that are inappropriate to their abilities, developmental level, adjustment problems, or motivation." [64] Consequently, when traditional high schools demand too much of students, students become frustrated, that frustration leads to maladjustment, and maladjustment leads to poor citizenship. Conversely, matching students with curricula appropriate to their abilities and interests guided by caring educational professionals would lead to positive adjustment and good citizenship.

These assumptions strongly supported the antiacademic conclusions and recommendations of the study. Indeed, in arguing for the importance of schools focusing on "a course of action capable of bringing about the satisfactory emotional adjustment of all children" Dimond specifically argued *against* a more discipline-based approach to civic education on both the elementary or secondary levels. As he put it, many people

> advocate more teaching of American history and government as a way of getting better citizens, not recognizing that some pupils who have studied these subjects at three different levels of school life still develop into bad citizens because parents, churches, and schools were not able to assist them in developing a satisfactory adjustment to themselves and to their society. Educators need to recognize that in developing good citizenship a most hopeful approach is to aid children and youth to be emotionally well adjusted.[65]

Dimond and the other researchers felt so strongly about this recommendation that they published a second report, *Emotional Adjustment: A Key to Good Citizenship*, the same year as the final report.[66]

Beyond its anti-intellectualism, the greatest problem with this conclusion was that the DCES researchers had found virtually no evidence to support it. Over the course of the study, the DCES group had worked with teachers in the two intermediate schools and the two high schools participating in the project, and got them to implement innovations that they thought would bring about substantial changes. These innovations included getting teachers to be "more understanding of the emotional problems of children and more expert in their treatment of such problems"; encouraging teachers to use more audiovisual materials in their classes; establishing, reorganizing, and improving student councils to get students more actively involved in democratic processes; urging teachers to give more attention "to problem-solving procedures, discussion techniques, and other aspects of critical thinking"; making guidance a central concern in all schools; implementing some form of "general education or core curriculum" in which several subjects such as social studies and English were combined in interdisciplinary courses.[67]

At the same time that they were introducing these changes, the DCES researchers also administered tests measuring "the quality of citizenship which has been designated as emotional adjustment" to graduating seniors in several Detroit high schools not in the DCES and compared those results to seniors in the two high schools in the study. They also tested for changes in problem-solving and critical thinking skills. Unfortunately, they found no positive significant changes in the schools in the study when compared to others, and in the areas of problem solving and critical thinking they found some modest negative results. In all, there was little evidence that the DCES reforms in the schools substantially influenced students' knowledge, attitudes, or behavior.[68]

Despite the lack of evidence, in the final report, Dimond showcased four broad "school practices that helped" in teaching citizenship based on a program for improving emotional and mental adjustment. The first of these practices involved changing school organization, specifically encouraging secondary schools to adopt team teaching structures especially in the intermediate grades (seven though nine), and keeping the same students and teachers together for more than one year. In addition, Dimond urged educators to think about a system that would link a group of teachers and counselors with a small group of students for their entire high school career as a way to reduce student alienation in large, impersonal urban high schools. He felt these approaches would reduce student alienation and provide more frequent and better personal interactions between students and teachers.

On the senior high school level, Dimond urged educational leaders to restructure general education by creating "core curriculum" or "common learnings" programs. At the time, these kinds of programs were becoming increasingly popular around the country, but there was little empirical evidence that they improved either academic performance or students' mental health.[69] Dimond based his recommendation on the dubious results of a core curriculum program introduced in one of the study's high schools. Despite opposition from subject matter department heads, teachers in this high school developed an "Effective Learning" course that combined English and social studies and met two periods a day. Unlike traditional English and social studies courses, the Effective Learning course included units about getting oriented to high school, reading a newspaper, and discussing "personal and group problems." At the end of the school year, tests comparing students in the new course with those in traditional English and social studies courses found no difference in subject matter achievement between the groups, but "better adjustment, as measured by a personality inventory" among the Effective Learning group. Dimond recognized the "inconclusiveness" of these findings, but nevertheless dealt with the results by raising the following rhetorical question: "Can a pattern of high school organization developed for college preparation goals be justified in view of the accumulating evidence that other methods of organization produce as good if not better results?"[70] For almost half a century, progressive educators had used such attacks on the supposedly college-oriented nature of American high schools in order to reduce the amount of academic courses taken by secondary students. In using this argument, Dimond was participating in this time-honored ritual, but he was also demonstrating that his reform efforts were based more on ideology than evidence.

The second "school practice that helped" involved improving and expanding the role of guidance counselors in the schools (again, another indication of the total-school approach). Dimond argued that this was an essential feature in democratizing schools because it would provide more personal attention for individual students and more expert advice to teachers in dealing with a broad-range students. Dimond, however, urged an even more expansive role for school guidance, modeled on the experiences of an experimental counseling center at one of the participating high schools. "The center staff included a counselor, a visiting teacher, a doctor, a dentist, a nurse, a stenographer, and a typist. Psychiatric aid was available on a limited basis. Private offices for interviews, and a room for testing composed the office suite."[71]

His third recommendation urged educators to provide more students with access to such extracurricular activities as clubs and organizations. These activities, in which students worked cooperatively with one another and their teachers, seemed to provide ideal situations for learning how to live in a democratic society. Singling out student government, Dimond enthused, "The student council is probably the most effective organization for education for democracy."[72] However, the DCES researchers found that despite the great promise of extracurricular activities they were for the most part quite undemocratic in terms of who participated in them. As Dimond described it, students from the "right" side of the tracks often dominated student council and after school organizations. He condemned the exclusion of working- and lower-class children as aristocratic, and urged school leaders to analyze and revise "the ways of selecting students for activities."[73]

However, even as Dimond delivered this thoughtful and egalitarian recommendation, he could not resist taking another swipe at what he believed was the overly academic character of traditional high schools. Dimond chastised schools that "do not allow participation [in extracurricular activities] if a high academic achievement is not maintained." He added,

> In our judgment this is a type of disenfranchisement of the student citizen. These exclusions are based on the premise that academic subjects are *the* most important aspect of a school. This premise is false; the *experiences* a school provides are the essentials. (emphasis in the original)[74]

Consequently, he suggested that decisions about whether a student should participate in extracurricular activities be left up to students and their counselors.[75]

The fourth and final recommendation, introducing "new subject matter," offers the best glimpse into the antiacademic bias of the final report. Despite concerns about seductive totalitarian ideologies or student ignorance about American democratic ideals and principles that had led to this study in the first place, the courses that Dimond urged high school leaders to add centered on such topics as "Home and Family Living," "Social Living," or "Personal Relations." These courses, he maintained, would be relevant and exciting and would provide students with opportunities to learn problem-solving and other skills. One of the high schools in the study introduced such a course, which devoted considerable attention to student problems. When questioned at the end of the course about the most interesting aspects of the class, students' top four responses were "manners, boy and girl relations, sex problems [and], clothes . . . ." Dimond also pointed to the Effective Learning course mentioned earlier as a model curricular approach for providing better adjustment for high school students.[76]

As with their recommendations for reforms on the elementary level, virtually all of the changes that the DCES researchers promoted on the secondary level involved weakening and/or marginalizing discipline-based citizenship education. This is despite the fact that their study provided no hard evidence that these changes actually improved the quality of citizenship education in the Detroit schools.

CONCLUSION

In 1963, a decade after the final DCES report had been published, Franklin Patterson, a leading scholar of citizenship education in the United States., summed up the study's significance, stating, "No other study of comparable depth in terms of teacher development and child study is available in the civic education field."[77] One year later, the lead editorial in the Fall issue of the *Journal of Negro Education* also drew on DCES findings to propose changes in civic education nationwide.[78] Given such responses, Stanley Dimond and other educators involved in the DCES must have felt that their huge investment in time and money was well spent. Yet, were these accolades due to the fact that the DCES had broken new ground in the field of civic education, that it reinforced the conventional wisdom about how best to teach citizenship to children and young adults, or that it found a thoughtful combination of both of these possibilities?

We argue that the most striking aspect of the DCES was the degree to which it followed and reinforced a wide range of educational assumptions that had developed since the Progressive Era, assumptions about how children learn and how they should be educated to become good citizens. These assumptions included the beliefs that discipline-based, teacher-centered instruction undermines high-quality education; that "active" leaning (e.g., taking a field trip) is always better than "passive" study (e.g., listening to a teacher read the Gettysburg Address); that children learn best when they begin with things close at hand in time and space rather than studying myths and fables, historical developments, or abstract principles; that the key to motivating students of all ages is finding subject matter that is relevant to their lives; and that all aspects of schooling are equally as educational as classroom instruction.

These assumptions inspired several innovative and pedagogically exciting recommendations from the DCES. On the elementary level, for example, the push for "real-world" activities could clearly be useful to "vitalize" abstract civic lessons. For example, teachers had students deal with such questions as "How can we stop boys from pushing us around?"[79] The DCES researchers believed that by discussing these questions, and then acting on possible solutions, children were engaged in civic-minded problem solving. On the secondary level, such ideas as keeping groups of students and teachers together for several years as a way of reducing young people's alienation and isolation in large, urban schools were well ahead of their time. Similarly, seeking ways to include more students from working-class backgrounds in high prestige extracurricular activities was a thoughtful response to a long-standing problem in American high schools. Finally, the recommendation that schools pay more attention to the mental and emotional aspects of students' lives in part by providing access to social workers and mental health professionals foreshadowed innovative programs that would appear decades later (e.g., the work of James P. Comer).[80]

The problem with the DCES was not so much its reliance on the pedagogical assumptions of progressive education or even its recommendations that were inspired by progressive ideas. In fact, we believe that some of these efforts may indeed have led to more engaging and active experiences for children, as it afforded them the opportunity to apply civic ideas "in practice." Rather, the great flaw in the program was its unrelenting disparagement of traditional subject matter, particularly discipline-based subjects such as civics, geography, and, most importantly, history. Despite the researchers' stated commitment that the DCES would address issues of political illiteracy and apathy, the DCES recommendations did little to improve the discipline-based knowledge and skills base of Detroit schoolchildren. Worse, as citizenship education became a "total-school experience" (the term that today describes a grab bag of social activities such as obeying school rules to playing nicely to washing dishes in the cafeteria), the direct teaching of democratic principles and U.S. history became increasingly marginalized. Indeed, even such thoughtful insights as how social class bias restricted opportunities for working-class students to participate in extracurricular activities that we noted above wound up being used as a way to undermine academic standards rather than an opportunity to find ways to improve the quality of discipline-based instruction for all students. In all, the authors of the DCES final reports sought to supplant the traditional civics curriculum with a new program that saw citizenship education as essentially teaching young people how to get along with others. These developments affected elementary and secondary education alike.

Nowhere was this trend more obvious than in the promotion of the most important claim made by the DCES, that emotional adjustment—the psychological well-being of children and young adults—should be the basis and the primary goal of citizenship education. Given the political and intellectual context of the time, this was not a far-fetched policy recommendation. During the 1940s and early 1950s, a growing body of literature produced by such writers as Hannah Arendt, Erich Fromm, and David Riesman argued that in the battle with totalitarianism, educational, and other civic leaders must be able to recognize and learn how to address the psychological appeal of fascism and communism.[81] As Hannah Arendt remarked, totalitarianism "bases itself on loneliness, on the experience of not belonging to the world at all, which is one of the most radical and desperate experiences of man."[82] In his well-known book, *Escape from Freedom* (which was reprinted almost annually from 1941 to 1965), Fromm went further, declaring that, "Any attempt to understand the attraction which Fascism exercises upon great nations compels us to recognize the role of psychological factors."[83] Thus, he stressed the importance of psychologically and socially nurturing citizens to help make them citizens who would resist the demands for conformity and submission that characterize totalitarian movements.

In a number of ways, the DCES conclusions about the need for good emotional adjustment as the basis for good citizenship actually fit quite nicely into this framework. By stressing the need to develop good group dynamics among school children, and by trying to ensure that students were socially and emotionally healthy and happy, the DCES researchers could be seen as addressing the kinds of concerns about young people and citizenship that these thinkers were raising. However, in the process of promoting good mental adjustment, the DCES researchers believed that educators had to diminish the importance of teaching traditional, discipline-based subject matter in areas like civics and history. Thus, the Detroit educators further marginalized one of the other vital areas in preparing young people to become knowledgeable defenders of democracy, learning the philosophical and historical roots of democratic ideals and practices. Totally missing from the DCES was the educational goal George Counts had described: making American young people feel "at home in the great liberal and humanistic heritage, in the thought and achievements of the thinkers, artists, prophets, and scientists of all ages and countries."[84]

Ironically, the DCES study, which was inspired in part by young people's lack of understanding of the ideals of democracy, did little to encourage schools to teach such content. The Detroit educators seemed genuinely concerned about the emotional and civic well-being of their charges and clearly recognized that young people needed to experience living democracy. However, their curriculum recommendations trivialized academic and content knowledge to such an extent that for them ideal of the good citizen came to mean little more than being a happy, "emotionally adjusted" person who was popular with others. In short, the animus toward discipline-based citizenship education that colored so many of the ideas and recommendations in the DCES ultimately led to an educational program that seemed determined to recreate exactly the kind of well-meaning, but ignorant, citizens whose lack of knowledge about democracy and the challenges to it had inspired the study in the first place. The greatest failure of the DCES was that it missed an incredible opportunity to show Detroit and the nation how educators could design a civics program that taught discipline-based knowledge and information using exciting and engaging pedagogy, thereby providing the students with the intellectual and affective tools necessary for good citizenship. Ultimately, and unfortunately, the DCES encouraged an educational program that seemed determined to produce young people who would intellectually defend the American way of life by arguing that we have the world's finest toilets.

NOTES

1. Stanley E. Dimond, "These Citizenship Clichés" *NEA Journal* 40:11 (January 1951), 10–11.
2. Ibid., p. 11. Along with educators Bradley also castigated an indifferent citizenry for the poor state of American civic education. Omar N. Bradley, "What You Owe Your Country" *Collier's* 123:9 (February 26, 1949), p. 38.
3. Dimond, "These Citizenship Clichés."
4. For example, Educational Policies Commission, *The Education of Free Men in a Democracy.* (Washington, DC: National Education Association, 1941).
5. *Detroit Board of Education Proceedings, 1944–45* (Detroit: The Board, 1945), pp. 207–08. The 2007 figure came from the U.S. Bureau of Labor Statistics Inflation Calculator, which can be found at http://www.bls.gov/cpi/.
6. Detroit Board of Education, *Progress Report: The Citizenship Education Study* (Detroit: Detroit Board of Education, 1947), p. 5.
7. Stanley E. Dimond, *Schools and the Development of Good Citizens* (Detroit: Wayne University Press, 1953), pp. 1–8.
8. Lester V. Chandler, *America's Greatest Depression, 1929–1941* (New York: Harper and Row, 1970), p. 39.
9. Newton D. Baker, "Homeless Wanderers Create a New Problem for America" *New York Times* (December 11, 1932) in David A. Shannon (ed.), *The Great Depression.* (New York: Prentice Hall, 1960), p. 58.
10. Arthur M. Schlesinger, Jr., *The Politics of Upheaval* (Boston: Houghton Mifflin, 1960), pp. 16–28, 69–95, 162–80.
11. Bell, *Youth Tell Their Story*, pp. 231–33, 299.
12. John Salmond, *The Civilian Conservation Corps, 1933–42* (Durham, NC: Duke University Press, 1967). See also, David Angus and Jeffrey Mirel, *The Failed Promise of the American High School, 1890–1995* (New York: Teachers College Press, 1999), pp. 59–62, 65–67, 203.

13. Homer Rainey to Laura Osborn, September 13, 1936 in the Laura F. Osborn Papers, Box 17, Folder 1, Burton Historical Library, Detroit Public Library, Detroit, MI.

14. For example, on April 24, 1939, a Committee for Democracy and Intellectual Freedom issued a "Manifesto to Educators" signed by more than 2,100 educational leaders that warned of the "grave threat" that "fascist dictatorships" posed to the United States and urged fellow educators accept their responsibility to lead the fight against totalitarian ideas. Committee for Democracy and Intellectual Freedom, "Manifesto to Educators" (April 24, 1939) in the R. Freeman Butts Papers, Box 1, Folder 1 in the Hanna Collection, Hoover Institution, Stanford University, Palo Alto, CA.

15. On the development of the EPC see Edward Krug, *The Shaping of the American High School, 1920–41* (Madison, WI: University of Wisconsin Press, 1972), pp. 252–54. For examples of the EPC publications on these issues, see, Educational Policies Commission, *The Unique Function of Education in American Democracy* (Washington, DC: National Education Association, 1937); Educational Policies Commission, *The Purposes of Education in American Democracy* (Washington, DC: National Education Association, 1938); Educational Policies Commission, *Education and Economic Well-Being in American Democracy* (Washington, DC: National Education Association, 1939); Educational Policies Commission, *Learning the Ways of Democracy* (Washington, DC: National Education Association, 1940); Educational Policies Commission, *The Education of Free Men in American Democracy* (Washington, DC: National Education Association, 1941). Examples of other books that addressed these issues are Elmer Ellis (ed.) *Education Against Propaganda* (Cambridge, MA: National Council for the Social Studies, 1937) and Harold Rugg (ed.) *Democracy and the Curriculum* (New York: D. Appleton-Century Company, 1939), which was prepared by the John Dewey Society.

16. Educational Policies Commission, *The Education of Free Men in American Democracy*, p. 9.

17. Ibid., p. 30.

18. Ibid., pp. 69–71.

19. A typical expression of this belief about the limited interests and capabilities of the new 50 percent can be seen in Forrest E. Long, "The High School in Competition" *Journal of Educational Sociology* 7:4 (May 1934), pp. 575–83. On these attitudes about students in the 1930s and their policy consequences see, Angus and Mirel, *The Failed Promise of the American High School*, pp. 57–101.

20. Jeffrey Mirel, *The Rise and Fall of an Urban School System: Detroit, 1907–81* (Ann Arbor, MI: University of Michigan Press, 1999), pp. 3, 152–56.

21. Steve Babson, *Working Detroit* (New York: Adama Books, 1984), pp. 59–60; Sidney Fine, *Sit-Down: The General Motors Strike of 1936–1937* (Ann Arbor: University of Michigan Press, 1969), pp. 64–65, 109–10.

22. Rachel Stutsman, *What of Youth Today?* (Detroit: Detroit Public Schools, 1935). The second study mainly focused on youth serving agencies in the city.

23. Stutsman, *What of Youth Today?* pp. 7–9, 101–06, 111–15, 120, 123.

24. Ibid., p. 176. The push for civic education as a means for addressing some of the problems arising from the depression was not new in Michigan. In 1931, for example, the state legislature mandated that no student could graduate from high school without passing a course in civics that concentrated on the "form and function of government" and the "rights and responsibilities of citizens." That same year, the Detroit Board of Education added a required course in economics for high school graduation. Elmer F. Pflieger, "Social Studies" in Paul T. Rankin (ed.) *Improving Learning in the Detroit Public Schools, V. II* (Detroit: Detroit Board of Education, 1969), pp. 488–9. As late as 1969, both courses, offered in the twelfth grade, remained as graduation requirements.

25. Alan Clive, *State of War: Michigan in World War II* (Ann Arbor, MI: University of Michigan Press, 1979), pp. 148–49, 156–62; Dominic Capeci, *Race Relations in Wartime Detroit* (Philadelphia: Temple University Press, 1984); Dominic Capeci, *Layered Violence: The Detroit Rioters of 1943* (Jackson, MS: University of Mississippi Press, 1991); Thomas Sugrue, *Origins of Urban Crisis* (Princeton, NJ: Princeton University Press, 1996), pp. 29, 73–75.

26. Ray Johns, *En Route to Maturity* (Detroit, MI: Detroit Board of Education, 1938), pp. 123, 19–26.

27. Clive, *State of War: Michigan in World War II*, pp. 207–13.

28. Jeffrey Mirel, "Politics and Public Education in the Great Depression: Detroit, 1929–1940" (Ann Arbor, MI: Ph.D. dissertation, University of Michigan, 1984), p. 389.

29. Stanley E. Dimond, *Schools and the Development of Good Citizens* (Detroit: Wayne University Press, 1953), pp. 1–8.

30. Arnold R. Meier, Florence Damon Cleary, and Alice M. Davis, *A Curriculum for Citizenship: A Total School Approach to Citizenship Education* (Detroit: Detroit Board of Education and Wayne University Press, 1952), p. viii.

31. Ibid., pp. 17, 171; Dimond, *Schools and the Development of Good Citizens*, pp. 17, 20–24, 159, 171; Harold J. Harrison, "A Study of the Work of the Coordinating Committee on Democratic Human Relations in the Detroit Public Schools from September, 1943 to June 1952" (Detroit: Ed.D. dissertation, Wayne [State] University, 1953), p. 37.

32. Detroit Board of Education, *Progress Report: The Citizenship Education Study of the Detroit Public Schools and Wayne University* (Detroit: Detroit Board of Education, 1947), p. 6.

33. Detroit Board of Education, *Progress Report*, p. 7.

34. Meier, Cleary, and Davis, *A Curriculum for Citizenship*, p. 12.

35. Julie A. Reuben, "Beyond Politics: Community Civics and the Redefinition of Citizenship in the Progressive Era," *History of Education Quarterly* 37, no. 4 (Winter 1997), p. 400.

36. Reuben, "Beyond Politics, p. 510.

37. Anne-Lise Halvorsen, "The Origins and Rise of Elementary Social Studies Education, 1884 to 1941," (Ph.D. dissertation, University of Michigan, 2006).

38. Dimond, *Schools and the Development of Good Citizens*, pp. 80, 78–108.

39. Ibid., pp. 150–70.

40. Meier, Cleary, and Davis, *A Curriculum for Citizenship*, p. 12.

41. Ibid.

42. Ibid., p. 13.

43. The researchers often used the phrases "critical thinking" and "problem solving" interchangeably.

44. Detroit Board of Education, *Exploring Your Community* (Detroit: Detroit Board of Education, 1949).

45. Grace Weston, Elmer F. Pflieger, and Mildred Peters, *Democratic Citizenship and Development of Children* (Detroit: Detroit Board of Education, 1949).

46. Detroit Board of Education, *Problem Solving* (Detroit: Detroit Board of Education, 1948).

47. Elmer F. Plieger and Grace L. Weston, *Emotional Adjustment: A Key to Good Citizenship* (Detroit: Wayne University Press, 1953).

48. Ibid., p. 5.

49. Ibid., p. 65.

50. Ibid., p. 4.

51. Ibid., pp. 37–39.

52. Ibid., pp. 67–69.

53. Ibid., p. 102.

54. The study produced a series of "guideposts" for teachers and schools to accomplish this. (I) Teachers need to know as much about developing emotional adjustment as they do about teaching subject matter; (II) Teachers need to accept the idea that all behavior is caused; (III) Good citizenship depends on the quality of the relationships among people; (IV) Teachers must give children the love and affection which they need; (V) Teachers must help to make children feel that they are important; (VI) Teachers and schools must find ways in which all children can experience success; (VII) Mentally healthy children learn better; (VIII) Administrators need to be more concerned about the mental health of teachers; (IX) Teachers and administrators need to give attention to their own mental health; (X) Both preservice and in-service training of teachers must emphasize the relationship of good mental health to citizenship; (XI) Schools need to permit more opportunities for children to satisfy their fundamental needs and to work out their normal mental disturbances; (XII) A changed school organization does not assure a better citizenship program or a better school; (XIII) Individuals should not be permitted to get lost; (XIV) Teachers need a clearer picture of their teaching obligations; (XV) Continuous evaluation of school and classroom practices is necessary to determine the values of citizenship education programs. Plieger and Weston, *Emotional Adjustment*, 131–143.

55. Weston, Pflieger, and Peters, *Democratic Citizenship and Development of Children*.

56. Ibid., p. 50.

57. Meier, Cleary, and Davis, *A Curriculum for* Citizenship, p. 398.

58. Ibid.

59. As the author of a 1957 textbook on secondary education in the United States explained, while some of the new students who had begun to enter or remain in high schools since 1930s adapted well to the "traditional" academic course of study, "it became increasingly apparent that many of the new recruits had neither interest in nor ability for the traditional course of study." William Marshall French, *American Secondary Education* (New York: The Odyssey Press, 1957), p. 149. For an almost identical quote about the majority of high school students 13 years earlier, see, A. Williams, *Secondary Schools for American Youth* (New York; American Book Company, 1944), pp. 119–20. See also, Angus and Mirel, *The Failed Promise of the American High School*, pp. 70–76.

60. Dimond, *Schools and the Development of Good Citizens*, pp. 151–57, 162, 169.

61. Ibid., pp. 158–60.

62. Ibid., pp. 93, 95, 99.

63. Ibid., pp. 104–06.

64. Ibid., p. 50.

65. Ibid., p. 40.

66. Pflieger and Weston, *Emotional Adjustment*. In neither this report nor the final report do the authors carefully define what they believe maladjustment is. However, from the text it is clear that their definition included children who were aggressive, sullen, angry, taciturn, arrogant, passive, and overly critical all provided examples of maladjusted individuals. It was hard to escape the notion that generally maladjusted pupils were ones who gave teachers a hard time, in short, discipline problems.

67. Dimond, *Schools and the Development of Good Citizens*, pp.175–6.

68. Ibid., pp. 178–83.

69. On a similar Common Learning course set up in Minneapolis in 1946. See Barry Franklin, "The Social Efficiency Movement Reconsidered: Curriculum Change in Minneapolis, 1917–1950 *Curriculum Inquiry* 12 (1982), pp. 9–33.

70. Dimond, *Schools and the Development of Good Citizens*, pp. 62, 59–63, 66–67. When the Common Learning program in Minneapolis came under attack in the late 1940s, educators there responded

with similar statement declaring that, " ... the whole school program cannot be geared to meet the needs of the few who expect to enter college." Franklin, "The Social Efficiency Movement Reconsidered," pp. 21–22.

71. Dimond, *Schools and the Development of Good Citizens*, pp. 63–64.

72. Despite the high hopes for the DCES researchers had for the democratic-participation approach, Dimond admitted, "we do not have statistical data to support this conclusion." Dimond, *Schools and the Development of Good Citizens*, pp. 99–101.

73. Dimond, *Schools and the Development of Good Citizens*, pp. 65–66.

74. Ibid., p. 65.

75. Ibid., p. 69.

76. Ibid., pp. 66–7.

77. Franklin Patterson, "Political Reality in Childhood: Dimensions of Education for Citizenship" *National Elementary Principal* 42: 6 (May 1963), pp. 19–20.

78. "We Learn What We Live" *Journal of Negro Education* 33:4 (Fall 1964), p. 367.

79. Alice Davis, Florence Cleary, and Arnold Meier, "Problem Solving: Discussion Groups Aim at Action," *Clearing House* 23 (1948), pp. 67–70.

80. James P. Comer, "Educating Poor and Minority Children" *Scientific American* 259 (November 1988), pp. 42–48.

81. Richard H. Pells, *The Liberal Mind in a Conservative Age: American Intellectuals in the 1940s and 1950s* (New York: Harper & Row Publishers, 1985), pp. 232–48.

82. Hannah Arendt, *The Origins of Totalitarianism* (New York: Harvest Book/Harcourt, [1948], 1994), p. 475. See also Ginia Bellafonte, "In the '24' World, Family is the Main Casualty," *The New York Times* (May 20, 2007), p. 30.

83. Erich Fromm, *Escape from Freedom* (New York: Avon Books, 1965 [1941]), p. 21.

84. Educational Policies Commission, *The Education of Free Men in American Democracy*, pp. 69–71.

CHAPTER TWO

Attainment amidst Adversity

Black High School Students IN THE Metropolitan North, 1940–80

JOHN L. RURY

The history of Black education in the postwar urban North generally has not been depicted as a happy one. The prevailing narrative of big city schools during this time has featured elements of crisis: crumbling buildings beset with problems of underqualified teachers, poorly prepared students, political turmoil and racial conflict, along with a host of social and economic problems associated with vast "ghetto" communities that appeared in the 1960s. By and large, Black students in big Northern cities also attended schools segregated due to sharply drawn racial residential settlement patterns, and despite controversial attempts at desegregation, this too contributed to the perception that their educational experiences were beset with problems. These issues have been highlighted in the historical record, which often presents the educational experiences of Black youth during these times as beset with disappointment and failure.

Even so, there were success stories in Black urban education during this period as well, perhaps most of which are not well known. One which has not garnered much attention is the growth of secondary attainment among African American youth. Their high school graduation rates increased at a pace faster than their White cohorts across the postwar era, but particularly after 1960, when the urban school crisis was arguably at its peak. It was a process of improvement that occurred when critical social and economic conditions in the big cities started to grow worse. Just how or why this happened is not altogether clear, but it does complicate the story of Black urban education that has been repeated for the past several decades. If there is a lesson about history in this, it may be that Clio is a multifaceted muse, and that the stories to be told of any large-scale process of change are rarely altogether good or bad. From the standpoint of history and policy, it suggests that inferences drawn from the past may have to be occasionally reexamined, especially as new information becomes available and new questions are posed about policies both past and present.

In this essay I examine the growth of secondary attainment among Black youth in the metropolitan North, and consider forces that may have contributed to its development. Drawing upon quantitative evidence that has not been previously used to examine these questions, I offer an account somewhat at variance with the dominant narrative of Black urban education during this era. While there were many challenges facing African American youth, their record of success in school improved remarkably. It was a change that appears to have gone largely unnoticed by contemporaries and historians alike, but which may have helped to lay the groundwork for even more momentous developments in Black education in the years to follow. It also was a process of change that may have important policy relevance for the present. As such, it seems an appropriate topic for a collection of essays such as this, which considers the shifting relationship between history and educational policy. If policymakers today want to narrow the contemporary achievement gap in urban education, after all, it would make sense to examine the experiences of earlier generations of Black students who closed the attainment gap. Before doing that, however, it is necessary to address the extant historical narrative on urban education to determine just whether such an examination is warranted.

THE PREVAILING VIEW OF AN URBAN EDUCATION "CRISIS"

There can be little question that conditions under which schools served Black children in large Northern cities through most of the latter twentieth century were difficult. In the decades immediately following the start of World War II, nearly five million African Americans migrated from the South to Northern and Western states, practically all of them taking up residence in large urban centers. While many of these migrants were relatively young and well educated by Southern standards, they were quite poor and unskilled in terms of the rest of the country. They were drawn by the prospect of employment in booming wartime industries and the robust economic expansion of the postwar era. They settled in established Black neighborhoods such as New York's Harlem, Detroit's Paradise Valley and Chicago's South Side, and somewhat later in newer Black settlements such as Brooklyn's Bedford-Stuyvesant or west side neighborhoods in Chicago and Detroit. Barred from many other neighborhoods, Black families crowded into these densely populated areas, straining the existing housing stock as well as city services.[1] One consequence of this was a growing problem of overcrowded schools in many large cities, resulting in large classes, double-shift instructional schedules, and overburdened staff and facilities. These issues became early points of conflict between community activists and urban school officials during the 1950s and 1960s. Almost from the start, there was a vivid perception that Black schools were inferior to those serving the White children of the major cities.[2]

Early clashes over the quality of schooling for Blacks drew attention to problems in nearly all areas of their lives. A host of commentators remarked on the poor conditions that Black students faced in their crowded and dilapidated schools, their high dropout rates, and the poor neighborhood and housing conditions they endured. A controversy erupted when Arthur Jensen suggested that genetic differences related to IQ made many Black children impossible to educate beyond a certain level.[3] Popular accounts like that of a young Jonathan Kozol, fresh out of Harvard and teaching Black children in a Boston elementary school, focused on the seeming indifference of White educators to the plight of Black students.[4] Social scientists invented new terminology to describe Black students, calling them "disadvantaged" or "culturally deprived," although both terms eventually became politically controversial and fell out of favor. But the idea that Black students had social and cultural deficits that made high levels of academic achievement difficult remained.[5]

Many commentaries focused on the high school dropout rate, which was much higher for African Americans than for Whites. This disparity seemed logical, because high school students suffered from cumulative educational experiences; those who had fallen behind in the earlier grades, or who had not received a solid education there, were at an obvious disadvantage in secondary schools. African American students had suffered the ills of inferior schooling throughout their lives, and could hardly be expected to succeed under such circumstances.[6]

Many of the observations documenting these trends were impressionistic, the results of individual experiences or fleeting glimpses of conditions based on visits to schools or chance encounters with students.[7] A few were grounded in more systematic and sustained study, however. James B. Conant visited a number of urban high schools with largely Black student bodies in the late 1950s and early 1960s, and highlighted the distinctions between those schools and their affluent suburban counterparts in his popular 1961 book, *Slums and Suburbs*. A few years later, Robert Havighurst conducted a survey of the Chicago schools, wherein he contrasted conditions of the high schools in various parts of the city. Racial differences in curricular offerings and test results were major components of his report. To little surprise, he found substantial differences in academic achievement in these settings. Havighurst's study was undertaken to strengthen the case for focusing additional resources on the needs of Black schools, but they also served to underscore the disadvantages that Black students faced in large urban school systems such as Chicago's.[8] These analyses, of course, contributed to the widespread public perception that Black education was substantially inferior to that of whites.

By the end of the 1960s these impressions were well established, and contributed to the extensively discussed phenomenon of "White flight" from urban schools. Widely publicized battles over desegregation added fuel to the fire. In some cities there was protracted conflict over questions of educational equity, curriculum change, and discrimination on the part of teachers and administrators. A widely cited national report declared that Blacks suffered from "racial isolation in the schools," but it did not seem that most White families objected to their own racial isolation, or wanted to help end it for Black students.[9] The general failure of desegregation in the urban North, fully consummated by the late 1970s, added further evidence to the perception that Black education was not the equal of whites. The urban schools that Blacks attended were for those students who had no other educational alternatives, and who were forced to suffer the consequences of an inferior educational experience.[10]

It was natural for historians to read the accounts of observers from the 1960s and 1970s, and to assign them considerable weight in constructing narrative portrayals of urban education in this period. Consequently, it is hardly a surprise that most of the historical treatments of Black education in the urban North have stressed the many problems that students and schools faced. In her widely read account of the Newark schools, for instance, Jean Anyon described the system as "bankrupt and dysfunctional" by the time that the city's first Black mayor, Kenneth Gibson, took office in 1970. Citing testimony before a governor's commission in 1968, she echoed the group's conclusion that the city's schools were in a state of "crisis." Noting the concerns of visiting accreditation teams with "watered down" content in certain courses, she highlighted the high degree of segregation in the schools and the relatively poor performance of Black students on standardized achievement tests. Most of the book's chapter on the 1960s focused on the poor credentials of teachers working in the Newark schools during these years, and the high turnover among both students and staff. The term used in the chapter's title to characterize the period is well suited to Anyon's treatment of such problems: "educational chaos." Elsewhere in the book she argues that conditions did not substantially improve in the years that followed.[11]

Anyon can conceivably be charged with dwelling on the negative aspects of urban education in her account, but even more carefully researched and balanced histories of the period sound similar themes. In his prize-winning study of the Detroit schools, Jeffrey Mirel focused on the city's high schools as critical sites of conflict over the quality of education and equity between Black and White students. Like Anyon, he cited contemporary reports deploring the quality of education in the Black high schools, noting racial disparities in achievement tests and community complaints about the inferior education received by African American students. In a particularly dramatic turn, he described the remarkable walkout staged by Black high school students in 1966 to protest the inferior education they were receiving. It was an event that electrified the city and fueled community anger at the school district, but it also pointed to the fact that many Black youth at the time were keenly interested in learning, and succeeding in school. Mirel acknowledged this, but the thrust of his narrative is concerned with the relatively poor conditions in many Detroit schools, the budget problems that beset them in the latter 1960s and 1970s, and community unrest over just how to best organize the district. These were all critically important issues, to be sure, but what was left out was just what happening to the students in the schools. Like Anyon, Mirel does not discuss graduation rates or attainment levels during these years.[12]

There are many other examples of this sort of treatment of Black urban education during this period.[13] It was an era of great conflict over issues of racial equity in schooling and a wide range of other issues in American life. Given this, the metaphor of crisis is certainly appropriate. The dominant historical narrative has accurately pointed to the many problems of urban education at this time; it is a literature that I have contributed to myself.[14] But it also has had some important limitations. Among the most telling may have been a tendency to overlook what was happening to students. This is a difficult question for historians to tackle, of course, for evidence is often fragmentary at best. But some data do exist, and they have not been fully exploited. In particular, there is the question of educational attainment, especially the numbers of students graduating from these urban systems. At the same moment that conflict and discord raged around the schools, it appears that something positive may have been occurring with their African American pupils.

ATTAINMENT IN THREE METROPOLITAN SETTINGS

As suggested above, the years following World War II witnessed a dramatic narrowing of the difference in educational attainment between Black and White youth. To examine just how this change was manifest in large Northern cities, I utilize data from the U.S. Census, obtained through the Integrated Public Use

Samples (IPUMS) data base at the University of Minnesota Population Center, to analyze patterns of educational attainment across three points in time. In particular, I examine U.S. decennial census returns in 1940, 1960, and 1980 to assess the educational experiences of 17-year-olds in central city and metropolitan settings. Since the focus is on large urban centers in the North, four states have been selected for analysis: Illinois, Michigan, New York, and New Jersey. Each of these states has historically been dominated by a single major metropolitan region: Chicago in the case of Illinois, Detroit for Michigan, and greater New York City for New York and New Jersey. While smaller metropolitan areas existed in each state, the vast majority of Black youth resided in these three urban settings in each of the census years considered herein. Indeed, most lived in the central cities of Chicago, Detroit, and New York, three of the most extensively researched and widely discussed urban school systems of the era. By examining trends in these states, in that case, it is possible to observe changes in educational attainment of Black students as they occurred in the most challenging of social and educational environments.[15]

The story of Black youth in these cities is generally a familiar one. The population in each city expanded rapidly during the 1950s and 1960s, as Blacks migrated from the South in search of jobs in the urban/industrial economy. For most, moving from the nation's least educationally developed region to the large urban centers of the North meant enhanced opportunities for educational attainment. In particular, secondary enrollment and graduation rates were considerably higher for African American youth in the North than in the South, even in the cities. This was partly a result of history; high schools were not provided for Black students throughout much of the South until after the war. Black youth in the 1960s were the first generation of African Americans for whom secondary enrollment was a majority experience, and attendance was highest in the metropolitan North and West. Consequently, for many, the big cities included in this study were settings that featured certain advantages, even if they also posed some daunting problems.[16]

Examining data from the U.S. Census, it is possible to identify several aspects of life for Black youth during this period in which they experienced considerable advancement. Table 1 presents figures from weighted IPUMS data on a number of critical social indicators for the states examined in this paper, and most Black youth lived in the larger cities. Poverty rates among them fell, and home ownership increased for their families. While there were Black communities outside of central cities in these metropolitan areas at the start of this period, the proportion of Black families living in the suburbs grew between 1960 and 1980.[17] Although many problems existed, often highlighted in the popular and academic accounts of the period, an expanding Black middle class also began to take shape in these urban areas.

For Black youth, however, perhaps the most striking development was a rather dramatic rise in educational attainment. As indicated in Table 2, the

Table 1 Social Characteristics, Metropolitan 17-Year-Olds, IPUMS Data, Four States

Census Year	Race	Homeowners (%)	Father Present (%)	Poverty (%)	In Suburbs (%)
1940	Black	15.9	63.8	NA	34.6
	Non-Black	41.1	83.4	NA	24.1
1960	Black	35.6	54.2	37.1	17.4
	Non-Black	66.5	84.4	8.6	52.6
1980	Black	46.3	47.2	30.7	25.8
	Non-Black	79	80.1	9.6	73.3

Table 2 Attainment Patterns, Metropolitan 17-Year-Olds, IPUMS Data, Four States

Census Year	Race	Enrolled Junior Year or Higher (%)	Enrolled Below Junior Year (%)	Dropped Out (%)	Junior or Higher, Central Cities (%)
1940	Black	23.7	34.6	41.4	24.1
	White	40.7	25.9	33.4	40.1
1960	Black	49.2	16.1	34.7	46.4
	White	72.3	7.1	20.6	68.8
1980	Black	66.9	16.3	16.8	64.6
	White	82.1	6.1	11.8	71.1

secondary attainment levels of African American youth increased most notably prior to 1960, but continued to improve in the following decades. During these years the gap between Black and White secondary graduation rates closed appreciably. As Jeffrey Mirel's account of the 1966 Northern High School walkout suggested, it was a time of rising educational expectations for Black communities in cities such as these.[18] As a group, Black youth were experiencing higher levels of educational success than ever before in history, and they appear to have wanted more. The data in table 2 also indicate that the racial attainment gap closed most dramatically in the central cities. Indeed, the gap between urban and suburban Whites (13 percentage points) was nearly as great as that of Blacks and Whites across the metropolitan regions. This suggests that race was less a factor in determining attainment than it had been in the past.

Other factors contributed to the positive outlook regarding education in many urban communities. Education was a major focal point of federal anti-poverty initiatives, and starting in the mid-sixties, Title I and other programs provided additional resources to urban schools.[19] While these funds often failed to offset declining local tax revenues, they did target new resources at students most in need of assistance. Indeed, during the late 1960s and 1970s, these federal dollars were a higher proportion of all urban education expenditures than any other time in U.S. history (they were cut significantly during the Reagan era). In addition to this, a wide range of educational programs were sponsored by private foundations, community organizations, and corporate partner programs. While many of these were episodic or even ephemeral in nature, their impact was probably greatest in the larger urban centers, and they did contribute to the impression that new levels of attainment were possible for "disadvantaged" Black students. [20] This also was a time when African American college enrollments began to increase rapidly as well, fueled in part by rising secondary graduation rates. In this respect, it was a time of excitement and new horizons. Contrary to popular perceptions, the higher reaches of the educational system, so long denied to African Americans, now appeared to be opening up on a massive scale. [21]

Of course there were problems too. The reports of the day were hardly exaggerating the many challenges facing urban schools, especially those serving Black students. With the rapid population increases, overcrowding was a critical issue. In Chicago, the district's decision to use portable classrooms—the infamous "Willis wagons"—in Black areas of the city became a decisive point of controversy. Similar policies incited debate elsewhere. Academic standards reportedly lagged in Black schools, but the evidence of this is largely impressionistic. Black test scores lagged Whites'; this was usually blamed on the schools, but African American students typically came from neighborhoods and households where adult education levels were far below those in White areas of the cities. [22] Poverty and family breakdown were critical issues as well. Given all of these factors, it is just not clear that the performance of Black schools at the time were significantly lower than that of other public institutions in the big cities at the time. It is also not clear just how much the tested performance of Black students represented a change from their previous levels of achievement. Contemporary measures of "growth" in achievement were not routinely conducted at the time. Nevertheless, widely reported differences in the test scores of Black and Whites contributed to the pervasive public impression that African American students were academically inferior to their White counterparts. [23]

School integration was a principal concern of the age, and in this respect too the urban schools were widely viewed as representing failure. Indeed, the notion that separate schooling was inherently unequal became deeply ingrained in the national consciousness, so that the very idea of a largely Black school often was seen as inherently problematic. Black and White students in most big city school systems remained sharply segregated throughout much of this period. In both Chicago and Detroit, the numbers of White students in the system plummeted dramatically across the period in question, a process given the popular name "white flight." Urban neighborhoods were slow to desegregate, and despite desegregation efforts, the schools exhibited even less integration. What social scientists came to term "racial isolation" continued to be seen as a major problem in the schools of these cities throughout the period in question. This too was widely interpreted as an impediment to academic improvement.[24]

Probably the most disturbing problem facing African American children in these settings at the time, however, was changes in family structure. As indicated in Table 1, the IPUMS data reveal that the number of African American households without an adult male father-figure increased sharply between 1940 and 1980, such that by the latter date more than half of all 17-year-old Black youth lived in households without one present. This was a condition that also garnered much commentary at the time, and engendered a national debate around Daniel Patrick Moynihan's controversial report on the question in 1965 (*The Negro Family: The Case for National Action*).[25] As documented in a wide range of studies (and below), living in a fatherless household was a powerful "risk" factor with respect to school completion during this time, as it is today.[26] Indeed, the fact that the proportion of Black youth living in such circumstances increased so much during these years makes their rapid growth of attainment an even more remarkable accomplishment. It also is a factor that must be taken into account when considering racial differences in educational achievement when comparing Black and White schools at the time.

Despite problems such as the ones described herein, there was reason to be quite positive about changes in Black schooling in the major cities of the North during the decades following World War II. Even if integration had largely failed and persistent racial differences in educational achievement existed, ever larger numbers of Black youth were making their way through the schools. In the discussion that follows, I take a closer look at shifts in educational attainment across the period in question, with a view to understanding the changing behavior of Black and White students.

THE CHANGING PROFILE OF METROPOLITAN ATTAINMENT

There are many factors that affect an individual's ability to attain a given level of education, and social scientists have devoted a great deal of attention to identifying the relative importance of these factors over the past several decades. One of the most important elements of such analyses is race, of course, but there are a range of other variables that affect educational attainment as well. Historians have devoted somewhat less thought to the question, although there has been considerable attention given to the determinants of school enrollment in the past.[27] In order to better utilize the statistical capacities of the IPUMS data, I perform an individual-level analysis of education attainment for metropolitan

17-year-olds in the states of Illinois, Michigan, New York, and New Jersey in 1940, 1960, and 1980. This makes it possible to identify variables associated with attainment at different points in time, and determine just how the social and economic correlates of success in school shifted across the period in question.

The statistical method employed in this analysis is logistic regression. This technique calculates the likelihood or odds of individuals in a given category of achieving a certain outcome. In this case, the outcome in question is attainment of junior status (grade 11) or higher in high school at the age of 17, and the various categories, or independent variables, represent individual characteristics reflecting different dimensions of metropolitan life in the mid to late twentieth century. The factors in this analysis are dichotomous categorical variables, meaning that individuals exhibiting a given characteristic are compared to those who do not. Coefficients represent the logarithmic expression of odds ratios, in this case the relative likelihood of individuals with a given characteristic of being enrolled with the status of a high school junior or higher. Like other forms of regression, this technique assumes independence between factors on the right side of the equation, and allows calculation of the effect of a given factor net of other variables in the analysis.[28] This is one of the features that make it a particularly useful statistical method for this study.[29]

Because the variables in IPUMS generally have been defined in the same way, and the samples are large and scientifically drawn, it is possible to examine results across years and different combinations of factors to identify broad trends in attainment for 17-year-olds during this 40-year period.[30] In this respect, logit coefficients can be considered analogous to OLS regression coefficients, insofar as they reflect effect size, or the impact of a given characteristic on those who exhibit or possess it. Unlike OLS regression, however, these coefficients should not be interpreted as predicting change in the outcome or dependent variable.

The results of this approach are presented in Tables 3, 4, and 5. Basically, the analytic strategy employed in each of these tables is the same. In each instance, three models of progressively greater complexity are specified. The first of these I have labeled "Race," and it contains just one element: being African American, dividing the sample into those identified as Black and all other 17-year-olds. The comparison group, in that case, is 17-year-olds who are White, Asian, or American Indian (numbers of the latter two groups were quite small in these IPUMS samples). As can been seen by examining coefficients in these models across the three tables, the bare (or uncontrolled) differences between Black and non-Black youth with respect to their likelihood of attaining this level of educational success appear to have remained substantial across the period in question. As noted above, the growing presence of African Americans in the metropolitan North, and their struggle for equity in education, employment, housing, and other areas, was a major concern. But even if there was substantial improvement in Black educational attainment, as indicated in Table 2, it still trailed non-Black attainment by a substantial margin in 1980. Thus it is hardly a surprise that the coefficients in the first models in Tables 3, 4, and 5 are robust, significant, and negative.

The second model, labeled "Race and Location," considers the effects of being African American and controlling for residence in a central city neighborhood (as opposed to the suburbs) in each of the decennial census years under consideration. In 1940, adding this geographic factor to the model has little effect on the disadvantage experienced by Black youth in terms of the odds of reaching grade 11 by age 17. In both 1960 and 1980, however, the coefficient is robust, statistically significant, and negatively associated with secondary attainment. At the same time, the negative coefficient on the Black variable in the Race and Location models declined in magnitude over time, as the negative effects of central city residence increased. Indeed, the two factors switch places in relative importance between 1960 and 1980. This undoubtedly is a reflection of the general process of urban educational decline that Jeffrey Mirel and other historians have documented so well. In 1980, controlling for living in the city raised the odds of a Black youth attaining this level of academic accomplishment substantially. Indeed, the odds of reaching this level of educational attainment were lower for central city residents than for Black youth in general. Certainly, controlling for the negative effects of living in a central city setting as opposed to the suburbs contributed to this, as urban schools and neighborhoods had fallen behind their suburban counterparts both in terms of resources and achievement levels.

The third model in Tables 3, 4, and 5 adds household resources of various kinds to the equation. These include factors ranging from family size and the presence of a male parent (typically denoting a two-parent household) to homeownership and

Table 3 1940 Logistic Regression, Metropolitan 17-Year-Olds, IPUMS Data, Four States

Variables	Race	Race & Location	Full Model
Black	−.989 **	−.762 **	−.646 **	
Central City		−.041	.008
Renter		−.652 **	
Father Present			.201
Youth Employed			−1.745 **
Father Pres, Renter			.392 *
Nagelkerke R/2	*.009*	*.009*	*.110*

N=4249
* significant at the .05 level
** significant at the .001 level

Table 4 1960 Logistic Regression, Metropolitan 17-Year-Olds, IPUMS Data, Four States

Variables	Race	Race & Location	Full Model
Black	−.998 **	−.877 **	−.494 **
Central City		−.334 **	.009
Renter			−.766 **
Father Present			1.072 **
Low Income			−.148
Youth Employed			−.514 **
Father Pres, Renter			.072
Father Pres, Low Inc			−.279
Nagelkerke R/2	*.029*	*.036*	*.150*

N=4749
* significant at the .05 level
** significant at the .001 level

Table 5 1980 Logistic Regression, Metropolitan 17-Year-Olds, IPUMS Data, Four States

Variables	Race	Race & Location	Full Model
Black	−.805 **	−.481 **	−.045
Central City		−.726 **	−.303 **
Renter			−.716 **
Father Present			.652 **
Low Income			−.461 **
Youth Employed			.149
Father Pres, Renter			.055
Father Pres, Low Inc			−.334 *
Nagelkerke R/2	*.030*	*.056*	*.150*

N=7129
* significant at the .05 level
** significant at the .001 level

an income threshold set at 200 percent of the poverty line (income data were not available for 1940). The factors with the biggest effects in both 1960 and 1980 were home rental and having a male household head. Both can be considered correlates of stability in the lives of youth, although the sign on each variable was different, and hence related in different ways to success in school.[31] Combined with the other "resource" factors in the equation, these variables had the statistical effect of controlling for many of the attributes that gave Black youth a disadvantage with respect to social and economic status. Statistically speaking, this had the impact of reducing the magnitude of race and location factors in all three equations, but most notably in 1960 and 1980. In particular, controlling for these factors diminished the disadvantage statistically associated with being African American with respect to educational attainment.

While the effect of being Black was negative and statistically significant in 1960, even controlling for these factors, including them in the 1980 equation had the effect of reducing the Black coefficient to statistical insignificance. This undoubtedly was a consequence of the substantial improvements in Black secondary attainment across the period in question. According to the findings presented in Table 5, by the end of the 1970s nearly the entire disadvantage due solely to race in high school attainment levels had been overcome, at least in these major metropolitan centers of the North. This was among the important and largely unheralded accomplishments of the age, and it is reflected clearly in Table 5.[32] This finding corroborates a number of other studies that found racial differences in secondary attainment to have largely disappeared by this time, when controlling for differences in income and family structure.[33]

These changing patterns of Black educational attainment appear to be indicative of a number of trends. The first, of course, is the rising levels of secondary attainment that Black youth in these urban areas—and across the country—exhibited in these years. By 1980, it had advanced to the point that purely racial differences in attainment at the secondary level had practically vanished. Second, the results point to a geographical dimension of inequality in metropolitan life in the postwar era. This is evident in the growing importance of the central city residence variable in models two and three. As metropolitan development unfolded during these decades, disparities in the status of central city and suburban residents grew wider.[34] Finally, the analyses in model three show the importance of social and economic facets of life that impact the educational attainment of youth in each of these periods. While employment competed directly with school in 1940, in subsequent decades its importance as an alternative to school diminished substantially.[35] At the same time, other factors loomed large in the lives of youth, especially the changing family structure, wealth, and income.[36] Not having a father present, not owning a place of residence, and living in a low-income household all lowered the odds of staying on track to graduate from high school. By 1980, controlling for these factors and the geographic location of one's residence has the statistical effect of virtually eliminating racial differences in secondary attainment. At the same time that social and economic inequality was growing more severe in many respects, the educational significance of race appeared to be declining.[37]

Thus the educational "crisis" that contemporaries and historians alike have pointed to during the 1960s and 1970s appears to be more a function of social class than of race. Of course, overall racial differences in educational attainment remained substantial throughout this period, especially in the cities. The broad process of spatial differentiation evident in Tables 3, 4, and 5 no doubt gave many observers the impression that conditions were deteriorating in many areas.

In particular neighborhoods, where the problems of rising poverty, increasing numbers of single parent households, and other facets of urban decline were most evident, it is hardly an exaggeration to say that an urban educational crisis affected the lives of thousands of Black children throughout this period. Those observing on the ground, after all, could hardly be expected to recognize the larger patterns of attainment that have been revealed in this and other statistical treatments of the question. As suggested in Table 5, conditions in urban schools did not improve as much as in other areas, at least with respect to attainment. In this respect the pictures painted in the prevailing historical narrative are broadly accurate. But they also are somewhat puzzling at the same time, given the trends in educational attainment.

The implications of the improvement in educational attainment for Blacks, both for grasping the manner in which the era of the 1960s and 1970s might be reinterpreted, and for present policy concerns in education, are hardly clear. But findings such as these do throw certain assumptions about the past, and the social and educational conditions that prevailed in earlier times, into doubt. And that can be a first step to identifying some new ways of looking at problems that might eventually be fruitful.

QUESTIONS OF EVIDENCE, THE EDUCATIONAL CRISIS AND POLICY

It is possible to think of a number of objections to the evidence presented in this essay, and to the idea that higher levels of Black secondary attainment was an important outcome of urban school system development during the 1960s and 1970s. One is that the attainment gains registered in these statistics were illusory, reported but not accomplished. Another is that they did not reflect substantial academic achievement due to social promotion or the widely reported low academic standards in Black schools. Both of these points are easily addressed with some additional information, outlined below. A somewhat bigger concern, though, is just what implications these findings hold for policymakers today, and for comprehending some of the bigger challenges facing urban school systems. What aspects of the educational crisis of that era have salience today, and how is this to be determined? Such questions are always a challenge for historians, but in this case the possibilities for finding relevance for historical research seem especially intriguing.

First there is the evidence. The possibility of misrepresenting attainment is a serious potential problem. Census data are self-reported, and infla-tion in attainment data, especially high school graduation reported by adults, is a well-known problem. There is reason to be a bit more confident of these data because they are focusing on attainment of a certain grade level and not graduation, and they are reported for 17-year-olds, rather than adults reporting on themselves. They also avoid confusion of secondary attainment or graduation with success on the General Educational Development certificate (GED) or similar credentials. Of course, it is always possible that adults in many households were not clear just what grade a given student had attained, a possibility made more likely by the indeterminateness of advancing through the levels in modern high schools, where it is possible to pass certain subjects and not others. Still, the patterns in these data correspond closely to self-reported state-level graduation rates for 19-year-olds in the IPUMS data, and with a number of data sources used in other studies.[38] Finally, the analysis performed in Tables 3, 4, and 5 above was focused on comparing Black and non-Black students in these metropolitan settings, and there is little if any reason to believe that errors due to misreporting are more likely among African Americans than other groups. For purposes of comparison, in that case, the Census data used in this analysis are arguably as good as other forms of statistical evidence on these questions.[39]

The question of social promotion or low educational standards is a more difficult one to address, and it is clearly a critical issue in assessing the legacy of the period in question. David Angus and Jeffrey Mirel have argued that academic standards in American high schools during this era were notoriously suspect for students from all racial backgrounds. In an analysis of course-taking trends in Detroit, they emphasized the stability of behavior across predominantly Black and White schools in 1960s and early 1970s. Despite some differences in mathematics, with White schools offering more high level courses, there appears to have been little further curricular differentiation by race.[40] While there is hardly any additional systematic evidence addressing the matter, there are a large number of observational reports and commentaries about it dating from the time that suggest standards were low in Black schools.[41] This evidence cannot be dismissed out of hand, but it certainly can be questioned, which most historical accounts have not done. As noted earlier, differences in reported achievement along racial lines during this period, which were often pointed to in making judgments about the quality of teaching and curricula, generally did not control for student background characteristics. Considered in terms of student growth, in that case, it is possible that many schools of the time were quite effective.

In the absence of systematic data, of course, it is impossible to say much about the efficacy of schools in these cities. But an uncritical acceptance of contemporary reports is hardly the sort of evidence that would pass muster in assessing the effectiveness of schools today. Should historians have different standards? Because of the uncertainty surrounding this question, I would suggest that we should treat it as an open question rather than an established fact. While I am certain that important differences did exist between Black and White schools in these cities with respect to academic standards, it is not possible to make broad generalizations about the quality of the schools serving either of these groups of students.

At the national level, there is at least one form of systematic achievement data that can be used to consider the performance of Black and White high school students. The National Assessment of Educational Progress (NAEP) has been collecting comparable test results broken down by race since 1970. While it is not possible to isolate scores for particular states from the early years (and probably not advisable even if the data were available), national trends do appear to tell an interesting story, one with relevance to the issues at hand. Specifically, there is the well-known but little-understood rise in African American 17-year-old mathematics and reading scores during the 1980s, the decade immediately following the final year in the analysis above. As Paul Peterson and others have pointed out, the Black-White gap on the NAEP tests shrank by about 50 percent in less than a span of 10 years.[42] Just why or how this occurred, however, is still something of a mystery.

Of course these are national data and trends might have been a bit different in the cities discussed herein, but there is little reason to believe that their students were radically different in this respect. Indeed, David Armor has shown that Black students in large cities were just as likely to exhibit achievement gains as those outside the cities.[43] There is also the question of timing. By and large, the period of dramatic improvement in Black NAEP scores lagged behind attainment increases by at least a decade, if not more. Peterson has suggested that a process of "generational change" may have been at work, whereby rapid improvements in attainment were followed by achievement gains in the children of high school graduates. Armor has advanced a similar argument. Although additional evidence is required to thoroughly test this proposition, this thesis is an intriguing possibility that bears further investigation. If true, it suggests that the effect of the attainment gains of the 1960s and 1970s was not so trifling after all. Even if Black achievement lagged that of Whites during these critical decades, improved attainment provided a foundation upon which further advances in academic achievement could be established. If the stories of improving Black attainment and achievement are thus linked, the attainment levels accomplished by students in the era of "urban educational crisis" marked the beginning of a critically important process, one that may deserve greater attention from historians than it has received to date.

Finally, there is the question of policy relevance. Just what bearing does all of this have on current policy concerns in education, if any? In at least one respect the answer to this question seems rather obvious. The so-called Black-White achievement gap is one of the major educational policy dilemmas of our age. Economists Roland Fryer and Stephen Levitt recently described it as "a robust empirical regularity" that appears to have grown more pronounced in the past two decades. There recently have been concerns registered about a growing attainment gap as well, at least for Black males. Derek Neal has argued that these trends suggest that continued progress on closing the "cognitive skills gap" between Black and White workers can no longer be assumed to be occurring. In light of these concerns, the historical experiences described above take on new meaning.[44]

The data presented earlier in this paper point to a time when attainment and achievement differences between Blacks and Whites closed rather dramatically, even in some of the most notoriously difficult circumstances for both students and the schools they attended. Just how this happened is not clear; the statistics just point to the outcomes. The "how," of course, is a critical policy concern, and it seems to be just the sort of question that carefully focused historical research can begin to answer. To do so, however, means going well beyond the existing historical accounts of "crisis" in urban education during the crucial decades of the 1960s and 1970s. It means formulating a new research agenda for historians of urban education, one focused on the ways in which students and teachers succeeded during these times and in these places, despite the many challenges they faced. It probably will entail identifying sources that have not been used much in the past, and which may be very difficult to locate, such as school records of success and failure for particular classes and students. It probably will also require the compilation of oral history data from significant numbers of students and teachers from that time, a task that probably ought to be started rather soon, as many of these people are getting old. In short, a careful, probing social history of success and failure in the urban schools of the time, one designed to shed light on the question of how larger numbers of Black students attained academic success. Such a program of historical research could go a long way to helping us understand how attainment was accomplished amidst adversity, potentially offering lessons and insights that may be useful to educators and policymakers—not to mention students and families—today.

NOTES

1. Thomas Sugrue, The *Origins of the Urban Crisis: Race and Inequality in Postwar Detroit* (Princeton, NJ: Princeton University Press, 1996) Chs. 5, 6 and 7; J.C. Teaford, Rough *Road to Renaissance: Urban Revitalization in America, 1940–1985*, (Baltimore, MD: Johns Hopkins University Press, 1990) Chs. 3, 4 and 5; K. Fox, *Metropolitan America: Urban Life and Urban Policy in the United States, 1940–1980* (New Brunswick, NJ: Rutgers University Press, 1985) Chs. 4, 5 and 6.

2. John Rury, "Race, space and the politics of Chicago's public schools: Benjamin Willis and the tragedy of urban education." *History of Education Quarterly*, 39, 2, 1999, pp. 117–142; H. Kantor & B. Brenzel, "Urban education and the 'Truly Disadvantaged': The historical roots of the contemporary crisis, 1945–1990." In M. B. Katz (Ed.), *The Underclass Debate: Views from History* (Princeton, NJ: Princeton University Press, 1993), pp. 366–402.

3. Jerome Hellmuth, ed. *The Disadvantaged Child, Volumes 1, 2 and 3* (New York: Brunner/Mazel, 1968) passim; H.J. Eysenck, *The IQ Argument. Race, Intelligence and Education* (New York: Library Press, 1971) passim.

4. Jonathan Kozol, *Death at an Early Age: The Destruction of the Hearts and Minds of Negro Children in the Boston Public Schools* (Boston: Houghton Mifflin, 1967) passim.

5. John Rury, "The changing social context of urban education: A national perspective." In J. L. Rury & Frank A. Cassel (Eds.), *Seeds of Crisis: Public Schooling in Milwaukee since 1920* (Madison: University of Wisconsin Press, 1993), pp. 10–41; Diane Ravitch, *The Troubled Crusade: American Education, 1945–1980*. (New York: Basic Books, 1983) Chs. 4 and 5.

6. Mark Temple and Kenneth Polk, "A Dynamic Analysis of Educational Attainment," *Sociology of Education*, 59, 2 (Apr., 1986), pp. 79–84.

7. Typical of this genre was a newspaper reporter in Detroit who wrote about conditions in one school after spending a week there as a substitute teacher, highlighting the poor facilities and low morale among teachers, described in Jeffrey Mirel, *The Rise and Fall of an Urban School System: Detroit, 1907–81* (Ann Arbor: University of Michigan Press, 1993), page 306.

8. James Bryant Conant, *Slums and Suburbs: A Commentary on Schools in Metropolitan Areas* (New York: McGraw Hill, 1961) Chs. 1, 2 and 3; Robert Havighurst, *The Public Schools of Chicago: A Survey for the Board of Education of the City of Chicago* (Chicago: Board of Education of the City of Chicago, 1964) Ch. X; Robert Havighurst, *Education in Metropolitan Areas* (Boston: Allyn and Bacon, 1966) Ch. 4.

9. U.S. Commission on Civil Rights, *Racial Isolation in the Public Schools, Vols. 1 & 2* (Washington, DC: Government Printing Office, 1967) passim.

10. Kantor & Brenzel, "Urban education and the 'Truly Disadvantaged,'" pp. 401–402 ; Rury, "The changing social context of urban education," pp. 35–36.

11. Jean Anyon, *Ghetto Schooling: A Political Economy of Urban Educational Inequality* (New York: Teachers College Press, 1997) Chs. 6 and 7.

12. Mirel, *The Rise and Fall of an Urban School System*, Ch. 6.

13. Ravitch, *The Troubled Crusade*, Ch. 5; Rury, "The changing social context of urban education," passim.

14. Rury, "Race, space and the politics of Chicago's public schools," passim.

15. I focus on 17-year-olds because the vast majority lived at home and can thus be connected to household variables that provide information about their families' social and economic status. These data were selected at the state level because information about individual metropolitan areas was not available for 1960. Individuals living in "group quarters" (institutions, jails, dormitories, the military, and boarding houses) were excluded. They represented less than 2 percent of 17-year-olds in these metropolitan regions in 1940 and 1980, and fewer than 4 percent in 1960. The data represented in tables 1 and 2 are weighted to be representative of the general population. I am grateful to the Minnesota Population Center, and the IPUMS program in particular, for making these data available.

16. Kurt J. Bauman, "Schools, Markets, and Family in the History of African-American Education, *American Journal of Education*, V 106, 4. (Aug., 1993), pp. 500–531; Sar Levitan, William B. Johnston, & Robert Taggert, *Still a Dream: The Changing Status of Blacks Since 1960* (Cambridge, MA: Harvard University Press, 1975) Ch. 4.

17. Harvey Kantor & Robert Lowe, "Class, race, and the emergence of federal education policy: From the New Deal to the Great Society." *Educational Researcher*, 24(3), 4–11, 1995; Harold Silver and Pamela Silver, *An Educational War on Poverty: American and British Policy-Making, 1960–1980* (Cambridge: Cambridge University Press, 1991) passim.

18. Mirel, *The Rise and Fall of an Urban School System*, pp. 300–304.

19. Adam R. Nelson, *The Elusive Ideal: Equal Educational Opportunity and the Federal Role in Boston's Public Schools, 1950–1985* (Chicago: University of Chicago Press, 2005) Chs. 3, 4 and 5; Kantor and Lowe, "Class, race, and the emergence of federal education policy," pp. 385–392; Ravitch, *The Troubled Crusade*, Ch. 5.

20. Nelson, *The Elusive Ideal*, Chs. 4 & 5; Kantor and Lowe, "Class, race, and the emergence of federal education policy," passim; Ravitch, *The Troubled Crusade*, Ch. 8; W.W. Goldsmith & E.J. Blakely, *Separate societies: Poverty and inequality in U.S. cities* (Philadelphia: Temple University Press, 1992) Ch. 5.

21. Dongbin Kim John L. Rury, "The Changing Profile of College Access: The Truman Commission and Enrollment Patters in the Postwar Era," *History of Education Quarterly*, 47, 3 (Aug, 2007), 302–327.

22. Mirel, *The Rise and Fall of an Urban School System*, pp. 307–308; Rury, "Race, space and the politics of Chicago's public schools," pp. 126–134.

23. Kantor & Brenzel, "Urban education and the 'Truly Disadvantaged,'" pp. 373–384.

24. John L. Rury Jeffrey E. Mirel, "The Political Economy of Urban Education," in Michael Apple, ed. *Review of Research in Education* 22 (Washington, DC: American Educational Research Association, 1997), pp. 49–110; Gary Orfield and Susan Eaton, *Dismantling Desegregation: The Quiet Reversal of Brown v. Board of Education* (Cambridge, MA: Harvard Civil Rights Project, 1996) Ch. 2; Kantor and Lowe, "Class, race, and the emergence of federal education policy" passim; David Armor, *Forced Justice: School Desegregation and the Law* (New York: Oxford University Press, 1995) Chs. 1, 2, and 3.

25. U.S. Department of Labor, Office of Planning and Research, *The Negro Family: The Case for National Action* (Washington, DC: Government Printing Office, 1965) passim; Lee Rainwater and William Yancey, *The Moynihan Report and the Politics of Controversy* (Cambridge, MA: MIT Press, 1967) passim.

26. Jay D. Teachman, "Family Background, Educational Resources, and Educational Attainment," *American Sociological Review*, 52, 4 (Aug., 1987), pp. 548–557; Alejandro Portes and Kenneth L. Wilson. "Black-White Differences in Educational Attainment," *American Sociological Review*, 41, 3 (Jun., 1976), pp. 414–431.

27. John L. Rury, "Social Capital and Secondary Education: Inter-urban Differences in American Teenage Enrollment Rates in 1950," *American Journal of Education*, 110, 4 (Aug., 2004), pp. 293–320.

28. For 17-year-olds, reaching the status of a "junior" in high school represents a level of attainment generally analogous to graduating at age 18 or 19. Across the four states examined in this analysis at the three decennial census dates, the correlation between 17-year-old attainment measured in this way and the 19-year-old high school graduation rate was 0.9, suggesting that it is a good general indicator of the likelihood of graduation. The data used for the analysis in tables 3, 4, and 5 are unweighted to avoid inflating sample sizes, so that accurate significance tests could be reported. Results of analyses with weighted data exhibited only very slight differences in the coefficients reported herein.

29. Fred C. Pampel, *Logistic Regression: A Primer* (Quantitative Applications in the Social Sciences) (Thousand Oaks, CA: Sage, 2006) passim.

30. It is necessary to exercise considerable caution in comparing coefficients across samples in analyses such as this. For purposes of the discussion herein, I only make note of general patterns in the magnitude of effects and the relative importance of various factors each year, along with the direction of effects (positive or negative) and statistical significance. See Glenn Hoetker "Confounded Coefficients: Accurately Comparing Logit and Probit Coefficients across Groups," University of Illinois-Champaign College of Business Working Papers, 2003; and Stephen W. Raudenbush, Leon Gleser, Larry Hedges, Eugene Johnson, and Eva Petkova, "Comparing Regression Coefficients Between Models: Concepts and Illustrative Examples." Research Triangle Park, NC: National Institute of Statistical Sciences, Technical Report Number 65, 1997.

31. For examples of studies examining this question with different data, see Steven Garasky, (1995) "The Effects of Family Structure on Educational Attainment: Do the Effects Vary by the Age of the Child?" *American Journal of Economics and Sociology*, 54, 1 (Jan., 1995), pp. 89–105; Teachman, "Family Background, Educational Resources, and Educational Attainment," pp. 548–9.

32. A parallel analysis was conducted using data from metropolitan Chicago, Detroit and New York (including New Jersey) for 1980, for which sizable IPUMS samples are available, and the results were virtually equivalent to those reported in Table 5.

33. Reynolds Farley, *Blacks and Whites: Narrowing the Gap?* (Cambridge, MA: Harvard University Press, 1999) Ch. 2; Kurt J. Bauman, "Schools, markets, and family in the history of African-American education," *American Journal of Education*, 106, 4 (Aug., 1993), pp. 500–531; M.T. Hallinan, "Equality of Educational Opportunity," *Annual Review of Sociology*, 14. (1988), pp. 249–268; Portes and Wilson, "Black-white differences in educational attainment," 414–416. Also see Kantor and Brenzel, "Education and the truly disadvantaged," pp. 382–383.

34. John R. Logan, Richard D. Alba, Tom Mcnulty, Brian Fisher, "Making a Place in the Metropolis: Locational Attainment in Cities and Suburbs," *Demography*, 33, 4 (Nov., 1996), pp. 443–453; D. Massey & N. Denton, *American Apartheid: Segregation and the Making of the Underclass* (Cambridge, MA: Harvard University Press, 1993) Chs. 4 and 5.

35. Marlis Buchmann, *The Script of Life in Modern Society: Entry into Adulthood in a Changing World* (Chicago: University of Chicago Press, 1989) Chs. 6 and 7; Robert D. Mare Christopher Winship, "The paradox of lessening racial inequality and joblessness among black youth: enrollment, enlistment, and employment, 1964–1981," *American Sociological Review*, 49, 1 (Feb., 1984), pp. 39–55; Robert D. Mare, Christopher Winship, Warren N. Kubitschek, "The transition from youth to adult: Understanding the age pattern of employment," *The American Journal of Sociology*, 90, 2 (Sep., 1984), pp. 326–358.

36. William J. Wilson, *The Truly Disadvantaged: The Inner City, the Underclass, and Public Policy* (Chicago: University of Chicago Press, 1987) Chs. 2 and 3.

37. Susan E. Mayer, "How economic segregation affects children's educational attainment," *Social Forces*, 81, 1 (Sep., 2002), pp. 153–176; Susan E. Mayer, "How did the increase in economic inequality between 1970 and 1990 affect children's educational attainment?" *The American Journal of Sociology*, 107, 1 (Jul., 2001), pp. 1–32.

38. Claudia Goldin, "America's graduation from high school: The evolution and spread of secondary schooling in the twentieth century," *The Journal of Economic History*, 58 2 (Jun. 1998), pp. 345–374; Sherman Dorn, *Creating the Dropout: A Social and Institutional History of School Failure* (Westport, CT: Praeger, 1996) passim; Robert Kominski, "Estimating the national high school dropout rate," *Demography*, 27, 2 (May, 1990), pp. 303–311.

39. On contemporary data issues regarding high school enrollments and graduation, see John Robert Warren & Andrew Halpern-Manners "*Is the glass emptying or filling up? Reconciling divergent*

trends in high school completion and dropout," *Educational Researcher*, 36 (2007), pp. 335–343. Also see Goldin, "America's graduation from high school," pp. 353–358; J. Miao, W. Haney, "High school graduation rates: Alternative methods and implications," *Education Policy Analysis Archives*, 12, 55, (2004) .http://epaa.asu.edu/epaa/v12n55/.

40. David Angus and Jeffrey Mirel, Jeffrey, *The Failed Promise of the American High School, 1890–1995* (New York: Teachers College Press, 1999) Ch. 5.

41. Anyon, *Ghetto Schooling,* Ch. 6; Mirel, *The Rise and Fall of an Urban School System,* Ch. 6; Ravitch, *The Troubled Crusade* Chs. 5 and 7.

42. Paul E. Peterson, "Toward the elimination of race differences in educational achievement." IN Paul E. Peterson, (Ed.) *Generational Change: Closing the Test Score Gap* (Lanham, MD: Rowman & Littlefield, 2006), pp. 1–25.

43. Armor, *Forced Justice,* pp. 92–98. In a recently published analysis, Ronald F. Ferguson has suggested that a number of school-related factors in the 1970s and 1980s may have accounted for most of these achievement gains, particularly smaller class sizes and exposure to more demanding coursework, especially in mathematics. Of course it is possible that even these changes were indirectly related to prior improvements in educational attainment, as Black parents with high school diplomas and college degrees demanded more of the schools and their children. See Ferguson's book, *Toward Excellence with Equity: An Emerging Vision for Closing the Achievement Gap* (Cambridge, MA: Harvard Education Press, 2007) Ch. 2.

44. Roland G. Fryer & Stephen D. Levitt, "Losing ground at school." in Paul E. Peterson (Ed.) *Generational Change: Closing the Test Score Gap* (Lanham, MD: Rowman & Littlefield, 2006), pp. 88–114; Will Jordan & Robert Cooper, "High school reform and black male students: Limits and possibilities of policy and practice," *Urban Education*; 38, 2 (Mar. 2003), pp. 196–216; Derek Neal, "How families and schools shape the achievement gap." In Paul E. Peterson (Ed.) *Generational Change: Closing the Test Score Gap* (Lanham, MD: Rowman & Littlefield, 2006), pp. 26–46.

CHAPTER THREE

When Wisdom WAS Better THAN Rubies

THE Public Schools OF Washington, DC, IN THE Nineteenth Century

WILLIAM J. REESE

America's public school system was born in the nineteenth century. By 1900, approximately a quarter of a million school houses testified to the nation's faith in the power and potential of formal education. Citizens often viewed the schools as a panacea: they would bind a nation nearly destroyed by a bloody civil war, melt the immigrant masses into a common core, and instruct children in Christian morals and basic literacy. Then, as now, what was intended was not always achieved. Americans invested considerable money and emotion in the educational system, so pupils, teachers, and administrators would often disappoint many people when schools proved less than perfect. Schools both reflected the gritty realities around them and generated utopian expectations. Garrison Keillor amuses his audience when he says that in Lake Wobegone all the women are strong, the men good looking, and the children above average. Like P.T. Barnum, an earlier entertainer, Keillor realizes that Americans often embrace humbug. It is comforting to think that whatever families, churches, communities, and government cannot solve might be fixed at school.[1]

The role of history in understanding the past and guiding the present has long been contested. However, as Howard Gillette, Jr., an important scholar of Washington D.C.'s history, has pointed out, "historical forces have a way of influencing ideas and attitudes long after an understanding of their context has been lost." Washington's schools are admittedly a unique place to study educational change in the nineteenth century. Poised between North and South and living in the shadow of the federal government, over which it has had incalculable influence, Washington was like no other city. Compared with many Northern cities, it had few factories or immigrants from distant lands. Washington also became a refuge for thousands of freed people escaping the terrors of Civil War and slavery, so it provides a special glimpse into the high hopes and lived realities of a newly liberated people. Despite their unique qualities, the Washington schools grappled with the major, divisive concerns of urban educators everywhere. Were schools for everyone, or only for the poor? How, and how well, should they be funded? Should White and Black children attend school together? Should the schools adopt the new ideals of progressive, child-centered education?[2]

PUBLIC SCHOOLS AND RACIAL INEQUALITY

One way to begin to understand the big issues that confronted Washington's schools is to revisit the dedication ceremonies of a locally famous school on the corner of M and Seventeenth Street, NW. Today it is a school museum. On September 2, 1872, it was the scene of a gala celebration. Named for the famous White champion of Black civil rights Senator Charles Sumner of Massachusetts, the Sumner School has a special place in Washington's history. In the early 1870s, the local racially segregated public schools were governed by separate school committees. The trustees of the colored schools, with White and Black members, controlled the schools attended by Black children. The dedication of Sumner school was a moment of great pride and promise for African Americans, but it also revealed the all-powerful nature of the color line.[3]

The dedication of a school was often a major community event in the nineteenth century. Education held particular importance to African Americans, who filled the Sumner auditorium to hear a range of inspirational speeches. Southern states beginning in the 1830s legally forbade teaching slaves to read or write, and free Blacks were also denied access to public education in antebellum Washington. The grand Sumner school, therefore, represented something of a triumph over history. The building itself was a wonder, its every feature noted in a speech by the Black superintendent of colored schools, George F.W. Cook. The dimensions and location of every room, the modern ventilation and heating system, the entry way, the Ohio sandstone trim by the doors and windows, the size of the Blackboards, the landscaping and playground: nothing escaped notice. The first story window sills were 9 feet 4 inches above ground—presumably to help keep children's eyes off the streets and on their lessons, and to help deter vandals when the school day ended! Everything was new, and the latest, and the best, reflecting "great credit upon the architect, Adoph Cluss, Esq., and Robert I. Fleming, builder."⁴

The dedication ceremonies reflected not only the power of Jim Crow at the high point of Reconstruction but also a Christian value system that permeated contemporary schools. At 2 o'clock in the "beautiful assembly room," Black children in their Sunday best opened with "the singing of 'Blessed Is He That Cometh'." A now-retired White superintendent, Zalmon Richards, read from the eighth chapter of *Proverbs*: "Receive my instruction, and not silver; and knowledge rather than choice gold. For wisdom is better than rubies; and all the things that may be desired are not to be compared to it." The Rev. Dr. Hill gave a benediction, followed by more singing, namely, "Guide me, O Thou, Great Jehovah." Superintendent Cook then spoke, tracing the long struggles of Black Washingtonians for freedom and learning. Cook pointed out that only a handful of pupils attended Washington's first Black public school, which opened in 1864. Seven teachers taught around 100 pupils in 1866; now there were eighty teachers instructing 4,000 of the estimated 9,000 African American children. If 5,000 still lacked a seat in any school, Sumner showed what was possible. "In this building," Cook concluded, children "will acquire habits of regularity in attendance, study harder, learn more, evince a higher sense of propriety, a more cheerful spirit, and develop a higher character."⁵

The builder of the school, Robert Fleming, shared these aspirations as he presented educators with the keys to the building. Fleming praised this "new temple to the cause of popular education." He added that "The child who years ago would have been brought up in ignorance will now have the same opportunities as others, which by the blessings of an all-wise Providence will be taught that elementary knowledge that leads to prosperity and happiness." Built by "colored mechanics," Sumner was likely the most impressive school building for African Americans anywhere in the nation.⁶

One of the Black school trustees, William H.A. Wormley, chairman of the building committee, took his turn at the lectern. Like other dignitaries, he praised the noble cause of human freedom championed by Charles Sumner, who unsuccessfully tried to legislate the integration of the local schools. For years, Wormley had worked tirelessly to improve Black education, and he recounted how children in the past attended classes in dank hovels, old stables, and unsanitary barracks. Proud of the new school but insulted by the legally mandated separation of White and Black pupils, Wormley said Sumner should admit everyone, whether "White or Black, high or low, rich or poor," for "if they seek for education, they shall be welcome. ... " One can only wonder what the White dignitaries on stage—including the U.S. Commissioner of Education—thought of his bold defense of equal access and civil rights. As the keys passed from speaker to speaker—to the chair of the school trustees, to a professor from Howard University—everyone praised Almighty God and the glory of public education. The audience of parents and friends of the new Sumner school repeatedly sang out, "Amen."[7]

As trustee Wormley had argued, racial segregation undermined the dream of equal rights and full citizenship for all. In that sense, schools followed the dominant racial norms of the city and nation. The Sumner school thus serves as an eloquent example of the promise and also the limitations of public education in the nineteenth century. So would other magnificent buildings that a soon-to-be world famous architect, Adolph Cluss, designed, such as the Franklin school for White children. Sumner had cost a princely sum of $70,000, Franklin a king's ransom, an amazing $187,000, a few years earlier. A kind of early command central, Franklin also held the rooms in which the board of school trustees, consolidated with neighboring Georgetown and the County in 1874, would hold its regular meetings, and where the White school superintendent and his staff were housed. For the rest of the century, an integrated board, with a Black and a White superintendent for their respective schools, would thus govern and supervise the world of Jim Crow education.[8]

Sumner and Franklin were akin to Romulus and Remus, whose statuary once greeted visitors at the gates of Rome. The schools were not twins but were handsomely built, quickly becoming the model schools of America's capital. They were often inundated with visitors who saw how high public education, whose status was once incredibly low, had literally and figuratively risen. These famous buildings were part of the larger story of American education in general and the local school system in particular. The founders of the schools and their successors over the course of the century were often deeply concerned about the quality of public education and its status relative to the private sector; school officials in the District often complained bitterly about the absence of direct democracy, home rule, and adequate funding; and the schools were also embedded in deeply divisive issues related to social class, race, citizenship, and pedagogy.

PAUPERS AND THE PUBLIC SCHOOLS

The founders of the first public, or free, schools in the District of Columbia, and in neighboring Georgetown, would have been shocked at the impressive size of the school system that emerged by the late nineteenth century. The first public schools built in the nation's capital in the early 1800s educated a small number of poor White children. Blacks were excluded from the benefits of tax-supported education, as were the vast majority of White children. Free education in America's cities was usually synonymous with charity schooling for the destitute classes. Washington was no different. While some of the founding fathers dreamed of establishing a national university there—which would have required feeder schools from below—the dream was never realized. Whether in New York City, Philadelphia, or nearby Baltimore, public schools before the 1840s were charity institutions for families unable to pay the tuition at private academies.[9]

In 1804, the Washington City Council mandated the creation of a board of school trustees. As historian Constance McLaughlin Green has written, it provided "$1,500 annually from the license fees for hacks, peddlers, taverns, dogs, and slaves." Civic-minded residents soon donated a few thousand dollars more, and two schools subsequently opened that had both charity and fee-paying pupils, the latter receiving some instruction beyond the Three R's. In a pattern repeated in the coming decades, the city soon cut the education budget, as the trustees pursued a popular strategy to educate the urban poor. They adopted a new educational plan, shaped by a variety of visionary schemes but perfected by an English Quaker school master named Joseph Lancaster, which promised to teach children effectively and cheaply.[10] Born in England in 1778, Lancaster established a famous model school in London that flourished in the early 1800s. He later enjoyed considerable influence in America where, as Carl F. Kaestle explains, he was often praised as a genius and public benefactor. The Lancasterian method of education reinforced the notion, prevalent outside of New England, that public or free schools were largely suitable for the poor, not all social classes. A prominent educational theorist, Lancaster believed with other reformers that the growth of cities, whether in England or America, necessitated concerted efforts to educate poor children, whose behavior frightened the respectable classes, in Christian morals and rudimentary literacy. In Washington as in other American cities, Lancasterian methods proved enormously popular among those trying to teach the many on few dollars. Lancaster's plan was simple: children would be assembled into large lecture rooms, with a single instructor aided by older, talented students who worked as pupil-teachers known as monitors. This lowered expenses, since a single master could teach a few hundred children, as monitors instructed pupils in smaller groups. Pupils could be classified in an orderly way by their achievement in different subjects, the spirit of emulation or competition encouraged, and the schools thus held accountable. If the teaching methods were didactic, the system of instruction and socialization had its enlightened qualities. Corporal punishment, for example, was discouraged. Lancaster preferred simple prizes and tokens—balls, dolls, cheap books—to reward the children who did well, and humiliation—dunce caps or sandwich board signs with indiscretions noted—to embarrass the ill-behaved and nonattentive. Thus would the motive to study, behave, and excel be instilled in the young without recourse to the birch or switch.[11]

By 1812, drawing upon public monies and charitable donations, two Lancasterian schools were operating in Washington. In 1813, one teacher, Henry Ould, an Englishman whose brother taught a Lancasterian school in Georgetown, proudly reported his accomplishments with 130 pupils: 82 boys and 48 girls. He claimed that "55 have learned to read in the Old and New Testament, and are all able to spell words of three, four, and five syllables. ..." Some memorized Methodist hymns, others "the first four rules of arithmetic. ... " Both Lancasterian schools closed due to financial woes in 1814 and 1815 and then reopened and limped along when a severe economic depression began in 1837. Congress had approved lotteries to raise a school fund, the interest on which largely financed these pauper schools, which only reached a fraction of the poor. A survey in 1839 discovered that there were about 5,200 White school-age children in Washington: 900 of them were in private schools, only 293 in the public charity schools, and the other 4,000 in no school at all.[12]

William W. Seaton, part owner of an influential newspaper and an activist mayor in the 1840s, watched with despair as the numbers of unschooled children grew. In annual mayoral messages; he championed more inclusive free schools—for Whites, that is—leading to a committee report in 1842 that favored "common" or public schools for everyone, including a free high school to teach advanced studies to the highest achievers. The committee had high hopes. Free schools were "calculated to improve society, to confer varied and lasting benefits upon the community, to arrest the progress of crime, to lessen the amount of poverty and suffering, to give firmness and stability to our republican institutions, and to perpetuate the blessings of a free government." Assuring citizens that they were neither egalitarians nor radical levelers, the committee argued that many illiterate youth populated the city streets, where they learned "habits of idleness and ignorance. ... " Schools, it confidently predicted, would uplift society, raising up the poor without leveling down the rich.[13]

Mayor Seaton and his allies wanted children to attend school to master the rudiments of learning and to become morally responsible, law-abiding citizens. In advance of popular sentiment, Seaton wanted free schools, supported by property taxes, for all White children. Slowly he built up political support, winning approval for a poll tax and other fees to fund more schools; a small property tax was finally approved in the 1850s. In 1845, the board of trustees operated a grand total of four schools; by 1853, however, they increased to 35, to 50 on the eve of the Civil War. This was a major accomplishment, though the majority of White pupils was still beyond the educational pale.[14]

THE CHARACTER OF THE SCHOOLS

With a few Lancasterian schools as the foundation, then, the Washington public schools—exclusively for White children—came of age between the mid-1840s and the onset of the Civil War. By many accounts, Washington's schools were underfunded, mostly patronized by poor Whites (though slowly embracing more of the children of better-off federal employees), and resembled one-room rural schools. By the 1820s, a rising number of Northern educators, however, criticized the social class stigmas attached to Lancasterian schools and monitorial instruction. Enlightened Washingtonians similarly began to favor age-graded classes, with one teacher responsible for every class. In 1846, Mayor Seaton, as president of the board of school trustees, urged educators to make "the proper distinctions of primary and grammar schools, suited to the ages and advancement of the children" and to provide enough classrooms for "all who might desire to attend." Efficient classification of pupils into perfectly age-graded classes was the goal, but financial crises persisted. And school supply could not meet pupil demand.[15]

No school could really have individual grades in which children could be examined and placed according to their abilities and merit. Pupil classification was based on rule of thumb methods—estimates by teachers of pupil ability and progress—and city schools continually absorbed children with little or no education of all ages from the countryside. Children were concentrated in beginning classes and often passed along despite their academic performance just to shorten the waiting list. Laboring in one- or two-room buildings, teachers were nevertheless encouraged to separate children into broad groups called "grades" to better help them ascend the ladder of learning. Parents were urged to buy the same textbooks and thus make instruction more uniform. Books, pens, and paper were, however, luxury items in a world where many families struggled to pay the rent and feed their children.[16]

Primary school pupils studied the Three R's, and a handful of advanced pupils also learned some history and geography. Large class sizes made keeping order a priority and a challenge and also reinforced didactic forms of instruction. Heavy reliance upon textbooks remained common. Most teachers were young women in their teens without a high school education or knowledge of pedagogy. Most were only a few steps ahead of their most advanced pupils. Teachers were paid a pittance and money was ever scarce for purchasing maps, globes, or other teaching aids. Some pupils saw arithmetic and grammar lessons worked out on Blackboards, then seen as a real innovation, but even after mid-century they worked out their sums and parsed sentences on slates, as in the older Lancasterian system. So children spent their time in partially-graded classrooms memorizing facts and rules and definitions and names and dates from their textbooks, recited the newly gained knowledge to their teachers, and, if they were available, then moved on to more difficult textbooks. Children likely left school with a smattering of book knowledge and rudimentary literacy and numeracy.[17]

Teaching was low pay, low status, and often very tedious. One contemporary in 1846 told the teachers not to lose faith, for their labors were of transcendent importance. "To the teachers, whose heads have ached, and whose nerves have been racked by their irksome labors, and whose lives are almost identified with the name of patience, we say be not discouraged or disheartened. The profession in which you are engaged is a noble one, for it has to do with the formation of mind, the character, and the soul—than which there is nothing higher or nobler on earth." Remember, he added: "The school is one of the great reforming and regenerating instruments by which the world is to be made better, the reign of peace and millennial glory ushered in. The children around you will soon be men and women, the fathers and mothers of the land." It was an inspiring way to be told not to expect a raise.[18]

As in the Lancasterian system, parents, taxpayers, and school officials wanted to know how well children fared in their studies. Citizens expected results. Exhibitions, public examinations, graduation ceremonies, parades, concerts, and other displays of erudition and the social graces helped to show, beyond rumor and anecdote, how a school was doing. Since the earliest charity schools, children had often joined in public parades, dressed in their finest, to demonstrate the civilizing effects of education. In 1846, Mayor Seaton praised the children who participated in a national manufacturing fair. The little paupers marched in a body with the trustees and their teachers to the Capitol, they then met the mayor and some congressmen. "The neat, well-dressed, healthy appearance of the pupils, and their correct deportment," the mayor said, "elicited many encomiums from those who saw them."[19]

By the 1840s, annual school exhibitions allowed everyone to take stock and show some pride in classroom achievements. As in other cities, local newspapers reported when the school trustees, who lacked the power to appoint a superintendent to serve as executive officer, visited and inspected the schools. The trustees and other dignitaries examined the pupils, peppering them with questions drawn from their school books. The reputations of students and their teachers were on the line. Oral—and increasingly over time, written—tests, helped reveal what the pupils learned. Teachers often prepped their pupils, hoping to anticipate the questions. Parents and friends of the schools sat in the audience, hoping that Mary and Johnny could display their knowledge. Sometimes, as in 1846, a trustee thought the pupils overall did well despite noticing some "egregious blunders." Pupils often memorized facts or concepts they did not understand. Many were no doubt nervous. Then, as now, not everyone learned their lessons. However, city officials usually praised the children and the teachers, saying this year's test results were better than the last, though there was always room for improvement. In addition, some students amazed their elders by their voracious appetite for learning and willingness to work hard. In 1850, one observer praised the scholars in Primary School No. 4. "The attainments of many of the pupils are respectable, and the improvement of several of them remarkable. Ten months since, one of the pupils scarcely knew her alphabet; she now reads with great accuracy, writes a fair hand, and is ciphering in some of the simpler rules of arithmetic." In a system born in the idea of educating the poor but now seeking a wider social embrace, points of pride and achievement received public notice.[20]

Teaching and learning were nevertheless expected to flourish in often dismal settings. In 1855, Washington's school trustees documented the distressing situation. Many school buildings lacked proper sanitation, heating and ventilation, proper desks, or teaching apparatus. By then the city owned 15 school buildings in various states of disrepair and rented 17 other sites. Listen to the laments of James G. Berret, mayor of Washington and ex-officio president of the board, in 1859: "Many of our schools are conducted in the basements of churches, from which the light of the sun is so excluded as to render the recitations [of the pupils] a duty of much difficulty. . . . " Little wonder that Black and White citizens were ecstatic when showcase schools such as Sumner and Franklin were built after the Civil War.[21]

Even though school budgets rose in the late 1840s after the economy revived following a severe depression and Mayor Seaton and his allies pressed for better educational provisions for Whites, the school population and other demands on the public purse grew faster. Washington lacked direct representation in the federal government, and a sizeable proportion of federal employees paid no taxes but used city services, including schools. Bitter complaints by city officials did not usually open up the federal coffers. Education was widely seen as a local responsibility.[22]

Despite the poor facilities, low pay for teachers, and chronic inability to know how to simultaneously raise salaries and rent or build enough schools for a burgeoning population, the school trustees soldiered on in the pre–Civil War era. By 1860, the prospects for education for White children had improved, though many were still shortchanged educationally: an estimated 2,800 children attended public schools, but there were 4,000 in private schools and perhaps 10,000 in neither. Soon thousands of ex-slaves poured into Washington seeking federal protection. The nation's capital now faced a long-evaded subject: public schooling for African Americans.[23]

AFRICAN AMERICANS AND THE SCHOOLS

The city fathers of Washington traditionally ignored the educational aspirations of African Americans. Since the early 1800s, White and Black charitable organizations, philanthropists, and churches had established a variety of private schools to help address high illiteracy rates among African Americans. An active center for the slave trade until it was banned at mid-century, Washington was home to 2,113 slaves in 1850 and a rising free Black community. By 1860, the total Black population of nearly 11,000 was 86 percent free. Local slaves were emancipated in 1862, and the Black population swelled by 222 percent in the 1860s, constituting a third of the city. Washington approved public schools for African Americans in 1864, which raised the inevitable, volatile questions: Who would establish, fund, and control these schools? Would the schools be integrated?[24]

The opening of model schools for both races—the Sumner and Franklin schools—during the Reconstruction period literally set in stone a policy that would ever plague the city: racial segregation. In the coming decades, African Americans fought for access to more and higher quality schools, something not easily achieved, and a minority of Black civil rights activists would challenge, unsuccessfully, the hegemony of Jim Crow. Sumner School, completed in 1872, was a source of great pride among Black citizens, even if it was less grand than its White counterpart. Sumner was also a very atypical Black school; its cost, $70,000, was impressive, but it nearly equaled the entire budget for *all* Black schools a few years earlier. For Black children, the cup of educational opportunity often remained empty or half full.[25]

As ex-slaves arrived in Washington during the Civil War, the educational needs of African American children became a pressing concern. During and immediately after the war, relief agencies from the North, often led by Protestant missionary groups and later aided by the Freedmen's Bureau, hired teachers, built schools, and fought for more educational opportunities for Black children. Such philanthropy dried up in the 1870s. Republican, Northern, and federal interest in civil rights withered, but federal dominance in Washington school governance intensified. When Washington created Black public schools in 1864, the federal government gave the Department of Interior the authority to appoint a board of colored school trustees. In 1870; the trustees appointed its own Black superintendent, George F.W. Cook. In 1874, four previously independent school boards—which had governed the colored and White schools of Washington, and the schools of Georgetown and of the county—consolidated into one board. This new board was something of an anomaly. While the schools were racially segregated, the school board had both White and Black members. For the rest of the century, a federally appointed board of commissioners named the trustees and tightly controlled and limited its budget.[26] Thus although African Americans in some respect controlled their own schools, they were ever dependent on powerful White politicians for the purse strings.

A member of Washington's leading Black family, Cook was retained in office and held his position as superintendent until he and his White counterpart were sacked in 1900 (see below). During his long tenure, he issued reports on the state of the schools, hired and fired staff, tested the pupils, listened to endless citizen complaints, and worked, sometimes contentiously, with the Black school trustees, themselves divided on the question of racial integration. Like the succession of White superintendents with whom he worked, Cook sought compliant teachers and deferential pupils. According to the 1873 rules and regulations for the "colored schools," a restatement of old edicts, teachers should teach their subjects well but also "inculcate the virtues of truthfulness, honesty, industry, cleanliness, respect for parents and teachers, and obedience to law." Students were warned not "to throw pens, paper, or anything whatever on the floor; to mark, cut, scratch, chalk, or otherwise disfigure or injure any portion of the school building, or anything connected with it; to use tobacco in any form; to use a knife in school; to play at any game within the school-room; to use any profane or indelicate language; to nickname any person; to throw stones or other missiles; to annoy or maltreat others; or do anything that may disturb the neighborhood of the school."[27]

Cook was in a subordinate position vis-à-vis the White power structure but an imposing figure in the African American community. Teaching appointments were coveted, high-status positions that offered educated Blacks, disproportionately drawn from the middle and upper reaches of society, some economic security in a racist economy. Being light-skinned, like much of the so-called colored aristocracy in Washington, Cook was regularly accused of playing favorites: of only hiring only the light-complexioned daughters of well-connected families. Moreover, as more teachers were hired, support weakened for the handful of Black leaders who championed integration. Everyone feared that integration would lead to the firing of Black teachers.[28]

Ultimately dependent on White patronage, Cook could not secure enough schools for the growing population of Black children. Moreover, separate but equal schools were a fiction, despite the endorsement of the concept by the U.S. Supreme Court in 1896. Along with the indignities of lower salaries and larger classes for Black teachers, African Americans had a longer waiting list than Whites for admission to school. In 1894, in the midst of the century's worst economic depression, a third of all Black children were excluded. While many Black children studied hard and gained the respectability and pride that comes from academic achievement, many in attendance had half-day sessions and studied in rented shacks. The opportunities to learn were clearly unequal. The curricula of the White and Black schools were virtually identical, though watering down the curriculum for the poor by adding vocational courses was already gaining traction. In 1900, most Black children in school dropped out after fourth grade, a reflection of the poverty and poor job prospects for well-educated Blacks. Despite these realities, Washington's Black middle class was substantial compared to most cities, its schools widely regarded as the nation's best for African Americans.[29]

The divide between the education of the masses of Blacks and wealthier families was often pronounced. Finding enough seats for every child, White or Black, was never accomplished. The board of trustees was not allowed to charge tuition to nonresidents—namely, numerous federal employees, usually White, who lived outside of the District. And the population of pupils in attendance, roughly two-thirds White and one-third Black, soared in the final decades of the century. Approximately 21,000 pupils came to school every day in 1880, 36,000 20 years later, when nearly 50,000 were enrolled. (Attendance was typically spotty, particularly among children from low-income families). As soon as a new school was built, it was filled, and a new waiting list generated. Similar to the era of charity education, school officials were expected to pay enough to retain experienced teachers, build more schools, improve the curriculum, and maintain reasonable academic standards. Perpetual supplicants before the district commissioners, the trustees were generally strapped for funds.[30]

By the dawn of the twentieth century, Jim Crow practices were firmly entrenched and unequal practices common in Washington's schools, not surprising since the era witnessed a general assault on Black civil rights throughout the South. Black leadership in the schools weakened further when a Senate investigation of the schools in 1900 led to their reorganization and the firing of both the White and Black superintendents. The conflict was not about money but ideology and politics. Only the White superintendent was replaced as White authority tightened its grip over the segregated system.

THE PERILS OF PROGRESSIVISM

The school crisis of 1900 was about 15 years in the making and rested primarily on the issue of progressive education. In 1885, the trustees appointed William B. Powell as the new superintendent for the White schools. Born in New York State and educated at Oberlin College, Powell was the former head administrator in the Aurora, Illinois, school system, and he soon earned a national reputation. Powell's critics claimed that he neglected the teaching of the basics in favor of the "new education." Earlier in the century, what was known as the new, and later, progressive, education traveled from Europe to America. Progressive, or child-centered, educators were a diverse, contentious lot, but they shared romantic views about children and the schools. Schools, they believed, should abandon teaching by rote memorization and recitation, end competitive exams, and add new programs to make school more inviting. This would include teaching the basics through objects, not simply by textbooks, and by providing more opportunities for learning by doing through manual training classes and kindergartens, which were introduced piecemeal into the system during Powell's tenure.[31]

Powell's annual reports to the board of trustees were suffused with romantic sentiments. With the trustees' approval in 1886, he ended the annual promotion examinations that traditionally determined who advanced to the next grade or was held back, or entered high school. Powell let the teachers decide, which horrified some parents, teachers, and principals, who apparently complained to the commissioners. Critics in the 1890s wondered why Powell and the board added nature study, manual training, and other innovations when thousands of children could not find a seat at school. Fads and frills, said critics, had supplanted the basics and squandered scarce resources. Photographers, especially the soon-famous Francis Benjamin Johnston, snapped pictures of pupils doing stretching exercises, on field trips, or enjoying a picnic lunch. Why, asked some citizens, were they being taxed to teach youth how to frolic and play?[32]

Other critics blamed Powell for allowing the local medical society to conduct a survey of students that asked embarrassing questions about their parent's personal habits. Still others said teachers cowered before him, fearing it was Powell's way or the highway. Powell's defenders praised his visionary ideals and said the Senators were angry because he would neither hire nor retain their cronies on the payroll. Rumors swirled around town in neighborhood meetings, eagerly covered by newspaper reporters, that the sandbox had replaced textbooks and that children no longer recited the times tables. Such hyperbole didn't square with reality, but in 1900 influential Senators launched a full-scale investigation. Powell prepared a lengthy defense of his ideas and leadership before the trustees in June. The board was so impressed that it ordered the printing of 5,000 copies of his report.[33]

In his defense before the board, restated before the Senate investigating committee, Powell admitted that for nearly 15 years children in the District had not faced competitive promotion examinations. He further admitted that many pupils could not pass a tough academic exam but said that this was hardly news; it had always been true. Children varied in terms of talent and ambition. "The schools," Powell insisted, "have been conducted on the theory that they were for the children and that they should be made to subserve the best interests of all the children, individually, that offer themselves for instruction." "We have sought to make the child love his school and like to come to school, but we have sought to do this, not by marks of percentage, not by credits, not by rewards, prizes—training to selfishness, every one of them—but we have sought to make him come to school by making school pleasant for him, by making learning not only agreeable, but delightful to him, by making school life a continuation of and a delightful adjunct to a cultivated home life." [34]

The idea that school and learning should be fun, and that objects should be studied and not simply books, had circulated in enlightened circles for decades. But parents, taxpayers, and politicians have often preferred the basics over so-called fads and frills. The Senators forced local pupils to take a competitive test on the Three R's, and they predictably found the results wanting. Alexander Stuart, a former supervisory principal who had worked under Powell, was named as his successor. Stuart was a former student in the schools and had also taught at Franklin. He regarded himself as a Three R's educator and no-nonsense administrator who promised to restore tradition and the primacy of textbooks. In a long interview published in 1905 in the *Washington Post*, he conveniently forgot that in the early 1890s he had championed Powell's advanced program of reform; obviously, Stuart had had a change of heart. "During the Powell regime," he concluded, "an educational fad swept over the country, which, in Washington, at least, has left a trail of bad spellers, poor grammarians, and indifferent arithmeticians. ... If I have a hobby, it is for reading, writing, spelling, grammar, history, and arithmetic." [35]

CONCLUSION

By the early 1900s, Washington's schools had evolved from a few pauper institutions into a modern, expansive, racially segregated system. Schools were often larger and better graded and had a more uniform course of study. Sumner and Franklin and other impressive school buildings stood as symbols of the ongoing struggle by the system for respectability, as it shed its pauper past, and an affirmation of racial inequality, as it retreated from the promise of Reconstruction. Tens of thousands of pupils, in facilities of varying quality, were taught time discipline, patriotism, respect for authority, basic literacy, and moral values. Like other major school systems, Washington's educational leaders had debated whether to embrace the new education or the traditional teacher and textbook authority. The curriculum had broadened along progressive lines, but traditional classes and pedagogy remained the norm.

What knowledge is worth knowing and how it should be taught would remain divisive questions. Wisdom may be better than rubies, but both are difficult to secure. Progressives still insist that the full measure of a school cannot be determined by test results, although many citizens prefer hard evidence on student achievement. Champions of back to the basics still battle the ideals of child-friendly pedagogy and curricular enrichment. The good life is impossible without access to a sound education, even though no one can agree on how to define either phrase or ensure their realization. And the establishment of high quality urban schools that educate the rich and the poor, White and Black alike, under the same roof, seems as elusive today as it was a century ago.

NOTES

1. Garrison Keillor, *Lake Wobegone Days* (New York, 1985). On the utopian aspirations of citizens and the schools, see William J. Reese, *America's Public Schools: From the Common School to 'No Child Left Behind'* (Baltimore, 2005).
2. Howard Gillette,. Jr., *Between Justice & Beauty: Race, Planning, and the Failure of Urban Policy in Washington, D.C.* (1995), xi. Basic sources on the history of Washington D.C. in the nineteenth century include the often-cited works by Constance McLaughlin Green, including *Washington: Village and Capital, 1800–1878* (Princeton, 1962), and *Washington: Capital City, 1879–1950* (Princeton, 1963). On the nonindustrial, native-born population, see Constance McLaughlin Green, *The Secret City: A History of Race Relations in the Nation's Capital* (Princeton, 1967), 120. Carl Abbott notes that Washington is not only atypical but an "extraordinary" city, in *Political Terrain: Washington, D.C., From Tidewater Town to Global Metropolis* (Chapel Hill, 1999), 5.
3. The speeches have been reprinted in *The Charles Sumner School* (Washington D.C., District of Columbia Public Schools, 1986).
4. *Charles Sumner School*, 3–5. On the importance of Cluss to the built landscape of the city, see Alan Lessoff and Christof Mauch, eds., *Adolph Cluss: Architect, From Germany to America* (Washington D.C., 2005).
5. *Charles Sumner School*, 13–16. For a biographical sketch of Edwards, a New England born and bred educator, read "Zalmon Edwards," *American Journal of Education* (March 1864): 14, 34 (American Periodical Series Online; hereafter referred to as APS).
6. *Charles Sumner School*, 16–18.
7. *Charles Sumner School*, 19; and Gillette, *Between Justice & Beauty*, 67. Cook and Wormley were members of old and prominent families. See Green, *The Secret City*, 126.
8. J. Ormand Wilson, "Eighty Years of the Public Schools of Washington, 1805 to 1885," *Records of the Columbia Historical Society* (October 30, 1896): 143.
9. Carl F. Kaestle, *Pillars of the Republic: Common Schools and American Society, 1789–1860* (New York, 1983), chapter 3. On the academy and seminary movement, see Margaret A. Nash, *Women's Education in America 1780–1840* (New York, 2005).
10. Green, *Washington: Village and Capital*, 43; and William Tindall, *Standard History of the City of Washington: From a Study of the Original Sources* (Knoxville, Tenn., 1914), 319–20.
11. This draws heavily upon Carl F. Kaestle, ed., *Joseph Lancaster and the Monitorial School Movement: A Documentary History* (New York, 1973), 1–49. Kaestle, 34, argues that Lancaster's system promised among other benefits "economy" in terms of cost, continuous student "activity" in terms of instruction, and "order" in terms of school discipline and organization.
12. Green, *Washington: Village and Capital*, 44, 76, 93, 140; and Wilson, "Eighty Years," 125. The quotes on Ould are from Wilson's essay, 127.
13. *Report of the Committee on Public Schools, In Relation to the Establishment and Support of Common and High Schools in the City of Washington* (Washington D.C., 1842), 2, 3; Green, *Washington: Village and Capital*, 161–62; Tindall, *Standard History*, 355–56; and Wilson, "Eighty Years," 126–27.

14. *Annual Report of the Board of Trustees of Public Schools, to the City Councils, August 23, 1846* (Washington, D.C.,1846), 3; *Report of the Board of Trustees of the Public Schools, of the City of Washington, For the Year Ending August 1, 1853* (Washington, D.C., 1853), 3; and *Sixteenth Annual Report of the Trustees of Public Schools, of the City of Washington* (Washington, D.C., 1860), 8. Seaton's support for an expanded public school system (for Whites) is a staple in Washington's historiography, as seen in the *Centennial History of the City of Washington, D.C.* (Dayton, Ohio, 1892), 492–93; and Wilson, "Eighty Years," 131.

15. *Annual Report of the Board of Trustees* (1846), 6; Kaestle, *Pillars*, 69, 70, 113, 125, 132–34, 220; Reese, *America's Public Schools*, 32–33, 57, 61–62, 109; and David B. Tyack, *The One Best System: A History of American Urban Education* (Cambridge, Mass., 1974), 70–71.

16. According to the *Annual Report of the Trustees of the City of Washington, August 13, 1849* (Washington, D.C., 1849), 4: "The Trustees have found no little difficulty in classifying the pupils. ... " There is an extensive literature on child labor and family sustenance. See, at least, John Bodnar, *The Transplanted: A History of Immigrants in Urban America* (Bloomington, In., 1985). 71–83, on the family economy.

17. Complaints about dull teaching and rote instruction were common in the D.C. school reports in the 1840s and 1850s, and object teaching and other progressive ideals inspired by European educators such as Johann Pestalozzi were often seen as superior. See, for example, *Annual Report of the Board of Trustees* (1846), 15, 19. On the curriculum, see *Annual Report of the Trustees of Public Schools of the City of Washington August 1850* (Washington, D.C., 1850), 44–46.

18. *Annual Report of the Board of Trustees* (1846), 22, 23.

19. *Annual Report of the Board of Trustees* (1846), 6. For more details on the fair, see Abbott, *Political Terrain*, 55–56, 113.

20. *Annual Report of the Board of Trustees* (1846), 18; *Annual Report of the Trustees of Public Schools* (1850), 11; and "The Public School Procession," *National Era* 4 (August 8, 1850): 127 (APS). The president of the school board noted that examining the pupils required considerable time and labor: "The annual examinations of the Public Schools have sometimes heretofore occupied the Trustees five afternoons of the week for nearly two months, each school being examined by the whole board." See *Annual Report of the Trustees of Public Schools of the City of Washington, August 1854* (Washington, D.C., 1854), 6.

21. *Fifteenth Annual Report of the Trustees of Public Schools of the City of Washington* (Washington, D.C., 1859), 9.

22. Tindall, *Standard History*, 355–56, 389, on funding and school reorganization. The former White school superintendent, Ormand Wilson, claimed that one-third of the pupils in the system by the 1870s were the children of federal employees. See Wilson, "Eighty Years," 137.

23. Green, *Washington: Village and Capital*, 257. A recent, comprehensive history that provides the broad context for educational developments in the 1860s is Ernest B. Furgurson, *Freedom Rising: Washington in the Civil War* (New York, 2004).

24. Green, *Secret City*, 63. The subject of private schooling for African-Americans in Washington in the nineteenth century has generated a rich historiography. See, for example, Leonard P. Curry, *The Free Black in Urban America, 1800–1850: The Shadow of the Dream* (Chicago, 1981), 159–60; James Oliver Horton, *Free People of Color: Inside the African American Community* (Washington, D.C., 1993), 188–89; and Gillette, *Between Justice & Beauty*, 35–36.

25. Office of the Trustees of Colored Schools, *Report of the Board of Trustees of Colored Schools of Washington and Georgetown, D.C.: Made in Compliance With a Resolution of The Senate of the United States, Passed December 8, 1870* (Washington, D.C., 1870), 5. The report stated that $72,000 had been spent on Black education.

26. On Reconstruction on the national level, see Eric Foner, *Reconstruction: America's Unfinished Revolution, 1863–1877* (New York, 1988). Green, *Washington: Village and Capital*, 387. The board also had women appointees later in the century, including Mary Church Terrell.

27. *Annual Report of the Superintendent of Colored Schools of Washington and Georgetown, 1871–'72* (Washington, D.C., 1873), 99.

28. According to Jacqueline M. Moore, the Cook family was the "most distinguished" in Washington; see *Leading the Race: The Transformation of the Black Elite in the Nation's Capital, 1880–1920* (Charlottesville, Va., 1999), 11. There is a large literature on Washington's so-called Black aristocracy, the economic, political, and cultured elite. See especially Willard B. Gatewood, *Aristocrats of Color: The Black Elite, 1880–1920* (Bloomington, In., 1990); especially 39–68, 162, 259; Allan Johnston, *Surviving Freedom: The Black Community of Washington, D.C. 1860–1880* (New York, 1993), 54–56; and Abbott, *Political Terrain*, 74–77.

29. On the high reputation of the Black schools in Washington, see Emmet D. Preston, Jr., "The Development of Negro Education in the District of Columbia," *The Journal of Negro Education* 9 (October 1940): 603; Gates, *Aristocrats of Color*, 259–63; Davison M. Douglas, *Jim Crow Moves North: The Battle Over Northern School Segregation, 1865–1954* (New York, 2005), 191; and Moore, *Leading the Race*, 21, where she writes: "Without a doubt, the District's Black public schools became the best of their kind in the country." The children of the Black elite, after graduating from high school or private academies, often attended college in the north or Howard University, established in Washington in 1867 during Reconstruction. On the overcrowding, half-day sessions, and lack of sufficient classrooms, see "This Ought Not To Be," *Washington Post* (December 10, 1894): 4. On the curriculum, in addition to the annual reports of the school board and superintendent, see Jennie S. Campbell, "Negroes in Washington," *New York Observer and Chronicle* (April 6, 1899): 77, 14 (APS).

30. *Report of the Board of Trustees of Public Schools of the District of Columbia to the Commissioners of the District of Columbia 1898–1899* (Washington, D.C., 1900), 34.

31. Powell's background and the controversies surrounding his ouster from office are described in Green, *Washington: Capital City, 1879–1950*, 56–57; and Jean Malia Pablo, "Washington, D.C. and Its School System, 1900–1906." (Ph.D. dissertation, Georgetown University, 1973), 15–37. On the national debates on the new education, see Reese, *America's Public Schools*, chapter 3.

32. On the elimination of competitive promotion examinations, see Powell's comments in *Report of the Board of Trustees of Public Schools of the District of Columbia 1886–'87* (Washington, D.C., 1887), 43, where he claimed that it was more important for the child "to learn and grow, rather than to stand high in examination, or even to be promoted." Powell provides a detailed endorsement of the new education in his annual reports, especially in *Report of the Board of Trustees of Public Schools of the District of Columbia to the Commissioners of the District of Columbia 1896–97* (Washington, D.C., 1897). Johnston's photographs of the Washington D.C. schools and Black and White children are available on line at the Library of Congress. As one of her biographers points out, her images of the "new education" should not be confused with typical classroom scenes. See Bettina Berch, *The Woman Behind the Lens: The Life and Work of Frances Benjamin Johnston 1864–1952* (Charlottesville, Va., 2000), 42.

33. Pablo, "Washington, D.C.," 37; and W.B. Powell, *Statement Made to the Board of School Trustees* (Washington, D.C., 1900).

34. Powell, *Statement*, 4. The controversy can be followed in these articles in the *Washington Post*: "Method is Practical," (October 25, 1899): 7; "Study System Wrong," (February 7, 1900): 2; "Defends Mr. Powell," (February 8, 1900): 10; "Thinks Critics Unjust," (February 9, 1900): 12; "Our Free School System," (February 15, 1900): 6; "Powell as a Witness," (February 20, 1900): 2;

and among the various letters to the editor that appeared, one written by the superintendent himself, "Supt. Powell's Statement," (May 31, 1900): 2.

35. On Stuart, see his comments on academic standards in the *Washington Post* in "Lack of School Drill," (February 21, 1900): 12; and the interview in "The Man Who Heads our Public Schools," (May 14, 1905): E7. On his earlier defense of the new education, when he was employed as a supervising principal, see *Report of the Board of Trustees of Public Schools of the District of Columbia to the Commissioners of the District of Columbia* (Washington, D.C., 1893), 57–62.

II. SCHOOL DISTRICTS AND STATES IN

EDUCATIONAL REFORM

CHAPTER FOUR

Democracy Undone

Reforming AND Reinventing THE American School District, 1945–2005

DAVID GAMSON

Perhaps one of the most criticized yet least understood institutions in the nation, the American school district has occupied a rather curious spot in our educational history. Once considered to be among the great democratic accomplishments of the early twentieth century, the large urban school district had apparently become defunct, a symbol of bureaucratic ineffectiveness—at least according to many observers of the 1960s and 1970s. Over the past few decades, reformers have offered a broad range of initiatives designed to correct what they see as the failings of local school systems. Many of these proposals for school improvement have viewed the school district as a barrier to fundamental reform. Some plans have sought to render the district powerless or obsolete through vouchers, charter schools, or school-based decision-making. Other reformers have often treated the school district as almost irrelevant to reform; for example, many of the whole-school reform projects established in the 1980s and 1990s tended to focus almost entirely on a reform through school-by-school networks. And throughout the 1990s, advocates of standards-based reform identified the state, rather than the district, as the appropriate engine of instructional change. In the early twenty-first century, the standards movement has transformed, or mutated, into the federal No Child Left Behind Act, complete with punitive measures directed at school districts not demonstrating adequate yearly progress.

When analyzing the traditions of schools and districts, historians address contemporary policy concerns with great reluctance; generally a cautious bunch, they know all too well the dangers of viewing the past through the distorting lens of the present. Nevertheless, I suggest that there are times when historians can— perhaps even *should*—speak to present concerns. This is all the more true when policymakers operate from misconceptions about our educational past, a condition that is hardly rare, for we all carry versions of the past in our minds, whether accurate or not. The historian's responsibility to adjust contemporary perceptions of the past becomes all the more imperative when, as I shall argue, reformers misconstrue the work of historians who have analyzed our educational traditions.

In other words, we need not flinch when asked to embrace the charge of this book, for, given the right conditions, history is often uniquely well-suited to help inform and improve education policymaking, especially when policies are drafted in the hope of recapturing an educational utopia that never truly existed. Historians have, for example, dispatched the portrait of the one-room school as the ideal of the nurturing, safe, and rigorous academic environment, just as they have dispelled the notion that there was once a "golden age" in education when respected and authoritative teachers taught challenging lessons to pupils who quietly and attentively learned them. To remind reformers of the contentious nature of our educational past, and of American education's darker chapters, is to advise them to be cautious, realistic, and humane in any endeavor they pursue.

It is around one particular historical misconstruction that I direct this chapter. Specifically, I suggest that a close historical analysis of the American school district offers us a revised conception, or at least a more nuanced view, of the nature of educational local control. At a general level, this chapter seeks to identify several specific aspects of district history that can be of use to policymakers. Or, to frame my focus somewhat differently, as Carl Kaestle once suggested I do, I could pose the question as: why do we still have school districts? After all, we might wonder, if the school district is as problematic and obsolete as its critics have argued, why has it not gone the way of the one-room school house?

One abiding assumption apparent in much of the rhetoric and research on the district, an assumption often held by historians and policymakers alike, is the view that the school district has remained something of a static entity over the past 70 or 80 years; the district is generally depicted as a holdover from the successful reforms of the Progressive Era. The middle decades of the twentieth century, in this view, are seen as an era of continued consolidation and centralization, with rural schools following the lead of city schools. David Tyack developed one of the most comprehensive and lasting analyses of the "organizational revolution" that took place in early twentieth-century schooling, and he argued that an inner circle of policy elites had advocated and implemented a "one best system" of education. This "one best system" was a district organized along bureaucratic lines borrowed from business models, which installed professional educators, replacing local, ward-based politics with a new form of middle class politics.[1] It is Tyack's "one best system" notion that has stood as the touchstone for many historians and policymakers who have been interested in examining the history of the district. The seeming ability of the school district to block fundamental change has frustrated reformers who believe that school districts have become patently undemocratic. Today, it is often the one best system that many reformers cite as one major problem in school reform.

Although we know a good deal about the development of the local control of schooling in the nineteenth century and about the rise of large, centralized, and bureaucratized school systems during the Progressive Era, we know remarkably little about the evolution of the school district, that fundamental democratic institution, since World War II.[2] I suggest that the pervasive view of district history—that the school district has remained a static institution since the early twentieth century—has shrouded a fascinating story of the ways in which districts have evolved in response to state and federal mandates, national reform movements, and a shifting political climate. The evidence I have collected to date about district reform indicates to me that many policymakers, and perhaps some historians, have stretched David Tyack's analytic conception of the "one best system" far beyond what Tyack intended, or that they have simply assumed too much consistency in twentieth-century district organization and function. Indeed, close examination of the evolution of the school district reveals that throughout the century the very notion of the "district" underwent redefinition and refinement, resulting in much greater historical variation than has been allowed for. In 1947, for example, the National Commission on School District Reorganization found 60 varieties of school districts throughout the country.[3] Well after World War II, many states and organizations continued to conduct their own studies, issue reports, and make recommendations on the best type of school district arrangement. I suggest that the expectations, mandates, and traditional authority of the school district have been significantly altered—if not eroded—through multiple, and often conflicting, demands over the past half century, beginning in the post-war period of 1940s and continuing through the rest of the century.

DISTRICT REORGANIZATION

This chapter focuses primarily on the origins and impact of "District Reorganization," a movement active in American education from the end of World War II through at least until the 1970s. I use the reorganization movement as a lens on how practitioners and policymakers viewed districts in relation to democracy and related concepts such as equal educational opportunity and local governance. Historians are familiar with the "consolidation" of schools and districts, the subject of much focus in the first several decades of the twentieth century. Although consolidation and reorganization shared some characteristics in common, consolidation tended to emphasize the combination of one or more individual school buildings, often through the merging of traditional enrollment boundaries, in the hope of creating larger schools that would boast professional staff and higher enrollments, whereas later reorganization efforts focused on larger administrative units containing multiple schools. The premise of school consolidation was that larger schools would be inherently more modern, more efficient, and more likely to meet the needs of different types of students. However, reformers recognized that their initiative had one significant shortcoming: consolidation could occur only when and where locals took the initiative to pursue it. With few policy levers at their disposal, administrative progressives often used the same methods of persuasion for rural communities that they had successfully employed in advocating for the reform of urban school systems—offering comparisons between good corporate principles and "sound" school organizational practices as evidence that efficiency and quality would follow proper consolidation.[4]

In general, administrative progressives, such as Ellwood Cubberley, were remarkably successful in selling their reform agenda: they must have felt they had a Midas touch when it came to educational reform, for so many of their recommendations were adopted in city after city. Nevertheless, when measured against other items on the administrative progressive agenda—whether intelligence testing, curriculum differentiation, or business and budget reform—the advance of consolidation outside of cities was comparatively slow. California offers a case in point. A 1920 *Report of the Special Legislative Committee on Education*, drafted in part by Cubberley, described California's system of schools districts as "expensive, inefficient, short-sighted, and unprogressive." In the 1930s, the California legislature passed provisions for unified school districts and encouraged districts to reorganize in a way that brought all levels of the local system into alignment. Yet a 1937 report, issued by the California State Department of Education in collaboration with the U.S. Office of Education, complained that Californians remained "content to 'muddle along' with a cumbersome, antiquated, and inefficient school district organization."[5] State leaders often stressed efficiency as a main goal, but certainly they had other motives as well; stronger, larger districts would mean that state could spend less on local educational institutions.

California was not the only state to tussle with consolidation. Depression-era policymakers in financially strapped states across the nation judged the situation dire, and the U.S. Office of Education—flooded with requests for assistance—organized a 1935 national conference on the organization of local school units. "As is well known, not only have schools suffered serious curtailments in length of school terms, instructional programs, supervision, and the like," federal officials reported, "but in many areas their very existence has been threatened." Acknowledging that the depression had aggravated conditions, the U.S. Commissioner of Education, J.W. Studebaker, nevertheless pressed educators to remember that the "fundamental causes" of local funding woes lay much deeper. "They are inherent in our systems of administering and financing schools through a multiplicity of small school districts inadequate in human and material resources." Permanent improvement, he said, would come about "through large-scale, generally State-wide, reorganization of school units." One outcome of that meeting was the creation of the Local School Units Office at the federal level. Within two years, representatives of this office had collaborated with state-level researchers on studies of school district organization in ten states. These reports, invariably recommending state-wide planning for redesigning local districts, became available to a national audience and were used by advocates in each of the ten states as proof of the need for organizational reform. A 1939 report summarized the results and made recommendations for other states based on the ten studies, but the Second World War temporarily stalled efforts to continue reorganization.[6]

In 1946, recognizing that much of the pre-war consolidation activity remained incomplete and arguing that "proper reorganization of local school districts is one of the most important needs for the provision of adequate public elementary and secondary schools in practically all states of the Union," researchers at the Rural Education Project at the University of Chicago and the Department of Rural Education of the National Education Association jointly organized the National Commission on School District Reorganization. At its inception, the commission laid out a broad agenda: survey the extant district organizational situations in various states, create a classification system for the different types of districts encountered, identify the factors necessary for district reorganization, apply the findings of related research, study the experience of reorganization in seven states (Arkansas, Illinois, Iowa, Kansas, New York, Washington, and West Virginia), and propose a program of action "most likely to result in timely and effective school district reorganization."[7] While the agencies sponsoring the commission clearly had a keen interest in rural reform, its reports moved beyond the kind of consolidation rhetoric characteristic of the 1920s and 1930s. Indeed, in Washington state and elsewhere leaders described their reorganization program as "a relatively new development."[8]

One noticeable shift that distinguished reorganization from earlier consolidation efforts was the commission's rejection of the older notion that there was one best model for district organization. "One thing is perfectly clear," the commission announced early in its official report, "school organization in our country has never been static. Scarcely anyone believes that there is any one kind of local school administrative unit that is clearly superior to all other kinds." And to those who might scoff at this, the commission replied, "school districts have continually been changing in the past; there is imperative need for additional reforms today; and other needed changes may be expected in the future as circumstances change and new conditions arise." In other words, by mid-century it was erroneous to believe that there was a one best system that would suit all needs, in all regions, at all points in time.

In reorganization, many states found something they could adopt with vigor. The commission offered a "program of action" laying out specific steps that states could follow to accomplish state-wide reorganization. Chief among these was the recommendation that each state pass legislation that would, first, formally create a state commission on reorganization and, second, make provisions for the establishment of local reorganization committees. The general idea was that the responsibilities would be divided between the state and local committees, such that each state commission would develop and promulgate organizational standards for districts that could then be used by local committees in planning for reorganization in their respective jurisdictions.

Cognizant that earlier consolidation efforts had often languished for years while state officials helplessly looked on, advocates of reorganization changed their strategies in some subtle but symbolically important ways. If the one best system notion was a casualty of the reorganization movement, so too were the characterizations of the role of the district and of the nature of democratic control. If the consolidation movement had relied too heavily on local voluntary initiative, reorganizers were determined not to make the same mistake, and they argued vociferously for state legislation that would be more likely to be rapidly efficacious. This meant doing away with "permissive" legislation—that is, laws that allowed local communities too much leeway in voting for or against reorganization. Although some observers reported some rapid accomplishments in the late 1940s, they were less sanguine about developments in the early 1950s. Permissive reorganization legislation of mid-century was often characterized by the requirement that a favorable majority vote be achieved in each of the districts that would make up the new, reorganized district—"that requirement alone has always been sufficient to restrain reorganization progress to a snail's pace," complained one federal official.[9]

Herein lay a dilemma for many advocates of reorganization. On the one hand, they argued that reorganization would give locals a stronger voice in both district and state educational policy, yet on the other they expressed deep frustration that democratic traditions—such as allowing a majority vote to determine policy—meant that locals could stifle the very reforms that state and federal policymakers argued were good for these same locals. Reformers found several ways to resolve this apparent dissonance. First, they argued that reorganizers should establish better communication with the public to help convince them of the logic of their proposals; this approach resulted in an avalanche of published reorganization pamphlets, reports, studies, and recommendations offered by state departments of education, the U.S. Office of Education, and a variety of other professional organizations. A second tactic was to argue that school districts were really agents of the state, that they existed to accomplish the state's educational functions. This attitude often emerged when state-level actors attempted to redefine districts as "creatures of the state"—in fact, that's just what the Washington State Research Council called them in 1957, in a public relations pamphlet entitled "What is a School District?" "Most people take their school district for granted," noted Washington state officials, who complained that allowing the local area to survey its own needs and then to prepare a proposed district pattern best suited to these requirements slowed the total statewide program "while local groups study and deliberate." "This indulgence by the legislature," as they phrased it, was "planned organization of a permissive nature." Reformers worried that too much community involvement would stymie progress, because it was "restrained by requiring a favorable majority vote." "Unfortunately," said reformers, "Washington now has the ... extremely restrictive [restrictive to their reform] provision as law (1957)." [10]

Some Californians evidenced a similar frustration with the pace of democracy. "Unification [California's version of reorganization] procedures are set along democratic lines and cannot be hurried," explained an administrator in one California county office of education. "In a democracy you discuss and discuss; you hold hearings to let every person have his say; you must refer your proposals to the State to be checked against standard criteria; then citizens in the areas to be affected by the change must be given a chance to vote on the plan. This all takes time, so don't expect any sudden miracles from unification studies in your county or your school district." This administrator warned his fellow reformers about the necessity of informing communities about the benefits of reorganization: "If John Citizen is given a reason to doubt your plan, he'll sock you right in the solar plexus with a 'No' vote come election day."

The "John Citizens" of California and other states often had reason to vote no on election day, and these reasons were not always fully appreciated by the reformers. First, reorganizers often ran roughshod over a community's sense of identity, coolly arranging tidy configurations of larger districts while ignoring the traditional affinities (or animosities) that had developed between neighboring towns. "Feelings are facts" when it comes to district reorganization, Roald Campbell perceptively reminded would-be reformers, and ignoring community sentiment could be fatal to local reorganization efforts. Second, state and county officials often relied upon local district superintendents to advance the cause of reorganization, yet these administrators often had little motive to support the movement. Not only did reorganization potentially mean that a superintendent of a smaller district could be out of a job but, if the local constituency was opposed to reorganization, that superintendent might put her or his own reelection or reappointment at risk, even if the reorganization effort failed. Third, state officials often overemphasized the cost savings that would result from larger districts and schools without appreciating the fear locals might have about what "big schools" could mean for their children or what new building construction would mean for their pocketbooks. And finally, many locals were not prepared to see their districts become agents of the state; concern regarding loss of "local control" often served as a major hindrance to reorganization.[11]

From our twenty-first-century perspective, reorganization seems an example of a successful reform. After all, the number of school districts in the country plummeted from roughly 130,000 in the 1930s to approximately 55,000 in the mid-1950s to under 18,000 by the 1970s; but, as always, success is in the eye of the beholder. As is the case with many reform movements, those most intimately involved with the innovation constantly perceive the distance between that which has been accomplished and that which remains to be done. Many reorganizers were vexed by the lack of local willingness to embrace their seemingly rational reforms, but it was their inability to perceive the resistance that was often their undoing. Nevertheless, the second half of the twentieth century is the story of states slowly wresting more and more power and responsibility from their local districts.

CONTINUED SHIFTS IN THINKING ABOUT THE NATURE OF LOCAL EDUCATIONAL CONTROL

By the late 1950s, observant commentators on education could detect how the traditional role of the school district had changed. Indeed, in 1959, Roald Campbell called upon Americans to strip away the "folklore of local control" and to face the realities of state and federal involvement in education. He pointed out, for example, that legislatures in 27 of the 48 states had enacted limits on local school taxation, that state departments of education had begun establishing curriculum standards for the states, and that the federal government had long been running educational programs, albeit often under departments or agencies that did not have the word "education" in their title.[12] Such recognition, Campbell hoped, would hasten constructive action.

Myron Lieberman weighed in a year later with a broadside against local educational control, arguing that its decline was long overdue: "Local control of the functions of education is largely responsible for the dull and uninspiring character of much school instruction. It enables local communities to protect dominant local points of view from analysis and criticism in the schools, while at the same time it deprives the teachers of any moral justification for refusing to be a party to indoctrination when it is sanctioned by a community. Teachers cannot criticize local points of view, no matter how much they may be questioned in the state or in the country." Lieberman felt sure of the source of this dismal state of affairs. "The most important causes of the ineffectiveness of public education are rooted in its anachronistic and dysfunctional power structure." In fact, Lieberman argued, local control was not only a "major cause of the dull parochialism and attenuated totalitarianism" of American schools but could not in practice "be reconciled with the ideals of a democratic society." Among his solutions, Lieberman proposed a national system of education. Centralization need not be synonymous with "totalitarian control," he said; indeed, "our present system of local control is far more conducive to totalitarianism than a national system of schools would be." [13]

Other reform-minded writers argued for alternative methods of reform. Peter Schrag's *Village School Downtown* depicted the Boston school system as antiquated, inbred, and resistant to new ideas.[14] In *110 Livingston Street,* David Rogers argued that the New York City school system typified the "sick bureaucracy"—its traditions, structure, and operations subverted their stated missions and prevented any flexible accommodations to changing client demands. "Many of the pathologies of the New York City school system," Rogers argued, "can be traced to the overcentralization of decisions, combined with the proliferation of specialized administrative units." Other observers joined the assault on urban school systems, charging that urban systems had mismanaged funds, removed parents from the decision-making process, and provided poor and minority children with an inferior education. Many agreed with David Rogers's conclusion about the New York schools: "Nobody can make the system work," he said, "if the bureaucratic structure is not radically altered." [15]

The 1968 yearbook of the National Society for the Study of Education, entitled *Metropolitanism* and edited by Robert Havighurst, gave scant attention to decentralization, focusing instead on metropolitan and regional concepts of school governance. But even before that volume was issued, centralized notions of educational administration appeared to be becoming passé. On March 30, 1967, the New York State Senate passed Act 4622, which provided increased state aid to New York City and also included a statement supporting decentralization: "Increased community awareness and participation in the educational process is essential to the furtherance of educational innovation and excellence in the public school system within the city of New York. The legislature hereby finds and declares that the creation of educational policy units within the city school district of New York for the formulation of educational policy for the public schools within such districts will afford members of the community an opportunity to take a more active and meaningful role in the development of educational policy closely related to the diverse needs and aspirations of the community."[16] Soon thereafter the New York City Board of Education adopted a decentralization policy statement.

Other proposed reforms went under the heading of choice. And so when Ronald Reagan declared in his 1981 inaugural address that "government was the problem, not the solution," he found a ready audience among those eager to shatter many of the traditions of public education. Yet many of these reforms were based on the premise that the one best system of schooling still existed. In their advocacy for choice in schooling, for example, John Chubb and Terry Moe identify the root of the problem as "the one best system." While policy debates rage and reforms target instructional practice, the "one best system," say Chubb and Moe, "has consistently stood above it all." Instead of being the target of critique itself, they assert, the one best system has provided the framework of democratic institutions within which "demands are expressed, problems identified, solutions explored, and policy responses chosen." In other words, the one best system has dictated the terms of critique and reform, rather than serving as the target of institutional reinvention.[17]

In 1995, the Education Commission of the States compiled a set of divergent views on what it would take "to re-engineer urban school districts." Some contributors to *The New American Urban School System*, such as Chester E. Finn Jr., felt that few of the reform efforts launched in the 12 years since the release of *A Nation at Risk* had succeeded and called for bolder and more fundamental changes to the educational system. Mixing a collection of metaphors to chastise current school systems, Finn characterized present structures as products of the nineteenth century, "when communications and transportation were limited to the distance one could physically move in a few hours on foot, horseback, or carriage"; as management structures that blended the "civil service model of 1895" with the "latest thing in scientific management circa 1925"; as smacking of the kind of top-down, centrally planned governance structures that had fallen out of favor by 1989, even in Eastern Europe.

Because of the disrepute into which the school district had fallen by the mid-1990s, educational researcher James Spillane felt compelled to entitle a study he had completed of district-state relations "School Districts Matter."[18] Despite reports of its demise, the school district turned out to be thriving, at least in some pockets of the country. Spillane's work coincided with new studies by scholars such as Richard Elmore, David Cohen, and Milbrey McLaughlin that examine how districts have used their leadership and coordination capacity for powerful and successful instructional change.[19] The school districts described by these researchers—especially New York City's Community School District #2—have led to something of a rebirth of interest in the district. After enduring decades of vilification, therefore, the American school district has recently been rediscovered as a mechanism for school reform. Across the country, cadres of practitioners and policymakers are returning to the once unfashionable notion that school districts are essential in fostering instructional improvement.[20]

Some policy analysts have begun to argue that public schools cannot exist without some kind of external organizational structure. Lauren Resnick and Thomas Glennan, for example, argue that despite traditionally lackluster efforts at intellectual and instructional leadership districts—primarily those that have been effectively reorganized and refocused on instruction and learning rather than on bureaucratic administration—"would be better positioned than any other agency" to fill the crucial role of providing leadership, capacity, and coherence in the instructional core of schooling. Resnick and Glennon make the point that, although organizations other than districts could carry out these essential functions, "these organizations would then function as virtual or quasi school districts." This is reminiscent of a comment by the Teachers College professor George Strayer: "If the intermediate unit of school administration did not already exist," he wrote in 1954, "someone would have to invent it."[21] Reformers who ignore the district or treat it as a outworn relic not only demonstrate a short-sightedness about the nature of educational change but also risk imperiling the very innovations they advocate due to their lack of understanding of the ways in which districts go about the delivery of educational services.

NOTES

1. David Tyack, *The One Best System: A History of American Urban Education* (Cambridge: Harvard University Press, 1974).

2. Tyack, *The One Best System*; for good examples of studies on specific cities see: Cohen, *Children of the Mill*; Raftery, *Land of Fair Promise*; Cuban, *How Teachers Taught*; Mirel, *The Rise and Fall of an Urban School System*.

3. National Commission on School District Reorganization, *A Key to Better Education: A Guide to School* District Reorganization (Washington, DC: National Commission on School District Reorganization, 1947).

4. Tyack, OBS; Cubberley on Consolidation, etc.

5. California State Department of Education, *Study of Local School Districts in California* (Sacramento: California State Department of Education, 1937).

6. Reorganization of School Units, 1.

7. *Your School District*, 13; The Commission primarily consisted of professors of education from rural states and administrators in national organizations focused on rural agendas.

8. National Commission on School District Reorganization, *Your School District: the report of the National Commission on School District Reorganization* (Washington, DC: Department of Rural Education, National Education Association, 1948), 8.

9. United States Department of Health, Education, and Welfare, *School District Reorganization* (Special Series No. 5, Washington, DC, 1957), 7.

10. Washington State Research Council, "What Is a School District?" (Seattle and Olympia: Washington State Research Council, 1957), 8–9.

11. Roald F. Campbell, "Feelings are Facts in School District Reorganization," *The Nation's Schools* 57(3), 1956; Robert R. Alford, "School District Reorganization and Community Integration," *Harvard Educational Review* 30(4), 1960.

12. Roald F. Campbell, "The Folklore of Local School Control," *The School Review* 67(1), Spring 1959, 8. On federal programs, Campbell wrote: "We suspect that dispersion of educational functions among more than a score of agencies ... helps congressmen preserve the delusion that the federal government does not interfere with the sacred rights of states and local communities to control our great public school system."

13. Myron Lieberman, *The Future of Public Education* (Chicago: University of Chicago Press, 1960), 5, 34, 37.

14. Peter Schrag, *Village School Downtown: Boston Schools, Boston Politics* (Boston: Beacon Press, 1967).

15. David Rogers, *110 Livingston Street: Politics and Bureaucracy in the New York City Schools* (New York: Random House, 1968), 267, 271, 266.

16. Baratta in Lutz, pp. 85–86.

17. John E. Chubb and Terry M. Moe, *Politics, Markets, and America's School* (Washington, DC: Brookings Institution, 1990), 6.

18. James P. Spillane, "School Districts Matter: Local Educational Authorities and State Instructional Policy," *Educational Policy* 10 (1996): 63–87.

19. Richard F. Elmore and Deanna Burney, *Investing in Teacher Learning: Staff Development and Instructional Improvement in Community School District #2* (New York: National Commission on Teaching and America's Future, 1997); David K. Cohen and Heather C. Hill, "Instructional Policy and Classroom Performance: The Mathematics Reform in California," *Teachers College Record* 102 (April 2000); Milbrey W. McLaughlin, "How District Communities Do and Do Not Foster Teacher Pride," *Educational Leadership* 50 (September 1992): 33–35.

20. See, for example, James P. Spillane, "School Districts Matter: Local Educational Authorities and State Instructional Policy," *Educational Policy* 10 (1996): 63–87; Richard F. Elmore and Deanna Burney, *Investing in Teacher Learning: Staff Development and Instructional Improvement in Community School District #2* (New York: National Commission on Teaching and America's Future, 1997); David K. Cohen and Heather C. Hill, "Instructional Policy and Classroom Performance: The Mathematics Reform in California," *Teachers College Record* 102 (April 2000); Amy Hightower, Michael Knapp, Julie A. Marsh, and Milbrey W. McLaughlin (eds.), *School Districts and Instructional Renewal* (New York: Teachers College, 2002), this volume contains a number of excellent studies of district reform. See also Annenberg Institute for School Reform, *School Communities that Work for Results and Equity* (Providence, RI: Annenberg Institute for School Reform, Brown University, 2002).

21. Strayer quoted in National Education Association, *Better Education through Effective Intermediate Units* (Washington, DC: National Education Association, 1963).

CHAPTER FIVE

Growing State Intervention IN Low-Performing Schools

Law AND Regulation IN Three Waves OF Reform

KATHRYN A. MCDERMOTT

For much of their history the states have taken a relatively small role in education governance, even though they have the primary constitutional responsibility for, and authority over, public education. During the 1970s, some states began expanding their education governance powers. By the early 1990s, the states were the main site of a reform effort intended to reorganize education policy around students' attainment of academic standards. Many states enacted policies that empowered the state government to intervene in schools and districts where student test scores fell short. In this chapter, I analyze the evolution of state sanctions against underperforming schools and districts in the 1980s and 1990s, emphasizing the strongest forms of accountability sanctions: state power to intervene in schools' staffing or shut them down entirely, and state receivership or direct operation of school districts.[1] I emphasize these policies because they appear to constitute a major shift in intergovernmental relations concerning education policy. I identify three waves of state intervention policy, defined by national-level organizing efforts and federal law. I conclude that advocates of these policies, and the standards-based education reforms into which they fit, did not so much learn from history as seek to escape from it.

WHY STUDY ACCOUNTABILITY IN THE STATES?

The expansion of the state intervention powers is a fruitful topic of research because of the states' position in the education governance system. Historically, the U.S. education governance system has been dominated by local school districts. The inequities in resources and needs generated by such a locally controlled system are well known. State laws themselves have also at times accepted, or even reinforced, inequity. The state laws that required racially segregated schools are the most egregious examples, but prior to state-level school-finance litigation, many states also had local-aid systems that increased, rather than mitigated, inequalities of wealth among communities. During the years following the *Brown v. Board of Education* decision, the main goal of federal education policy was equal treatment for certain vulnerable populations, such as students with disabilities and students whose native language was not English. Many states enacted similar policies. Advocates for students in low-spending school districts challenged states' systems of funding public education. Where these plaintiffs won their cases, state legislatures enacted new systems with more egalitarian funding formulas. However, state policymakers—especially legislators—were reluctant to challenge the system of local control that produced financial inequality in the first place.[2]

In the last quarter of the twentieth century, the standards-based reform model (SBR) became popular among state education policymakers. The core idea of SBR is to replace the tangle of often-conflicting educational policies with a single idea: all students should master a common core of academic material, and if they do not, then the state should hold teachers, administrators, and sometimes the students themselves accountable. Instead of regulating "inputs" such as class sizes, or time spent on certain subjects, the state should concentrate on setting standards and maintaining accountability through a system of rewards and punishments.[3] These ideas were consistent with ideas about public management that were gaining in favor at the time, such as performance measurement and program-based budgeting.[4] For many legislators in state that were increasing their education spending, accountability for results was an appealing quid pro quo.

Initially, the SBR idea traveled around the states through personal connections among reform-minded governors and staffers, and also through the work of regional organizations. During a second period, beginning in 1986, the National Governors Association (NGA) took up the cause. In 1994, SBR went from a national movement to a federal law, as that year's reauthorization of the Elementary and Secondary Education Act required states to enact some form of SBR in order to receive federal Title I funds. This third wave set the stage for the 2001 passage of the No Child Left Behind Act.

ACCOUNTABILITY BEFORE THE STANDARDS
MOVEMENT: THE EARLY 1980s

In the 1970s and early 1980s, discontent with the quality of U.S. public schools was widespread. The "high school graduate who could not read his diploma" (who, sadly, was probably not apocryphal) made regular appearances in public debate,[5] and a *Time* magazine cover story in 1980 reported on Americans' growing belief that their schools were in trouble. State and regional efforts to boost educational quality preceded the federal commission that produced *A Nation at Risk*, the 1983 report that increased national pressure for reform.[6] One response to this discontent about school performance was for legislatures to enact minimum-competency testing programs, designed to certify that students were functionally literate and able to do basic mathematics. Some states even began requiring students to pass minimum-competency tests before they could earn high school diplomas.

The concern for quality was particularly acute in the southern states, which historically had not had especially strong commitments to public education. In many cases, the states had compounded their educational disadvantages by disinvesting in public schooling during conflicts over school desegregation. Mississippi, the last state in the U.S. to have made schooling mandatory, went so far as to repeal its mandatory-attendance law in 1956 and did not reinstate it until 1977.[7] Southern governors advocated education reform as an economic development tool, believing that they could attract businesses by producing a better-educated workforce. For example, a 1984 education reform package advocated by Tennessee governor Lamar Alexander (a future U.S. secretary of education) often gets credit for General Motors chosing to locate its new Saturn assembly plant in that state.[8] Another ambitious southern governor, Bill Clinton of Arkansas, made economic competitiveness through education reform an early focus of his administration.[9] The southern states were especially likely to adopt policies that attached serious consequences, or "high stakes," to test results. Of the ten states that enacted graduation tests prior to 1980, six were southern.[10]

In addition to having graduation tests aimed at students, some states also began using test scores to evaluate the performance of schools and districts, and threatening strong state action where performance fell short. Under Arkansas law, a school or district where fewer than 85 percent of students met a "mastery" level score on state tests had to participate in a school improvement program, after which it would lose its accreditation if scores did not rise.[11] Texas required all school districts to be accredited by its Central Education Agency, according to standards that included test scores.[12] In Texas, loss of accreditation could lead to state appointment of a "master to oversee the operations of the district,"[13] and in Arkansas, it could lead to a district's being dissolved and annexed by another district.[14] Georgia schools and districts classified as "nonstandard" after failing a state review had to implement a corrective plan, which could include court appointment of a trustee to ensure implementation.[15] South Carolina districts where the state determined that the quality of education was "seriously impaired" were also subject to corrective action. If the district failed to implement a corrective action plan successfully within six months, the state superintendent of education could then escrow state funds or recommend that the governor of the state declare the district's superintendency to be vacant, with an interim replacement to be appointed by the state superintendent.[16]

All these sanctions resembled the ones that other states would enact later in the history of standards-based reform. However, in the early 1980s, the states' criteria for intervention had not completely broken with the idea that states should monitor educational inputs. Georgia's state reviews included a long list of input and process requirements, from which schools could be exempt if they had particularly high performance on tests, but also exempted any school already accredited by the Southern Association of Schools and Colleges. Texas required school districts to document the quality of their staff evaluation and in-service training, while also complying with paperwork reduction requirements (a mixed message, perhaps). South Carolina lists "accreditation deficiencies" as one of the elements that would be taken into consideration in identifying "seriously impaired" school districts. Georgia law additionally departed from what would later become the SBR orthodoxy by requiring schools and districts to compare themselves to others that were "comparable in terms of demographic characteristics," and reserving the "nonstandard" designation for those who were unsuccessful "relative to comparable units," which suggests that the state accepted different standards of performance for institutions serving different populations of students.[17]

Research on the spread of policy ideas among the states has typically concluded that wealthy, industrialized states are the most frequent innovators.[18] However, contrary to this general pattern, most of the southern states were neither wealthy nor industrialized in the late 1970s. What accounts, then, for the region's being in the lead in this particular policy area? Part of the answer may be institutional. The Southern states already had relatively centralized systems of education governance, many of which included state approval of textbooks. Of the 22 states that currently have the power to approve public-school textbooks, 13 are in the South, in contrast to only two of the 28 states that do not approve textbooks.

Where the state approves textbooks, there is a precedent for a larger state role in shaping curriculum, including setting standards and evaluating school and district performance. Three of the first four states (all but South Carolina) to enact strong accountability sanctions against school districts were states that

Table 1 Strength of Accountability Systems in Textbook Adoption versus. Non-adoption States, 2002

Value of Acct. Index (per Carnoy & Loeb, 2002)	Non-Adoption States	Adoption States	Total
5	2 (NJ, NY)	3 (FL, NC, TX)	5
4	1 (MD)	4 (AL, CA, KY, NM)	5
3 or 3.5	1 (OH)	5 (IN, LA, MS, SC, WV)	6
2 or 2.5	4 (AZ, MA, MN, WI)	4 (GA, IL, OR, VA)	8
1 or 1.5	18 (AK, CO, CT, DE, HI, KS, ME, MI, MO, MT, ND, NH, PA, RI, SD, VT, WA, WY)	6 (AR, ID, NV, OK, TN, UT)	
0	2 (IA, NE)	0	2
Total	28	22	

also approved textbooks. States with textbook approval power, regardless of their region, still tend to have more extensive accountability systems than states without. Table 1 shows states categorized by their presence or absence of textbook adoption powers, along with the "accountability index" assigned to the state's policies by Martin Carnoy and Susanna Loeb in a 2002 *Educational Evaluation and Policy Analysis* article.[19] Although there are nontextbook-adopting states with strong accountability systems, and textbook-adopting states with less extensive accountability, the textbook-adopting states are likelier than the others to have an accountability index above 2.5, and less likely to score below 2.5. Of the 16 states rated higher than 2.5, 12 (75 percent) have textbook-adoption power, compared with 10 of the 34 (29 percent) rated 2.5 or lower. Sixteen of the twenty-two textbook-adoption states (73 percent) score above 2.5 on the accountability scale, and none score zero.

THE STATES RESPOND TO A NATIONAL MOVEMENT, 1986–1994

By the middle of the 1980s, "education reform" in general, and standards-based reform in particular, had gone from being a goal of a few policy entrepreneurs in a few states to being the main priority of the NGA. Historically, oversight of public schools had been entrusted to state superintendents and state boards of education, in the belief that professionals rather than governors or legislators should run the schools. However, as education became a larger part of state budgets, and public concern about school quality rose, governors became less willing to leave education to educators. In 1986, the NGA, then co-chaired by Tennessee governor

Alexander, announced a seven-point, five-year education agenda entitled *Time for Results*. The seven elements of the agenda included strengthening school leadership and management and helping at-risk students meet high educational standards. Governor Alexander likened SBR to "old-fashioned horse trading" and said, "we'll regulate less, if schools and school districts will produce better results." In other words, the governors would work to reduce regulations on what schools and districts did, so long as their state governments could hold those schools and districts accountable for the results of their deregulated activities. The NGA also convened an "education summit" for its members and President George H.W. Bush in Charlottesville, VA, in 1989, after which NGA leaders (including Bill Clinton), President Bush, and U.S. Secretary of Education Lauro Cavazos jointly announced a set of National Education Goals.[20]

The NGA's education agenda emphasized accountability for student performance, rather than monitoring of resources and processes, as the goal of state education policy. However, standards and accountability were only one of the NGA priorities. The others were professionalizing the teacher workforce, enhancing parental involvement and choice, improving the use of technology, using resources more effectively, and making higher education institutions more mission-driven and effective.[21] During the late 1980s and early 1990s, more states enacted accountability policies with sanctions, but they often combined accountability policy with other policy ideas such as the ones advanced by the NGA. The most lasting development during the late 1980s was the enactment of omnibus reform laws intended to reorganize a state's entire education system around performance standards. Where earlier laws had sometimes targeted only districts or only schools, the new reform laws included both in a common accountability system. They were often based on the NGA's "horse trade" idea.

Despite the new emphasis on student performance, inputs and processes remained prominent in states' reviews of schools and districts. Indiana, for example, enacted a new "performance-based accreditation system" section of the state code in 1987, but the system was not *exclusively* performance-based.[22] In addition to stipulating that schools and districts must attain their expected performance levels in order to earn full accreditation, Indiana's statute also required review of "minimum time requirements for school activity," staff-to-student ratios, staff evaluation plans, and internship programs for beginning teachers. West Virginia's "performance-based" accreditation system also included evaluation of school districts' "average class size; pupil-teacher ratio; number of exceptions to pupil-teacher ratio requested by the county board and the number of exceptions granted; the number of split-grade classrooms; pupil-administrator ratio; and the operating expenditure per pupil."[23] A 1991 California law required the state superintendent of public instruction to review county education budgets, a process that could culminate in the state's developing a fiscal plan for a county, rescinding its spending decisions, and monitoring the county office of education.

Even in states with standards-based systems, in which low test scores alone could put a district or school on a warning list or identify it for further scrutiny, intervention happened only after a review of resources and/or management practices. For example, New Jersey's State-Operated School District law of 1987 required a "comprehensive compliance investigation" including "a thorough and detailed examination of a district's educational programs, fiscal practices, governance and management"[24] prior to an administrative law hearing on whether the state should take over.

During this period, several states enacted laws that specifically targeted a single school district for intervention, rather than creating more generally applicable intervention powers. In 1993, the California legislature passed a law that approved a state loan to the Compton public schools, while also requiring the school district to take corrective actions that included improvement of services for Latino students and others with limited proficiency in English.[25] New Jersey's state intervention law, although written to apply generally, was widely understood at the time as targeting just a few urban districts. To date, the state has intervened only in Newark, Paterson, and Jersey City.[26]

The comprehensive reform laws enacted during this period all used students' test scores as the main criterion for judging school and district performance, but they often differed in their definitions of the kind of performance that would trigger state interventions. The Massachusetts Education Reform Act of 1993 left the definition of "underperformance" up to the state board of education but did specify that the criteria must "include, but not be limited to," results on state tests.[27] Oklahoma law called for sanctions when a school's test performance put it in the lowest quartile in the state *and* its students scored below the national average on any norm-referenced test for three consecutive years.[28] The Kentucky Education Reform Act targeted the two-year change in student scores, labeling a school as "in crisis" and imposing sanctions if the proportion of its students scoring at a level considered "successful" declined by more than 5 percent.[29]

In contrast to the SBR principle that all students, regardless of poverty or minority group status, should be held to identical academic standards, which would later become central to federal policy, some of the accountability policies enacted in the 1980s took student demographics into account in determining whether a school's test scores were satisfactory. Under a law passed in 1987, Indiana's state education agency was to determine "the level of performance expected for each school in light of the socioeconomic factors of and resources available to the school," which was to serve as the minimum level for the school to attain.[30] A 1989 Texas law stipulated that the state's performance indicators for school districts were to include "a comparison of the district's performance to a projection of the district's expected performance."[31]

During this same period, plaintiffs in school-finance lawsuits were beginning to have some success with legal arguments based on the education guarantees in state constitutions.[32] Beginning in the early 1990s, states often addressed finance reform and SBR at the same time, because responding to a finding that the existing system did not produce an adequate education, or a "thorough and efficient" one, logically seemed to require criteria for judging adequacy, thoroughness, and efficiency. Statewide tests based on curriculum standards promised to provide the needed evidence. The best-known example of a state law that included SBR in a response to a finance lawsuit was the Kentucky Education Reform Act of 1990, enacted after the plaintiffs prevailed in the state-level *Rose* lawsuit.[33] The Massachusetts Education Reform Act of 1993 was modeled in part on Kentucky's, and passed by the state legislature before its Supreme Judicial Court had even decided its finance suit.[34]

School and district sanctions enacted during this period were mostly variations on the theme of replacement of staff, or of limits or changes to local powers. Illinois and Kansas both could declare a district "nonrecognized," which would lead to its being dissolved, and districts in Oklahoma and Texas could be annexed by another district. New Jersey could place a district within state control, and other states could place districts in various types of receivership. In Massachusetts, the state could remove the principal of a chronically underperforming school and grant broad personnel powers to the new principal.[35] It could also place a chronically underperforming district into receivership.[36] Kentucky and Michigan both gave students the right to transfer out of a school with poor performance, a way of bringing market pressures to bear.

Despite the growing popularity of laws that threatened to sanction schools and districts for poor performance, states actually showed little interest in actually using the most extreme sanctions. (New Jersey represents an exception to this rule, since its legislators assumed that the intervention power they were creating would be immediately used against several urban districts.) Typically, sanctions such as replacement of a superintendent, disbanding a school district, or reconstituting a school do not take place automatically but rather require a lengthy administrative process. States' use of the strongest forms of sanctions remains rare. In 2004, the Education Commission of the States reported that only 54 school districts nationwide (out of about 15,000 total) had ever been taken over by their states, and only 18 of these takeovers were for primarily academic reasons.[37] A 2005 study funded by the federal Institute for Education Sciences concluded that only five states had ever taken over a school.[38]

There was clearly a common theme in the accountability policies of the late 1980s and 1990s, in that they were all grounded at least partially in student performance on statewide tests and employed many of the same sanctions against schools and districts, most of which were not used but rather held in reserve as threats. However, the diversity of the laws was at least as important as the common tendencies. It is also important to remember that in 1994, well into the "national movement" for standards-based reform, only nineteen states had the strongest forms of sanctions in place for schools, and only 14 had them for districts. SBR advocates' interest in pushing their agenda forward led to the next main development in the history of sanctions policies, the enactment of the federal Goals 2000 and Improving America's Schools Acts in 1994.

MODEST RESPONSE TO NEW FEDERAL REQUIREMENTS, 1994–2001

The Goals 2000: Educate America Act and the Improving America's Schools Act (IASA), both enacted in 1994, wrote SBR into federal policy. Although Congress spent more time debating Goals 2000, which was based on the goals identified at the 1989 Charlottesville governors' summit,[39] the IASA had the greater impact in the states. Goals 2000 made new federal funds available to states and school districts to support SBR projects. IASA, in contrast, attached new SBR-inspired conditions to the Elementary and Secondary Education Act Title I funds, on which many states and districts had come to rely. Thus, the IASA was harder to ignore or resist than Goals 2000.[40] Some state accountability laws enacted during this period show the influence of the IASA conditions; however, the state responses did not add up to a convergence of policies around a single model.

While, IASA imposed new SBR conditions on states receiving Title I funds, these conditions brought federal policy into better alignment with existing state SBR legislation. Paul Manna points out that the basic design of federal education policy had influenced the balance of power within state governments by channeling federal funds into state education agencies, beyond the direct control of governors and legislators.[41] The new federal requirements had the blessing of many governors because they were consistent with the governors' own education agendas. According to Mike Cohen, a Clinton administration official who was a staffer at the NGA in the late 1980s,

> The main message ... we didn't have the word standards just yet, but it was very much results-focused, outcome based, accountability, so on and so forth, and we need your help

in lining up your programs to support our agenda. So even then, they [the governors] were quite specifically saying to the feds, help us hold schools accountable for results.[42]

When Bill Clinton, who had been one of the leaders of the NGA's education reform efforts, became president in 1993, he brought many alumni of those efforts—most prominently, U.S. Secretary of Education and former South Carolina governor Richard Riley—into his administration.

The new testing and accountability requirements in the IASA were more extensive than previous reauthorizations of the Elementary and Secondary Education Act, but they still left a great deal up to the states. The states had to set standards, administer tests based on those standards at least once in the elementary grades, once in the middle grades, and once in high school and use these tests both for Title I and non-Title I students. The states also had to determine what would constitute "adequate yearly progress" in student achievement for schools and districts. The law required that the definition of adequate yearly progress be linked "primarily" to student performance on state assessments but left the rest of the definition to state discretion.[43] If schools or districts failed to make "adequate yearly progress" with two years, they were to be subject to a range of sanctions that grew more stringent for each year of inadequate progress. The precise sanctions, however, were mostly left to the states to determine.[44] Although IASA said that a state "may" take corrective action as early as the second consecutive year a school district does not make adequate progress, the law did not *require* corrective action until the fourth year, and even then the corrective action could consist of "a joint plan between the State and local educational agency" for improvement, rather than any of the more dramatic measures.[45] This flexibility meant that many states did not need to make major changes to existing SBR laws in order to comply with IASA.

Several states, including Alabama, Texas, North Carolina, Vermont, South Carolina, Rhode Island, and California, enacted omnibus SBR laws between 1995 and 2001. Some of these laws revised existing accountability policies. For example, the new Texas Education Code enacted in 1995 made the state's accreditation policies more clearly performance-based than they had previously been.[46] States such as Vermont, Rhode Island, and Pennsylvania, all with strong traditions of local control, enacted accountability laws for the first time. Vermont's Act 60 of 1997 built accountability into an unusually redistributive revision of its education finance system following the Vermont Supreme Court's decision that its education finance system was unconstitutional.[47] Pennsylvania's Act 2000–16, the Education Empowerment Act, provides an example of how SBR laws sometimes frame an expansion of state power as also "empowering" locally. Act 2000–16 directed the Pennsylvania state department of education to compile an annual list of school districts with histories of low test scores, entitled the "Educational Empowerment List." If a district remains on this list for three consecutive years, the law states that it "shall be certified by the department as an education empowerment district and a board of control shall be established," which "[e]xcept for the power to levy taxes … may exercise all other powers and duties conferred by law on the board of school directors."[48] School districts already classified as financially distressed under an earlier law were to go directly to the control-board stage as soon as the 2000 law took effect. Clearly this law did not "empower" the local boards of education; presumably, "empowerment" referred to the law's effect on the state department of education, acting on behalf of local citizens and students.[49]

Following the model outlined in IASA, state laws enacted during this period phase in progressively more aggressive interventions as schools and districts spend more time classified as low-performing.[50] Some states enacting post-IASA laws established performance categories for schools and districts. Based upon percentages of students scoring proficiently on state tests, plus satisfactory attendance and drop-out rates, Ohio classified school districts as "effective," "needs continuous improvement," under "academic watch," or in a "state of academic emergency."[51] South Carolina divided its schools and districts into five categories of performance and improvement. Districts rated below average were subject to being declared in a "state of emergency," which could trigger state removal of the district superintendent or direct state management of the district.[52] North Carolina chose to base its school accountability system mostly on student achievement growth, rather than on absolute levels of achievement.[53]

IASA permitted, but did not require, states to use school choice policies to permit students to leave schools and districts targeted for improvement.[54] For the most part, state sanctions employed administrative means rather than market pressure, but legislation in Florida, California, and West Virginia did require that students in underperforming or low-rated schools be permitted to transfer to other schools.[55] In 1999, the Florida legislature expanded school choice to the private sector by creating the Opportunity Scholarships program.[56]

Despite the new federal requirements, and the flurry of state legislative activity, by 2001 only about half of the states had the power to replace school staff, close schools, place districts in receivership, eliminate districts, or directly operate districts. About half of the state laws empowering states to intervene strongly in schools and forward slash or districts were actually passed prior to IASA, as Figure 1 shows.

The state-level results of the federal IASA disappointed some SBR advocates. From the advocates' point of view, the problem was both that the IASA was too

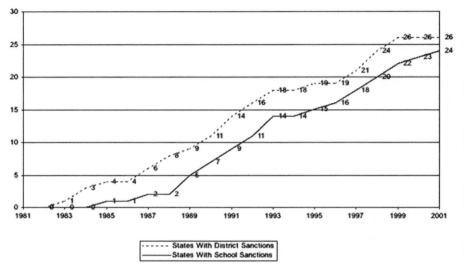

Figure 1 Ultimate State-Level Sanctions for Schools and Districts

Source: Author's data on state policy enactments.

flexible and that the USED did not aggressively enforce the requirements the law did contain. Part of the Republican Party's campaign strategy for the 1994 midterm elections was an attack on the expanded federal authority in education; thus, when the Republicans gained control of Congress after the elections, they reduced funding for IASA and Goals 2000.[57] Facing congressional opposition and retaliation, USED granted waivers and did not insist on strict compliance with IASA as a condition of receiving funds. As Mike Cohen, by then Assistant secretary of education, recalled, "it's really hard for the leadership ... to focus on the details of enforcement, when they're in fact responding to attacks to eliminate the agency entirely."[58] As late as 2002, only 19 states had full federal approval of their accountability systems, five had entered into compliance agreements, and 27 were operating under waivers.[59]

In some states, federal pressure was not especially influential in shaping educational legislation. For example, Connecticut did not greatly expand its powers in the 1990s in response to IASA, although it did pass laws enabling state takeover of the Hartford Public Schools and requiring the state to develop a list of underperforming schools. The chief lobbyist for the Connecticut Association of Boards of Education and the state deputy commissioner in charge of assessment both recalled that requirements attached to federal funds had been one impetus for the underperforming-schools legislation. However, Ted Sergi, who was then Connecticut commissioner of education, said that state legislators' own preferences had driven the agenda, and that the state "generally ignore[s] the feds." The Senate co-chair of the state legislature's education committee also did not recall federal pressure.[60] More dramatically, in 1995, Alabama enacted a comprehensive reform law whose testing provisions put the state out of compliance with IASA .[61]

OVERALL EFFECTS OF ACCOUNTABILITY POLICY ON DISTRICT, STATE, AND FEDERAL GOVERNANCE

The complexity of intergovernmental relations in education policy makes it quite difficult to generalize about how an expanded state role in sanctions and accountability has affected the overall balance of authority in the system. States' governance institutions and policies vary considerably, even when trends towards more centralized funding and state accountability are considered. For example, although the 50-state average proportion of total education revenue from state sources has increased since the early 1970s, in the 2003–04 school year the actual figures still ranged from 29.6% in Nevada to 86.6% in Hawaii.[62] Some of the earliest accountability enactments did not entail large net increases in state power, since most of them happened in the southern states that already had more centralized systems, often including state-level approval of textbooks. Even in the more locally controlled states, state-level sanctions against schools and districts could be understood as an implementation of existing state constitutional power in public education, rather than as an assertion of new powers. Many states did not enact school or district sanctions. States that did expand their powers to sanction have used the strongest sanctions sparingly.

It is also important to keep in mind that U.S. school districts range in size from a few dozen students to over one million students, and that a "school district" is not the same sort of governmental entity in all states. Most are fiscally independent of any other local government, but many are not. Thus, broader state powers do not necessarily affect settled patterns of state-local interaction in the same way in all states. Furthermore, state education departments typically have limited enforcement and implementation capacity,[63] so a law whose effect seems large on paper may be less significant in practice.

The flurry of state policymaking that followed enactment of the federal IASA in 1994, to say nothing of No Child Left Behind seven years later, suggests that the relationship between federal and state policymaking is not zero-sum.[64] According to Fuhrman and Elmore, increased state policymaking may actually increase policymaking at the local level.[65] However, quantity of policies made is probably not the best indicator of whether activity at one level crowds out activity at another. We should also ask whether there is evidence that state-level accountability policies pushed local policy agendas in directions that local officials and voters would not have chosen on their own. If the answer to this question turns out to be yes, then it leads to another question that is even more difficult to answer: is it necessarily a bad thing for one level of government to change another level's agenda or priorities? This sort of change has been a major goal of federal education policy, which has used constitutional rights, rights created by statute, and granted conditions to compel state and local governments to pursue equitable treatment for disadvantaged populations.[66]

Influence travels upwards in the system as well. Congress based the IASA, and later NCLB, on states' standards and accountability policies.[67] Indeed, Lorraine McDonnell has argued that the federal role could not have expanded as it has without the states' standards-based policies, on which the federal role was modeled. McDonnell argues that the two Bush administrations and the Clinton administration "took advantage of political conditions and policy directions developing outside the federal role."[68] Manna describes the mutual influence of state and federal education policies as the result of policymakers "borrowing strength," in the form of license and capacity to act, across levels of the federal system.[69]

WAS CLIO AT THE TABLE? DID ANYBODY LISTEN TO HER?

States' enactment of accountability policies does not appear to be the result of learning from history. The idea of standards and accountability diffused so fast, and the strongest sanctions have been used so infrequently, that state policymakers could not possibly have been observing the laws' effects in other states before enacting their own sanctions. Essentially, many states enacted accountability sanctions because other states had already done so, because organizations such as the NGA backed them, and because the basic logic behind them made sense to policymakers.

State legislative debate on SBR policies combines idealistic rhetoric about ensuring that all children learn what they need to know in order to succeed economically and participate politically with occasional flashes of a tendency to blame victims of the local-control system for their situation.[70] History sometimes enters these debates in the form of allusions to a time in the past when every high-school graduate learned the classics. These allusions leave out the uncomfortable fact that the high schools of the early twentieth century were elite institutions, enrolling a relatively small segment of the relevant age group and graduating their students at rates far lower than contemporary high schools.[71] Some proponents of SBR policies acknowledge that public schools have never actually done what we presently ask them to do: educate all children to high standards, regardless of their socioeconomic status. However, this acknowledgement generally comes in the course of an upbeat "we can do better than we did in the past because the global economy demands it" argument, essentially treating the historic short-comings of U.S. public schools as if they were easily overcome, or irrelevant to the current situation. We want to believe that our nation's public schools can be for all what they have been for some: sources of economic mobility and civic education, independent of children's place in existing social hierarchies. Doing so means somehow transcending our history, never an easy task.

NOTES

I gratefully acknowledge financial support from the Spencer Foundation and the William and Flora Hewlett Foundation, through the Advanced Studies Fellowship Program at Brown University. The research was also supported by the Center for Public Policy and Administration of the University of Massachusetts, Amherst, and by a Faculty Research Grant from the University of Massachusetts, Amherst.

1. Generally, I began with the legislative and regulatory citations in Todd Ziebarth, *ECS StateNote: Accountability—Rewards and Sanctions* (Denver, CO: Education Commission of the States, 2002), and then searched for the laws' original texts and enactment dates. Much of this information was available in the LEXIS online database related to state codes, or on the states' own legislative websites, but where I could not find information on-line, I got it in law libraries' state legislative collections, and in some cases, directly from the state legislative or reference library staff. Staff members at the University of Massachusetts' W.E.B. DuBois Library, the Massachusetts State Library, the Suffolk University Law Library, the New England School of Law Library, and numerous other states' libraries and education departments assisted in locating enactment dates and texts of policies. Karen Addesso, Bernice Clark, and Kathy Naito provided additional research assistance.

2. See Douglas S. Reed, *On Equal Terms: The Constitutional Politics of Equal Opportunity* (Princeton: Princeton University Press, 2001).

3. See, for example, Marshall S. Smith and Jennifer O'Day, "Systemic School Reform," in Susan H. Fuhrman & Betty Malen, eds., *The Politics of Curriculum and Testing: Politics of Education Association Yearbook 1990* (New York: Falmer, 1991), pp. 233–67.

4. I am indebted to Carolyn Herrington for pointing out the performance-based budgeting connection in her Division L Vice-Presidential Address at the 2007 AERA Annual Meeting. On performance measurement and SBR, see Kathryn A. McDermott, "Incentives, Capacity, and Implementation: Evidence from Massachusetts Education Reform," *Journal of Public Administration Research and Theory* 16(2006): 45–65.

5. For example, at a 1979 hearing on a graduation test bill in New Jersey, the bill's sponsor told his colleagues about a recent high-school graduate who had had to ask his 9-year-old sister to read his diploma to him. Public hearing before Assembly Education Committee on Graduation Standards (S-1154), held February 28, 1979, p.8.

6. Thomas Toch provides a helpful summary of these early reports in Chapter 1 of his book *In the Name of Excellence: The Struggle to Reform the Nation's Schools, Why it's Failing, and What Should be Done* (New York: Oxford University Press, 1991).

7. Robert L. Jenkins & William A. Person, "Educational Reform in Mississippi: A Historical Perspective," in David J. Vold & Joseph L. DeVitis, eds., *School Reform in the Deep South: A Critical Appraisal*, pp. 75–108 (Tuscaloosa, AL: University of Alabama Press, 1991), p.79 and p.82.

8. Toch, *In the Name of Excellence*, p. 18.

9. See David Osborne, *Laboratories of Democracy* (Cambridge, MA: Harvard Business School Press, 1988), ch. 3.

10. The ten states are Alabama, Florida, Georgia, Hawaii (since repealed), Maryland, Nevada, New Jersey, New York (the Regents' Competency Test), North Carolina, and Virginia.

11. Acts of Arkansas 1983, Act 54, Section 8.

12. Texas Education Code 21.751 and 21.753, as enacted by 68th Texas Legislature, 2nd Called Session, Chapter 28, Article V, Part A, Section 1 (1983).

13. Texas Education Code 21.757, as enacted by 68th Texas Legislature, 2nd Called Session, Chapter 28, Article V, Part A, Section 1 (1983).

14. Acts of Arkansas 1983, Act 445, Section 2.

15. Georgia Statutes sec. 20–2-283(a), as enacted by Georgia Laws of 1985, Act 770 (Quality Basic Education Act) (1985).

16. Education Improvement Act (South Carolina Act 512 of 1984), Part II, Section 9, Division II, Subdivision E, Subpart 4, Section 1.

17. Contrast these policies with the federal government's later insistence that all students, including those with limited proficiency in English, should score "proficient" on the same state English test.

18. See Virginia Gray, "Innovation in the States: A Diffusion Study," *American Political Science Review* 67(1973): 1174–1185; J. L. Walker, The Diffusion of Innovations Among the American States, *American Political Science Review* 63 (1969): 880–899.

19. Martin Carnoy & Susanna Loeb, "Does External Accountability Affect Student Outcomes? A Cross-State Analysis," *Educational Evaluation and Policy Analysis*, 24 (2002): 305–332.

20. This account is drawn from Maris A. Vinovskis, *The Road to Charlottesville: The 1989 Education Summit* (Washington, DC: National Education Goals Panel, 1999). The Lamar Alexander quotation appears on p. 18.

21. Vinovskis, *The Road to Charlottesville*, p. 17.

22. Indiana Code 20-1-1.2

23. WV Stat. Sec. 18-2E-5(b).

24. NJ Stat. 18A:7A-14(c) and (e), as enacted by Laws of 1987, Chapter 398.

25. California Laws of 1993, Chapter 455, Sec. 1.

26. Kathryn A. McDermott, "'Expanding the Moral Community' or 'Blaming the Victim?': The Politics of State Education Accountability Policy," *American Educational Research Journal* 44 (2007):77–111.

27. Massachusetts General Laws Chapter 69, Section 1J, as enacted by Massachusetts Acts and Resolves of 1993, Chapter 71, Section 29.

28. Oklahoma Laws of 1989, Chapter 335, section 14.

29. Kentucky Education Reform Act (KY Laws of 1990, Chapter 476), Section 5.

30. The quotation is from Indiana Code 20-1-1.2, Section 7(b). Indiana Code 20-1-1.2, Section 7(a)(2)(G)(iii) establishes the performance expectation.

31. 71ˢᵗ Texas Legislature, Regular Session, Chapter 813, Sec. 2.20.

32. This strategy contrasts with earlier cases argued on state or federal equal-protection grounds. See Deborah A. Verstegan and Terry Whitney, "From Courthouses to Schoolhouses: Emerging Judicial Theories of Adequacy and Equity," *Educational Policy* 11(1997):330–352; also Reed, *On Equal Terms.*

33. See *Kentucky Education Reform Act: A Citizen's Handbook* (Frankfort, KY: Legislative Research Commission, 1998).

34. See Kathryn A. McDermott, "A National Movement Comes Home: State Politics and Educational Accountability in the 1990s," in Carl F. Kaestle & Alyssa E. Lodewick (Eds.), *To Educate a Nation: Federal and National Strategies of School Reform* (Lawrence, KS: University Press of Kansas, 2007).

35. Massachusetts General Laws Chapter 69, Section 1J, as enacted by Massachusetts Acts and Resolves of 1993, Chapter 71, Section 29.

36. Massachusetts General Laws Chapter 69, Section 1K, as enacted by Massachusetts Acts and Resolves of 1993, Chapter 71, Section 29.

37. Todd Ziebarth, *State Takeovers and Reconstitutions* (Denver, CO: Education Commission of the States, 2004). Online: http://www.ecs.org/clearinghouse/51/67/5167.htm.

38. L. Steiner, *State Takeovers of Individual Schools* (Naperville,IL: Learning Point Associates, 2005).

39. John Jennings, *Why National Standards and Tests? Politics and the Quest for Better Schools* (Thousand Oaks, CA: Sage, 1998).

40. Kathryn A. McDermott & Laura S. Jensen, "Dubious Sovereignty: Federal Conditions of Aid and the No Child Left Behind Act," *Peabody Journal of Education* 80(2005): 39–56.

41. Paul Manna, *School's In: Federalism and the National Education Agenda* (Washington, DC: Georgetown University Press, 2006), p. 145.

42. Mike Cohen, author's interview, November 6, 2003.

43. Improving America's Schools Act, P.L. 103–382, Sec. 1111(b)(2)(B)(ii).

44. NCLB would later use much of the same terminology, but with less discretion for the states. See Kathryn A. McDermott & Elizabeth DeBray-Pelot, "Accidental Revolution," in Bruce Cooper & Bonnie Fusarelli, eds., *The Rising State* (Albany: State University of New York Press, forthcoming).

45. Improving America's Schools Act, P.L. 103–382, sec. 1116(c)(6).

46. Texas Acts of 1995, 74ᵗʰ Legislature, Chapter 260.

47. *Brigham, et. al., v. State of Vermont*, 166 Vt. 246, 692 A.2d. 384, 1997 VT LEXIS 13.

48. PA Act 2000–16, Sec. 8.

49. For an explanation of how legislators in other states appear to have understood the connection between increased state power and political "empowerment," see McDermott, "'Expanding the Moral Community' or 'Blaming the Victim'?".

50. See Alabama Public Law 313 of 1995, sec. 3; California Statutes sec. 52055.5, as enacted by Public Schools Accountability Act of 1999 (First Extraordinary Session, Chapter 3X); Indiana Public Law 221–1999, sec.3; Arkansas Act 999 of 1999, sec. 10; Georgia A+ Education Reform Act of 2000, sec. 93; Colorado Statutes 22–7–609, as enacted by Laws of 2000, Chapter 107; Pennsylvania Act 16 of 2000; Texas Education Code, sec. 39.131, as

enacted by Acts of 1995, 74th Legislature, Chapter 260.

51. 1997 Ohio Senate Bill 55, amending Ohio Statutes Section 3302.02.

52. South Carolina Educational Accountability Act of 1998, Section 2, amending 1976 South Carolina Code, Chapter 18, Title 59, section 59–18-1580.

53. North Carolina Statutes 115C-105.38, as enacted by Laws of 1995, Chapter 716.

54. Improving America's Schools Act, P.L. 103–382, secs. 1116(c)(5)(B)(i) and 1116(c)(6)(B)(i).

55. Florida Laws of 1996, Chapter 369, creating Florida Statutes Sec. 229.0535; California Public Schools Accountability Act of 1999 (1st Extraordinary Session, Chapter 3X), sec. 52055.5; West Virginia Laws of 2001, Chapter 104, enacting WV Code Section 18–2E-5(k).

56. Fl. Stat. 1002.38, as enacted by Florida Laws of 2002, Chapter 387, sec. 103.

57. See Jennings, *Why National Standards and Tests?*

58. Cohen interview.

59. Erik W. Robelen, "States, Ed. Dept. Reach Accords on 1994 ESEA," *Education Week*, April 17, 2002, p. 1, 28–29.

60. Kathryn A. McDermott, "A National Movement Comes Home: State Politics and Educational Accountability in the 1990s," in Carl F. Kaestle & Alyssa Lodewick, eds., *To Educate a Nation: Federal and National Strategies for School Reform* (Lawrence, KS: University Press of Kansas, in press).

61. Robelen, p. 29.

62. National Center for Education Statistics, *Digest of Education Statistics 2007* (Washington, DC: Institute for Education Sciences), Table 164.

63. Thomas B. Timar, "The Institutional Role of State Education Departments: A Historical Perspective," *American Journal of Education* 105(1997): 234–60.

64. Manna, ch. 5.

65. Susan H. Fuhrman & Richard F. Elmore, "Understanding Local Control in the Wake of State Education Reform," *Educational Evaluation and Policy Analysis* 12(1990): 82–96.

66. To get a sense of how complex this process has been, see Adam Nelson, *The Elusive Ideal: Equal Educational Opportunity and the Federal Role in Boston's Public Schools, 1950–1985* (Chicago: University of Chicago Press, 2005).

67. See Jennings, Why National Standards and Tests; also McDermott & DeBray-Pelot, "Accidental revolution: State policy influences on the No Child Left Behind Act."

68. Lorraine M. McDonnell, "No Child Left Behind and the Federal Role in Education: Evolution or Revolution?" *Peabody Journal of Education* 80(2005): 19–38.

69. Manna, ch. 2.

70. See McDermott, "'Expanding the Moral Community' or 'Blaming the Victim'?".

71. See David F. Labaree, *How to Succeed in School Without Really Learning: The Credentials Race in American Education* (New Haven: Yale University Press, 1997), ch. 3.

CHAPTER SIX

Learning FROM Head Start

Preschool Advocates AND THE Lessons OF History

ELIZABETH ROSE

Today's advocates for preschool education have taken two major lessons from the history of Head Start, the nation's oldest and best-known public program for preschool children. The first lesson is that programs targeted at the poorest children will not build a strong enough base of political support to thrive, and the second, that a stand-alone federal program will be vulnerable to the winds of political change. These negative lessons from Head Start's history have helped to shape the current movement by focusing it on making pre-kindergarten available to all children, and integrating it into the state-based system of public K-12 education. In seeking direction from history, however, advocates can run into trouble, both by simplifying the past and by ignoring positive lessons in the rush to focus on the past's failures.

This movement for universal pre-kindergarten has seen remarkable growth in recent years: there are now more children enrolled in state pre-kindergarten programs than in Head Start (see Figure 1).[1]

This expansion in public education does not follow the historical pattern of the nineteenth century, with northeastern states setting the standard for reform. Here the South has taken the lead, in both enrollment and quality of programs.[2] Oklahoma and Georgia are the leaders in offering pre-kindergarten to all four-year olds whose parents wish to enroll them, while states such as Tennessee, Texas, and Arkansas have dramatically increased access to pre-kindergarten

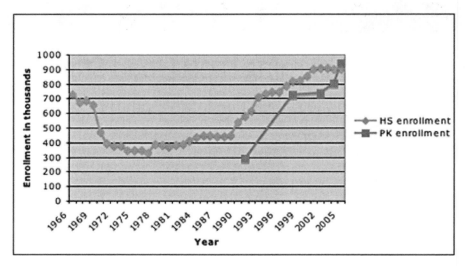

Figure 1 Head start and state pre-K enrollment, 1966–2005

by expanding targeted programs. Florida, West Virginia, Illinois, New York, Iowa, and Massachusetts are also in the process of implementing universal pre-kindergarten (see Figure 2).

This growth in state pre-kindergarten programs has roots in a strategic shift that many advocates made, starting in the mid-1990s. Rather than pushing at the federal level for more money to expand Head Start programs for poor families, they embraced a universal approach, arguing for state programs to provide "preschool for all." This was simultaneously a shift from a targeted program to a universal one, from the federal to the state level, and from an antipoverty to an educational mission. This chapter focuses on how this shift was informed by lessons from the past, and questions whether these lessons are an adequate guide for policy decisions today.

LESSON 1: BUILD A UNIVERSAL PROGRAM

When they talked about this strategic shift, preschool advocates often discussed the "lessons" they had learned from the history of Head Start. Most of all, they pointed to the difficulty of building political support for a program that only served the nation's poorest children. For instance, Susan Urahn of the Pew Charitable Trusts, which launched a multimillion dollar campaign for universal preschool in 2001, questioned the political logic of targeting services for low-income children. "I think the long experience we've had with Head Start sends a pretty clear message," Urahn explained, "that when the programs are designed for poor

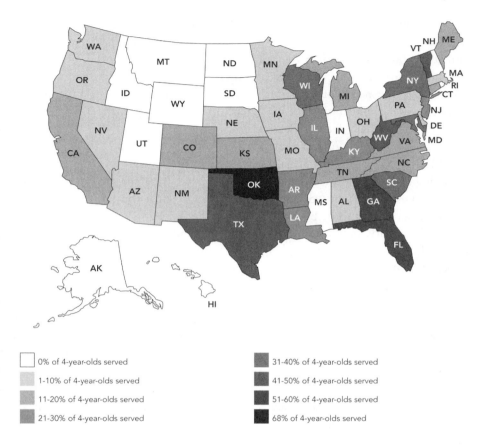

Figure 2 Percent of 4-year-olds served in state pre-K

Source: W. Steven Barnett, Jason Hustedt, Laura Hawkinson, and Kenneth Robin, *The State of Preschool 2006: State Preschool Yearbook* (New BrunswickNJ : National Institute for Early Education Research, 2006), p. 15.

kids, they never develop the constituency, and they never reach the level of quality that we, in the middle-class, would want for our kids. And I think that if you want a good program then you make it something that the middle class develops an investment in." Head Start champion Edward Zigler has written recently that Head Start's history shows the dangers of developing a program just for the poor. After more than 40 years, it only serves 60 percent of the eligible children, and there seems to be little hope of expanding it to serve all eligible children, not to mention those just above the poverty line. Furthermore, the quality of the programs has never been consistently as high as it should be. Graciela Italiano-Thomas, who spent ten years working in Head Start and now directs Los Angeles' universal preschool effort, commented in 2006, "We are at a point where we need to go beyond Head Start. ... If we are going to aim at high quality we have to aim at all children. ... When you only aim at those in greatest need, history tells us that the programs lose the political support they need to survive, and therefore those in greatest need don't benefit." [3] Head Start has thus become a compelling piece of evidence illustrating the inadequacy of targeted approaches.

The lesson that advocates learned from Head Start is one that scholars like Theda Skocpol and William Julius Wilson offered in the late 1980s. Skocpol argued that only universal social policies have been, over time, successful at garnering enough political support to be sustainable. Targeted programs raise the difficult question of "why working-class families just above the poverty line should pay for programs for those below it." On the other hand, universal programs such as Social Security, public education, Civil War soldiers' pensions, and maternal health efforts in the 1920s proved popular because they benefited broad categories of people. Once created, these universal programs built broad coalitions of support and also provided a framework within which extra benefits could be offered that helped the poor more. Similarly, Wilson argued in his 1987 book *The Truly Disadvantaged* that the way to benefit the poor was to develop universal policies (such as family allowances and employment programs) that would benefit a large segment of the population. Targeted programs, which tended to be perceived as benefiting poor minorities rather than white taxpayers, were at once less effective and more vulnerable. Policymakers could actually help the poor more by not talking about them, but rather, by pursuing policies that addressed their needs alongside the needs of the middle class and the stable working class. Noting that Social Security proved over time to be a much more effective antipoverty tool than War on Poverty programs, Skocpol and Wilson urged policymakers to look for universal, rather than narrowly focused, targeted programs. [4]

Whether they ever read Skocpol or Wilson's work, advocates seem to have come to a remarkably uniform conclusion about Head Start: that a program targeted to poor children will inevitably have shaky political support, struggle for funds, and offer lower-quality services. This negative lesson from Head Start's history was reinforced by the positive example of Georgia's universal pre-kindergarten program. Georgia's program started in 1993 as a program for at-risk children, but seemed politically vulnerable. When the new state lottery he had championed produced more revenue than expected, Governor Zell Miller decided to open the pre-kindergarten program up to all families in 1995, thus creating a broader base of support. An administrator reflected several years later, "With the political conservative environment that we are living in, if we come out and try to push a program for poor kids, we're not going to get a whole lot of support. And so, what we made the decision to do is push a program that would touch all Georgians." Another commented, "You can't mount a sustainable program without support from the middle-class that votes."[5] As a universal program, Georgia's pre-kindergarten program has flourished, and now serves slightly more than half of the state's four-year olds. Because it has grown in size, it serves more disadvantaged children now it than it did when it was restricted to serving only those children.

Supporters of a universal approach also pointed to the example of France, where a system of *écoles maternelles*, open to all children, enjoys strong public support. When Delaine Eastin, California's superintendent of education and a member of a group of U.S. experts visiting in 1999, asked a local mayor which of France's political parties would suggest cutting funding for preschool during a recession, he laughed and said "No one would dare!" Eastin commented, "It's as if someone here were running for office and wanted to discontinue public education. You'd run him out of town."[6] Moreover, children in disadvantaged neighborhoods could receive earlier and more intensive services, thus offering targeted services within a universal framework. For American advocates, universal preschool was an idea that could appeal across class lines, increasing access to preschool for poorer families while also relieving middle-class families of the expense of paying to send their children to private programs. As one scholar wrote, providing preschool for all could be both "popular in the suburbs and good for the poor."[7]

This argument for the political benefits of a universal approach has been influential, undergirding the campaign for expanding access to preschool that has been spurred by the Pew Charitable Trusts and other organizations in the past six years. The Pew-funded National Institute for Early Education Research at Rutgers University specifically references Skocpol's historical argument in favor of universal programs in a policy brief on universal and targeted approaches, and continues to encourage policymakers to pursue a universal approach Libby Doggett, director of Pre-K Now (the advocacy group supported by Pew), wrote in 2007, "History has proven that targeted pre-k programs are more vulnerable to chronic underfunding and political attacks," pointing to the history of Head Start as the prime example. Pew's president Rebecca Rimel gave this explanation in a 2002 speech: "Why focus on universal access—not just for poor children who need it most? Let me be candid. We see it as an issue that appeals to a broad range of American families. Middle-class families care just as much about this issue as poor parents. Like those who were so successful winning support for Social Security and Medicare, we must appeal not just to the disenfranchised, but to the broad base that can compel policymakers to act in the best interest of all. In pushing for universal access we improve education for all kids."[8]

The first lesson that preschool advocates have learned from the history of Head Start—that universal programs will be more successful than targeted ones—is helping to shape the current movement to provide "preschool for all." Yet if advocates take away only a simplistic version of this lesson, it will not serve them well. Convinced that "history tells us" that universal programs will garner broader public support, advocates may be surprised by the opposition that some proposals for universal pre-kindergarten have aroused. For instance, the ambitious "Preschool for All" 2006 ballot initiative in California would have raised an estimated $2.3 billion annually to provide preschool to all four-year olds, by increasing the state income tax on the wealthiest taxpayers. The initiative started with substantial support, including the endorsement of the Los Angeles Chamber of Commerce, which had never before in its 188-year history supported any income tax increase. But in the balloting, voters rejected the measure by a margin of 61 to 39 percent. One of the opposition's main objections was that the proposal, because it was universal, would subsidize middle-class families who could afford to pay for preschool rather than helping those who needed it most.[9] Opposition to universal preschool in Virginia, Illinois, Tennessee, and elsewhere has also focused on the question of universality, contending that it is a waste of public funds to pay for preschool for families who can afford to pay tuition costs themselves. In these states, a universal approach actually created more opposition, rather than generating immediate political support. The *Chicago Tribune* wrote that while "Preschool for Some" did not make as good a slogan as "Preschool for All," it was a more responsible approach, especially given other pressing educational needs.[10] Indeed, if advocates are convinced by their historical analysis that it is critical to launch a universal preschool program, they may focus on this at the cost of other essential needs, a questionable policy priority.

A closer look at the historical case for building political support for universal social programs shows that simply making a program universal is no guarantee that it will become popular, well-funded, and sustainable. Scholars like Skocpol who argue for universal programs cite the example of common schools in the nineteenth century and Social Security in the twentieth. But neither of these universal programs was met with immediate acclaim. Indeed, the idea of providing free public schools to the children of the affluent as well as the poor was a controversial move in many places in the nineteenth century, while the Social Security Administration worked for years to "sell" Americans on the idea of Social Security, which did not become broadly popular until 20 twenty years after its creation. In both these cases, public attachment to these programs was a gradual process, shaped over time as much by the ideas that made them appealing and legitimate public endeavors as by the fact that they were universal.

Not all universal programs are popular, and not all popular programs are universal. Some targeted programs draw broad support from the perception that their recipients are "deserving" of assistance, or from the way the program meshes with social values. Aid to the disabled, or to military veterans, for instance, did not carry the stigma of welfare, because its recipients were seen as deserving. The Earned Income Tax Credit, targeted to low-income workers, has also generated a broad coalition of political supporters who like the idea of providing incentives to working poor families through the tax structure.[11] Programs such as these that embody popular ideas can be sustainable under the right political circumstances, even though they benefit only a small proportion of the voting public.

Indeed, Head Start itself is an excellent illustration of this point. Despite the limitations to which many advocates point, Head Start has enjoyed remarkable popularity with both policymakers and the broader public throughout its existence. Having outlived most other Great Society programs, Head Start was protected from major cuts during the Reagan years, and enjoyed a resurgence of funding and support in the 1990s. By the early 1990s, as a *Newsweek* reporter wrote, it seemed that "everybody loves Head Start"[12] and presidential candidates were vying to see who could promise the program more funding, as they sought "photo opps" in Head Start centers. Funding did expand significantly during this period, allowing the program to go from serving approximately 30 to about 60 percent of eligible children. A survey by the President's Management Council in 1999 found that Head Start received the highest customer satisfaction rating of any government agency or private company (including BMW and Mercedes-Benz).[13] In 2000, the *New York Times Magazine* reported that Head Start is "thought of as the one Great Society program that really worked."[14] Its broad support across the political spectrum came from the popularity of the idea of aiding young disadvantaged children, from research findings endorsing the concept of early education for disadvantaged children, from the program's multiple goals, which could appeal to liberals and conservatives alike, and from the activism of Head Start parents and staff, who mobilized effectively at key junctures to protect the program.

Head Start has faced more challenges under the George W. Bush administration, which sought to restructure the program by shifting control to the states and strengthening its academic component. Head Start supporters, however, were ultimately able to generate enough pressure to block these changes in 2003, and to keep them out of the 2007 reauthorization of the program. Indeed, there was a widespread sense that in attacking Head Start, Bush was going after one of Washington's sacred cows. Liberal columnists referred to Bush as "a schoolyard bully" picking on younger children, and referred to the measure as "spanking Head Start," while a columnist in the business journal *Bloomberg Report* asked, "Can Bush Touch an Untouchable Federal Program?" In the face of protests from Head Start supporters, even some Republicans were worried that they would come across as "voting against 5-year olds learning."[15] Meanwhile, the program's popularity with the general public has endured: a national survey in 2003 found that four out of five respondents favored expanding Head Start to serve more children.

The question, however, is not *whether* targeted programs can garner support, but rather a question of how much. Although congress is unlikely to dismantle Head Start, it seems equally unlikely to dramatically expand it, or increase its funding enough to significantly raise quality. Anthropologist and policy "framing expert" Axel Aubrun, who studied how to best communicate to the public about early childhood policy, commented, "It is possible to generate a certain amount of good will and sacrifice on behalf of unfortunate 'Others,' but no more" than that. From this assessment, Edward Zigler and Walter Gilliam conclude that Head Start will "remain vulnerable and its target population will remain underserved" as long as it is about "other people's children." [16]

Indeed, some argue that Head Start serves largely as a *symbol* of the nation's commitment to poor children, rather than as a solution. In a 1989 article that questioned the research base claiming the long-term effectiveness of the program, Ron Haskins nevertheless called for its continuation, in part because "Head Start has come to symbolize the nation's commitment to helping poor children advance through the traditional American route of self-improvement." [17] Sociologist Jeanne Ellsworth wrote in 1998 of Head Start's "enduring appeal" and its "privileged place among 'welfare' programs in the public imagination ... Among all the sad and disgraceful stories about poverty, Head Start's charm and reputation can inspire us to believe that something ... is being done." Exploring why the program remained popular even as welfare was attacked, Ellsworth concludes that Head Start tends to reinforce the popular idea that poverty and school failure are a result of the personal failings of poor parents, which can be remedied through compensatory education for their young children. "What sets Head Start apart from other social programs, perhaps, is that a folk wisdom has developed that *supports*, even celebrates, the program, while most other 'welfare' programs have been attacked by another set of cultural myths." [18] Similarly, foundation head Ruby Takanishi commented in a 2003 interview that people "see [Head Start] as a way of saying, 'We're doing something.' And the fact is, we're not." [19]

What can advocates take from this history? Universal programs do, over time, have the *potential* to create broad political support, establishing a system in which many different citizens have a stake, and which can make a bigger difference than a small program that only seeks to serve those most "in need." However, there is no immediate or simple relationship between a program's universality and its political stability or longevity. Simply making a pre-kindergarten program universal will not necessarily make it popular; indeed, Head Start has achieved remarkable popularity and longevity precisely because it is targeted at the neediest children. The negative lesson that advocates say they have learned from Head

Start—that restricting a program to poor children limits it in the long run—is a legitimate one. But translating this directly into policy today by insisting on making state pre-kindergarten programs universal is difficult, as the example of California's "Preschool for All" initiative shows. If advocates and legislators can adopt a historian's long-term perspective, they may find different ways of arriving at the goal of building broad support for their pre-kindergarten programs.

LESSON 2: INTEGRATE PRESCHOOL INTO K-12 EDUCATION

The second lesson that preschool advocates have learned from Head Start (although they are less explicit about it) is that it matters how public programs are funded and organizationally structured. For example, Georgia's pre-kindergarten program thrived not only because it was universal, but also because of how it was set up. Rather than being subject to yearly appropriations process in the legislature, it was funded through a dedicated (and unexpectedly successful) state lottery, which was administered through a commission controlled by the governor. This meant that the program could expand dramatically without raising taxes or taking money away from other needs in the state budget. It also mattered where the program was located administratively: when the pre-kindergarten program came under fire, Miller moved it out of the politically hostile territory of the state department of education and appointed one of his trusted advisors to administer it. Similarly, in arguing from historical examples of successful universal programs, Theda Skocpol notes that the success of programs like Social Security, public schools, and Civil War pensions lay not only in their universality, but in the fact that they were structured as fixed entitlements rather than yearly appropriations.

When Head Start was created, it was part of a new commitment from the federal government to fight poverty and promote equal educational opportunity for all children. When that context changed, however, Head Start was subject to the winds of political change in Washington, as a federal program that required yearly appropriations and regular reauthorizations. Furthermore, Head Start often stood alone. In establishing the program in 1965, expert planners and Office of Economic Opportunity (OEO) staffers agreed that the new program needed to be autonomous from the public schools, which were often seen as hostile to minority and poor children and parents. Believing that only community-based, grassroots efforts could mobilize the poor and create change, OEO channeled federal aid directly to local community action agencies, bypassing the usual structures of state and local government. In the long run, this meant that rather than relying on the existing infrastructure of local school districts and state departments of education, Head Start developed its own, separate systems for administering programs, creating quality standards, and providing monitoring and technical assistance. Head Start maintained its autonomy as a federal program, and never—for good or for ill—became fully integrated with the public education system. Its location outside the structure of the public schools allowed great creativity and flexibility in addressing the needs of poor children and their families, in spurring organizing in poor communities, and in employing poor parents, but also made it vulnerable politically and isolated it from the schools for which it was supposed to be preparing children.

The current state-level campaign for pre-kindergarten takes the opposite approach, aiming to make preschool part of the existing K-12 education system. While Head Start grew out of a context in which the federal government was taking bold action to fight poverty, advocates in the 1990s and 2000s saw their efforts as part of the crucial task of K-12 school reform, which was focused on the state level. Armed with substantial research evidence that high-quality preschool could have a long-term impact on children's educational performance, they cast preschool as an important tool for education reform. By linking preschool to public education, reformers hoped to benefit from the K-12 system's infrastructure, relatively stable funding, and professional standards and compensation for teachers. Most of all, they sought to cast preschool as part of the system of public education, which taxpayers see as a legitimate public expense and responsibility. As an education initiative, pre-kindergarten makes a stronger claim on the public purse and can become part of the structure of public education. The state pre-kindergarten programs that grew during the past 20 years are almost all administered by state departments of education and they are school districts, and connected more tightly to public schools than is Head Start.

Foundation director Ruby Takanishi, who was involved with Head Start from the beginning of her career in child development, now believes that Head Start is no longer a sufficient approach. She commented in a 2003 interview, "Given what we know about [children's] development, given the huge achievement gaps that occur at the kindergarten door, why, given current knowledge and changing work patterns of families and so on, why shouldn't education, publicly-supported education, begin at least at three?" Though she recognized that "hitching our wagon to the public education system, with all of its inequities and flaws" carried some risks, she also believed that an effective system of early childhood education had to be connected to a broader system: "if you don't hitch your wagon to that, what are you going to hitch it to? There's nothing to hitch to."[20]

Oklahoma, which now enrolls more of its four-year olds in state-funded pre-kindergarten than any other state, is the best example of how public pre-kindergarten programs can benefit from being "hitched" to the public schools. Preschool developed in Oklahoma as an integral part of public education.

Starting from a pilot program in 1980, Oklahoma's pre-kindergarten became part of a large education reform bill passed (amid great controversy) in 1990. After some changes in 1998 that increased funding and opened the program up to all children, enrollment grew dramatically. By 2006, 70 percent of four-year olds in the state were attending public pre-kindergarten classes. Pre-kindergarten in Oklahoma is treated as part of public education: it is funded through the state aid formula, administered by school districts (although classes may also be located in community settings), and taught by certified teachers who are paid at the same rate as teachers in other grades. Essentially, over time Oklahoma has added pre-kindergarten as a grade to its public education system—albeit one that remains optional for both families and districts.

Although no other state has gone as far as Oklahoma in offering pre-kindergarten for all as part of its system of public education, some national organizations have embraced the idea that pre-kindergarten should be seen as part of school. For example, the National Association of Elementary School Principals issued a guide in 2005 championing pre-kindergarten as a core of public education, urging principals to support a continuum of learning from age three through the primary grades. Curriculum guidelines developed by the National Council of Teachers of Mathematics in 2006 started with pre-kindergarten as the foundation for future math work. The Commission on the Skills of the American Workforce, which called in 2007 for a restructuring of public education in the United States, saw offering high-quality preschool to all four-year olds as a crucial investment in improving education—more important than the last two years of high school, which it recommended eliminating.[21]

New York's Universal Pre-kindergarten program, launched in 1997, also reflects a desire to integrate preschool into public education. Local school districts administer the programs, which were intended to ensure that all children would be "ready" for school on kindergarten entry. Standards for teachers and curriculum were similar to those for K-12 education, as the measure sought to raise the educational level of preschool to match that of the regular schools. The program was to be universal like public education, not restricted to the poor. One key advocate noted that even though the state already had a good program for poor children (created around the same time as Head Start), it "still was a poor kids' program and it will never enjoy wide public support." People would not necessarily oppose it outright, but they would not work hard to expand it enough to serve all those in need. Creating a universal program linked to public education seemed to be a more promising strategy. When Governor Pataki proposed eliminating the program as part of a package of drastic budget cuts in education in 2003, advocates found that fighting for the program's life helped intensify its connection to the public schools. As a result of banding together with other education supporters to fight the proposed cuts, the advocate said, "pre-K has an identity as a part of education in New York State. And regardless of these miserable battles, and all the things that we have to do, that is something that once it is well established, once it's there in people's minds, it doesn't go away. It is something that for kindergarten, probably took a hundred years."[22]

Funding pre-kindergarten through the state aid formula helps protect it from swings in a state's economic health or political equilibrium, and guarantees that funding will keep pace with the number of children in the state, since it is tied to enrollment. States that include pre-kindergarten in the school aid formula thus typically gain some stability for their pre-kindergarten funding by defining these programs as part of public education. A different approach to attaining stable funding is to create a dedicated funding stream for pre-kindergarten, such as a state lottery (Georgia, Tennessee, and North Carolina), or "sin" taxes (California's on cigarettes, or Arkansas' on beer). Even in the majority of states that rely on regular appropriations through the ordinary budget process, defining pre-kindergarten as part of education has led to remarkable growth in state programs even as the federal government has cut funds for Head Start and other social programs.[23]

Focusing on pre-kindergarten rather than on Head Start also means shifting from the federal to the state level. Since the federal government took the lead in establishing Head Start in the 1960s, and has the capacity to support large-scale programs across the country, advocates have tended to look to the federal level to support programs for young children. The federal role in special education (which eventually came to include mandating services for preschoolers) was another example of how federal action could transform education for a particular population of children. In recent years, however, proponents of universal pre-kindergarten have argued that preschool should not be seen as a special federal program, but rather as an integral part of public education, which is properly the domain of the states. Not coincidentally, this argument gained attention at a time when it seemed particularly unlikely that the federal government would move to expand its support for Head Start or other early education efforts.

Some reformers have laid out an ideal division of labor between states and the federal government for achieving a real system of preschool education, consistent with the U.S.'s federalist structure for providing public education. Preschool policy expert Anne Mitchell wrote in 2001 that the federal government should pursue its established role of promoting equity, by supporting states with funding and conducting research, while states should work on building "a unified preschool education system" by integrating, improving, and expanding existing programs.[24] The Committee for Economic Development (CED)'s 2002 blueprint, *Preschool for All*, building on a similar understanding of state and federal roles, proposed a specific mix of state and federal responsibilities. Its authors envisioned a system of preschool education administered by the states, but with significant federal support to ensure equity and high program standards. The federal government would subsidize pre-kindergarten for low-income families and help states develop an infrastructure for providing "preschool for all," as well as creating an independent body to certify standards for early education, and helping to collect and analyze data. The states would be responsible for building systems to actually provide preschool, monitor the quality of these programs, and fund pre-kindergarten for those children not covered by a federal subsidy. As approximately half of all children in the United States. currently fall under low-income guidelines, the responsibilities of federal and state government would be roughly equal. Noting that expanding access and opportunity in education has long been seen as a special federal role, the CED authors argued that it was appropriate for the federal government to share the costs of providing preschool with the states.[25] By giving the federal government a larger role than it has in the current K-12 system, the group sought to improve on the existing structure for financing education. Janet Hansen of the CED explained in 2003, "It's been hard to overcome the inequities embedded in the K-12 system because of the traditions and so on, but you don't have those traditions in early ed[ucation]. We wanted to be really explicit about that, which is one of the reasons that we called for a much bigger federal role than is true for K-12."[26]

In practice, however, there has to date been relatively little interest from the federal government in leading a push for universal pre-kindergarten. (Leading up to the 2008 presidential campaign, candidate Senator Hillary Clinton proposed an ambitious plan for federally supported universal pre-kindergarten. Several other members of congress have also proposed legislation to support state efforts, but to date none of these bills have attracted broad support.[27]) So far, early education has remained a matter for the individual states to pursue, without significant guidance, support, or pressure from Washington. In the absence of federal direction, the task of developing standards for state pre-kindergarten programs has fallen to national organizations. The National Institute for Early Education Research thus developed ten benchmarks for quality pre-kindergarten, and it has produced a "yearbook" for the past four years, measuring where states fall on these benchmarks, as well as on access and funding for pre-kindergarten.[28] Responding to a question about establishing federal standards, Libby Doggett of Pre-K Now said in 2006, "There are fifty states, and fifty ways to do pre-K. We're advocating that states come up with new dollars, not just depend on federal funding." She was also willing to leave standards and regulation up to the states, feeling "that states and the local level knows best."[29] Doggett's stance reflected not only advocates' assessment that there was little hope of significant action at the federal level, but also a belief that integrating preschool into states' responsibility for public education was a more sustainable path over time. This state-by-state strategy, however, also ran the risk of creating wide variability from state to state. If there were "fifty ways to do pre-K," not all of them would be equally desirable: some of them included not doing pre-K at all, and others included not doing it very well. But this is the trade-off that preschool advocates have made as they work to build pre-kindergarten at the state level, rather than waiting for the federal government to act.

A MISSING THIRD LESSON: PARENTAL ENGAGEMENT

We have seen that today's preschool advocates have drawn two negative lessons from Head Start's history: first, that programs targeted to the poorest children will not build enough political support and second, that a stand-alone federal program will be vulnerable to the winds of political change. These are legitimate conclusions, and may be important guides for the future. They have been influential in shaping a movement that seeks to provide "preschool for all" rather than just for the neediest and to integrate preschool into the structure of state-funded public schooling.

It would be a mistake, however, to think that these are the only two lessons that Head Start's rich history has to offer. By focusing on some lessons but ignoring others, advocates and policymakers run the risk of impoverishing the programs they are now creating. Preschool advocates can surely learn from Head Start's remarkable accomplishments over the past 43 years as well as from its difficulties. Among the lessons to be learned, one of the most important is how Head Start made a federal program feel like a grassroots effort marked by parent involvement and community volunteerism. Public opinion researchers reported in 2003 that while people distrusted state and federal programs as a rule, they perceived Head Start positively as a neighborhood or community program.[30] This may explain what sociologist Jeanne Ellsworth calls "a fierce loyalty to Head Start—a love, really, for *the program*, if not for every regulation, every individual, every policy or practice."[31] State pre-kindergarten programs seem unlikely to generate this sort of loyalty, which is rooted in Head Start's success at involving parents in program activities, hiring them as staff members, enabling them to create social networks with other parents, and mobilizing them to defend the program when necessary.

Indeed, one of the striking themes in Head Start's history is the number of occasions when the activism of Head Start parents influenced policymakers in Washington to "save" the program from specific threats. For instance, when the Senate was voting to move Head Start to the Office of Education in 1968, parents signed petitions and traveled to Washington to urge legislators to vote against the idea.[32] In the early 1970s, Head Start parents often rallied when federal officials were speaking about Head Start, protesting cuts to the program. For instance, in 1970, Edward Zigler was confronted with 800 protesting parents when he stopped in Marin City, California, and he found 500 parents outside his Washington office, chanting "Zigler must go!" Parents also became a major force within the National Head Start Association, which was established in 1973 to lobby for the program, and became a strong force in the fight against Jimmy Carter's efforts to move Head Start to the new Department of Education in 1978. Head Start advocates protested his plan, fearing that the move would mean dismantling the program by simply handing it over to the schools. Zigler tried to persuade Senator Abe Ribicoff of Connecticut, a personal friend, not to support the measure, but Ribicoff said he was "carrying water for the president" and could not switch positions. A busload of Head Start mothers from Hartford and New Haven, who had traveled all night to talk with Ribicoff, however, did change his mind; after meeting with them, he joined the rest of his committee in voting to delete Head Start from the bill creating the new department. Head Start administrator Bambi Cardenas Ramirez, who had worked behind the scenes to oppose the transfer, noted that this victory for the program really belonged to the parents, who were the ones who "got the message across. It's a miracle that the least empowered parents took on a president of the United States they liked and won."[33] Throughout the 1980s and 1990s, the National Head Start Association continued to organize parents in letter-writing, petition-signing, and rallies to support the program.

More recently, the 2003 campaign against George W. Bush's plan to give states control of Head Start shows the continued power that Head Start parents can exert to defend the program when it seems to be under attack. The National Head Start Association and its allies campaigned intensely against the proposed changes, which they feared would dismantle Head Start. Advocates mobilized a large grassroots base to bombard representatives in congress and state government with emails and faxes, and to demonstrate at local and national rallies to oppose the legislation. Many lawmakers from both parties were convinced to oppose the bill; Republican leadership in the House pulled the bill from the floor schedule in mid-July, fearing that with several members absent, they would not be able to pass it. A week later (after midnight, on the last night of the session), the bill did pass the House by one vote, but the reauthorization died in the Senate, and it is only now moving through congress again, without the provisions that the administration had supported in 2003.[34]

This history of parent activism in Head Start complicates the argument made by some reformers today about the need to include more affluent parents in pre-kindergarten programs to benefit from their political clout. For instance, Head Start champion Edward Zigler has written recently, "Programs for poor children are susceptible to the whimsical support of policy makers, changing national priorities, and political strategizing—events that middle-class parents would not stand for if they affected their children's care and education." Universal programs, Zigler argued, would benefit from the clout and knowledge of middle-class parents accustomed to exerting pressure on policymakers, ultimately creating higher-quality programs.[35] Although cross-class alliances may indeed help expand a program's political support, Head Start's history shows that poor parents can be quite effective advocates on their own. Indeed, the impact of their activism on behalf of the program since the 1960s has often surprised administrators and legislators. Pre-kindergarten advocates today may well want to consider how to nurture in parents a similar kind of dedication to defending their programs in the years ahead. To reproduce the level of parent engagement that has marked Head Start, state pre-kindergarten program directors will have to work hard and deliberately seek ways of overcoming the barriers that often separate parents and schools. If advocates ignore this and other positive lessons from Head Start's history, they risk creating weaker programs for the future.

Activists in today's movement to expand preschool education are quite aware of historical parallels to their efforts. While they take key lessons from Head Start, some also look to those in the past who pushed to expand public kindergarten, created the high school, or established common schools earlier in the nineteenth century. This is encouraging for those of us who believe that understanding the past can help us to make better policy in the present. Drawing lessons from the past, however, is not as simple as it appears, for strategies, ideas, and structures cannot be imported intact from one historical context to another. Thus, what worked in creating the common schools of the nineteenth century may not be the best blueprint for creating a system for preschool in the twenty-first century. The strengths of a program like Head Start cannot be separated from its weaknesses, for they flow from the same source. Lessons based on a simplistic or partial understanding of Head Start's history are not likely to provide an adequate guide to shaping preschool policy for the future. A closer look at this history may produce multiple lessons that do not all point toward the same course of action, but may spur a more nuanced debate about how history can inform the decisions we make today. Perhaps rather than providing *answers* in the shape of "lessons from history," the best contribution that history can make to those engaged in shaping policy is to draw our attention to the most important *questions* that we can ask about the present.

NOTES

1. Administration for Children and Families, "Head Start Program Fact Sheet Fiscal Year 2006". Accessed at http://www.acf.hhs.gov/programs/hsb/research/2006.htm on 5/18/07. Data on

state pre-kindergarten enrollments for 1991 comes from Gina Adams and Jodi Sandfort, *First Steps, Promising Futures: State Prekindergarten Initiatives in the Early 1990s* (Washington, DC: Children's Defense Fund, 1994); for 1998, Karen Schulman, Helen Blank, and Danielle Ewen, *Seeds of Success: State Prekindergarten Initiatives, 1998–1999* (Washington, DC: Children's Defense Fund, 1999); for 2001–2005, National Institute for Early Education Research, *State of Preschool Yearbook* (New Brunswick, NJ: National Institute for Early Education Research, 2006, 2005, 2003). The Children's Defense Fund reports counted programs somewhat differently from the more recent NIEER reports, so the recent growth is probably more dramatic than these figures indicate.

2. *Pre-Kindergarten in the South: The Region's Comparative Advantage in Education* (Southern Education Foundation, 2007). Accessed at www.southerneducation.org on 5/19/07.

3. Edward Zigler, Walter Gilliam, and Stephanie Jones, *A Vision for Universal Preschool Education* (Cambridge: Cambridge University Press, 2006), p. 247; telephone interview with Susan Urahn, October 2, 2003; Carolyn Goossen. "Preschool in L.A. County: A Multilingual Universal Approach," *Pacific News Service* (March 9, 2006). Accessed at *http://news.pacificnews.org*.

4. Theda Skocpol, *Social Policy in the United States: Future Possibilities in Historical Perspective* (Princeton,NJ: Princeton University Press, 1995), pp. 259–267; William Julius Wilson, *The Truly Disadvantaged: The Inner City, the Underclass, and Public Policy* (Chicago, IL: University of Chicago Press, 1987), pp. 118–124, 152–155.

5. Quoted in Anthony Raden, *Universal Prekindergarten in Georgia: A Case Study of Georgia's Lottery-Funded Pre-K Program* (Foundation for Child Development, 1999), pp. 67–68. Accessed at www.ffcd.org on 4/18/00.

6. Candy Cooper, *Ready to Learn: The French System of Early Education and Care Offers Lessons for the United States* (New York: The French-American Foundation, 1999), p. 36.

7. Anne McGill-Franzen. "Literacy and Early Schooling: Recursive Questions of Child Development and Public Responsibility," (Ed.D. dissertation, Albany: State University of New York at Albany, 1988). p. 222.

8. W. Steven Barnett, Kirsty Brown, and Rima Shore, "The Universal vs. Targeted Debate: Should the United States Have Preschool for All?," *Preschool Policy Matters* Issue 6 (April 2004), p. 12; *Pre-K Post* [Pre-K Now email newsletter] (February 26, 2007); Rebecca Rimel, "More to Do: Unfinished Business for America's Children" (Address given at the Children's Circle of Care Leadership Conference, 2002). Accessed at www.pewtrusts.org on 9/18/03.

9. Jill Tucker. "Reiner Initiative Qualifies for Ballot," *Atlanta Daily World* (January 14, 2006); Dana Hull, "Should California Pay for Preschool?," *Bradenton [FL] Herald* (February 12, 2006); Dana Hull. "Voters Reject Prop. 82," *San Jose Mercury News* (June 7, 2006).

10. Editorial, "Preschool for Some," *Chicago Tribune* (February 16, 2006).

11. Christopher Howard, *The Hidden Welfare State: Tax Expenditures and Social Policy in the United States* (Princeton University Press, 1997), p. 159.

12. Connie Leslie. "Everybody Likes Head Start," *Newsweek* (February 20, 1989), pp. 49–50.

13. U.S. Department of Health and Human Services, "Head Start Bests Mercedes and BMW in Customer Satisfaction," (press release December 13, 1999). Accessed at http://www.acf.hhs.gov/news/press/1999/hssatisfies.htm on 5/4/07.

14. James Traub, "What No School Can Do," *New York Times Magazine* (January 16 2000), p. 55; quoted in Josh Kagan, "Empowerment and Education: Civil Rights, Expert Advocates,

and Parent Politics in Head Start, 1965–1980," *Teachers College Record* 104, no. 3 (2002), p. 552.

15. Miriam Markowitz, "Head Hunter," *American Prospect* (July 10, 2003). Accessed at http://www.prospect.org/webfeatures/2003/07/markowitz-m-07-10.html on 5/4/07; Jennifer Niesslein, "Spanking Head Start," *The Nation* 277, no. 12 (October 20, 2003), p. 8; Andrew Ferguson, *Can Bush Touch an Untouchable Federal Program?* (Bloomberg News, June 30, 2003). Accessed at quote.bloomberg.com/apps/news?pid=10000039&cid=ferguson&sid=a XZNu93ADdXM on 7/7/03.

16. Zigler, Gilliam, and Jones, *A Vision for Universal Preschool Education*, p. 247.

17. Ron Haskins, "Beyond Metaphor: The Efficacy of Early Childhood Education," *American Psychologist* 44, no. 2 (1989), p. 282.

18. Jeanne Ellsworth. "Inspiring Delusions: Reflections on Head Start's Enduring Popularity." In *Critical Perspectives on Project Head Start*, eds. Jeanne Ellsworth, and Lynda Ames (Albany: State University of New York Press, 1998), pp. 319–320, 324.

19. Interview with Ruby Takanishi, New York City, October 23, 2003.

20. Interview with Ruby Takanishi, New York City, October 23, 2003.

21. Pre-K Now, "Moving Forward: The Role of Pre-K in Education Reform" (National Conference Call, February 21, 2007); National Association of Elementary School Principals, *Leading Early Childhood Learning Communities: What Principals Should Know and be Able to Do: Executive Summary* Accessed at www.naesp.org on 5/26/05; Sean Cavanaugh, "NCTM Issues New Guidelines to Help Schools Home In on the Essentials of Math," *Education Week* (September 12, 2006).

22. Telephone interview, January 9, 2004.

23. Head Start has experienced budget strains in the past several years with cuts in the federal budget and rising operating costs translating into an effective cut of 11 percent. This has forced the closing of some local programs and a reduction in slots, staff, operating hours, and services such as transportation and family support in half of all programs, according to the National Head Start Association. Linda Jacobson, "For Head Start, a Marathon Run," *Education Week* 26, no. 34 (April 25, 2007); pp. 28–31.

24. Anne Mitchell, *Education for All Young Children: The Role of States and the Federal Government in Promoting Prekindergarten and Kindergarten* (Foundation for Child Development, 2001), pp. 18–22. Accessed at www.ffcd.org on 12/18/01.

25. Committee for Economic Development, *Preschool for All: Investing in a Productive and Just Society* (New York: Committee for Economic Development, 2002), pp. 30–34.

26. Telephone interview with Janet Hansen, September 9, 2003.

27. Brendan Farrington. "Clinton Pushes Pre-Kindergarten Proposal," *San Francisco Chronicle* (May 21, 2007).

28. W. Steven Barnett, Jason Hustedt, Laura Hawkinson, and Kenneth Robin, *The State of Preschool 2006: State Preschool Yearbook* (New Brunswick NJ: National Institute for Early Education Research, 2006). Accessed at http://nieer.org/yearbook2006/ on 9/7/08.

29. Comments of Libby Doggett, "Effective Advocacy in the Pre-K Movement" (Pre-K Now Satellite Conference, September 30, 2006).

30. Phil Sparks. "What the Public Thinks about Early Care and Education," Yale Center in Child Development Social Policy Luncheon Series, New Haven, January 24, 2003.

31. Ellsworth, "Inspiring Delusions," p. 319.

32. New Haven parents met with Senators Weicker and Dodd, both of whom voted in their

favor. Kagan, "Empowerment and Education," p. 539.

33. Quoted in Edward Zigler and Susan Muenchow, *Head Start: The Inside Story of America's Most Successful Educational Experiment* (New York: Basic Books, 1992), p. 186. See also Maris Vinovskis, "The Carter Administration's Attempt to Transfer Head Start Into the U.S. Department of Education in the Late 1970s," (2002), which argues that the case for including Head Start in the legislation may have already collapsed by the time Ribicoff made this decision.

34. Kate Schuler and Jonathan Allen. "Head Start Vote Pulled From Friday's House Floor Schedule," *Congressional Quarterly Today* (July 16, 2003); AP Wire Service, "Head Start Overhaul Heads to Senate" (July 25, 2003). Accessed at abcnews.go.com/wire/Politics/ap20030725_127.html on 7/30/03; National Head Start Association, "House Head Start Reauthorization Vote Lauded by National Head Start Association," (press release May 3, 2007). accessed at http://www.saveheadstart.org/ on 5/30/07.

35. Zigler, Gilliam, and Jones, *A Vision for Universal Preschool Education*, p. 247.

III. EQUITY AND THE ROLE OF THE FEDERAL GOVERNMENT IN ELEMENTARY AND SECONDARY EDUCATION

CHAPTER SEVEN

Education Interest Groups AND Policy Agendas IN THE 109th AND 110th Congresses

Applying AN Advocacy Coalition Framework

ELIZABETH DEBRAY-PELOT

This chapter uses an Advocacy Coalition Framework to analyze coalitions and alliances in the national education interest group and think tank sectors between 2005 and 2007, a period before the reauthorization of the No Child Left Behind Act (NCLB). I examine the basic sources of agreement and conflict among the major education interest groups and think tanks in the national education policy subsystem. The foundations for these questions lie in changes in interest group involvement in the formation of federal education legislation during the prior reauthorization period I studied.[1]

The Elementary and Secondary Education Act reauthorization process between 1999 and 2001, which spanned two Congresses and two presidential administrations and ultimately produced NCLB, was marked by interparty competition over education policy, as well as a shift in the kinds of actors and interest groups involved in the policy process. The rise in ideological tensions about education resulted in a weakening of institutional relationships among the executive branch, education committee staff, and interest groups. Groups representing professional educators and researchers saw their influence diminished in the legislative process. In their stead, a nascent but well-organized mobilization of several conservative coalitions outside of Congress, frustrated by more liberal-leaning groups' access to the Democratic-controlled congressional committees for 30 years, sought a proactive role in the legislative arena.[2] Congressional aides generally turned to newer, right-of-center think tanks that advocated for block grants and vouchers in Title I, as their positions were aligned with many Republican members' own ideology. In addition to the new dynamics between the two political parties, the reauthorization period was also a time when new institutional dynamics were in play—new actors and sources of influence, and the breakdown of the previously stable "iron triangle."[3] The influence of think tanks on the final legislation was apparent, particularly proposals for decentralization and public-school choice.

The identification of these factors led to a fresh set of questions about education interest groups and coalitions in the post-reauthorization period: What kinds of institutional relationships would replace the formerly stable coalitions? Would the interest groups that had been shut out of the deliberations around NCLB, such as teacher unions and administrator groups, attempt to renegotiate their access? Would new coalitions form in the inter-reauthorization period? Would party control of Congress and the presidency make a difference in which groups gained access to the policymaking process? In other words, was interest groups' involvement in (and think tanks' more indirect engagement with) the policy process a function of partisanship, or simply a change in the nature of the expanded interest group and think tank sectors themselves?

In the aftermath of the passage of NCLB, party politics and education policy became intertwined in unpredictable ways. Certainly, the conventional wisdom in 2006 was that the bipartisan consensus that had produced NCLB was so powerful that its major provisions would remain intact in the next reauthorization. Frederick Hess and Michael Petrilli, analysts with the American Enterprise Institute and the Thomas B. Fordham Institute, respectively, argued that a powerful new agreement among members of Congress, the Bush administration, and major interest groups, about testing and accountability, signified that the law's core provisions would not be changed. They termed this the "Washington Consensus." "So long as there remains a centrist consensus for the principles of NCLB, it will be difficult for legislators to call for drastic change without leaving themselves open to charges that they are `anti-accountability' or that they don't believe all children can learn," they wrote.[4] In other words, even though educators' or the public's discontent with the law might rise, it was the inside-the-Beltway political agreement about accountability that would be decisive in keeping its core provisions intact.

Because an analysis of education interest group activity in the post-NCLB passage period would only be meaningful if it were done in comparison to conditions before 2001, it was necessary to employ a theoretical framework that allowed for an examination of patterns over a relatively long period of time. For this reason, I utilized an Advocacy Coalition Framework (ACF), developed by Sabatier and

Jenkins-Smith,[5] to investigate interest group activity during the 109th and 110th Congresses. Because the Democrats controlled Congress following the 2006 mid-term elections, the two Congresses provided a natural setting for investigating whether and how partisanship played a role in interest group activity.

APPLYING THE ACF TO THE NATIONAL EDUCATION POLICY SUBSYSTEM

In the field of political science, advocacy coalitions are "defined as actors from a wide variety of institutions who share policy core beliefs and coordinate their behavior in a variety of ways."[6] Thus, coalitions embody beliefs and theories about how to achieve policy objectives. A policy "subsystem" in a given domain consists of "actors from a variety of public and private organizations who are actively concerned with a public problem or issue," and includes not just the traditional "iron triangle" of interest groups, the executive agencies, and the Congress, but also "journalists, researchers, and policy analysts, all of whom play important roles in the generation, dissemination, and evaluation of policy ideas."[7]

The ACF posits that the policy "core" remains stable over a period of time, generally a decade or more.[8] For purposes of this analysis, the policy "core" could be viewed as the fairly stable congressional consensus from 1994 on that funds under Title I of ESEA ought to be tied to requirements for the state-level administration of standards, assessments, and accountability requirements for schools, as both the Improving America's Schools Act of 1994 and NCLB mandated. External factors, such as fiscal constraints or political upheavals, also affect the policy subsystem. For instance, during this time period, education policy at the federal level was shaped by the reality of a constrained domestic budget, which meant more limited federal education dollars for K-12 programs than in the recent past. In addition, the imminent congressional elections of 2006 also played a role.

The ACF framework distinguishes between "core" and secondary aspects of belief systems. For instance, in education policy, if, as noted above, a core aspect of a belief system is that for states to receive federal compensatory education funds, they need to administer some sort of centralized assessment of students' academic performance, the secondary aspects of that belief system would specify how much or what kind of testing ought to be required, or what stakes for schools states ought to attach to testing outcomes. The framework posits two hypotheses about coalitions: first, that "actors within an advocacy coalition will show substantial consensus on issues pertaining to the policy core, though less so on secondary aspects"; and second, that "an actor (or coalition) will give up secondary aspects of a belief system before acknowledging weaknesses in the policy core."[9] Secondary aspects of belief systems are considered relatively easy to change, whereas core beliefs are considered much harder to change.

The hypotheses about core and secondary belief systems are central to this study's exploration of advocacy coalitions. For instance, it is a matter of interpretation whether the coalitions of interest groups weighing in on aspects of the NCLB reauthorization disagreed sufficiently about core beliefs to be viewed as true advocacy coalitions. I will argue that the "tinker" versus "overhaul" NCLB coalitions' disagreements were more over secondary aspects of belief systems, although some core beliefs were clearly in dispute.

Policymaker "learning" is also a central of the ACF, which posits that interest groups and actors in a policy subsystem "learn" from the challenges posed by new policies or institutional boundaries and then adapt their strategies accordingly order to achieve their policy objectives. Sabatier and Jenkins-Smith write:

> Coalitions seek to learn about how the world operates and the effects of various governmental interventions in order to realize their goals over time. Because of resistance to changing core beliefs, however, such "policy-oriented learning" is usually confined to the secondary aspects of belief systems. Changes in core elements of public policies require the replacement of one dominant coalition by another, and this transition is hypothesized to result primarily from changes external to the subsystem.[10]

Thus, I expected to see examples of policymaker "learning" in the study, as policymakers reacted to the limitations of NCLB to achieve its purported goals of closing the achievement gap. The emphasis in the ACF on changes external to the education policy subsystem also becomes directly relevant to this study, as will be seen, because of the gaining momentum of the competitiveness agenda in interest groups and Congress, which broadened the education policy agenda significantly between 2005 and 2007.

THE ACF AND THE EDUCATION POLICY SUBSYSTEM:
DEVELOPING INITIAL HYPOTHESES

There were several broad hypotheses about education interest group behavior that guided my examination of advocacy coalitions during this period. First, I posited that partisanship in Congress in general, and within the House and Senate education committees in particular, would be a major factor affecting the way federal policy is made and the kinds of groups/researchers/coalitions that gained access to the process. This hypothesis was derived from my earlier research in the 106th and 107th Congresses about the formation of NCLB, as well as from theories of unified party government, for example, the alignment of presidential party and congressional control of both House and Senate.[11] A corollary of this hypothesis about partisanship was that the practitioner-based coalitions would work together to try to regain some access to the process that they had lost with NCLB. These coalitions would be expected to learn from and mediate their relative exclusion and "out-group" status with respect to party control.[12]

A second initial hypothesis concerned the behavior of governmental groups, especially those representing state-level policymakers. As the regulatory pressure and compliance demands of NCLB were high relative to financial resources available, I expected to see a fresh mobilization of and possible coalition in the education policy subsystem of groups such as the National Governors Association (NGA), the Council of Chief State School Officers (CCSSO), the National Conference of State Legislatures (NCSL), and the National Association of State Boards of Education (NASBE). Research by Cammisa supports the tendency of governmental lobbies to form strategic alliances, particularly when greater federal resources are sought.[13] At the time of study initiation in 2006, state-level leaders had already emerged as a central outside-the-Beltway "opposing coalition" with political demands. State leaders in Connecticut had sued the federal government over NCLB's testing demands, for instance, and numerous state legislatures, including Virginia's and Utah's, had passed resolutions opposing NCLB's regulations.

One of NCLB's most vociferous opponents and a central figure in the legislative rebellion against the law was David Shreve, education program director at the NCSL. Shreve, who had worked on labor and workforce development issues at NCSL since 1987 and had been education program director since 1997, had written to congressional leaders at the time of the law's passage that NCLB was "seriously and perhaps irreparably flawed."[14] In 2005, he convened a task force of state legislators, who issued a report, *Delivering the Promise: State Recommendations for Improving No Child Left Behind*, which was critical of the law's provisions on teacher quality, special education, and limited English proficient students and stated that the law had "questionable constitutional underpinnings."[15] In this context of intense and widespread state-level opposition to the law, which constituted a kind of emergent "policy network,"[16] I sought to investigate the question of whether or not the inside-the-Beltway state governmental lobbies would find the incentives to behave like a coherent coalition with common goals and strategies.

Third, as the states and federal government negotiate and implement NCLB's regulations and productivity demands, I hypothesized that the national coalitions would have to confront the fact that many parts of the implementing system did not have the capacity to rise to the challenge of these productivity and performance demands.[17] Pressure on members of Congress, as well as continued dissent in state legislatures, were two factors I anticipated as I began this study.

METHODS

The qualitative research involved a mix of participant-observation methods, interviews, and document collection and analysis appropriate to the longitudinal nature of the ACF.[18] This investigative method identified: first, trends in the education policy subsystem, both those that were a continuation from the previous reauthorization, as well as new key events and political changes; and second, the content of coalitions' beliefs about the policy core. During this period, from September 2005 through May 2006, and again from March through June 2007, the author conducted interviews with legislative and governmental relations directors (as well as executive directors), focused on the various groups' and institutions' plans and proposals about the upcoming ESEA reauthorization (see appendix A for list of interviews conducted and meetings attended). Many questions focused on strategies for building support for their legislative priorities, including formation of coalitions. Other questions centered on perceptions of how partisanship affected the individual groups' or coalitions' strategies for enacting their goals. Three congressional aides were also interviewed about their perceptions of interest group and national commissions' influence. In addition to the interviews, other data sources included interest groups' and think tanks' policy reports and position statements on NCLB; field notes at meetings I attended; and selected media accounts. Because not all of my data came from interviews, but also from informal conversations, writing analytic memos during and after fieldwork was central to my strategy.[19] The investigative method drew on these memos, along with official document and media source analysis and coding of interviews, to identify:

1. Patterns of coalition formation, that is, which interest groups and institutions were working in concert;
2. Perceptions of interviewees' about interest groups' access to Congress; and
3. The emergence of new education agendas within the subsystem.

These policy-related and political trends allowed comparison with the prior period studied, i.e., 1999 to 2001.

FINDINGS: COALITIONS EMERGE

As Patrick McGuinn and I have written, there had already been changes in the political environment that produced NCLB; but, to use Theda Skocpol's formulation, the new policies of NCLB also bred new politics.[20] The present study reveals that coalitions of interest groups and civil rights groups advocating the overhaul of NCLB's testing and accountability provisions did form and mobilize during this period. While these "pro" and "anti" coalitions and the change of party control in Congress did shape the emerging agenda, there was an even more powerful factor in play in the policy subsystem: renewed calls for national standards. As alarms about international competitiveness reemerged, members of Congress began to recognize the limitations of some of the policy mechanisms of NCLB. In fact, when Democrats took control of Congress in 2007, the "Washington Consensus" appeared to begin to weaken as several national commissions, as well as congressional leaders, pointed to NCLB's inadequacies in solving the perceived competitiveness problems.

Further, the growing collaboration of think tanks across the ideological spectrum, the presence within them of a core of relatively young policy-savvy analysts, and their convergence on a platform of national standards also worked to shape congressional action. Thus, in support of my previous findings, I saw that new kinds of institutions and interest groups were more prominent than the practitioner-based associations. I found, however, that the debate in Congress and in the think tank sector was less ideological and partisan-driven than it had been in the 106th and 107th Congresses (1999–2001).

This inter-reauthorization period was marked by the expansion of the trend of pluralism in the education policy arena; a decline in partisan tensions, as the two parties' traditional ideological priorities begin to reemerge; and the strong re-emergence of the "competitiveness" and national standards agendas, both distinct from debates over the NCLB reauthorization.

Table 1 above provides a comparison of major political differences between this period and the prior one studied.

While there were policy trends common across both Congresses, I present my findings in chronological order, starting with the 2nd session of the 109th.

Table 1 Political Comparison between Reauthorization and "Inter-Reauthorization" Periods

---

1999–2001 (106th and 107th Congresses)

Republican-led Congresses
New Republican stance on policy
Groups' access contingent on ideology
New kinds of groups and coalitions
Ideologies get subsumed by partisanship w/NCLB
Think tank sector relatively limited

2005–2007 (109th and 110th Congresses)

Congress switches party control with 110th
NCLB on defensive/Ideologies begin to reemerge
Think tank sector has broadened—diversification of voices
Reenergized, organized coalition of practitioner and civil rights groups
Three areas of education policy: NCLB, standards, and competitiveness
Partisanship less a factor in interest group access

EDUCATION POLICY IN THE 109TH CONGRESS

Congress, rather than the White House, took the lead in setting the agenda for education in the 109th Congress. The competition between parties over message on education continued to some extent, but without control of the committees, the Democrats' ability to use the media to gain an advantage on the issue with the electorate was diminished significantly. As with all other areas of the federal domestic budget, the education budget for the first time was cut. The chairmanships of the education committees also changed hands. Senator Mike Enzi (R-WY) replaced Sen. Judd Gregg (R-NH) as chair of the Senate Committee on Health, Education, Labor, and Pensions. Rep. Howard "Buck" McKeon (R-CA) replaced Rep. John Boehner (R-OH) in 2006 as House Education and the Workforce Committee chair when the latter was tapped to become the House Majority leader.

One of the notable shifts in the education policy arena in the 109th Congress was a direct result of heightened concerns about international competitiveness in mathematics, science, and technology, particularly with respect to the emergent and highly technologically proficient workforces of China and India. Concerns about economic competitiveness as an impetus for education reform were, of course, not a novelty in the realm of federal education policy. Thomas Friedman's 2003 book, *The World is Flat*, which offered a vivid portrait of the workforces of these emergent economic competitors, was widely read by policymakers and raised concerns about the skills of the workforce overall, but particularly America's highest achieving students. As policy analysts Frederick Hess and Andrew Rotherham observe about the attention to Friedman's work: ". . . his point is hardly new. Robert Reich, secretary of labor under President Bill Clinton, made many of the same arguments in his influential 1992 book, *The Work of Nations*. The fears about China and India today are more than a little reminiscent of—and tinged with the same hysteria as—discussions of `Japan, Inc.' in the 1980s."[21] And the 1983 *Nation at Risk* report famously invoked military metaphors to describe the United States's so-called "unthinking, unilateral educational disarmament."[22] However, as Hess and Rotherham note, "off-shoring" of service jobs has added extra concern about America's production of engineers and scientists. Despite evidence that off-shoring was overwhelmingly a byproduct of the abundance of relative low-wage workers abroad, policymakers' attention once again became focused on the U.S. education system. Congress became rapidly involved in trying to identify solutions.

In response to a congressional request for specific recommendations about what actions the federal government could take to enhance the nation's competitiveness, the National Academy of Sciences published a report in 2005 entitled *Rising above the Gathering Storm: Energizing and Employing America for a Brighter Economic Future* (also referred to as the Augustine report, after its chairman, Norman Augustine). Unlike past calls for U.S. economic competitiveness, the report was very specific about the costs of the 20 action items in four interlinking policy areas: K-12 math and science education, basic research, higher education, and technology and innovation policy. In the wake of its release in fall 2005, with the strong encouragement of the Science, Technology, Engineering, and Mathematics (STEM) coalition (an "umbrella group" of national organizations representing business, academic, and technology-related members), the science committees in the House and Senate developed bills that called for a wide range of competitiveness measures, including awarding four-year scholarships to students obtaining a bachelor's degree in the physical or life sciences, engineering, or mathematics who would commit to teach for a minimum of five years in public schools.[23] In the Senate, all 20 of the report's action items were introduced with 65 cosponsors as the Protecting America's Competitiveness Edge (PACE) Act, while President Bush announced the less-comprehensive (and less expensive) American Competitiveness Initiative.

None of the legislative initiatives were passed during the 109th Congress, though some eventually would pass in the 110th, as will be discussed. The "competitiveness agenda," however, had already reshaped the contours of the education policy subsystem, as it brought in new "players" from business, higher education, and technology. For instance, the already-influential Business Roundtable forged alliances with groups such as the Business-Higher Education Forum and the Council on Competitiveness. As each of these groups had staff assigned to work on K-12 education policy, it naturally followed that they began to take positions on NCLB. Hess and Rotherham contend that there are inevitable political tensions between NCLB's equity-oriented, "gap closing" agenda and the competitiveness agenda for education, which is necessarily more focused on advanced instruction in mathematics and science for high-achieving students. Business groups realize that "from any short- or even medium-term perspective, K-12 schooling is a flimsy tool for addressing competitiveness in science and engineering. It is akin to signing promising preschoolers to a baseball team's farm system rather than bringing in top-tier free agents—even when those free agents make it clear they're eager to sign with your team at a discounted price ... consequently, the ability of NCLB to gradually broaden the pipeline is more relevant to our competitiveness in 2030 than to our standing in the next decade or so."[24] It is inevitable, these authors argue, that there will be some tension between the equity-geared and the competitiveness agendas once debates over resources heat up.

In my study, however, education policy directors in business groups, while drawing the same distinction as Hess and Rotherham, did not characterize the two policy agendas as being in conflict with respect to their own priorities. Susan Traiman, director of education policy at the Business Roundtable, when asked why these business groups were intensifying their focus on competitiveness issues at this particular moment, responded:

> It's been bubbling for a long time. In the emphasis on both pre-K and K-12, the notion is that we need to have a long-term effort to raise student achievement in the United States. And I think the business community understands that that's long term. But they also feel a very pressing and immediate need, and worry that if we only look at the long term, other countries are racing forward so quickly, especially China and India, that it could be too late for us. And they really worry that without a Sputnik to galvanize Americans, or to make them realize that we have a problem, that by the time we wake up to it, the number of years it takes to produce a scientist or engineer or mathematician, you won't be able to compress that … They're really concerned that we need a more concerted focus on what people in education call STEM [Science, Technology, Engineering, and Mathematics].[25]

Yet despite this new focus of business groups on STEM, I found no evidence that there were two opposing coalitions forming during this period pitting NCLB against competitiveness. Rather, the business groups continued their advocacy for preserving NCB's core provisions while simultaneously promoting "competitiveness"-related reforms.

GROWTH AND DIVERSIFICATION OF THE THINK TANK SECTOR IN EDUCATION POLICY

A second observable development during this period was the continued growth and diversification of the think tank sector of the education policy community. In contrast to the prior period I studied, where the major sources of new ideas in the legislative process emanated from The Education Trust, the Fordham Institute, the Progressive Policy Institute, or the Heritage Foundation, there were new and visible entrants in the later period, particularly on the left. Examples of the latter included the Center for American Progress, conceived of by former Clinton chief-of-staff John Podesta as a progressive, left-leaning think tank; and the New America Foundation, whose education program director, Michael Dannenberg, was a former education aide to Senator Edward Kennedy (D-MA). In addition, the Center on Education Policy, led by former congressional aide Jack Jennings, while not a new entrant to the education policy subsystem, produced annual reports about NCLB's implementation that were known for their nonpartisan orientation. Another active new entrant was Education Sector, cofounded in 2005 by former Democratic Leadership Council/Progressive Policy Institute policy analyst (and former Clinton education aide) Andrew Rotherham and former U.S. News and World Report journalist Thomas Toch. Many of these new interest groups and think tanks took advantage of recent advances in communications technology to disseminate their views through e-mail lists, Web sites, webcast conferences, and blogs.

Despite some political differences, the education program directors across these and other think tanks' staff began to "cross-pollinate" policy ideas and even build new agendas. An example of a think tank's leader attempting to challenge conventional wisdom was Robert Gordon, the education program director at the CAP, writing in *The New Republic* in 2005: "It's stunning to see Democrats lose their edge on education." Criticizing the party for what he saw as its sole demands for "money, money, and money," he proposed that the Democrats' first task in building an affirmative education policy agenda should be

> ... to stop the unprincipled attacks on NCLB. At its heart, this is the sort of law liberals once dreamed about. In the 1970s, liberal litigators fell one vote short of a Supreme Court decision requiring evenhanded education funding. NCLB doesn't guarantee funding, but it goes one step further by demanding educational results. It says that, when states accept federal funding, they must ensure that all children (except the most disabled) meet "challenging academic standards." This has made achievement a legal command, not just a gauzy aspiration. The law requires a form of affirmative action: States must show that poor and minority students are achieving proficiency like everyone else, or else provide remedies targeted to the schools those students attend. The law's unyielding demands have created a powerful tool to raise both expectations and money.[26]

NCLB had spurred the think tank sector in education to grow, innovate, and disseminate new proposals for federal policy. Indeed, it was within this sector that true advocacy coalitions with competing ideologies were truly evident; that is, there were emerging categories of neoconservative and neoliberal organizations. While it is beyond the scope of this Chapter, a large part of the battles within this arena were less about NCLB than they were about choice and privatization.[27] Although the think tank sector had plenty of ideological diversity, it was also true that on some issues, such as national standards, otherwise rather ideologically different think tanks began to unite. For instance, the education program directors at the Center for American Progress and the Thomas B. Fordham Institute began a joint initiative to work on state-level standards and teacher-quality initiatives, and the two organizations cosponsored a symposium in fall of 2006 about the feasibility of national standards.

THE DEVELOPMENT OF NCLB-RELATED COALITIONS

During the 109th Congress, a wide range of groups across the political spectrum increased their public activities in response to the contentious initial implementation of NCLB's performance-based accountability model. Part of these efforts involved the formation of new coalitions to defend or challenge particular parts of the law. For instance, the Achievement Alliance, a consortium of five pro-NCLB groups based at the Citizens Commission for Civil Rights (CCCR), launched a Web site that refuted the claims of groups such as the NCSL, which released a report critical of NCLB, and the National Education Association (NEA), which had filed suit claiming the law's mandates were inadequately funded. The other four members of the Alliance were the National Council of La Raza (NCLR), the Education Trust, the Business Roundtable, and Achieve, Inc.

As the Citizens Commission's leadership in the Achievement Alliance indicates, the groups in the civil rights community are not unified on their political stances with respect to NCLB. The Civil Rights Project issued research reports about the law's uneven enforcement [28] but the CCCR and the NCLR continued to strongly endorse the law's accountability measures, and the Mexican-American Legal Defense and Education Fund (MALDEF) did not join the major coalition advocating an overhaul of the law. Another major endorsement of the law came from the National Association for the Advancement of Colored People (NAACP) in early 2006. When Connecticut filed suit against the U.S. Department of Education, objecting to the federal government's denial of waivers that would allow it to test students in every other grade, rather than in grades three through eight, and alleging that the federal government was underfunding the law by approximately $50 million, the NAACP sided with the United States on the grounds that states do not have the right to ignore federal legislation aimed at helping minorities.[29] Victor L. Goode, the NAACP's assistant general counsel, cited the importance of federal protections: "One can't help but remember back in the Dixiecrat period when certain Southern states asserted that they were not required to comply with certain federal civil rights laws designed to protect people's rights." The president of the Connecticut branch of the NAACP, Scot X. Esdaile, stated that the organization was aligned with the Bush administration "on this particular issue and only this particular issue."[30]

Another prominent example of a new coalition was the Forum on Educational Accountability (FEA), organized by the National Center for Fair & Open Testing (FairTest) Executive Director Monty Neill. Neill's organization had been involved in opposing the Clinton administration's national testing proposals in the 1990s. By April 2008, there were 144 education, civil rights, disability, and religious groups who had signed a joint statement outlining "core principles" of assessment and accountability—an eclectic and extremely diffuse coalition. The FEA's major premise was that the federal government ought to assume a less punitive and test-based version of accountability than NCLB. Politically, Neill explained, the best strategy for changing the law was to keep the major groups in the education establishment and the civil rights groups in dialogue with each other, even if all principles could not be agreed upon:

> There are two critical issues. One is, it was very clear there was going to be a lot of anger about this law. So how does one focus that anger so the Congress responds? And the other is, there's going to be an ESEA, the feds are going to do something—so what should they do? And unless we have a "what should they do" to replace the current things they are doing, it's much harder to win. The default position perhaps is to go back to the 1994 law, which would be a great improvement by and large. [31]

Neill further explained that if there was a tension within the coalition, it was between " ... the civil rights folks who desire a strong federal role, and that shows up in the statement, that we're for a strong federal role. On the other side are those who don't want micromanagement, such as the National School Boards Association and the American Association of School Administrators."[32] Neill pointed out that the Black and Hispanic caucuses in Congress had opposed NCLB; and that while most of the education interest groups had shared those views, they had not been very vocal about them. He attributed this relative silence to the CCCRs' support for the law, and the American Federation of Teachers' (AFT) passive support for it. (While certainly not a close ally of the Bush administration, the AFT had not officially opposed the law's passage back in 2001. Instead, the union's leadership assumed a cautious approach to criticism of the law, opting to launch a campaign in 2006 called "NCLB: Let's Get it Right.") Overall, Neill said of the coalition: "An alliance of education and civil rights groups is probably not sufficient to change things, but it's necessary. And so how does one create that alliance? Well, you have to get them talking with one another."[33]

Several of the most powerful education interest groups did not sign the Forum's Joint Statement, which was posted on its Web site: the National PTA, the Council of Great City Schools, and the state leaders' groups all declined to participate. While the number and diversity of the groups in the coalition were impressive, as Neill's comments above make clear, there appear to be fundamental disagreements among the member groups, and it remains unclear how united they are behind specific reforms to NCLB.

THE 110TH CONGRESS: THE DEMOCRATIC MAJORITY AND THE GROWING CONSENSUS OF "IDEA BROKERS" ON A NATIONAL STANDARDS AGENDA

The 2006 elections, which reestablished Democratic control over both houses of Congress, also placed Rep. George Miller (D-CA) and Senator Kennedy in the chairmanships of the House and Senate education committees, respectively, in the 110th Congress. This development not only moved the two Democratic sponsors of NCLB into the key positions for the bill's reauthorization, it also favorably altered the prospects for interest groups' renegotiation of their prior access. Even as presidential politics were increasingly assuming center stage by spring of 2007, the committees moved forward with hearings for the reauthorization. And the three interest group coalitions that had begun to formulate positions on NCLB in the previous Congress—the FEA; the state leaders' coalition comprised of governors, state board members, and chief state school officers; and the Achievement Alliance—solidified their positions and agendas. Meanwhile, support for national standards gained political momentum, and the House and Senate in April 2007 enacted part of the competitiveness coalition's agenda in the form of bills supporting resources for recruiting and training mathematics and science educators.

NATIONAL STANDARDS COALITION

The revived debate over national standards, as mentioned earlier, had largely incubated in the think tank sector since President Clinton's proposal of 1997 had failed to win congressional support. In the 110th Congress, these proposals were introduced as legislation, forcing interest groups to stake out their rationales for supporting or opposing voluntary national standards. In ACF terms, these positions were another "secondary aspect" of belief systems.

The core beliefs of the coalition supporting national standards were that there needed to be "pressure" on the system to deliver higher levels of content, and that NCLB had been an insufficient policy instrument for applying that pressure. Supporters of national standards invoked discrepancies between state scores on the National Assessment of Educational Progress (NAEP) and their own tests. In September 2006, for instance, *The Washington Post* reported that Virginia had announced that 86 percent of its fourth-graders were proficient in reading, while NAEP data showed 37 percent at or above proficiency.[34] Policymakers and experts in this coalition argued that NCLB was creating a downward pressure on states to lower their standards, and that national standards were the only way to ensure that all states maintained the same expectations for students. Diane Ravitch of New York University, a former U.S. assistant secretary of education and long-time proponent of national standards, argued that "the more discontented the public is with confusing and dumbed-down standards, the more politically feasible it will be to create national standards of achievement."[35]

The core beliefs of the groups opposing national standards were that the federal government, before being entrusted to assume a new authority in the area of standards, needed to fix the problems with NCLB accountability. The NCSL was one group that strongly opposed the development of national standards.[36] Conservative think tanks such as the Cato Institute also opposed them on grounds that they were a harmful expansion of federal authority.

In January 2007, Sen. Christopher Dodd (D-CT) and Rep. Vernon Ehlers (R-MI), introduced legislation called the Standards to Provide Educational Achievement for All Kids (SPEAK) Act. The bill would require the National Assessment Governing Board to create voluntary U.S. education standards in mathematics and science for grades K-12, and it would provide competitive grants to states that adopted the standards. It would also permit the U.S. Secretary of Education to extend NCLB's 2014 deadline for "all students proficient" in reading and math by up to four years.[37] Sen. Kennedy also introduced a bill, the "SUCCESS Act," that would offer incentives for states to benchmark their standards and tests to the NAEP.

Ideologically diverse think tanks that often did not share common priorities found common ground in supporting national standards. When Dodd and Ehlers introduced their bill, the New America Foundation and Thomas B. Fordham Institute cosponsored an event that featured advocates such as Michael Casserly, Executive Director of the Council of Great City Schools, John Engler, former governor of Michigan and President of the National Association of Manufacturers, and Bob Wise, President of the Alliance for Excellent Education. Michael Dannenberg, Director of the Education Policy Program at New America, described the think tank consensus on national standards:

> There is a consensus among folks who have worked in this policy field for a while, and has been for some time, that national standards is the right policy and necessary. I don't think that's a new idea; when the Goals 2000 Educate America Act was passed, it included a system to consecrate voluntary national standards. So there's been this long-standing view among policy wonks that national standards are the right education policy to have. In fact, I would submit that the history of the standards movement indicates that the country is on an inexorable march toward national standards. The question is not if, it's when and how do we get there.[38]

Yet popularity in the think tank sector was hardly a predictor of national standards' legislative success. As Andrew Rotherham of Education Sector stated, "when you get outside some policy elites, who are big on this, you don't see a real groundswell of support" for national standards.[39]

For the most part, congressional aides did not view the national standards agenda as competing with NCLB; indeed, part of the strategy was to attempt to blend the two legislatively.[40] Yet Michael Petrilli of the Fordham Institute saw the two agendas as mutually exclusive ones. In an address to the National Association of State Boards of Education, he described the embrace of national standards as a way for groups to disavow NCLB's regulations without falling into the political trap of disavowing accountability: "If you are tired of the micromanaging federal government a la NCLB, the best way to get the federal government off your backs may be to sign up for national standards and tests." Before NCLB, most conservatives and state education leaders saw national standards as a dangerous expansion of federal authority. In the wake of NCLB, however, as Petrilli's statement shows, the political terrain and policy discourse have shifted in ways that these same groups now view national standards as a way to *limit* federal micromanagement in schools.[41]

Forty groups endorsed the Dodd/Ehlers SPEAK bill, including the NEA and the Council of Great City Schools. The AFT walked a political fine line; when Dodd-Ehlers was introduced in January, executive vice president Antonia Cortese said the bills were "definitely a step in the right direction,"[42] but as of mid-May, the union had still not officially signed on as a supporter.

Within a month of the introduction of the Dodd/Ehlers and Kennedy bills, another call for national standards came from the independent Commission on NCLB, funded by the MacArthur and Gates Foundations, convened by the Aspen Institute, and cochaired by former governors Tommy Thompson of Wisconsin and Roy Barnes of Georgia. The Commission called upon Congress to set up a process for developing national academic standards and requiring states either to adopt them or to measure their own standards against the national benchmarks. Releasing its report on February 13, 2007, Barnes stated: "Fairness requires—particularly in math, science, and reading—that there be national standards."[43] The response to the report was mixed, with more conservative members of Congress, interest groups, and think tanks arguing that its recommendations constituted too much regulation. Yet the congressional Democratic leadership claimed that they were entirely receptive to the NCLB Commission's ideas. At the press conference at which the Commission released its report, Sen. Kennedy said, "I believe so many of their recommendations are going to see life."[44]

Figure 1 shows some of the major alignments for national standards during early 2007. The FEA is shown to highlight that there was virtually no overlap with the supporters of national standards measures in Congress (the NEA being the sole and major exception).

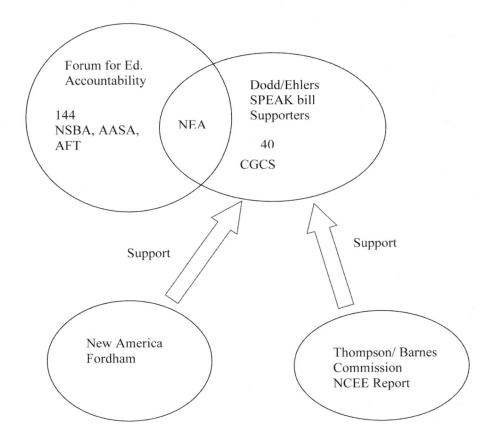

Figure 1 National standards: Political Alignments

SPRING 2007: THE HIGH-LEVEL, IDEOLOGICAL SPLIT

Along with the bipartisan revival of proposals for national standards was the reassertion of ideological differences. In March, three conservative Republicans, Rep. Peter Hoekstra and House Minority Whip Roy Blunt (R-MO) and Sen. Mel Martinez (R-FL) introduced bills that would allow states to vote to "opt out" of the requirements of NCLB but instead direct the federal dollars toward narrowing of the achievement gap. Rep. Blunt stated that "the over-whelming intrusion of No Child Left Behind is too large to deal with unless you fundamentally change the legislation."[45] In the House version, states could opt out of NCLB's regulations via either a referendum or a decision by a combination of state-level education officials. Except for the fact that it came in direct opposition to NCLB, it was, in many ways, a "redux" of the Straight A's proposal that passed the House of Representatives in 1999 during the ESEA reauthorization debate, which called for consolidation of federal program funds in selected states.

The legislation made clear that conservative ideology in favor of a scaled-back federal role had begun to reassert itself. Of all of the policy proposals that had thus far emerged, it was the one that represented a split with what the ACF calls the "near" policy core, or what Hess and Petrilli called the "Washington Consensus." Despite the continued support for this consensus among President Bush and the two Democratic chairs of the education committees, Miller and Kennedy, the Blunt-Martinez bill showed that the bipartisan spirit that produced NCLB was splintering.

STATE LEADER LOBBIES FIND COMMON GROUND: CHIEFS, NGA, AND NASBE

The groups representing governors, chief state school officers, state legislators, and state boards of education gradually staked out common ground as the reauthorization hearings gathered steam. This coalition-building transformed the influence of each of the groups.

During the prior ESEA reauthorization, the NGA had taken a fairly active role, helping Senate HELP committee chairman James Jeffords (then a Republican) to draft legislation in 2000. By contrast, the NGA did not issue any major position papers on education policy at all during the Bush presidency—until 2007. This was largely because the Bush administration had attempted to marginalize the NGA as whole during its first three years. According to the former education program director there, the White House attempted to fire the Executive Director, Ray Sheppach, and instead got the second-in-command fired.[46] NGA's education program, however, had received a large infusion of cash from the Bill & Melinda Gates Foundation to focus on the redesign of high schools, and proceeded to work on influencing state policy in that arena, rather than on legislation. After the 2006 elections, however, there were thirty-five Democratic governors, and the new education chair, Democratic Governor Christine Gregoire of Washington, promised to take an active role in the reauthorization.[47]

Similarly, following the passage of NCLB, the CCSSO experienced what was considered a "slump" in political power. Having accepted significant grant monies from the Education Department to support NCLB's implementation, the Chiefs did not have an organizational incentive to take an oppositional stance to the law. As a result, unlike other associations, the Chiefs did not vociferously attack the law; the Executive Director, Thomas Houlihan, preferred to negotiate issues with the administration in a non-confrontational style.[48] However, in the 110th Congress, the CCSSO's new legislative director, Scott Frein, and Houlihan's successor, Gene Wilhoit, sought alliances with the NGA, NASBE, and the NCSL.

In April of 2007, the Chiefs, NASBE, and the NGA endorsed a set of joint principles for the reauthorization, including a plan to allow states to measure school progress through "growth models," revisions to the accountability requirements for special education and English language learners, and a proposal to allow differentiation of state-level consequences for schools not making adequate yearly progress. The NCSL, which had been part of the initial negotiations, did not sign onto the proposal. NCSL's senior education program director, David Shreve, noted that the proposals had been developed "unilaterally and internally" at the NGA, and that the conference had been unable to express its own concerns in what had been a "flawed process."[49] The inside-the-Beltway split of state legislators with chiefs, board members, and governors reflects the legislatures' more oppositional stance to the law. NCLB has in many ways reinforced the education agendas of, and in some cases, accrued greater centralization of political power to, chief state school officers and governors.[50]

None of the state leaders' groups signed the Forum for Educational Accountability's Joint Organizational Statement on the NCLB Act, signifying that they wanted to retain their collective influence to fight for very specific changes to the law.

It is useful to consider these findings in terms of each of my initial hypotheses about the ACF. However, as it applies to this case (NCLB), there is one crucial underlying observation to be made about the ACF's application to education interest groups and think tanks during this time period: the framework seems most useful for understanding tensions in the *secondary aspects* of belief systems. That is, no major coalition during this time period was calling for a radical overhaul of the dominant paradigm of federal policy— that is, standards, assessment, and accountability—that would have signified "the replacement of one dominant coalition by another."[51] The major coalition that emerged to challenge NCLB, the FEA, did call for a retooling of the law's assessment provisions. However, the FEA itself was broad enough to encompass groups with wide-ranging ideologies with respect to the law. Indeed, the NAACP Legal Defense and Education Fund was one of the FEA signatories, and, as discussed earlier, had come to NCLB's ardent defense in the Connecticut lawsuit.

While central elements of the policy "core" were being debated by the FEA and the Achievement Alliance (such as the appropriate balance of responsibilities between states and the federal government, and the kinds of policy instruments that ought to be used), these elements more closely fit the "information concerning program performance" and the "decisions concerning administrative rules" corresponding to the secondary aspects of belief systems.[52] Thus, we could say that both the FEA and the Achievement Alliance were broadly part of the larger K-12 "equity" coalition—they just differed on the details of how the federal role should best support that goal. Yet by the end of 2008, the groups' statements about NCLB seemed more convergent than they had in 2005. These were indicators that perhaps the eventual reauthorization debates would be microbattles about the fine-tuning of some aspects of assessment and accountability, rather than true broad philosophical battles about the nature of the federal role in education (which were more in evidence in the think tank sector).

Then what about the reemergence of the competitiveness and national standards agendas? Did they constitute new advocacy coalitions in the education policy subsystem competing against the pro-NCLB coalitions for resources and attention? I have argued against this interpretation, because at least during this particular period, I did not find evidence of overt competition between the national standards/competitiveness agendas on the one hand and the pro-NCLB coalition on the other. A group's being part of the FEA did not necessarily predict its opposition to the national standards bills, with the NEA's endorsement of both as the strongest example. While some policy analysts, such as Fordham's Petrilli, framed national standards as an exit strategy of sorts from NCLB's regulations, it was more common to hear congressional aides speaking in terms of a "both/and" strategy, that is, adopt incentives for standards while "fixing" NCLB.

Given this, in the analysis that follows, my use of the term "coalitions" refers generally to groups banding together in support of secondary aspects of belief systems.

I return now to my three initial hypotheses about the ACF. The first was the relationship between partisanship and interest group access to the process, which as I argued earlier was quite marked in the 1999–2001 reauthorization process. Starting in 2005, there was an abatement of partisan tensions, and this had the effect of increasing interest group participation in the policy process. This was partially due to the reestablished link between the Democratic majority and the practitioner-based coalitions. But even before the 110th Congress, policymakers were looking for concrete solutions to problems—notably, international competitiveness, students displaced by Hurricane Katrina, and perceived shortcomings of NCLB's design—and it became more necessary and made pragmatic sense to run a policy process in which the experiences of practitioners and state and local-level policymakers could be utilized. The collective power of the interest groups, new actors, and external reports brought pressure on Congress to run a more open and transparent process than it had in the 1999–2001 process.

The diversification of the players in the policy arena during this time period—of interest groups, think tanks, and external commissions—corresponded with a broadening of the education policy agenda overall. That is, while my initial questions focused on clear-cut delineations of "pro" and "anti" NCLB groups, the conversation had broadened by 2007 to include both national standards and competitiveness. The competitiveness and national standards agendas transcended partisanship even further.

The second hypothesis, regarding the likely mobilization of state-level groups as a cohesive coalition, was also supported by my research findings. By the spring of 2007, the NGA, CCSSO, and NASBE were working in unison to enact common goals.

The third hypothesis was that actors across the various coalitions would "learn" from the documented capacity shortfalls of states and localities in implementing NCLB, and would modify their strategies accordingly. While this chapter has not been able to treat this topic in any depth, the results of the National Assessment of Educational Progress (NAEP) became central to the opposing coalition's claims about NCLB's failure to raise student achievement, that is, that even in states where scores on state tests were rising, student learning gains, as measured by NAEP, were flat. Political dissatisfaction with NCLB's regulation and testing coincided with renewed concerns about international competitiveness, and this created the opening for a new and expanded focus on national standards. Thus, policy-oriented learning about NCLB's limitations did occur, but attempts to apply the learning were limited by the timing of the political process and the upcoming presidential election.

CONCLUSION

This paper has presented an initial mapping of the status of political coalitions in the national education policy subsystem on the eve of the next ESEA reauthorization. This inter-reauthorization period was a fertile one for policy innovation and entrepreneurship, both among interest groups and think tanks. NCLB had provided the impetus for state leaders' groups to mobilize on behalf of greater flexibility, for coalitions opposing the law's mandates to form, and for think tanks to develop new agendas with greater sophistication—all indicators that, as Patrick McGuinn and I have argued, NCLB is an example of "new policies creating new politics."[53] What I find in this period is further confirmation that the passage of NCLB did far more than just rearrange party politics in education by giving the GOP an active voice in education policy. The law itself was enough of a shift in equilibrium[54] to spur new entrants, sharpen the message of older organizations, and forge new coalitions.

I found that a new advocacy coalition—comprised of business interests, associations of K-12 mathematics and science educators, organizations promoting science, technology and engineering, organizations specifically focused on economic competitiveness (e.g., the Council on Competitiveness), as well as some higher education leaders through the Business-Higher Education Forum—solidified and actively pursued education policy goals centered on improving the competitiveness of U.S. students in mathematics and science. While I found no evidence of competition between this coalition's agenda and that of the equity-geared coalition supporting and seeking improvements to NCLB, the next studies on the politics of the federal role will have to examine whether the two coalitions do begin to compete, especially as domestic budgetary resources become scarcer. Whether a non-incremental change occurs in education policy depends on how much weight policymakers continue to give the claims of those organizations highlighting the U.S.'s declining competitiveness. Congress received sufficient signals from the various coalitions between 2005 and 2007 to continue to treat both "gap closing" in the K-12 system and competitiveness for the highest achieving students as priorities. However, conservative Republicans' dissent about the NCLB regulatory model raised questions about how strong the "Washington Consensus" actually was.

This study's initial mapping of the configuration of interest groups raises several questions for the reauthorization, specifically: How would the debate among the civil rights groups in the opposing coalitions unfold? In particular, how would the long-standing, close connections between the Education Trust and the CCCR, both members of the Achievement Alliance and close allies of Rep. Miller and Sen. Kennedy, affect the substance of the proposals? Would national standards initiatives be introduced into the reauthorization bill, and if so, how? Even under strengthened Democratic control of Congress following the 2008 elections, would the practitioner-based coalition, including the National Education Association, the National School Boards Association and the American Association of School Administrators, regain any of their former levels of influence on the Hill?

The larger question for policy research on federal education legislation remains *what substantive effects* the profusion of new players in the national education policy arena will have on the outcomes of the policy process, for example, the next ESEA reauthorization bill.

APPENDIX A

List of Interviews Conducted and Meetings Attended

*Indicates taped interview conducted

2005
*Lawrence Patrick, Black Alliance for Educational Options
*Cindy Brown, Center for American Progress
Lucy Gettman, Reading Recovery Council
Sally McConnell, Elem. School Principal
*Reggie Felton and Kathleen Branch, National School Boards Association
David Shreve, National Conference of State Legislatures
Bethany Little, Alliance for Excellent Education
Andrew Rotherham, Education Sector
Rachel Tompkins, Rural School and Community Trust
Arnold Fege and Guitele Nicoleau, Public Education Fund Network
*Susan Traiman, Business Roundtable
*Tonya Clay, People for the American Way
*Susan Nogan, National Education Association
*Edward Kealy, Committee for Education Funding
Civil Rights Project Roundtable on NCLB and High Schools
Michael Petrilli, Thomas B. Fordham Institute
Jodi Peterson, National Science Teachers' Association/STEM Coalition
Meeting of the AACTE Governmental Relations Committee
Ruth Wattenberg, American Federation of Teachers
Cindy Brown, Center for American Progress
Maite Arce, Hispanic CREO
Patricia Sullivan, Center on Education Policy
Richard Long, National Association of State Directors of Title I

2006
*Mary Kusler, American Association of School Administrators
*Debbie Stine, National Academy of Sciences
Matt Sonnesyn, Sen. Alexander's Subcommittee on Education Reform
*Chris Roe, Business-Higher Education Forum
*Jim Wilson, House Science Committee
*David Attis, Council on Competitiveness
*David Griffiths, National Association of State Boards of Education

Monty Neill, FairTest
Joel Packer, National Education Association

2007 (110th Congress)
Jill Morningstar (Democratic Committee)
Scott Frein, Council of Chief State School Officers
Michael Dannenberg, New America Foundation
Debate on National Standards at National Association of State Boards of Education Meeting between Michael Petrilli (Fordham Institute) and David Shreve (National Conference of State Legislatures), 3/16/07

NOTES

I.   The author gratefully acknowledges the support of the Spencer/National Academy of Education postdoctoral fellowship. She also thanks Sandra Vergari, Jay P. Scribner, and Kevin Welner for comments on a draft of this paper.

1.   Elizabeth DeBray, *Politics, ideology, and education: Federal policy during the Clinton and Bush administrations* (New York: Teachers College Press, 2006).

2.   DeBray, *Politics, ideology, and education*; Patrick J. McGuinn, No Child Left Behind and transformation of federal education policy, 1965–2005 (Lawrence, KS: University Press of Kansas, 2006).

3.   Elizabeth DeBray-Pelot, "Dismantling education's `iron triangle': Institutional relationships in the formation of federal education policy between 1998 and 2001." In C. Kaestle and A. Lodewick eds. *To educate a nation: Federal and national strategies of school reform* (Lawrence, KS: University Press of Kansas, 2007), 64–89.

4.   Frederick Hess and Michael Petrilli, "The politics of No Child Left Behind: Will the coalition hold?" *Educational Policy*, 185 (3), 2006, 11.

5.   Paul A. Sabatier and Hank C. Jenkins-Smith, *Policy change and learning: An advocacy coalition approach* (Boulder, CO: Westview Press, 1993).

6.   Paul A. Sabatier and Hank C. Jenkins-Smith, "The advocacy coalition framework: An assessment." In Paul A. Sabatier, ed. *Theories of the policy process* (Boulder, CO: Westview Press, 1999), 130.

7.   Paul A. Sabatier, "Policy change over a decade or more." In Sabatier and Jenkins-Smith, *Policy change and learning*, 17.

8.   Ibid.

9.   Ibid., 32–33.

10. Sabatier and Jenkins-Smith, *Policy change and learning*, 5.

11. DeBray, *Politics, ideology, and education*; Sarah Binder, "Congress, the executive, and the production of public policy: united we govern?" In L. Dodd and B. Oppenheimer, ed. *Congress reconsidered*, 7th ed. (Washington, DC: Congressional Quarterly Press, 2001), 293–313.

12. James G. Gimpel, "Grassroots organizations and equilibrium cycles." In Paul Herrnson, Ronald Shaiko, and Clyde Wilcox, eds. *The interest group connection: Electioneering, lobbying, and policy-making in Washington* (Chatham, NJ: Chatham House, 1998)

13. Ann Marie Cammisa, Governments as interest groups: Intergovernmental lobbying and the federal system (Westport, CT: Praeger, 1995).

14. "State group: ESEA rules 'seriously flawed'." *Education Week* 21 (6), October 10, 2001, 31.

15. National Conference of State Legislatures *Delivering the promise: State recommendations for improving the No Child Left Behind Act* (Washington, DC: National Conference of State Legislatures, 2005).

16. See, for example, Michael Mintrom and Sandra Vergari, "Policy networks and innovation diffusion: The case of state education reforms" *Journal of Politics* 60 (1), February 1998 126–148.

17. James G. Cibulka, "The changing role of interest groups in education: Nationalization and the new politics of education productivity," *Educational Policy* 15(1), January 2001, 12–40.

18. Sabatier, "Policy change over a decade or more"; Jack D. Douglas, *Investigative social research.* (Beverly Hills, CA: Sage, 1976).

19. Joseph A. Maxwell, *Qualitative research design: An interactive approach* (Thousand Oaks, CA: Sage, 1996).

20. E. DeBray-Pelot and P. McGuinn (forthcoming), The new politics of education: Analyzing the National Education Policy Landscape in the Post-NCLB Era. *Educational Policy.*

21. Frederick Hess and Andrew Rotherham, "NCLB and the competitiveness agenda: Happy collaboration or collision course?" *Phi Delta Kappan* 88(5), January 2007, 345.

22. National Commission on Excellence in Education, *A nation at risk* (Washington, DC: U.S. Department of Education, 1983).

23. National Research Council, *Rising above the gathering storm: Energizing and employing America for a brighter economic future* (Washington, DC: National Academies Press, 2005).

24. Hess and Rotherham, "NCLB and the competitiveness agenda," 349.

25. Personal communication, October 11, 2005.

26. Robert Gordon, "Class struggle: What Democrats need to say about education." *New Republic.* June 6, 2005, 24.

27. The fact that this chapter does not treat the growth of the national advocacy coalition for privatization in education in detail, as it was not yet a major force in what I examined with respect to NCLB, should not diminish that coalition's power or significance to policy. In fact, the growth of this part of the education policy subsystem during this period was considerable. See Elizabeth DeBray-Pelot, Christopher Lubienski, and Janelle Scott, "The institutional landscape of interest group politics and school choice." *Peabody Journal of Education* 82(2).

28. Gail Sunderman, *The unraveling of No Child Left Behind: How negotiated changes transform the law.* Cambridge, MA: The Civil Rights Project at Harvard University, 2007.

29. A. Salzman, NAACP is Bush ally in Connecticut school case. *New York Times* [online edition] (February 1, 2006).

30. Quoted in A. Salzman.

31. Personal communication, March 21, 2006.

32. Ibid.

33. Ibid.

34. Ibid.

35. Jay Mathews, "National school testing urged: Gaps between state, federal assessments fuel call for change." *Washington Post*, September 3, 2006, p A01.

36. David Shreve, National standards: What do national standards have to do with ESEA/NCLB reauthorization? Presentation to National Association of State Boards of Education Legislative Conference, Washington, DC, March 16, 2007.

37. Lynn Olson, "Standards get boost on the hill: Bills before Congress aim to raise the bar in states." *Education Week* January 17, 2007 (online edition).

38. Personal communication, March 15, 2007.

39. Quoted in Olson, "Standards get boost on the Hill."

40. M. McGuire, personal communication, April 21, 2007.
41. See DeBray-Pelot & McGuinn (forthcoming).
42. Quoted in Olson, "Standards get boost on the Hill."
43. David Hoff, "NCLB panel calls for federal role in setting national standards." *Education Week* February 13, 2007 [online edition].
44. Quoted in Amit Paley, "'No Child' commission presents ambitious plan," *Washington Post*, February 14, 2007, p A03.
45. Quoted in Amit Paley, "GOP bills would relax test requirements of `No Child' law." *The Washington Post*, March 16, 2007, A6.
46. Patricia Sullivan, personal communication, November 2005.
47. Allison Klein, "Governors enter fray over NCLB: State chiefs, boards join plan for revisions to law." *Education Week*, April 11, 2007, 1.
48. Patricia Sullivan, personal communication, November 2005.
49. Quoted in Klein, "Governors enter fray over NCLB," 28.
50. Lance Fusarelli, Gubernatorial reactions to No Child Left Behind: politics, Pressure, and education reform, *Peabody Journal of Education*, 80, 124.
51. Sabatier and Jenkins-Smith, *Policy change and learning*, 5.
52. Sabatier, "Policy change over a decade or more," p. 31.
53. DeBray-Pelot & McGuinn (forthcoming).
54. Frank Baumgartner and Bryan Jones, Agendas and Instability in American Politics (Chicago, IL: University of Chicago Press, 1993).

CHAPTER EIGHT

Equity AND Special Education

Some Historical Lessons FROM Boston

ADAM R. NELSON

What has the keyword *equity* meant in contemporary educational policy debates? Common sense might suggest that, substantively, the word *equity* should carry the same meaning for all students, but in fact, the word has substantively different meanings for different groups. Owing to a series of exigencies that have emerged in state and federal law, the substantive meaning of equity differs, for example, for students in regular and special education. In a sense, all students in public schools are entitled to equitable, adequate, or appropriate education, but in an Orwellian twist, some are entitled to more equitable, adequate, or appropriate education than others.

To explain how different groups came to warrant different services in public schools, this chapter looks at evolving concepts of "equal educational opportunity" in one urban district. Specifically, it uses the case of special education to examine the meaning of equity for diverse groups in Boston since the 1960s. Over time, various policies arose at the local, state, and federal levels to guide the provision of special education services in Boston, but these policies did not serve all groups equally; more often than not, they perpetuated *inequalities* in the schools. The result has been confusion about the meaning of equity in both special and regular education.

Embedded in special education debates in Boston have been complex questions about race and social class, as well as difficult questions about the best way to provide "appropriate" education for all students. In a city known for troubled race relations and enduring class tensions, the politics of special education in Boston have long reflected broader conflicts in the city and its schools. Inasmuch as the very concept of "disability" has (too often) been associated with notions of racial difference and social disadvantage, special education in Boston has provoked constant and sometimes bitter controversy (as it has in other cities as well).

Over time, as special education policies emerged at the local, state, and federal levels, the key questions in Boston were these: who exactly would be eligible for special education? What exactly would special education programs involve? And how would the cost of special education affect the overall distribution of resources in the city's schools? As special education programs expanded (in the city as well as the suburbs), many asked how their claim on resources—supported by legal mandates—would affect students *not* enrolled in special education. In the end, would special education policies help or hinder the larger goal of equity in the public schools?

WHO EXACTLY WOULD BE ELIGIBLE FOR SPECIAL EDUCATION?

This story begins in the 1960s, when congress authorized federal grants to states to improve education for mentally retarded children. In 1963, the Massachusetts Mental Retardation Planning Project received federal aid to encourage local schools to provide better care for students with mental retardation and other cognitive disabilities.[1] Sensing an opportunity to receive aid by serving a neglected population, Boston school officials set out to diagnose all children who could be placed in aid-eligible programs. Many with below-average academic achievement, including large numbers of low-income and racial minority students, were found to be eligible for special education.

One reason Boston placed so many students in special programs for the mentally retarded was that federal aid was not available for "regular" classes. In the early 1960s, Boston's school enrollments had surged, and the education budget had become strained. Although the state had revised its school-aid formula to direct more aid to urban areas—areas with growing numbers of minority (both in-migrant and immigrant) students—the state had not collected enough tax revenues to fulfill its aid promises; consequently, the schools had looked to the federal government for help. In 1963, help arrived in the form of grants to special education.

Two years later, congress passed the Elementary and Secondary Education Act of 1965, which directed aid to special "compensatory" programs for low-achieving students. Congress hoped this aid would meet the needs of disadvantaged (often minority) students and reward local districts for pursuing racial desegregation (a goal thwarted in part by the ESEA's automatic distribution formula and in part by the federal government's inability to monitor civil rights violations). Boston, desperate for aid, applied for ESEA grants—and, like other cities, used these grants to fund special compensatory programs targeted at low-achieving students.

While local officials considered these "concentrated" programs an efficient use of funds, Massachusetts passed a law in 1965 to withhold state aid from racially imbalanced schools, many of which received ESEA grants. Hoping to evade the effects of this racial-imbalance law, Boston found that, by establishing special education programs in certain schools and justifying placements in these schools on the basis of "disability" (as well as race), it was possible simultaneously to improve "racial balance" *and* to increase aid for special education. One example of this strategy was the manipulation of "Chapter 750," which funded programs for emotionally disturbed children.

Starting in 1965 (five years after the passage of Chapter 750), the schools began to diagnose more and more low-income minority children with emotional disturbances. Since no minority neighborhood in Boston had a Chapter 750 class, diagnosed students were bused to predominantly white neighborhoods, where they were placed in separate—and racially imbalanced—classes within those schools. As one study explained, minority students assigned to predominantly white schools "were being classified as retarded or emotionally disturbed and removed from the classes they were [otherwise supposed] to integrate."[2]

J. Edward Conners of the Harvard School of Public Health investigated Chapter 750 in this period and discovered that 60 percent of students diagnosed as emotionally disturbed came from poor, minority, and/or limited-English-proficient families—though minority families comprised only 20 percent of the city's total population. Conners also found that low-income children were likelier than high-income children to be placed in programs with few academic services. Arguing that racially imbalanced programs were inherently discriminatory, Conners appealed for better diagnostic procedures to prevent the disproportionate enrollment of minority students in special education.[3]

Yet, special education was eligible for state and federal grants, whereas regular education was not; thus, schools desperate for aid continued to place large numbers of students—especially low-income minorities—in aid-eligible classes. And, once enrolled, students remained in these classes indefinitely, because the schools did not retest them to see if they could move back into regular classes (despite a state law mandating retests). "It's against the law," admitted the state director of special education, but "when the superintendent of schools and the school committee chairman in Boston swear—under penalty of perjury—that [retesting] is done, what can you do? They don't retest them, but they say they do."[4]

In 1967, parents in Boston took action to stop the disproportionate placement of minority students in special education. Two community groups, the Parents' Association for South End Schools and the United South End Settlements, charged the schools with misdiagnosing poor, minority, and limited-English-proficient students and placing them in remedial classes for the mentally retarded or emotionally disturbed. In a report titled "End Educational Entombment," they alleged that (mis)diagnoses and (mis)placements had occurred without parents' consent—and indeed, without reliable evidence of actual cognitive or behavioral difficulties.[5]

The parents followed their report with a legal petition to bar schools from using "racially discriminatory tests" to place children in separate remedial tracks.[6] Echoing a recent federal court decision in Washington, DC (in the case of *Hobson v. Hansen*), the parents argued that any standardized test resulting in the disproportionate placement of minority students in special education was legally suspect. (The federal judge in *Hobson v. Hansen* had asserted that "the practical effect" of Washington, DC's testing/tracking policy was "to group students largely according to their socio-economic status and, to a lesser but observable degree, to their racial status.")[7]

Despite the parents' legal protest, Boston's public schools continued to diagnose large numbers of low-income minority students with mental retardation. An official from Massachusetts's department of mental health commented: "Looking at the normal range of human intelligence, we know that a fixed percentage of a school population will score below a certain point on an I.Q. test. In Boston, for example, there should be about 1,500 children so retarded that they need special educational services; but [the public schools] have about 4,000 children instead. It's obvious they've got a lot of children who aren't retarded at all."[8]

It was no secret that Boston used special education to garner aid (and to mitigate the effects of the state racial imbalance law), but in the late 1960s a growing number of observers pointed to racially disproportionate enrollments as clear evidence of intentional discrimination. Noting that Boston's special education programs did little to help students academically, critics said that, more often than not, special education *hampered* students' intellectual development. While special educators claimed to meet their students' "needs" regardless of race, accusations of discrimination mounted.[9]

Allegations that special programs were dumping grounds for poor, minority, and limited-English-proficient students circulated widely in this period. For example, in the case of *Diana v. State Board of Education* (1970), limited-English-proficient students in California asked to be removed from classes for the mentally retarded—classes in which they had been placed because of diagnosed "language deficiencies." School officials said these classes helped limited-English-proficient students, but the federal court sided with the students, who said that placement in these classes carried a negative stigma. The court ordered the schools to place these students in regular classes.[10]

Before the case of *Diana v. State Board of Education* was decided in California, parents in Boston filed suit in federal court accusing the city's schools of discriminating against minority students by placing them in special education. The named plaintiff in this case was Pearl Stewart, the mother of a South End child who had been "entombed" in classes for the mentally retarded. The defendants in the case were the department of educational investigation and measurement and the state departments of education and mental health. Stewart claimed that discriminatory tests had led to the (mis)diagnosis of black children who were thus denied "equal opportunities" in the public schools.[11]

According to Stewart, "equal opportunities" hinged on accurate diagnoses, which in turn led to appropriate placements and meaningful educational programs. If the schools found disproportionate evidence of "disability" among racial minorities, then, she argued, something must be amiss with the schools' diagnostic methods. Only methods leading to *proportionate* (or at least randomly distributed) diagnoses across all groups—regardless of race, income, or language background—could be nondiscriminatory. In effect, Stewart claimed, any test leading to disproportionate enrollments in special education was legally dubious.[12]

In February 1971, the federal court ruled in Stewart's favor and ordered Boston to develop new procedures for diagnosing and placing students in programs for the mentally retarded. This decision was soon joined by another, *Larry P. v. Riles* (1972), in which a federal court in California found I.Q. tests to be racially discriminatory and prohibited the schools from using I.Q. scores to place black students in classes for the disabled. Each of these cases from the early 1970s—*Diana v. State Board of Education*, *Larry P. v. Riles*, and the Boston case of *Stewart v. Phillips*—sought to decrease the number of minority students (mis)placed in special education.[13]

At the same time, however, other cases sought to *increase* students' placements in special education. The best-known case from this era was *Pennsylvania Association for Retarded Children (PARC) v. Pennsylvania* (1971). In this case, children diagnosed with mental retardation sued for access to publicly funded schools (from which they had been categorically excluded). A federal court affirmed a consent decree in which the schools agreed to provide all mentally retarded children with a "free appropriate education" in the "least restrictive environment," that is, the most inclusive or mainstreamed class possible, given each child's unique needs.[14]

Shortly after the decision in *PARC*, a related decision came down in Washington, DC. In the case of *Mills v. Board of Education* (1972), a group of low-income minority students with mental and emotional disabilities accused the city's board of education of excluding them from the public schools. The board countered that, given severe budget constraints, it could not afford the programs the plaintiffs required. To accommodate the plaintiffs' needs, the board held, congress (which funded Washington's schools) would have to grant "millions of dollars to improve special education services in the District of Columbia." [15]

The court sided with the students, ruling that Washington, DC, must provide appropriate services to all disabled students and insisting that financial difficulties were no excuse not to do so. In the judge's words, "If sufficient funds are not available to finance all of the services and programs that are needed and desirable in the system, then the available funds must be expended equitably in such a manner that no child is entirely excluded from a publicly supported education consistent with his needs and ability to benefit therefrom." [16] In other words, Washington, DC, had to provide full and complete access to disabled students *even* if it had to cut other services to produce an "equitable" distribution of resources.

While the court in *Mills* did not specify exactly what an "equitable" distribution of resources might be, it did say that disabled students were legally entitled to "adequate alternative educational services suited to [their] needs." Moreover, the court held, "The inadequacies of the District of Columbia public school system, whether occasioned by insufficient funding or administrative inefficiency, certainly cannot be permitted to bear more heavily on the 'exceptional' or handicapped child than on the normal child." The implication was that "inadequacies" in the budget must not keep schools from providing disabled students with "adequate" educational services. [17]

Mills was an important ruling, but it left two questions unanswered. First, would the public schools be required to provide *all* students, including the *nondisabled*, with an equivalent level of service—that is, "adequate" services "consistent with [students'] need and ability to benefit therefrom"? Second, would an "equitable" distribution of resources be measured in terms of the resources spent on each student or in terms of the measurable "benefits" each student received from his or her placement in a special or regular class? Answers to both questions were necessary to discern when a school had in fact produced equitable, adequate, or appropriate educational benefits for all.

WHAT EXACTLY WOULD SPECIAL EDUCATION PROGRAMS INVOLVE?

The questions noted above applied directly to the debates over special education in Boston, where minority parents had sued to remove their children from special education classes in hopes that regular classes would yield greater "benefits." If it turned out that students in regular classes were not entitled to the same benefits as students in special education, or if it turned out that regular education was held to some lower standard of "equitable" spending or adequate services, then it was conceivable that minority students would gain little by moving from special to regular education. In fact, they might actually *lose* more than they gained.

This predicament—whereby minority students might renounce special education only to receive inadequate (as well as inequitable) treatment in regular education—was precisely what happened in Massachusetts in subsequent years. In the summer of 1972, Massachusetts's state legislature responded to special-education lawsuits with a massive increase in state aid to special education. A new law, Chapter 766, promised to reimburse 110 percent of the "excess" costs associated with special education services and required all schools to provide "appropriate" services to ensure that disabled students reached their "maximum feasible potential."

Addressing complaints about discriminatory placements, Chapter 766 pledged to monitor schools' diagnoses to see that only *truly* disabled students were placed in special education. The law stated that, "until proven otherwise, every child shall be presumed to be appropriately assigned to a regular education program and presumed not to be a ... child requiring special education."[18] Chapter 766 held that disabilities were evenly distributed across the student population (rather than concentrated in specific groups), and it required diagnosticians to use strictly cognitive rather than cultural criteria to make placements. In this way, the new law hoped to avoid racial imbalance in special education programs.

Chapter 766 brought extensive—and unexpected—changes to special education in Massachusetts. In the wake of the new law, schools across the state revisited their special education policies. Some, fearing charges of overdiagnoses, quickly reduced enrollments in special classes. Others, fearing charges of underdiagnoses, put unprecedented numbers of students in these classes. To show why some erred on the side of overdiagnosis while others erred on the side of underdiagnosis, analysts pointed to the financial incentives created by Chapter 766. In particular, they pointed to the specific procedures Massachusetts used to allocate state aid to special and regular education programs.

In 1969, seeking to meet the needs of the disabled, Massachusetts had prioritized special over regular education in the state's budget, which meant that the state met all its obligations to special education *before* it spent anything on regular education. Intended to assist urban schools with large enrollments in special education, this prioritization had an unintended effect after the passage of Chapter 766. Since aid for both special and regular education drew on the same revenue (a sales tax), and since aid for special education was assured while aid for regular education was pro-rated based on remaining tax revenues, schools had an incentive to shift costs into guaranteed-reimbursable special education programs.[19]

Under Chapter 766, schools could maximize their state aid by maximizing special education placements. This incentive applied to all school districts, but it applied most powerfully to affluent districts, which stood to receive more aid under Chapter 766 than they received under Chapter 750, the state's general aid program (which steered funds to poorer districts). As one analyst observed, "it is no secret ... that wealthier communities increase state aid by identifying and serving more children in special education programs. They increase their state aid by shifting expenditures to the more lucrative Chapter 766 formula for reimbursement."[20]

As long as funds for special education received top priority in the state education budget, wealthy districts took advantage of this system—and reminded their critics that recent court rulings made access to special education a legal right. The practical effect of this strategy was predictable: special education enrollments (and expenses) skyrocketed in suburban districts. So-called resource rooms swelled with affluent white students eligible for special accommodations. Indeed, policy researchers at the Huron Institute in Cambridge, Massachusetts, found that nearly every suburb around Boston received state aid for reading specialists, hearing experts, and school psychologists under Chapter 766.[21]

Similarly, researchers at the University of Massachusetts-Amherst discovered that suburban parents were far more aggressive than urban parents in their pursuit of special education resources. They reported that "wealthier communities have more sophisticated resources (programs and personnel) to take advantage of the services provided by state agencies. State employees more readily respond to school systems that have the expertise to demand responses and underserve those who do not."[22] In this way, special education programs in the suburbs gradually—and legally—siphoned resources away from urban schools.

This situation was fraught with historical irony. For years, poor minority students in Boston had been overdiagnosed as mentally retarded and/or emotionally disturbed. The city had been under intense court pressure to *reduce* enrollments in special education. Yet the Boston Public Schools started to curb diagnoses just when state aid began to flow in large sums to special education programs. It was in 1969 (the year South End parents sued to "end educational entombment") that special education had been placed above regular education in the state budget, and when aid became available, relatively wealthy suburbs rushed to enroll as many students as possible in aid-eligible programs.

After the passage of Chapter 766, enrollments in special education rose to record heights. This expansion resulted not only from the incentives created by Chapter 766 but also from the prospect of larger *federal* grants to special education. The federal Education Amendments of 1974 boosted aid to special education (even as these amendments *barred* aid to pay for court-ordered busing in cities such as Boston). The next year, congress passed the landmark Education for All Handicapped Children Act of 1975 (P.L. 94–142), which promised unprecedented sums for special education. (Significantly, this aid went to local districts regardless of their wealth or racial balance.)

With a price tag of $3 billion to $4 billion over five years, P.L. 94–142 authorized funds to cover the excess costs of special education on a steadily increasing annual basis, from 5 percent reimbursements in the first year to 10 percent in the second, 20 percent in the third, 30 percent in the fourth, and 40 percent in the fifth and all subsequent years. In keeping with the framework of Chapter 766, the new law offered reimbursements only to students who had been accurately diagnosed; it sought to control expenses by capping the total number of students whose costs would be reimbursed at 12 percent of a district's average daily attendance.

Despite this cap, local school districts in Massachusetts placed larger and larger numbers of students in special education—and reimbursable expenses rose accordingly. Between 1973–74 and 1976–77, total expenditures on special education in Massachusetts rose 130 percent (even as overall expenditures on education increased only 35 percent). Since the state reimbursed all excess costs of special education *first* and *in full*, special education consumed an ever-larger portion of the state's education budget. Meanwhile, regular classes—particularly those in urban districts seeking to reduce special education placements—faced growing financial shortfalls.[23]

Chapter 766 and P.L. 94–142 gave schools a clear incentive to shift enrollments into special education, because, even if budgets had to be cut in other areas, programs for the disabled were legally protected. The costs, however, were staggering. As one editorial in the *Boston Herald* noted, "this state is now embarked on a special education spending spree that boggles the mind and threatens taxpayers, regular students, and teachers."[24] In the years between 1974 and 1977 (an era of deepening recession), the number of special education teachers in Boston grew by 187 while the number of regular education teachers fell by 350.

Adding to budget woes was the fact that P.L. 94–142 failed to keep its promises, so state and local agencies had to pick up the tab for legally mandated services. As early as 1977, the National Education Association (NEA) anticipated the likely consequences of underfunding P.L. 94–142. "In order to fulfill federal mandates," the NEA speculated, "local school districts would have to compensate by … slashing other programs. These cutbacks would seriously undermine the quality of education provided for all children and would generate hostility and outrage [among] parents of normal children, parents of handicapped children, and teachers."[25]

Making this situation more complicated was a provision in P.L. 94–142 (and other federal education laws) that penalized school districts if they cut state or local spending on federally supported programs. So-called maintenance-of-effort regulations stipulated that any district reducing its local commitment to special education would lose a portion of its federal aid. By protecting special education from cuts, maintenance-of-effort rules virtually guaranteed that reductions would come from regular education. In cities hoping to shift resources *into* regular education, maintenance-of-effort regulations struck a hard blow. (Meanwhile, suburban districts continued to expand aid-eligible special classes.)[26]

Frustration with special education escalated in the late 1970s when the state revised its school-aid formula. In 1976, two years after Chapter 766 took effect, the legislature changed Chapter 750 aid from an "automatic" distribution set by statute (at 80 percent of sales-tax revenues) to a "variable" distribution set by majority vote. Thereafter, even as Chapter 766 remained a guaranteed distribution, Chapter 750 aid was increasingly susceptible to political negotiations—and cuts. In the wake of this change, schools had an even greater incentive to shift enrollments into the legally and financially protected area of special education.[27]

By the late 1970s, the protections afforded special education led to criticism. As the *Boston Globe* reported, "Few ... have criticized Chapter 766 for its intent to provide educational services for physically, mentally, and emotionally handicapped children in Massachusetts. Quite a few, however, are highly critical of its enormous financial impact on local communities at a time when their school costs are soaring and the state's fiscal crisis is worsening. The results are coming through loud and clear: less state money for general school purposes and rising expenses in scores of cities and towns that could force cuts in spending for regular school programs in favor of Chapter 766 children."[28]

Despite concerns about runaway costs, it was hard to curtail enrollments, because Chapter 766 and P.L. 94–142 both included "zero-rejection clauses," which meant that all disabled students, regardless of their degree of disability, were entitled to individualized services unless they explicitly opted out. In Massachusetts, even mildly disabled students were entitled to aid to reach their "maximum feasible potential" before other (nondisabled) students were entitled to *any* state aid. Between 1974 and 1978, as Chapter 766 expenses climbed from $143 million to $243 million—a jump of 70 percent in four years—some in Massachusetts began to ask what equity in education really meant.[29]

It was a difficult question, because one had to gauge not only whether students in special education were genuinely better off than they might have been in regular classes but also whether students who *remained* in regular classes were better off than they might have been had they been diagnosed with, say, a mild disability that warranted specialized assistance. Since the line separating "mildly disabled"

EQUITY AND SPECIAL EDUCATION | 167

from "nondisabled" students was not clear, a truly equitable system would have to be one that afforded *both* groups "equal benefits." A system that granted substantively greater benefits to mildly disabled students in special education in the suburbs than it granted to nondisabled students in regular education in the city was not equitable.

Looking back on the first years of Chapter 766, policy analysts John Pittinger and Peter Kuriloff surveyed Massachusetts's predicament in an essay for *The Public Interest.* "Because parents who were wealthy or well-educated tended to live in the more affluent districts (districts that complied more faithfully with the law [Chapter 766]), and because such parents were better able to articulate their concerns, demand evaluations, and appeal when necessary [for still more services], the effect of the law was to increase the disparity between the special education services available to children at opposite ends of the social ladder." In the end, they noted, "Boston children ... were probably least well served."[30]

HOW WOULD THE COST OF SPECIAL EDUCATION AFFECT THE OVERALL DISTRIBUTION OF RESOURCES?

By the fall of 1977, special education placements had increased exponentially— not only in Massachusetts but nationwide. Before the passage of P.L. 94–142, fewer than 5 percent of the nation's school-aged children had been diagnosed with disabilities, but after federal aid became available, that number had climbed to 9 percent. In Chicago, the number was 11.7 percent; in Philadelphia, 12.4 percent; in Baltimore, 14.9 percent. In Boston, the proportion of students who had been diagnosed with disabilities stood at 18.4 percent—more than twice the national average and more than six times the city's average three years earlier.[31]

While some felt these figures represented an accurate count of disabled students, others raised questions about diagnostic procedures. Two scholars, Richard Weatherly and Michael Lipsky at Harvard, showed that, in Massachusetts, "[t]he chances of a child's being referred, evaluated, and provided with special education services were associated with presumably extraneous factors: the school system and school attended, the child's disruptiveness in class, his or her age and sex, the aggressiveness and/or socio-economic status of the parents, the current availability and cost of services needed, and the presence of particular categories of specialists in the school system."[32]

According to Weatherly and Lipsky, many diagnoses in Massachusetts stemmed from economic rather than educational criteria. "As for cost considerations," they wrote, "school systems continue to be concerned about expenditures, but now try to assign many regular education items to the special education budget, since Chapter 766 expenditures have first claim in the state's educational-reimbursement program."[33] Bruce Perlstein, an economist completing his doctorate at Brandeis University, concurred. He noted that "a large number of districts were shifting significant numbers of pupils and resources from regular ... to special education programs in response to ... financial incentives."[34]

School districts succeeded in this ruse because it was so difficult to ascertain how many students were actually or legitimately "disabled"—and therefore legally entitled to special education. In 1977, the Stanford Research Institute reviewed 400 studies of the "prevalence" of different types of disability in the general population and found that "no single set of prevalence figures can be accepted as fact."[35] Different states used different criteria to identify the same disability; moreover, different states used different formulae to reimburse schools for services, which created different incentives to identify different categories of disabled students in the first place.

One study found that "learning disabled" students accounted for 19 percent of the total population of disabled students in New York but 63 percent in Hawaii. Since it was unlikely that "learning disabilities" were three times more prevalent in Hawaii than New York, analysts sought other explanations for the disparity. The most plausible explanation had to do with money: New York offered higher reimbursements for "mentally retarded" than "learning disabled" students, so local schools placed more students in the financially advantageous "mentally retarded" category; Hawaii covered 100 percent of the costs for all groups, so officials placed students in the cheaper "learning disabled" category.[36]

In states that used different reimbursement formulae for different categories of disabilities, schools had a financial incentive to place students in categories that brought the most generous reimbursements. Particularly in an era of budgetary constraints when diagnoses were subject to easy manipulation, administrators seized the opportunity to pad their balance sheets with special education reimbursements. As one analyst noted, "with more than one category of aid available, administrators tend to 'play the percentages' in developing programs."[37] Put simply, school officials placed students in programs likely to maximize state and federal grants.

Some categories of disability grew faster than others. Nationwide, for example, the population of students diagnosed as "learning disabled" jumped 83 percent between 1976–77 and 1980–81. One policy analyst observed, "Whereas in school years 1976–77, 1977–78, and 1978–79, the largest sub-population of handicapped students were those having speech impairments; beginning in 1979–80, the largest number of handicapped children now served are the learning disabled."[38] By 1980, nearly 37 percent of students diagnosed as disabled in Massachusetts were considered to have some form of learning disability.[39]

Part of the explanation for this rapid increase in diagnoses was that Chapter 766 never defined the word *disability*. State legislators hoped to avoid the "stigmatization" associated with "labeling" disabled students, but the consequence of leaving the law's operative term undefined was that an enormous range of students qualified for services. As policy analyst Milton Budoff wrote in the *Harvard Educational Review*, "no definition of the child with special educational needs was ever established. Consequently, the districts had difficulty establishing the number of children potentially eligible for services. ... "[40]

According to Budoff, some of the confusion regarding diagnosis, eligibility, and placement may have been intentional, an effort on the part of special education advocates to expand their constituency. "With the emphasis on labeling removed," Budoff asserted, Chapter 766 "opens the way for a dramatic expansion of eligibility for special services. The law takes the radical step of dealing with all children in actual or potential risk. Thus if a child is in danger at midyear of not being promoted, or indeed fails, he or she can be referred for services."[41] This strategy of manipulating diagnoses to increase enrollments (and reimbursements) arose not only in the suburbs but, increasingly, in the city as well. It seems that, in the wake of *Larry P. v. Riles* (1972), which cast doubt on the validity of I.Q. tests, schools found other diagnostic tools that could facilitate placements without triggering legal scrutiny.

Realizing that suburbs were placing large numbers of students in special classes, Boston opted to play the same game. The difference was that Boston reverted to its old tactic of placing low-income minorities in special education in disproportionate numbers. In the late 1970s, the Massachusetts Advocacy Center (MAC) found "separate programs in Boston that are comprised entirely of black students." Investigators also found large numbers of black students cited for disciplinary problems and relegated to classes for the emotionally disturbed. For the MAC inspectors, such findings offered clear evidence of racial discrimination.[42]

Yet, school officials reminded the MAC that the best way to boost state aid was to increase enrollments in special education. If the city chose not to increase its enrollments, then suburbs less averse to special education placements would continue to claim larger and larger portions of the school aid budget. Given the widespread view that Boston was not receiving its fair share of state aid, officials did not apologize for the disproportionate enrollment of minority students. Rather, they pointed to "poverty, transiency, and cultural differences as the reasons for the generally higher rates of placement of minority students in special education."[43]

What distinguished special education placements in the suburbs from placements in the city was the fact that white parents in the suburbs usually accepted their children's diagnoses and felt that special programs would serve their children's educational needs; they believed special education would offer "meaningful," "appropriate," or "beneficial" services and would equalize their children's educational opportunities. Minority parents in the city did not share this view. Influenced by prior experiences, they distrusted their children's diagnoses and feared that special education would actually *limit* their children's academic opportunities. They were probably right.

In Boston, black students were enrolled in special education at higher rates and placed more often in physically isolated programs with limited academic resources. In 1975–76, physically isolated programs enrolled 41.9 percent of white special education students but 44.2 percent of all black special education students. Two years later, the gap had widened. In 1977–78, physically isolated programs—now funded by Chapter 766 as well as P.L. 94–142—enrolled 41.3 percent of white special education students and 47.1 percent of black special education students.[44] To many black parents in Boston, the signs of discrimination were obvious.

But these signs were not unique to Boston. In 1976–77, black students comprised 15 percent of total enrollments in the United States but 21 percent of special education enrollments and 38 percent of enrollments in special classes for the "educable mentally retarded." Two years later, in 1978–79 (after funds became available under P.L. 94–142), black students comprised 17 percent of total school enrollments but 23 percent of special education enrollments and *41 percent* of enrollments in classes for the educable mentally retarded. While some insisted these figures reflected "true" rates of disability across the school-aged population, others saw evidence of racial discrimination.[45]

Unfortunately, any rate of placing minorities in special education was likely to be criticized for being either too high or too low—and discriminatory in both cases. Hence, school officials expanded special education services with an eye toward maximizing state and federal aid. This strategy appeared to benefit schools (if not students) in the short run, but eventually, as placements grew and costs mounted, taxpayers balked. In 1979–80, the Boston Public Schools faced a $10 million deficit, and the Boston Municipal Research Bureau attributed a large part of this deficit to the approximately $1 million in annual expenses for private residential facilities mandated under Chapter 766. As deficits grew, it was clear that something would have to give.[46]

Efforts to bring the overall school budget under control were repeatedly foiled by legally mandated special education programs. In 1980, the Boston Public Schools had a budget of $228 million, $205 million of which was "the result of legislative mandate—for such services as special education and bilingual [classes]—or double-digit inflation."[47] In the eight years since the passage of Chapter 766 and the five years since the passage of P.L. 94–142, local expenditures for special education had increased threefold, from $12 million to $38 million.[48] (The next year, 1981, local outlays for special education were projected to rise another 21 percent, to $46 million.)[49]

By the fall of 1980, special education programs enrolled 12,000 students, or 18 percent of the student population, and the fiscal outlook was bleak. Yet, after the November elections that year, the outlook was even bleaker.[50] Voters passed a statewide initiative, Proposition 2½, which dramatically restricted property tax rates—and, thus, revenue for schools. Proposition 2½ had a drastic effect on education (which absorbed 60 percent of property tax revenues in the state), but its effects did not fall evenly across the education budget. Most seriously threatened were *regular* education programs, which had no legal safeguards.[51]

Proposition 2½ passed by wide margins in precincts throughout Massachusetts, but it hit urban areas hardest. State Commissioner of Education Gregory Anrig explained that Proposition 2½ would affect "most heavily our largest and poorest communities. ... Boston's budget, for instance, if you use the current recommended property valuations and current year tax levy, would have to [be reduced] ... by 70 percent."[52] Such a huge reduction in the city's budget would obviously force major cuts in the city's schools—especially in vulnerable regular education programs.

Proposition 2½ was not, however, the only factor shaping Boston school policies after 1980. Coinciding with Proposition 2½ was a push for greater "accountability" in the public schools. The accountability movement had been mounting for several years—ever since 1973–74, when state officials began collecting statewide data on academic performance. The goal was to develop "specific measures for evaluating the progress of each student and the success of each educational program."[53] The goal, in other words, was to spur the public schools to produce superior results with fewer resources—to get them to do more with less.

In the summer of 1981, the state required all districts receiving aid to give "basic skills competency tests" in reading, writing, and mathematics to students in elementary, middle, and high schools. This exercise, intended to produce baseline data for later achievement standards, had an immediate effect. As one editorialist observed, "the mere appearance of the 1981 scores has apparently been enough to generate an irresistible pressure to go statewide with a mandatory testing system."[54] Yet, two crucial questions soon emerged. First, would the state impose sanctions on schools if students failed to meet specific achievement standards? Second, would the state track scores for students in both regular *and* special education?

EQUITY AND ACCOUNTABILITY IN SPECIAL AND REGULAR EDUCATION

From the beginning of the accountability movement, students in special education had been exempt from tests used for accountability purposes. The underlying assumption was that standardized tests were inappropriate for students in special education, whose learning programs were tailored to their unique individual needs. Instead, policymakers assumed, both norm-referenced and criterion-referenced basic skills tests should be given only to regular education students who could be expected to master particular standards from year to year or grade to grade. Schools would then be held accountable only for the scores of regular education students.

Yet, the exemption of special education students raised a number of questions in Boston, where more than 30 percent of all students in the public schools were enrolled in either special or bilingual education—and most of these students were racial minorities. If the schools exempted more than 30 percent of students from accountability tests, and if most of these students belonged to racial minority groups, then how would officials discern when—or whether—minority students in the district had received "equal educational opportunities," or whether they were instead subject to inappropriate (or discriminatory) treatment?[55]

How could the state discern the relative "equity" or "adequacy" of special versus regular education placements? One possible answer was to require all students to sit for the same test, but this solution had flaws, because no test could determine *ex post facto* whether students in special education might have produced higher scores had they been placed in regular education, or vice versa. No test could tell whether a particular student might have benefited *more* from some *other* placement. But since it was obviously discriminatory to give different tests to different groups, many believed the only way to determine "equal benefits" (or equal opportunities) was to give the same test to all.

Herein lay a key dilemma of assessing equity across special and regular education programs. Over time, schools had placed large numbers of students in special education, but the state had no way to measure the relative benefits of these placements. It could not measure when—or whether—students in special education had reached their "maximum feasible potential," nor could it gauge when students had received "adequate" or "equitable" treatment, because it could not answer the question, *adequate or equitable compared to what?* With no way to assess the hypothetical benefits of alternate placements, it was impossible to measure the "equity" of placements in special or regular education.

Despite this dilemma, special education placements continued to grow. By 1991–92, Boston's special education classes enrolled nearly 22.9 percent of all students in the city's public schools. Special education and bilingual education together enrolled nearly 35 percent of all students and claimed 40 percent of the total school budget (meanwhile, regular education claimed only 23 percent of the budget). Nationally, from 1967 to 1991, the share of instructional expenses going to regular education *decreased* from 80 percent to 59 percent while the share going to special education *increased* from 4 percent to 17 percent. (Special education students were, however, still exempt from state accountability tests.)[56]

Schools took particular advantage of the vague category of "learning disabilities." From 1980 to 1991, the proportion of handicapped students in Massachusetts diagnosed as learning disabled climbed from 36.7 percent to 61.0 percent. This percentage (the highest in the country) was 21 percent higher than the national average. State officials admitted this percentage was fishy. According to a report published by the Massachusetts department of education in 1992, "the large percentage of students with learning disabilities may not reflect actual disabilities, but the decreased capacity of regular education to appropriately meet the needs of diverse learners." [57]

Indeed, given persistent budget cuts in the wake of Proposition 2½, regular education programs had slowly deteriorated. One analyst from the conservative Pioneer Institute noted, "Boston's regular and special education programs function in a vicious cycle. As the regular classroom declines, students are shunted into special education. Since special education's small class sizes and generous staffing levels are guaranteed by state regulations, costs skyrocket as enrollment burgeons. As a larger portion of the district's budget flows to the mandated program, the resources for regular education diminish further. Remedial programs are eliminated ... and regular education programs [are] debilitated, leading to still more special education referrals." [58]

It was indeed a vicious cycle. Over time, as special education costs rose, relative spending on regular education fell. As spending (and perceived quality) in regular education declined, schools funneled more students into special education programs where aid (if not quality) was legally assured. Growing enrollments and expenses in special education put further strain on regular education budgets, which accelerated the decline of regular classes and drove schools to shift more students into special education programs (which, of course, had the added benefit of being "exempt" from standardized tests).

Under these conditions, special education spending continued to escalate. In 1980, state reimbursements for special education in Massachusetts totaled $266.9 million; by 1985, reimbursements had risen to $389.2 million; and by 1990, reimbursements stood at $739.5 million (an increase of 177 percent over ten years). Federal aid was supposed to cover 40 percent of these costs, but in Massachusetts in 1989, federal aid covered only 6 percent. Meanwhile, Chapter 766 was supposed to cover *all* excess costs associated with special education, but in 1989 the state covered only 5.8 percent. Thus, local districts in Massachusetts covered, on average, 88.2 percent of special education costs. [59]

If local districts covered such a large percentage of special education costs, why did they not seek to control these costs more effectively? Why did they allow costs to get so high? The growth of special education programs even after it became clear that state and federal aid would not cover their costs was puzzling until one realized that regular education was even *less* assured of receiving adequate resources. Indeed, this situation—whereby students in special education had more reliable access to funds than students in regular education—was a pivotal development in public school finance. Even if special education was expensive, it was more likely than regular education to be funded with the resources available.

Not only were students in special education guaranteed aid but they were exempt from accountability sanctions: it was the perfect combination of incentives for schools to place as many students as possible in special education programs. But it could not last. In 2000, faced with continuing budget strains, Massachusetts abandoned its commitment to helping all disabled students reach their "maximum feasible potential." Legislators voted instead to adopt the federal standard that required schools only to offer "appropriate" or "adequate" services, which the Supreme Court had defined as "basic minimum" services to help mainstreamed students progress from grade to grade with passing marks.[60]

Also in the year 2000, Massachusetts adopted new placement rules that rendered 30,000 "mildly" disabled students ineligible for special education and forced them back into regular classrooms—where, unfortunately, they had no legal guarantee of receiving an "appropriate" education. But would these students, now in regular classes, receive an "equitable" education? Would they receive "benefits" equal to the "benefits" guaranteed their counterparts in special education? Would they have access to "adequate" programs or services, "consistent with their need and ability to benefit therefrom"? Or, to reframe the language of *Mills*, would their schools be allowed to let budget inadequacies "bear more heavily" on students in regular education?

History did not bode well for these students. As the story of special and regular education in Massachusetts since the 1960s revealed, students in special education had a legal right to make substantive claims to "adequate" or "equitable" services—with *adequacy* and *equity* defined in terms of both financial resources and learning outcomes—but students in regular education had no such right. Put simply, while all students were ostensibly entitled to an "equal" education, some were apparently entitled to a more equal education than others.

Given this situation, was it any surprise that officials steadily increased enrollments in special education? Given the persistent budgetary constraints in the public schools and the ease of diagnosing students, both the suburbs and the city placed more and more students in special classes and gladly accepted state and federal reimbursements for their "excess" costs—even as these reimbursements fell short of covering expenses, and even as special education classes escaped accountability oversight. The result was a growing diversion of financial resources away from regular education and, it seems, a digression from the larger goal of "equity" in Massachusetts's public schools.

Some believed the only way to know for sure if students in special and regular education were receiving "equitable" education was to give both groups the same tests and see if their scores were equal (or at least to see if their scores were rising or falling at equal rates, such that any "gaps" in achievement did not grow). In 2002, the federal No Child Left Behind Act (NCLB) moved a step closer to measuring "equity" in this way by requiring all schools receiving federal aid to give all students in all programs in grades three through eight the same (state-approved) tests and to disaggregate students' results by race, language, and disability status.

NCLB said nothing about the equitable distribution of financial resources across subgroups, nor did it stipulate which test(s) a state must use to measure achievement. It simply demanded that schools receiving aid produce "adequate yearly progress" for each subgroup. If the scores of a particular subgroup failed to improve, any student in the school could demand private supplemental services, transfers to different schools, or ultimately a takeover of the school by the state. Each of these interventions was supposed to foster the equalization of scores across programs. In effect, NCLB made "equity" a function of equal—or gradually equalizing—test scores.

It remains unclear how judgments of equity in special and regular education will be made in the future. Certainly, the criteria used to determine equity in special education had changed many times in the past. In the 1960s, judgments of equity hinged in part on determinations of racial balance, or racial proportionality, in special education placements. In the 1970s, as urban and suburban districts competed for limited resources, the emphasis shifted from racial proportionality in placements to greater funding for special education programs. Eventually, in the 1980s and 1990s, as calls for "accountability" emerged, the emphasis shifted from racial proportionality and financial redistribution to academic achievement. Whether test scores offer the best measure of "equity" across regular and special education programs remains to be seen.

CONCLUSION: EQUITY AND SPECIAL EDUCATION

What can this brief history of special education in Boston tell us about improving current educational policy? Four answers come to mind. First, it would seem that, going forward, determinations of "equity" in special education will hinge not so much on racial disproportionality in enrollments but on measures of the relative academic gains of students in special and regular education. If enrollments are racially disproportional but academic results improve equally across subgroups, then placements in special education are not likely to be considered "discriminatory" (racially or otherwise). In short, both equity and discrimination will be assessed in terms of test scores.

Second, and somewhat paradoxically, it would seem that, if schools continue to see financial incentives in special education placements, they will continue to make these placements, *regardless* of the relative academic gains of the students in these programs. As in the past, economic considerations are likely to trump educational considerations in school policy, so if the equalization of test scores is a goal, then financial incentives must be structured in a way that *rewards* the gradual equalization of scores. For years, Massachusetts rewarded enrollments, not academic gains, and, unsurprisingly, both suburban and urban schools responded by maximizing enrollments rather than achievement.

Third, and perhaps unfortunately, it would seem that schools will place students in programs that are most likely to maximize aid, *even* if this strategy results in racially disproportionate enrollments or, as the case of special education in the suburbs reveals, even if this strategy puts disadvantaged students in the city at even further disadvantage. When a state finance system allows wealthy suburbs to divert funds from urban schools and weakens its own aid-equalization formula in order to subsidize wealthy schools (on grounds of protecting disabled students' civil rights), then nondisabled students enrolled in regular classes in the city will have little hope of an "equitable" allocation of resources.

Finally, and most regrettably, it would seem that, even if gradually "equalizing" academic gains were a desirable goal, this goal may be difficult—if not impossible—to achieve. Schools have limited influence over students' academic performance; myriad other factors affect test scores, many of which have little to do with student experiences in school. It may therefore be unwise to require schools to pursue equalized achievement. Since equalized achievement is (psychometrically) unlikely, such a demand may lead to further erosion of trust in the "equitability" of public schools. In the long run, setting the schools up to fail in this way might do more harm than good.

NOTES

1. Massachusetts Mental Retardation Planning Project, *Massachusetts Plans for Its Retarded* (Boston, 1966).
2. Alicia Caban Wheeler, "Public Policy Formulation: Chapter 766, Education of the Handicapped Act (Qualifying Paper, Harvard Graduate School of Education, June 1980), 25. See also Wheeler, 12. "In spite of the good intent behind the development of Chapter 750 and its regulations, an examination of political and social history, including data from the Project 750 follow-up study, reveals that Chapter 750 was used to: a) misclassify and exclude minority and bilingual children [from regular classes], b) perpetuate racial segregation, and c) discriminate by race and social class." Boston's Chapter 750 classes were investigated for possible malfeasance in 1968. See Herbert J. Hoffman, *Take a Giant Step: Final Report of*

Evaluation of Selected Aspects of Project 750 (Boston: Massachusetts Advisory Council on Education, September 1969), 1, 20–21. "The present regulations and forms [governing Chapter 750] make no provision for recording the child's color. This is understandable in terms of accepted philosophies and practices at the time the regulations were developed in the early 1960s. [But] Times, philosophies, and concerns have changed. Events in the black communities over the past five years (black-white confrontations and several federal promulgations) have [now] made it [necessary] for responsible public officials to know what the distribution of clients and employees is by color."

3. See Massachusetts Institute for Intergovernmental Services, *The Children's Puzzle: A Study of Services to Children in Massachusetts* (February 1977), 7.

4. Wheeler, 31.

5. Parents Association for South End Schools and the United South End Settlements, "End Educational Entombment" (1967).

6. "Aid to Handicapped Pupils to Be Probed," *Boston Globe* (25 December 1969).

7. *Hobson v. Hansen* 269 F. Supp. 401 (1967).

8. Quoted in Task Force on Children Out of School, *The Way We Go to School: The Exclusion of Children in Boston* (Boston 1970), 37.

9. In 1970, congress passed the Elementary and Secondary Education Act Amendments of 1970 (P.L. 91–230), which added a new law, "Part B," to provide grants to states to expand special education services for disabled students.

10. *Diana v. California State Board of Education*, Civil No. 70–37 RFP (N.D. Calif. 1970),

11. *Stewart v. Phillips*, Civil No. 70–1199-F (D. Mass, February 8, 1971), reprinted in Harvard University Center for Law and Education, *Classification Materials* (Cambridge, MA: Author, 1972), 234.

12. *Stewart v. Phillips*, Civil No. 70–1199-F (D. Mass, February 8, 1971).

13. *Larry P. v. Riles* 345 F. Supp. 1306 (N.D. Calif. 1972), affirmed 502 F. 2nd 963 (9th Cir. 1974).

14. *Pennsylvania Association for Retarded Children (PARC) v. Pennsylvania*, 343 F. Supp. 279 (E.D. Pa. 1972).

15. *Mills v. Board of Education*, 348 F.Supp. 866 (D. D.C., 1972).

16. Ibid.

17. Ibid.

18. Chapter 766 was signed into law on July 18, 1972. It created Chapter 71B of the Massachusetts General Laws but was popularly known as Chapter 766.

19. Charlotte Ryan, "The State Dollar and the Schools: A Discussion of State Aid Programs in Massachusetts and Promising Reforms" (Boston: Massachusetts Advisory Council on Education, 1970), 17.

20. Bruce W. Perlstein, "Taxes, Schools, and Inequality: The Political Economy of the Property Tax and School Finance Reform in Massachusetts (Unpublished Ph.D. dissertation, Brandeis University, 1981), 430.

21. James McGarry, *Final Report: Implementing Massachusetts' Special Education Law: A Statewide Assessment* (1982), 25.

22. University of Massachusetts Institute for Governmental Services, *The Children's Puzzle: A Study of Services to Children in Massachusetts* (February 1977), 4.

23. Perlstein, 441.

24. Warren T. Brookes, "What Chapter 766 is Doing to City's Regular Education," *Boston Herald American* (15 May 1977) quoted in Caroline Marie Cunningham, "Special Education: A Cost Analysis of the Financial Impact of Chapter 766 on Local School Systems" (Unpublished Ph.D. dissertation, Boston College, 1979), 7.

25. Paul W. Cox, "The Impact of State Funding of Special Needs Programs, Under Chapter 766, Acts of 1972, on the Funding of Other State and Local Educational Programs in Massachusetts" (Unpublished Ed.D. dissertation, Boston College, 1980), 29–30, 34–36.

26. Catherine Flynn and George McDowell, *Cutback Management: Coping with Proposition 2½* (Cooperative Extension Service, University of Massachusetts-Amherst 1981), 9. See also John Lawson, *Report on Federal Aid to Massachusetts School Districts* (19 October 1983).

27. See Massachusetts Department of Education, *Taxes, Schools, and Inequality in Massachusetts: Chapter 70 School Aid and School Finance* (June 1977), 15.

28. "Special Education—Plenty of Problems," *Boston Globe* (12 June 1975).

29. Richard A. Weatherly and Michael Lipsky, "Street-Level Bureaucrats and Institutional Innovation: Implementing Special Education Reform," *Harvard Educational Review* 47:2 (May 1977), 102, 114.

30. John C. Pittinger and Peter Kuriloff, "Educating the Handicapped: Reforming a Radical Law," *The Public Interest* (Winter 1982), 81.

31. Joseph P. Viteritti, *Across the River: Politics and Education in the City* (New York, Holmes and Meier, 1983), 183.

32. Weatherly and Lipsky, 102, 114.

33. Ibid., 115–116.

34. Perlstein, 441.

35. Stearns, M., Norwood, C., Kaskowitz, D., and Mitchell, S., *Validation of State Counts of Handicapped Children*, 2 vols. (Menlo Park, Calif.: Stanford Research Institute International, 1977).

36. Jeffrey J. Zettel, "Implementing the Right to a Free Appropriate Public Education" in Joseph Ballard, Bruce A. Ramirez, and Frederick J. Weintraub, *Special Education in America: Its Legal and Governmental Foundations* (Reston, Va.: Council for Exceptional Children, 1982), 28–29.

37. Ryan, 17.

38. Zettel, 25.

39. Massachusetts Department of Education, "Students with Special Needs in Massachusetts by Federal Disability Category for the Year 1991–1992" (Boston, March, 1992), 20.

40. Milton Budoff, "Engendering Change in Special Education Practices," *Harvard Educational Review*, 45:4 (November 1975), 518–519.

41. Budoff, 516.

42. Massachusetts Advocacy Center, "Double Jeopardy: The Plight of Minority Students in Special Education" (1978), 28, 1.

43. Ibid., 7.

44. Ibid., 28, 1.

45. Zettel, 34.

46. Boston Municipal Research Bureau, "Boston Does It Again: Budget Overspent by $18.3 Million in FY 1979" (4 October 1979).

47. "Wood Asks $227 Million School Budget," *Boston Globe* (17 June 1980).

48. "Special Education Target of Cuts," *Boston Globe* (31 March 1980).

49. "Boston Schools in Crisis: A School System Caught in the Chapter 766 Crossfire," *Boston Globe* (12 February 1981).

50. "Boston Schools in Crisis: A School System Caught in the Chapter 766 Crossfire," *Boston Globe* (12 February 1981).

51. See Lawrence E. Susskind and Jane Fountain Serio, eds., *Proposition 2½: Its Impact on Massachusetts* (Cambridge, Mass. 1983); and Helen Ladd and Julie Wilson, *Proposition 2½: Explaining the Vote* (Boston: Program in City and Regional Planning, 1981).

52. Untitled, *Boston Globe* (6 October 1980).

53. Joseph M. Cronin, "Plan for Reorganization" (Boston: Executive Office of Educational Affairs, January, 1973), 29.

54. "Testing Competently," *Boston Globe* (27 December 1981).

55. "Now and Then a Different System; Schools Changed, But For Better or Worse?" *Boston Globe* (4 September 1985).

56. Steven F. Wilson, *Reinventing the Schools: A Radical Plan for Boston* (Boston: Pioneer Institute, 1992), 201–203; Paul T. Hill, "Getting It Right the Eighth Time: Reinventing the Federal Role" (Unpublished paper, March, 1999). See also Hamilton Lankford and James Wyckoff, "Where Has the Money Gone? An Analysis of School District Spending in New York," *Educational Evaluation and Policy Analysis* 17:2 (Summer 1995), 195–218.

57. Massachusetts Department of Education, "Students with Special Needs in Massachusetts by Federal Disability Category for the Year 1991–1992" (Boston, March, 1992), 20.

58. Wilson, 212.

59. State Auditor's Report on Special Education in Massachusetts (March 1991). See also Julie Berry Cullen, "The Impact of Fiscal Incentives on Student Disability Rates," *National Bureau of Economic Research Working Paper* 7173 (1999).

60. See *Board of Education of the Hendrick Hudson Central School District, Westchester County v. Rowley* 458 U.S. 176 (1982).

CHAPTER NINE

Examining THE Federal Role IN Education

FROM Reagan's Excellence Movement TO Bush AND No Child Left Behind

GAIL L. SUNDERMAN

The federal role in education has always been a sensitive one in American politics. Traditionally, the federal government has played a limited role and federal legislation has normally contained prohibitions against federal control of education. Indeed, local control of education is deeply engrained in the rhetoric and practice of American politics, where concerns about local control and liberty have far outweighed concerns about policy objectives.

Suspicion about federal power has been particularly strong among conservatives. Conservative views of federalism emphasize the prerogatives of state and local governments as the legitimate sources of policy and support the devolution of social programs to the states. This view supports local decision-making without interference from the federal government and assumes that states will invest funds in ways that will achieve particular policy goals. Others have been less opposed to a federal role. Civil rights advocates and researchers supported a federal role in ending discrimination and desegregating public schools. Public education supporters have long seen the federal government as a means to improve the education of disadvantaged students and equalize funding for schools. The federal education programs enacted in the 1960s and 1970s expressed these aims by allocating federal funds for the education of previously neglected groups of students.

With the No Child Left Behind Act of 2001 (NCLB) the objectives of Republican reformers changed from limiting the federal bureaucracy and decentralizing decision making to the states toward an activist bureaucracy that assertively promotes particular political and policy goals. NCLB expands federal authority over core educational functions—assessment, curriculum, teacher qualifications, and school intervention—traditionally under local control. Implementation proceeded with very little time for states to prepare for the provisions and did not follow the normal protocol of federal-state relationships that depended on intergovernmental coordination and cooperation between state educational officials and federal administrators.

In a true federal system where the state and national governments have their own independent political and legal systems, there is always tension over the division of power and authority. These issues have been particularly salient in struggles over school policy. Since all members of Congress as well as state officials are elected or appointed at the state or local level, disgruntled state and local officials and citizens have channels for changing federal programs, since all federal programs depend up on appropriations and laws from Congress. Because members of the House and Senate depend on state and local electorates for their survival, the administrative and professional struggles over implementation of a controversial federal law are very likely to enter into politics. This has surely happened with NCLB, as many legislatures expressed their displeasure with the law and elected and appointed officials in some states actively criticized the law. As political pressure mounted, the federal government began to move from a posture of imposition of rigid requirements to negotiation, permitting many changes that it previously resisted.[1]

Federalism is deeply engrained in the United States, where there are 50 independent state education systems with 15,700 local variations at the district level that are loosely regulated by the states.[2] Even so, this role has been evolving since the Reagan administration. This chapter examines how the federal role in education has changed and the forces that have pressed the United States toward greater federal involvement in education. Central to understanding this evolution are the Republican administrations of Ronald Reagan and George W. Bush. It argues that, as Republican administrations have gained an understanding of the political saliency of education, they have expanded the federal role in education to meet political and policy goals. First, during the Reagan administration, the release of the *A Nation at Risk* report was instrumental in shifting the policy agenda from equity to excellence and providing the administration a platform for advancing other policy preferences favored by conservatives.[3] The administration recognized the saliency of education as a political issue, but maintained a policy focus on a limited federal role and decentralized governance. Indeed, the interesting thing about the excellence movement was that while *Risk* initiated a national educational movement, it was the states that enacted many of the *Nation at Risk* reforms. Second, the George W. Bush administration reversed long held conservative principles of limited government and a preference for local decision making. This new paradigm includes a significant expansion of federal authority over the instructional core of education and conflicted federal-state relationships. States were marginal to the adoption of NCLB and the administration's approach to implementation has generated a particularly strong response from state and local governments in defense of federalism and the expanded federal role in education.

POLICY SHIFTS UNDER THE REAGAN ADMINISTRATION: FROM EQUITY TO EXCELLENCE

The Elementary and Secondary Education Act of 1965 (ESEA) marked the creation of an intergovernmental policy system where the federal government provided additional resources targeted on particular students. The ESEA, and other federal education policies that followed, were important in expanding the federal government's provision of sustained categorical aid to elementary and secondary education and addressed national policy priorities that, for the most part, were neglected at the local level. These policies sought to equalize educational opportunity through integration and compensatory education and to redistribute resources to students who were deprived or who had been discriminated against under a system financed and controlled by state and local governments.

These federal education programs were based on New Deal assumptions that the great majority of the unemployed or impoverished were not personally to blame for their conditions. Instead, structural inequalities, resulting from racial discrimination, unemployment or under-employment, low wages, lack of education, and inadequate transfer payments were considered to contribute to the high unemployment and poverty of a particular group of people.[4] Differences between the educational experiences of black urban students and their white counterparts, for example, were seen to derive from the racial isolation of black students in urban schools and from the unequal resources available to students in urban schools, which contributed to high dropout rates, low achievement, and unemployment among black students.[5]

Many of the Great Society programs, enacted in the 1960s, relied heavily on educational strategies to reduce poverty and equalize economic opportunity. These programs emphasized the provision of resources and skills through education and training programs that would allow low-income individuals to compete more effectively for jobs. The 1964 *Economic Report of the President* state this view emphatically: "If children of poor families can be given skills and motivation, they will not become poor adults."[6]

Under this paradigm, the federal government was considered essential in addressing these problems. The use of federal authority to remedy social and economic problems gained saliency in the 1960s as policies were adopted to address a number of national problems. Through a combination of federal grants-in-aid to assist in the financing and provision of educational programs considered to be in the national interest, national commissions, and media campaigns the federal government sought to persuade state and local governments to address these national concerns. Major interest groups and the responsible state and local officials were actively involved in shaping federal grant programs and in determining how they were implemented.[7] A rare exception to this collaborative approach was the use of federal power to advance civil rights in the 1960s.[8]

The Reagan administration challenged both the workings of the intergovernmental system and the prevailing federal ideology. Consistent with conservative principles of a limited federal government, the administration sought to reduce the size of government through a reduction in entitlement spending and devolution of responsibility for service delivery to state and local governments. Called "new federalism," the administration policy sought to replace categorical aid—under which the federal government determined the way funds should be spent—with block grants, which gave state and local governments more responsibility over the use of federal funds. There was an emphasis on deregulation and on weakening guidelines that restricted state and local discretion over program implementation. Decentralization was coupled with efforts to reduce federal aid, eliminate national programs, and cut the rate of growth in education and social spending.[9] Through these actions, the Reagan administration sought to decrease the federal role in education policy and programs and establish a clear division of intergovernmental responsibility. The commitment, however, was to a shift in authority rather than a release of it[10] and reinforced the trend towards greater state level activity in the governance of education.

At the same time, the administration challenged the assumption that structural inequalities contributed to social and economic problems. The administration diagnosed the problem as the low overall performance of the schools rather than the needs of particular types of students. Low morale, bureaucratization and centralization of the public school system, and politicization of educational issues were identified as major causes of educational deficiencies. Under this orientation, structural causes of educational inequality (i.e., concentration of poverty, racial segregation) were replaced with an emphasis on individual and cultural deficiencies and the failure of educational bureaucracies. Two themes—moral conduct and the intrusion of government bureaucracy in the lives of Americans—were consistent throughout the administration. For example, Reagan's discourse on the problems plaguing the schools concerned the morality of conduct where "learning has been crowded out by alcohol, drugs, and crime."[11]

The belief that the market, rather than government, was the solution to education problems also gained ground under the Reagan administration. The administration considered that the market would be more efficient and produce better outcomes than federal policy or spending, and led the administration to favor educational excellence reforms over equity reforms. If vouchers were adopted, for example, Reagan argued, "the potential for competition for enrollment and resources will raise the quality of both public and private education."[12] This message appealed to a political culture and rhetoric that assumed the superiority of private sector solutions to public solutions. By privatizing education decisions, vouchers lessen public control over schools and separate policy decisions from public input, making it easier for public officials to advance ideas that might not have widespread public support.[13]

Education gained greater national visibility after the release of the *A Nation at Risk* report in 1983 and the report provided momentum for shifting the education debate to a focus on excellence. This report linked the nation's economic problems to the poor performance of the schools and argued that education played a crucial role in preparing students for the workplace. It recommended a broad set of policies to improve the school system that were aimed at enhancing educational productivity and efficiency. These reforms emphasized increasing achievement testing to measure student progress, the adoption of rigorous standards for all students coupled with increasing the teaching of basic skills, and improving the teaching profession by requiring higher teacher standards and competency testing. Consistent with conservative views of federalism, it identified state and local officials as having the primary responsibility for financing and governing the schools and called on local government to "incorporate the reforms we propose in their educational policies and fiscal planning."[14]

THE POLITICS OF EDUCATIONAL EXCELLENCE

While *A Nation at Risk* was instrumental in shaping the education agenda during the Reagan administration, the impact this report was to have on the public debate on education was not readily apparent to Reagan. The idea to appoint a national commission to study the problems of American education was advanced by Education Secretary Terrel Bell. Bell was unsuccessful, however, in persuading senior White House staff to support the idea of a presidentially appointed commission, which would optimize public exposure. Appointment of a federal commission was contrary to the administration's belief that education was a state and local responsibility and might imply there was a significant federal role in education. When the report was released, the president did little other than offer verbal encouragement for reform. It was only after *A Nation at Risk* became front-page news and received wide coverage in both local and national media that the administration recognized the political saliency of the issue to the American people.

The public response to the *Risk* report impressed on the administration the importance of education as a political issue. By invoking education as an issue of national concern, the administration helped mobilize support for reform at the state level and had a platform to advance its own policy preferences, which included support for tuition tax credits, vouchers, school prayer, and a reduced federal role in education. Over time, the administration refined its education message to themes of morality and a lack of discipline and broader concerns about the deterioration of the schools. It continued its strategy of calling on state and local policymakers to lead the reform effort. This strategy had an immediate impact of focusing the national education debate on the themes enumerated by the administration and the *Risk* report.

Both the administration's philosophy of local control and the recommendations of *A Nation at Risk* contributed to an educational reform movement spearheaded by the states. This was the unconventional aspect of the excellence movement— that the states would adopt federally established policy goals. This was a reform movement where, within two years of the publication of *A Nation at* Risk, most states had initiated or enacted some of the educational reforms measures suggested in the report—without federal fiscal incentives attached. Until the excellence movement, there was an assumption, held by both policymakers and researchers, that states responded to local conditions with policies that conformed to these conditions. Policy diffusion across states was a slow process that could take years if there were no federal fiscal incentives or sanctions attached to new ideas.

The excellence reforms gained widespread acceptance because they provided state policymakers with a set of solutions that were carefully attuned to the political and economic exigencies of the time. By linking the excellence reforms to economic concerns about the changing position of the United States. in the international economy, job security, and the future economic prosperity of the country, the report provided a powerful argument that these policies could correct the perceived problems in the educational system and real problems in the economy. This argument, also taken up by the Reagan administration, appealed to a public that has long believed that education could solve social and economic problems.[15]

While the *Risk* report provided state lawmakers with a set of clearly articulated and easily understood issues, political factors created the conditions for their widespread adoption.[16] For one, the popular rebellion against the prevailing fiscal structure of the late 1970s and early 1980s translated into a declining willingness of taxpayers to support continued increases in educational spending, especially funding that was redistributed.[17] Slow economic growth, inflation, and unemployment persisted along with the increasing financial burden of higher taxes and government spending. By adopting the excellence reforms, many of which were low cost, state leaders could respond to electoral pressures for tax relief as well as the continued demand for government services to address the changing economic conditions.

Second, the ascendancy of the business community in the educational policy arena transformed the constellation of interests contending for influence. Business interests coincided with the change in the ideological orientation of the electorate toward reduced government spending and a heightened concern with economic issues. At the same time, interest groups with a direct stake in the public schools lost influence in the policy process as their positions were perceived as defending narrow self-interests. Education groups, particularly the unions, were further disadvantaged by structural changes in state government that concentrated policy initiation in the hands of legislative leaders and governors. As education policy-making increasingly became the prerogative of state legislatures and governors, many of the avenues that education groups used to influence policy, such as education commissions, departments of education, or state boards, were neutralized. Under these new arrangements, education groups had to compete with other actors for influence over the education policy agenda.

Finally, support for the excellence reforms benefited from demographic changes, population shifts that concentrated political power in the suburbs, and the loss of political clout within the Democratic Party. The suburbs and Republican Party were the primary beneficiaries of these demographic changes and population shifts, as the suburbs gained in population, cities and rural areas lost population, and the minorities and low-income residents were increasingly concentrated in the cities. The *Risk* recommendations resonated with this emerging suburban constituency and encouraged state-level policy activism among Republicans. To adapt to these changing political conditions, Democratic leaders abandoned traditional positions in favor of the more popular excellence reforms.

The widespread adoption of the excellence reforms also served to reinforce the role of federal policymakers in defining and shaping an educational policy agenda and the central role of the states in education policy. As such, it helped set the stage for the development of a formal national education agenda under the first Bush administration. Although the Reagan administration continued to adhere to the traditional conservative position of a limited federal role and support for local control, George H.W. Bush pledged to be an education president and made education a centerpiece of his domestic agenda. In 1989, President Bush and the nation's governors met and formulated six education goals to be achieved by 2000. While this was a nationwide effort, the strategy was local and focused on bringing local communities into a network to learn about the goals and how to meet them. Governors were instrumental in advancing the concept of educational goals. When President Clinton took office in 1993, these initiatives continued as Goals 2000, which encouraged states and school districts to set high content and performance standards in exchange for federal school-reform grants. Both these initiatives included the idea of educational standards but relied on local adoption and implementation (and included federal incentives for states to develop and adopt standards). They strengthened the state role in regulating education with states introducing laws and regulations designed to monitor local compliance with state requirements. While the regulations were demanding, they left districts with considerable discretion to implement the standards and align them with instruction.

The passage of the Improving America's Schools Act (IASA) in 1994, which reauthorized the ESEA, provided further federal support for the standards movement by requiring that the same standards apply to all students. This law encouraged states to set high content and performance standards aligned with state assessments in exchange for federal aid. But the law left it up to states to develop and implement curriculum standards and assessments and allowed states full autonomy to make instructional, governance, and fiscal policy decisions to support their academic and performance standards. Moreover, the law was weakly enforced and few states made substantial progress in meeting its requirements: as of 2001, only 16 states were fully in compliance with the IASA.[18] These factors prevented widespread state and local opposition to an expanded federal role in education and permitted states to mold the requirements to fit their local policy priorities and the capacity of their state agencies. As chronicled by the *Education Week* yearly report, *Quality Counts*, adoption of strong standards and accountability systems and the extent of state testing varied widely across the nation.[19]

THE BUSH ADMINISTRATION AND NO CHILD LEFT BEHIND: AN EXPANDED FEDERAL ROLE

NCLB departs from this history of educational policymaking in both its requirements and its sponsors. First, NCLB expanded federal authority over core educational functions. NCLB continues the federal role in providing supplemental funds to states and districts through a system of grants-in-aid, but it marks a significant expansion of federal authority over the programmatic aspects of education and departs in significant ways from its predecessor, IASA.[20] Second, to meet the administration's political and policy goals, NCLB reversed long-held

Republican positions on education that supported reducing the federal role and that called for the devolution of responsibility for education to state and local governments. Finally, NCLB changed the politics of education and raised fundamental questions about who controls education.

EXPANDING FEDERAL EDUCATION REQUIREMENTS

While many of the NCLB concepts were present in a less developed way under IASA, NCLB departs from its predecessor in significant ways: it marks an expansion of federal authority over programmatic aspects of education and raises the expectations of federal policy. In contrast to IASA, states must adhere to federally determined timelines for identifying failing schools and improving student achievement. States must establish performance standards and define adequate yearly progress goals that all schools, including Title I schools, must meet. Instead of reforms targeting special populations, states are required to bring all students up to a state-defined proficiency level by 2013–14. By emphasizing this goal of equal educational outcomes, NCLB raises expectations for what schools must accomplish. Indeed, an important goal of NCLB is to close "the achievement gap between high- and low-performing children, especially gaps between minority and non-minority students, and between disadvantaged children and their more advantaged peers."[21]

To meet these goals, states must test all students annually in grades 3 through 8 and one high school grade in reading and mathematics (beginning in 2007, states were required to add a test in science in at least three grade levels). Schools were required to demonstrate "adequate yearly progress" (AYP) toward the state-defined proficiency goal, both for students overall and for subgroups of students (i.e., students from major racial and ethnic groups, economically disadvantaged and limited English proficient students, and students with disabilities). More so than IASA, NCLB narrowly defines proficiency as test scores in reading and mathematics; although AYP includes other factors, such as high school graduation rates, the chief aim is to measure academic performance on state tests. The testing requirements extend to all students in public schools, and not just those receiving Title I funding, as in the past. By linking the progress of schools and teachers to AYP, NCLB helped ensure that these tests, and by extension, federal education policy, drive curriculum and instruction in the classroom.

In addition to mandating testing, NCLB specifies accountability measures for schools. Schools failing to make AYP targets overall or for any subgroup for two consecutive years are identified as "in need of improvement" and subject to a series of sanctions specified in the law. These include a series of state-driven reforms that include state takeovers, state intervention in poorly performing schools, options for families to transfer to another school, and the implementation of supplemental educational services. The idea was to provide an array of strong tools states could use to force change in failing schools and districts. Moreover, through the use of sanctions, NCLB introduces the idea of exit from the public schools and the transfer of money away from poorly performing schools as strategies for school improvement.[22] This contrasts sharply with the idea of reform embraced under previous federal education policy, where low performing schools were given additional resources and flexibility to coordinate Title I programming.

AN ACTIVIST FEDERAL ADMINISTRATION

Conservative views of federalism emphasize the prerogatives of state and local governments as the legitimate sources of policy and support the devolution of social programs, through block grants and other means, to the states.[23] This view supports local decision-making without interference from the federal government and assumes that states will invest funds in ways that will achieve particular policy goals. While Republicans have used the federal bully pulpit to change the education agenda or to meet international and economic goals, which was the case during the Reagan administration, education policy retained a focus on core conservative principles.

With NCLB, the objectives of Republican reformers changed from limiting the federal bureaucracy and decentralizing decision making to the states toward expanding the federal role with an activist bureaucracy that assertively promotes particular political and policy goals. However, the rationale of the Bush administration for reversing long-held Republican doctrines and expanding the role of the federal bureaucracy in education has not been fully stated. The administration has dodged the issue of local control by asserting that the law gives local school districts greater flexibility in the use of federal funds and by arguing that the new testing requirements do not dictate what is taught or how it is taught.[24] Rather, much like the Reagan administration, the Bush administration has taken an activist role in education policy because NCLB is meeting the administration's political and policy goals. Since Bush campaigned on an education agenda, the enactment of NCLB fulfilled his campaign promise. Until Medicare reform in November 2003, it was his only domestic policy accomplishment and an important issue of political symbolism. Politically, NCLB allows the administration to say it did something to improve education, an issue that the american public cares about. And, much as the Reagan administration did during the educational excellence movement in the

1980s, by adopting an issue that traditionally was dominated by the Democrats, the administration was able to claim education as one of its own.

Several provisions in NCLB also appeal to the ideological agenda of the administration's constituencies. Support for supplemental educational services and public school choice are the prime examples. Supplemental services are additional academic instruction provided outside the regular school day by public and private organizations.[25] Public school choice allows students attending schools identified as in need of improvement to transfer to another public school within the local educational agency. Support for these policies reflects a faith in market approaches that is a consistent theme in conservative politics. There was a belief, for example, within the administration that supplemental services "is going to bring schools out of improvement status as student achievement goes up."[26] The testing and accountability provisions appealed to the business community, another Bush administration constituency. The business community had been advocating stronger accountability since the Reagan administration, when it was instrumental in advancing the excellence reforms.[27]

Finally, NCLB reinforces the idea that social and economic causes of poverty can be discounted as causes of poor performance. As Kantor and Lowe argue, the idea that economic and racial inequities are connected to schooling inequality is replaced with a rhetoric that students of all racial, ethnic, and class backgrounds can learn. Instead of addressing structural causes of inequality, low achievement will improve if students, teachers, and schools work harder. While this rhetoric may suggest a greater focus on equal educational opportunity, it allows policymakers to make education the sole social and economic policy.[28]

FEDERAL-STATE RELATIONSHIPS: COLLABORATION OR CONFLICT?

NCLB was passed with very limited consultation with leading educational experts, either researchers or professional leaders, or input from state and local officials.[29] Unlike the excellence or the standards movements, where the major education groups and the responsible state and local officials were actively involved in the shaping of federal grant programs, NCLB was developed by a small group of Congressional leaders, the president, and a few groups acceptable to the Republicans and sympathetic to their ideology. This approach is consistent with a political process that increasingly relies less and less on the political participation of its citizens and more on the bureaucracy and a closed group of elites to accomplish its goals.[30]

When it came to implementation, the administration similarly ignored the traditional protocol of intergovernmental relations. By 2005, as it became increasingly evident that the law's requirements would be strictly enforced and backed by sanctions against states for noncompliance, there was severe conflict over implementation. What might have been a minor objection to a more intrusive federal role in education escalated into major political battles between a White House intent on enforcing the letter of the law and state officials pushing back to retain their prerogative over educational policy.

Under IASA, enforcement by the federal government was lax as states were granted broad waivers through the Education Flexibility Partnership Program. When NCLB was enacted, the U.S. Department of Education (ED) had granted timeline waivers to 28 states and entered into compliance agreements with five states.[31] There was no serious enforcement of the federal requirements under IASA and no states lost federal money for non-compliance. In contrast, NCLB severely curtailed the possibility of timeline waivers and specified the withholding of federal funds for states out of compliance.[32] Early on the Bush Administration indicated that it would strictly enforce the new requirements, particularly the implementation timelines. The presumption of this Administration was that unless the Administration took a firm stand, states will "game the system." Nonetheless, the Administration recognized that some areas would be easier to enforce than others. According to the director of policy in the Office of the Under Secretary:

> We recognize that we are limited by the statute in some respects and we can't go after states that don't make adequate yearly progress on that front. But, in terms of actually doing what the law requires—providing choice and not playing games—there is a serious commitment to seeing the law implemented well.[33]

The challenge of implementing the NCLB requirements produced angry reactions by state and local officials. These were initially rejected by ED officials, who took a rigid approach to enforcing the NLCB requirements that did not recognize the complexity of state responsibilities. As political opposition to the law intensified, however, ED loosened some of the regulations governing the law and followed a process more typical of federally funded grant programs. Many of the changes ED allowed were a sign of the stress the NCLB requirements placed on state education systems. States were given additional time to meet the highly qualified teacher requirements in part because of questions about the validity of state data and the time it took states to develop the data systems needed to track teacher requirements. In response to the rapidly increasing number of schools and districts identified for improvement and subject to the law's sanctions, a situation likely to overwhelm the capacity of states to intervene, ED negotiated numerous changes in state accountability plans that reduced the number of schools or districts identified for improvement, at least temporarily.[34] Other changes allowed by ED acknowledged the difficulties of holding English language learners and students with disabilities to grade-level standards and the lack of adequate assessments needed to assess these two subgroups. Yet despite these nods to the challenges of implementing NCLB, there was no serious debate among federal officials about the expanded federal role in education, what might be an appropriate arena for federal involvement, and where states should be given the prerogative.

By adhering to the basic principles of NCLB and negotiating changes with individual states, ED officials followed a process that lacked transparency and created more dissension among states as they discovered what concessions ED granted other states. For example, ED delayed approving amendments to Virginia's accountability plan, most of which had been granted to other states. The approval process took five months, causing state Board of Education president Thomas M. Jackson, Jr., to issue a statement calling ED's approach one that "undercuts support for NCLB in the Commonwealth and encourages confrontation."[35]

The conflict over implementation initiated a debate over the proper role of the federal government among state and local officials, which became a dominant theme of the state and local opposition to NCLB. In Utah, state representative Margaret Dayton, a Republican, defined NCLB as a "states' rights issue" and introduced legislation that required state and local education officials to give first priority to meeting Utah's educational goals when they conflict with NCLB and to minimize the amount of additional state resources used to meet the NCLB requirements.[36] The Utah legislature passed the bill in April 2005, and the governor signed it. This followed 15 months of negotiations between ED and Utah officials and threats from ED to withhold the $107 million that Utah received in federal education funds.[37] While the state backed away from earlier legislation to opt out of the law altogether, the Utah law remained among the strongest anti-NCLB legislation in the country.

Other states continued to challenge the federal role as well, with one source identifying 47 states that had taken action to amend or fix the law or limit its impact in their state.[38] Connecticut attorney general Richard Blumethal said "the federal government's approach with this law is illegal and unconstitutional" and sued the federal government over the cost to the state of implementing the NCLB testing provisions.[39] The Texas Education Agency (TEA) continued to follow state law when determining AYP by allowing districts to follow state rather than federal rules for counting the test scores of students with disabilities.[40] In a bipartisan review of the law, the National Conference of State Legislatures (NCSL) issued a consensus report on NCLB in February 2005 that was highly critical of the federal role in education under NCLB. Further highlighting the limited support from state legislators, this report was critical of the expanded role of the federal government in education and what the report called "a coercive relationship between states and the federal government."[41]

THE FUTURE OF FEDERALISM IN EDUCATION

The limits of a regulatory approach to education directed from Washington are no more apparent than with the highly qualified teacher requirements of NCLB. The hopes of the provisions' authors were that establishing standards (albeit, minimum ones) for teachers would push states to upgrade the teaching force and allow them to get rid of poorly performing teachers. The deadline for having all teachers "highly qualified" was the end of the 2005–06 school year. When it was clear that states were not going to meet this deadline, it was extended to 2007. Still, states have not met the requirements.[42] The options for the federal government are limited. It could withhold funds from states that are out of compliance, but this would risk intensifying the political backlash. It could retreat from the 100 percent target, but this would signal a retreat from the basic premises of NCLB. Besides, determining what percent of teachers could be "unqualified" and still teach would be politically problematic. The administration's current approach is to require states to develop a plan for meeting the requirements and to monitor those states furthest from meeting the 100 percent target. A similar scenario is likely to repeat itself as the nation approaches 2013–14 and the 100 percent proficiency target.

The unworkability of many of the NCLB requirements is one factor likely to constrain an expanded federal role in education. As is already evident, it has forced the administration to modify its approach to implementation and adopt an approach more typical of past federal-state relationships, where the federal government deferred to state and local priorities.

Continuing an activist federal role in education also depends on whether the bipartisan consensus that passed NCLB holds. Since the 2006 election, signs from Congress indicate that this bipartisan consensus cannot be taken for granted. Indeed, despite strong support for quick reauthorization of NCLB from the respective chairs of the education committees, Representative George Miller (D-CA) and Senator Edward Kennedy (D-MA), both Republicans and Democrats in Congress have responded to local concerns about the law. Republicans have reasserted the traditional conservative position of limited government, thus reintroducing federalism into the debate over reauthorization. In March 2007, 50 Republicans introduced legislation calling for block grants and the ability of states to opt out of the law and continue to receive federal funds. While this view is unlikely to prevail, it does exert counter-pressure for Congress to reassess the federal role. The Democratic leadership continues to support NCLB conditioned on additional funding, but other Democrats have raised questions about its core provisions and are seeking to broaden the debate beyond one centered primarily on funding. A letter to members of the Senate education committee signed by ten Democratic senators recognized issues related to federalism when it said: "Every state and every school district is different, and we are concerned that the mandates of the law and the Department's rigid approach to its implementation over the past five years do not take into account, and could even undermine, the variety of successful and innovative teaching methods that exist around the country." [43]

Nonetheless, the allure of education as both a political and policy issue will remain strong for both parties. The current pushback against the expanded federal role is sending some signs that federalism may still resonate in education and that some aspects of NCLB may be changed. The more collaborative approach adopted by the Administration towards implementation, albeit reluctantly, suggests that the realities of implementation must be addressed if the law has any chance of being implemented. In the long run, however, the political saliency of education as an issue important to the American people will continue to shape the federal role in education.

NOTES

1. Ellen Forte and William J. Erpenbach, *Statewide educational accountability under the No Child Left Behind Act: A report on 2006 amendments to state plans* (Washington, DC: Council of Chief State School Officers, 2006); Gail L. Sunderman, *The unraveling of No Child Left Behind: How negotiated changes transform the law* (Cambridge, MA: The Civil Rights Project at Harvard University, 2006).
2. U.S. Census Bureau, *Statistical abstract of the United States* (Washington DC: Author, 2006).
3. Gail L. Sunderman, *The politics of school reform: The educational excellence movement and state policymaking.* Unpublished Dissertation, The University of Chicago, 1995.
4. Carl F. Kaestle and Marshall S. Smith, "The federal role in elementary and secondary education, 1940–1980." *Harvard Educational Review, 52*(4), Winter 1982, 384–408; Harvey Kantor, "Education, social reform, and the state: ESEA and federal education policy in the 1960s." *American Journal of Education, 100* (1), November 1991, 47–83; Henry M. Levin, "Federal grants and educational equity." *Harvard Educational Review, 52*(4), Winter 1982, 444–460; Norman C. Thomas, "The development of federal activism in education: A contemporary perspective." *Education and Urban Society, 15*(3), May 1983, 271–290.
5. Rachel Carson, *Silent Spring* (Greenwich, CT: Fawcett Publications, 1962); Council of Economic Advisors, *The annual report of the Council of Economic Advisors* (Washington, DC: U.S. Government Printing Office, 1964); Michael Harrington, *The other America* (New York: Macmillan, 1962).
6. U.S. President, Economic report of the president together with the annual report of the Council of Economic Advisors (Washington, DC: U.S. Government Printing Office, 1964).
7. Russell D. Feingold, *Feingold part of Senate coalition calling for improvements to NCLB testing mandates.* Retrieved March 26, 2007, from http://feingold.senate.gov/~feingold/releases/07/02/20070215nclb.html; Paul E. Peterson, Barry George Rabe, and Kenneth K. Wong, *When federalism works* (Washington, DC: The Brookings Institution, 1986); Randall B. Ripley and Grace A. Franklin, *Congress, the bureaucracy, and public policy* 5th ed. (Belmont, CA: Wadsworth Publishing Co., 1991).

8. Gary Orfield, The reconstruction of Southern education: The schools and the 1964 Civil Rights Act (New York: Wiley-Interscience, 1969).

9. David Walker, "The nature and systemic impact of 'creative federalism.'" In Marshall Kaplan and Peggy Cuciti (Eds.), *The Great Society and its legacy: Twenty years of U.S. social policy* (Durham: Duke University Press, 1986).

10. Theodore J. Lowi, "Ronald Reagan—revolutionary?" In Lester M. Salamon and Michael S. Lund (Eds.), *The Reagan presidency and the governing of America* (Washington, DC: The Urban Institute Press, 1984).

11. Ronald Reagan, Remarks at the National Association of Independent Schools annual meeting, February 28, 1985. Weekly compilation of presidential documents 21, no. 9 (Washington, DC: U.S. Government Printing Office, 1985).

12. Ronald Reagan, Message to the Congress of the United States, March 17, 1983. *Congressional Quarterly, 9,* 715–716.

13. Matthew A. Crenson and Benjamin Ginsberg, *Downsizing democracy: How America sidelined its citizens and privatized its public* (Baltimore: The Johns Hopkins University Press, 2002).

14. National Commission on Excellence in Education. *A nation at risk: The imperative for educational reform* (Washington, DC: U.S. Department of Education, 1983).

15. Sunderman, *The politics of school reform*; David Tyack and Larry Cuban, *Tinkering toward utopia: A century of public school reform* (Cambridge, MA: Harvard University Press, 1995).

16. Sunderman, *The politics of school reform*.

17. David O. Sears and Jack Citrin, *Tax revolt: Something for nothing in California* (Cambridge, MA: Harvard University Press, 1985).

18. Eric Robelen, "States sluggish on execution of 1994 ESEA." *Education Week, 21*(13), November 28, 2001: 1, 26–27.

19. Boser, U. (2001, January 11). Pressure without support. *Education Week, 20,* January 11, 2001: 68–84; Greg F. Orlofsky and Lynn Olson, "The state of the states." *Education Week, 20,* January 11, 2001: 86–106.

20. Patrick McGuinn, "The national schoolmarm: No Child Left Behind and the new educational federalism." *Publius, 35*(1), 2005: 41–68; Gail L. Sunderman and James S. Kim, "The expansion of federal power and the politics of implementing the No Child Left Behind Act." *Teachers College Record, 109*(5), 2007: 1057–1085; Kenneth K. Wong and Gail L. Sunderman, "Education accountability as a presidential priority: No Child Left Behind and the Bush presidency." *Publius: The Journal of Federalism,* 37(3), Summer 2007: 333–350, doi:10.1093/publius/pjm1011, accessed May 5, 2008; Patrick McGuinn, *No Child Left Behind and the transformation of federal education policy, 1965–2005* (Lawrence, KS: University of Kansas Press, 2006).

21. P. L. 107–110, Sec. 1001, (3).

22. A.O. Hirschman, *Exit, voice, and loyalty* (Cambridge, MA: Harvard University Press, 1970).

23. Richard P. Nathan, Thomas L. Gais, and James W. Fossett, *Bush federalism: Is there one, what is it, and how does it differ?* Paper presented at the Association for Public Policy Analysis and Management, Washington, DC, November 7, 2003.

24. Kenneth Godwin and Wenda Sheard, "Education reform and the politics of 2000." *Publius: The Journal of Federalism, 31,* Summer 2001: 111–129.

25. U.S. Department of Education, *Supplemental education services, non-regulatory guidance (final draft).* (Washington, DC: Author, 2003).

26. Cheri Yecke, personal communication, November 15, 2002.

27. Sunderman, *The politics of school reform*.

28. Harvey Kantor and Robert Lowe, "From new deal to no deal: No Child Left Behind and the devolution of responsibility for equal opportunity." *Harvard Educational Review, 76*(4), Winter 2006: 474–502; Richard Rothstein, *Class and schools: Using social, economic, and educational reform to close the black–white achievement gap* (New York: Teachers College Press, 2004).

29. Elizabeth H. DeBray, *Politics, ideology, and Congress: The formation of federal education policy during the Clinton and Bush Administrations* (New York: Teachers College Press, 2006).

30. Crenson and Ginsburg, *Downsizing democracy.*

31. Erik Robelen, "States, Ed. Dept. reach accords on the 1994 ESEA." *Education Week*, April 17, 2002. Retrieved September 17, 2002, from Education Week http://www.edweek.org/ew/ew_printstory.cfm?slug=31esea.h21

32. NCLB specifies timelines for states to meet the new requirements and allows for one-year extensions of these deadlines only in the event of "natural disaster or a precipitous and unforeseen decline in the financial resources of the State" (P. L. 107–110, Sec. 1111 (b)(3)(C)(vii)). It also specified that ED must withhold 25 percent of the state's administrative funds until the state meets the 1994 requirements.

33. C. Wolfe, personal communication, December 10, 2002.

34. Sunderman, *The unraveling of No Child Left Behind.*

35. Virginia Department of Education, Statement of board of education president Thomas M. Jackson, Jr. regarding USED response to Virginia's request for NCLB flexibility, June 4, 2005. Retrieved June 17, 2005, from http://www.pen.k12.va.us/VDOE/NewHome/pressreleases/2005/jun14b.html.

36. George Archibald, "Utah set to reject No Child Left Behind." *The Washington Times*, February 23, 2005; Joetta L. Sack, "Utah passes bill to trump 'No Child' law." *Education Week, 24*, April 27, 2005: 22, 25; Implementing federal educational programs, Utah State Legislature, 2005 First Special Sess.(2005); R. Lynn, "Utah bucks feds on schools." *The Salt Lake Tribune*, April 20, 2005.

37. Michelle R. Davis, "Utah is unlikely fly in Bush's school ointment." *Education Week,* February 9, 2005: 1, 21; Sam Dillon, S. (2005b, April 20). Utah vote rejects parts of education law. *New York Times*, April 20, 2005: 14.

38. This information is available from Communities for Quality Education, a national advocacy organization, at http://www.qualityednow.org/reports/revolt/index.php. The website covers actions states had taken through August 2005 (site last visited on October 3, 2005).

39. Sam Dillon, "Connecticut to sue U.S. over cost of testing law." *New York Times*, April 6, 2005: B-1.

40. David J. Hoff, "Texas stands behind own testing rule." *Education Week,* March 9, 2005: 1, 23.

41. National Conference of State Legislatures, Delivering the promise: State recommendations for improving No Child Left Behind (Washington, DC: Author, 2005).

42. Bess Keller, "NCLB rules on 'quality' fall short." *Education Week,* May 16, 2007: 1, 16–17.

43. Feingold, *Feingold part of Senate coalition.*

IV. STANDARDS, LITERACY, AND POLICY IN U.S.

HISTORY

CHAPTER TEN

Standards-Based Reform

Lessons FROM THE Past, Directions FOR THE Future

MARGARET E. GOERTZ

The pending reauthorization of the No Child Left Behind Act has renewed calls by groups across the ideological spectrum for national standards. The bi-partisan Commission on No Child Left Behind recommended the development of voluntary model national content and performance standards and tests in reading/language arts, mathematics, and science based on the National Assessment of Educational Progress (NAEP) frameworks. If states did not adopt these standards and tests, states would have their own standards and assessments subjected to public review against the national model. The Fordham Foundation also supports the concept of voluntary national standards and assessments with federal regulatory relief as an incentive for state adoption. The Education Trust suggests incentives for states to adopt "college-and career-ready" assessments and performance standards and sanctions for states with large discrepancies between proficiency rates of the own assessments and NAEP. In contrast, state and local education organizations have adopted positions calling for greater flexibility, multiple assessments, and measures of accountability, and a focus on capacity-building in NCLB.[1]

The arguments in support of national standards today echo those of the past: they will promote democracy, equity and economic competitiveness. The arguments against national standards are also familiar: they will lead to the establishment of a national curriculum; one size does not fit all; and local communities, not the federal government, know what is best for their students.

The context for the debate differs, however, from earlier years. The extent of the federal government's involvement in elementary and secondary education is unprecedented. Many disciplines have national standards, developed by professional organizations and/or by the federal National Assessment Governing Board (NAGB) for the NAEP framework. NAEP's proficiency levels have become de facto national performance standards, benchmarks against which the performance of states is judged (or confirmed). Indeed, it is the disparity between state and NAEP proficiency standards that has been a driving force in the current push for national standards.

If the nation already has de facto content and performance standards, it would appear that the adoption of incentive-driven, voluntary national standards is a logical next step in federal education policy. Yet, the same underlying issues bedevil the adoption of national standards now as in the past: what kinds of standards, whose standards, and with what effect? More specifically, policymakers must reach consensus on the type, content, and specificity of the standards; determine who will develop the standards; and facilitate the implementation of the standards. This chapter discusses what we have learned over the years about standards and standards-based reform in an attempt to inform and improve future policy. It is organized around six points that have implications for future policy:

1. The United States has a long history of education standards, and standards-driven reform, but the type, target, and use of these standards has changed over time.
2. Standards matter.
3. Incentives to use standards matter.
4. Who establishes the standards and incentives matters even more.
5. Consensus over standards remains elusive in our highly fragmented and decentralized education system.
6. Standards are necessary but not sufficient to change teaching and learning.

The chapter begins with a very brief overview of the history of standards in the United States. The second section discusses the implementation and effect of the standards movement over the past 30 years. The final section raises a set of issues facing policymakers who advocate national standards (or any standards) as the keystone of education reform in the years to come.

A BRIEF HISTORY OF EDUCATION STANDARDS

While the current focus on education standards seems fairly recent (dating to the 1985 National Governors Association report, *Time for Results,* and the 1989 Charlottesville summit), education standards have been expressed through laws, common curriculum, and textbooks, and entrance requirements for over 200 years.

The type (content, performance, input),[2] target (students—all or differentiated; teachers; schools; districts), and use (improving educational quality, increasing educational opportunity, monitoring, gatekeeping) of the standards, however, have changed over time.

One could argue that our founding fathers delineated the first education standards in their writings about the purpose of education and in the education clauses of early state constitutions. For example, Article 83 of the New Hampshire constitution of 1783 spelled out not only the purposes and focus of public education, but a set of education outcomes as well.

> **[Art.] 83. [Encouragement of Literature, etc.;]** Knowledge and learning, generally diffused through a community, being essential to the preservation of a free government; and spreading the opportunities and advantages of education through the various parts of the country, being highly conducive to promote this end; it shall be the duty of the legislators and magistrates, in all future periods of this government, to cherish the interest of literature and the sciences, and all seminaries and public schools, to encourage private and public institutions, rewards, and immunities for *the promotion of agriculture, arts, sciences, commerce, trades, manufactures, and natural history of the country; to countenance and inculcate the principles of humanity and general benevolence, public and private charity, industry and economy, honesty and punctuality, sincerity, sobriety, and all social affections, and generous sentiments, among the people.* (Italics added)[3]

Ravitch argues that schools in the nineteenth century had common content and performance standards as defined by relatively similar curricular materials (e.g., readers, geography books), grading systems, and, for high schools, college admission requirements, and examinations.[4] In 1893, the Committee of Ten, a group of college presidents and professors who wanted to bring some order to the hodge-podge of high school curriculum and to improve and standardize preparation for college, established high standards for *all* high school students, whether college- or work-bound. Similar to the current standards-based reform movement, they recommended what should be taught and how in each subject area, how student knowledge should be assessed, and how teachers should be prepared to teach the content. These standards affected few students, however, as only one in ten youth were enrolled in high school at the turn of the twentieth century. In a sense, schools had common standards in the nineteenth century, but the extent of students' common schooling was determined by the duration of their time in school and their access to educational opportunities.

During the first half of the twentieth century, program and content standards for students became differentiated. The Cardinal Principles of Education, issued by the National Education Association's Commission on the Reorganization of Secondary Education (CRSE) in 1918, called for a differentiated, rather than a common, curriculum—one that would adapt the school program to individual differences in interest and ability. This approach seemed well-suited for the expanding population of high school students who came from working, class and immigrant families and trends set in motion by this report dominated the mainstream of the education profession through the 1940s. Thus, although more students attended and completed high school, they did not experience a common curriculum. As Ravitch has noted, the principles of the Committee of Ten and college admission standards defined the content of the academic track in high schools, while those of the CRSE applied to the general and vocational tracks.[5] Periodic attempts to increase the rigor of curriculum and instruction in selected subjects, such as mathematics and science in the 1950s and 1960s, were targeted primarily on the high achieving students.

At the same time, the administrative progressives focused on upgrading and standardizing the qualifications of teachers, physical plants, the length of the school year, types of instructional materials, and libraries. States implemented these input standards in non-Black schools through legislation, regulations and school accreditation, but the type and level of educational opportunities available to students continued to differ by district urbanicity, size, wealth, and racial/ethnic composition.

Since 1965, policy has focused on equalizing educational opportunity, first through input standards and resource equalization, and then through content and performance standards. The ideal is similar to that of the Committee of Ten, to ensure that all students have access to a common, rigorous education.

The equity movement of the late 1960s directed new attention to inequities in school inputs, particularly for schools in poor and minority communities. At the same time, increased state fiscal support of education and concerns about students' inability to read and compute ("Johnny Can't Read") led many states to implement testing and other policies in the 1970s to hold educators accountable for the operation and performance of their schools and to hold students accountable for the mastery of basic skills through high school graduation tests. When states instituted minimum competency tests in the 1970s, teachers paid attention to the competencies and prepared students for the tests. In New Jersey, for example, as the percentage of students passing minimum competency tests rose, the state incrementally increased the rigor of the tests, although it continued to test basic skills. This emphasis on basic skills (an example of low-level standards-based reform), coupled with federal funding for compensatory education through the Elementary and Secondary Education Act (ESEA), increased the performance of minority students and, to a lesser extent, students from educationally disadvantaged families.[6] Concerns were raised then, however, as now, that teachers narrowed the curriculum to the tested content, which was low-level mathematics and reading. And the basic skills movement primarily impacted students in low-income schools and communities.

Success in raising basic skills was not matched by a commensurate rise in student performance on higher-order skills or in performance that was on par with the country's international competitors. This situation triggered the next round of education reform—one focused on higher quality input standards (*A Nation at Risk*) and, increasingly, on more rigorous content and performance standards (e.g., *Time for Results*; *National Education Goals Report*).[7] The standards-based reform movement, which emerged in the late 1980s and early 1990s through the work of a group of education leaders, governors, businessmen, researchers, and professional organizations such as the National Council of Teachers of Mathematics (NCTM) and the American Association for the Advancement of Science (AAAS) was designed to address the shortcomings of input-driven education reforms. Under the theory of standards-based reform, states establish challenging content and performance standards for all students and align key state policies affecting teaching and learning—curriculum and curriculum materials, preservice and inservice teacher training, and assessment—to these standards. Then, states give schools and school districts greater flexibility to design appropriate instructional programs in exchange for holding schools accountable for student performance.[8]

These ideas initially received the support of President George H.W. Bush who, in the aftermath of the 1989 education summit, unsuccessfully proposed a system of voluntary national standards and tests. The Clinton administration subsequently took a "carrot and stick" approach to promote and support nascent state standards-based reform efforts. The Improving America's Schools Act of 1994 (IASA) required states to develop challenging standards in at least reading and mathematics, create high quality assessments to measure performance against these standards, and have local districts identify low-performing schools for assistance. The Goals 2000 legislation and programs like the National Science Foundation's State and Urban Systemic Initiatives provided funds for states and localities to design the components of a standards-based system and to build the capacity of local districts to implement these reforms.

During the mid- and late-1990s, states and school districts began to move in the direction of standards-based reform, consistent with the intent of IASA. But state policy responses were uneven. While all states developed assessments, standards, performance reporting, and in most cases, consequences for performance, states found different ways to define what it meant for schools to succeed, what indicators to include in their definition of success, and what the consequences would be.[9] The No Child Left Behind Act (NCLB) of 2001 was designed, in part, to address this variability in state policy. With the enactment of this law, the federal government expanded its role significantly, requiring states to test more and set more ambitious and uniform improvement goals for their schools, and prescribing sanctions for schools that fail to meet these goals. The substance of academic content and proficiency standards remains the responsibility of states, however. Federal law forbids its agencies from mandating, directing, or controlling the specific instructional content, curriculum, programs of instruction, or academic achievement standards and assessments of states, school districts, or schools, although it can and does use grants to support the adoption of instructional programs with a particular focus.[10]

In summary, the current standards movement has many things in common with the past. There have been periodic pushes for common standards over the centuries and the call for higher standards for all students is not new (e.g., the Committee of Ten). What is new, however, is that the talk of high standards takes place in a context where all students are expected to attend and complete high school. Accountability for the outcomes of schooling has shifted from a primary focus on students to schools and school districts, and the purposes of assessment have expanded from placing and promoting students to generating indicators of performance of the education system, motivating educators to change their instructional content and strategies, and aiding in instructional decisions about individual students. In addition, states are moving from school finance systems focused on inputs and equity to those focused on adequacy; that is, ensuring that school districts have sufficient resources to provide all students a quality education as defined by state standards.

IMPLEMENTATION OF STANDARDS-BASED REFORM

Standards-based reform is designed to establish clear goals for student achievement through the establishment of standards and related assessments, generate data to improve teaching and learning, create incentives for change through rewards and sanctions, and provide assistance to low-performing schools. Studies of standards-based reform conducted over the past 10 to 15 years show that standards and accountability systems are driving educational change.

Standards Matter

Although the public is divided in its support of the No Child Left Behind Act,[11] there is general acceptance of the concept of higher academic standards among the public, educators, and policymakers. Most parents support continuing to raise standards and most students say requiring them to meet higher standards for promotion and graduation is a good idea.[12] Teachers also believe in the intrinsic value of standards. They feel that state standards identify what their students should know and be able to do, the standards are compatible with good educational practice, and the public should hold students and educators to account for meeting certain outcomes. Teachers like common measures to calibrate teachers' expectations, and find standards useful for bringing focus and consistency of instruction within and across schools. They also find standards helpful for guiding their own instruction and align their instruction to them, although they feel that standards include more content than they can cover in a year, and are, in some cases, too vague to provide useful guidance.[13]

The legitimacy of state assessment systems is much lower, however, particularly among teachers. Teachers do not believe that state tests are necessarily a good measure of their students' mastery of content, and many raise concerns about the lack of alignment among standards, assessment, and curriculum. But teachers report they align instruction to assessment and focus more on standards.[14] Teachers, schools, and districts are also paying attention to the data generated by assessments. Teachers review assessment results to identify students who need additional help, topics requiring more emphasis, and gaps in curriculum and instruction. Districts and schools are increasing their use of student data in school improvement planning to change curriculum and instructional materials and to focus on professional development.[15] Although teachers feel that their students are over-tested,[16] teachers, schools, and districts want more information on student achievement. Since the mid-1990s, districts and schools have supplemented state tests to measure continuous progress toward district and/or state standards, provide instructional feedback to teachers, offer student-level information for parents and teachers, reinforce constructivist teaching through performance assessments, and/or evaluate programs.[17] With expanded state testing under NCLB, districts have turned to interim or benchmark assessments to track student progress during throughout the school year.

Incentives to Use Standards Matter

Accountability has gotten people's attention, for better or worse. Educators are responding to the press of performance-based accountability even though they feel that accountability and assessments narrow the curriculum and constrain their teaching approaches, and even when they do not feel an immediate threat from sanctions or see the possibility of rewards.[18] Stronger accountability has also focused educators' attention on traditionally underserved populations of students. While some educators still question whether all students can learn to high standards, their expectations for these students are considerably higher than in the past. Teachers report they search for more effective teaching methods, focus more on standards and on topics and formats emphasized in assessments, and change some elements of their instructional practice in response to state assessments.[19] And districts have responded to accountability press by providing assistance to schools, although not always the kinds of intensive support envisioned under NCLB.[20]

Consequences, however, are not sufficient in and of themselves to motivate action consistently across districts or schools. Staff in some low-performing schools feel little press and react only minimally. An important factor in whether or not staff are responsive is whether their district leaders take a strong stand on accountability, mandating or in other ways encouraging their schools to take action. Professional pride and the acceptance of the intent of reform are other factors that explain changes in teacher behaviors.[21]

Researchers have identified negative consequences of increased accountability press as well. High-stakes accountability has led to more time on test-preparation activities, narrowing of the curriculum, and increased attention to "bubble kids"—those who perform just below the proficiency level.[22] For example, nearly two-thirds of the nationally representative sample of school districts surveyed by the Center on Education Policy in 2006 reported that they had increased time for English/language arts (ELA) and/or mathematics in their elementary schools since 2001–02. The average increase for these districts was about 30 minutes a day in ELA and 18 minutes a day in mathematics. About 40 percent of districts reported they had decreased time in other elementary subjects.[23] In some cases, districts were responding to state guidelines for more time on primary grade reading instruction. Concern over the negative impact of more difficult tests on students, particularly students of color and English language learners, has slowed the development of new high school tests aligned with higher standards and led some states to delay when passage of these tests would be required for high school graduation.[24] And, under the press of NCLB sanctions, states have called for changes in ways that schools are identified for improvement, such as increasing the size of subgroups required to report results, incorporating confidence intervals in the measurement of proficiency, and using growth models.

Who Sets Standards and Incentives Matters Even More

States use different processes for setting and updating academic content standards, setting proficiency standards, and designing accountability systems.[25] Who sets standards can affect the legitimacy of standards among educators and the public. Teachers are more likely to support standards set by other educators or their professional associations than by government. In Pennsylvania, for example, opposition to standards introduced in the late 1980s under the name Outcomes-Based Education left a legacy that standards generated by the state were tainted by politics. This dampened educators' support for state standards introduced in the early years of the twenty-first century.[26] Kim has argued that, without the imprimatur of exemplary classroom teachers, the National Reading Panel's recommendations lacked legitimacy with some professional organizations and practitioners, slowing their adoption in the classroom.[27] The composition of this and other national consensus reading panels raised the issue of whose research was most valued—that of university academics or that of practitioners.

However, standards-setting by educators can leave standards politically vulnerable. For example, literacy and mathematics standards developed by teachers, professional organizations, and state departments of education in California and Arizona in the late 1980s and early 1990s shifted pedagogy and related assessments toward a less traditional approach to teaching and learning. These states developed performance-based assessments designed both to measure new kinds of learning and to expand constructivist modes of teaching. Implementation of the new standards was supported by networks of like-minded teachers. Low student scores and technical problems with the tests in both states, and poor performance on the 1992 and 1994 NAEP tests in California, triggered intense public and political scrutiny of the content of the standards as well as the format of the assessments. This led to a call by the governors, state boards of education, and legislatures of Arizona and California for revised standards developed by more broadly representative groups. The resulting standards placed greater emphasis on basic skills and traditional pedagogy and assessment formats.[28]

Tensions also exist between the accountability requirements of NCLB and state-designed accountability systems in several states. Although all states have developed accountability policies that meet the requirements of NCLB, at least 11 states have their own way of rating schools. These state systems differ from federal policy in several ways: inclusion of additional subject areas and/ or nonacademic indicators; use of performance indices to combine performance on multiple state assessments; application of growth measures; and exclusion of subgroup performance. These policy design decisions—particularly the use of growth models and lack of subgroup accountability—result in the identification of many fewer low-performing schools than under NCLB and have created a public relations nightmare for states, particularly in suburban school districts which are highly rated under state measures.[29] As a result of these differing accountability determinations, many states have requested that NCLB be amended to permit the use of growth models for demonstrating academic gains, even if these gains fall short of what is required for students to meet NCLB proficiency targets.

CONSENSUS OVER STANDARDS REMAINS ELUSIVE

Although professional organizations such as NCTM and AAAS have used consensus processes to develop standards, consensus over the content of standards remains elusive both within and outside the education community. States have faced philosophical battles over what should be taught (e.g., evolution, social science content) and how (e.g., different approaches to teaching mathematics and reading). For example, after gaining control of the Kansas State Board of Education—twice—religious conservatives voted to change that state's science standards to include alternatives to the teaching of evolution. The teaching of mathematics became the subject of heated controversy in California and other states, with traditionalists (including university mathematics professors) battling reformers over appropriate pedagogy (teacher-directed versus student-constructed knowledge), and curricular emphasis—process (problem-solving and mathematical reasoning) versus content (facts, computation, and algorithms). Similar fights took place over reading curriculum policy: what is the best way to teach reading—through the direct instruction of phonics and skills, using controlled text, or indirect instruction through students' interaction with authentic literature, in an approach called "whole language"?

These battles are not new. Schoenfeld argues that the underlying issues being contested in mathematics education are more than a century old.[30] Is mathematics for the elite or for the masses? Should mathematics be studied because it develops the ability to reason, for its cultural value, or for its economic value? Controversy over the role of phonics instruction in reading instruction dates back to Horace Mann, who argued that children should first learn to read whole words, an approach dubbed "look-say" in the late 1940s.[31] And the debate over the teaching of evolution pre-dates the Scopes trial of 1925. Standards-based reform has shifted the venue for these battles, however, from local school boards to state boards of education and state legislatures. While skirmishes continue in local communities and debates rage in the academic and practitioner communities, combatants now mobilize to influence the content of state curriculum frameworks, and, in many states, the selection of instructional materials.

Standards are Necessary But not Sufficient to Change Teaching and Learning.

Rigorous standards require teachers to teach different content and to teach that content differently. Building teachers' knowledge and skills is a crucial component of the change process, and the theory of action underlying standards-based reform, including NCLB, assumes that states and local school districts possess, or can develop, the capacity to assist school improvement efforts, to bring all students to proficiency, and to pay for these efforts. Under the NCLB Act, states and local school districts are to share responsibility for supporting low-performing schools. States must establish statewide support systems composed of school support teams, distinguished educators, and principals from successful schools. Local school districts must provide technical assistance in analyzing data, identifying and implementing effective professional development and instructional strategies, and revising school budgets. Districts must take specified actions with Title I schools in corrective action, such as instituting a new curriculum with appropriate professional development, decreasing management authority or restructuring the internal organization of the school, appointing outside experts to assist the school, and extending the length of the school day or year.

Districts have been aligning curriculum and instruction, both vertically to state standards and horizontally to other elements of district and school policies and procedures, for over a decade. Many districts have taken additional steps to align instruction by developing more specific local standards, publishing curriculum guides with standards, frameworks, and pacing sequences, and issuing documents that mapped the content of required textbooks to standards and assessments.[32] Most districts with schools identified in need of improvement report using other strategies such as school improvement planning, the use of data and research to inform instruction, increasing the quantity or quality or professional development, providing extra time for and/or more intensive academic instruction to low-performing students, and increasing instructional time in reading and mathematics, particularly in elementary schools. Districts are also restructuring the elementary school day to teach core content areas in greater depth. Identified schools have adopted new curricula in support of curricular alignment; teachers have participated in professional development focused on alignment of curriculum, standards and assessment, reading and mathematics instruction, and, to a lesser extent, data use and instructional strategies for specific student subgroups.[33]

States and districts lack capacity, however, to provide *intensive* support to low-performing schools and students, the kind of support they need to meet the high academic standards as envisioned under NCLB. Only half of the districts with schools in need of improvement report they have school support teams and only one-third provide additional full-time school-level staff to support teacher development and/or mentors or coaches for the principal.[34] Furthermore, this support has not been available to all schools in improvement status. For example, in districts that provided these services, less than half (43 percent) of continuously identified schools reported they received help from their district's school support teams and only 14 percent received a principal mentor or coach. About two-thirds

(63 percent) of the schools received assistance from a school-based staff developer and only half (55 percent) of the schools reported receiving special grants to support school improvement. In some cases, districts targeted limited resources to their lowest-performing schools; in others, low-performing schools volunteered to participate in district initiatives.[35]

These averages mask considerable variation in the capacity of districts to assist their low-performing schools. In 2003–04, the latest year for which data are reported by district type, schools in larger districts were more likely than schools in smaller districts to report they received resource-intensive support. For example, three-quarters of continuously identified Title I schools in the largest districts (more than 38,000 students) received assistance from school-based staff developers compared to only one-third of schools in small districts (fewer than 3,500 students). Similarly, half of schools in the largest districts received help from school support teams compared to only 29 percent in the small districts. About one-fifth of identified Title I schools were located in districts that did not provide any school-based staff developers, school support teams, or principal mentors to these schools. Only half of small and rural school districts provided any form of on-site assistance, yet these kinds of districts accounted for 20 percent of identified schools. Intensity of support also differed by district size. Large districts assigned more full-time equivalent (FTE) school-based developers to low-performing schools, and school support teams in the larger districts spent more days in each identified school than those in small districts.[36] Other research has shown that large school districts have greater capacity to support standards-based reform, although the positive effects of size may be moderated in high-poverty districts.[37]

This variable level of support is worrisome because most technical assistance comes from school districts. Districts report they turn to multiple organizations for help: their state departments of education (98 percent), education service agencies or local consortia (77 percent), institutions of higher education (56 percent), regional educational laboratories (53 percent), and comprehensive regional technical assistance centers (45 percent).[38] The most frequently used state strategies are special grants to districts to support school improvement efforts, alignment of curriculum and instruction with standards and assessments, professional development through the federal Reading First program, and provision of school support teams and educational or management consultants.[39] As with districts, however, resource-intensive state assistance covers only a portion of low-performing schools. In 2003–04, only 46 percent of districts with identified schools reported that their state was the source of additional professional development staff or school support teams. Few districts received full-time staff to support teacher development or mentors for principals from their state.[40]

Both states and districts report that they have insufficient staff or funds to serve all identified schools and districts. While state departments of education (SEAs) report that they are becoming more focused on technical assistance, only 11 states felt in 2006 that they were able to provide assistance "to a great extent" to districts with schools in improvement, corrective action, or restructuring. Thirty-one states responded they were "moderately" able and eight states were "minimally" able. Half of the states reported that their capacity to provide needed support was affected "to a great extent" by insufficient numbers of staff (27 states) and inadequate federal funds (twenty-three states); another eighteen states reported that their capacity was affected "moderately" by each of these two factors. Thirty-six states felt constrained by a lack of state funds. States in which at least one-quarter of schools did not make AYP reported challenges to providing technical assistance more often that states with fewer low-performing schools.[41] States with large or growing numbers of schools and districts identified for improvement are focusing support on their most challenged schools. This situation has generated calls for differentiated treatment of and consequences for schools under NCLB. One proposed revision to NCLB would create two separate and distinct school improvement and assistance systems: one for chronically struggling schools, and one for schools that miss AYP in only one or two student groups and need only minor interventions.[42]

THE FUTURE OF STANDARDS-BASED REFORM

Education policy in the United States has changed considerably in the past 20 years. All states have content standards, assessments, and accountability systems that include all students and focus attention on student learning. In most states, the rigor of standards is higher than in the past, although many groups, such as Achieve, the Commission on No Child Left Behind, Education Trust, the Thomas B. Fordham Foundation, and the New Commission on the Skills of the American Workforce, argue that current standards are not rigorous enough. If low standards are the problem, then the solution lies in generating higher quality academic standards (perhaps national standards), getting states to adopt them, and supporting schools and districts in implementing more challenging curriculum. The theory of action underlying standards-based reform remains the same; only the standards change. The push for national standards-based reform raises five issues for policymakers, however.

First, what *is* the nature of the problem? Are standards too lax? Are they too general? Are they too incoherent? Critics charge that standards in most states are not as challenging as those in high-performing nations and too few students are gaining the knowledge and skills they need to succeed in college and the workplace.[43] In contrast to other countries, our state academic standards are unfocused, lack coherence, and have led to a curriculum in the United States that is "a mile wide and an inch deep."[44] Or, have we established suitable standards but set our expectations for student performance too low? States vary widely in the percentage of students who are proficient on their state standards, ranging from 87 percent in Mississippi to 34 percent in Missouri.[45] Is this range due to variation in content standards or in proficiency standards? Is there a problem with the quality and coverage of state assessments? If we establish national standards, must we also create national assessments and proficiency standards (such as NAEP) to accurately measure what students know and are able to do?

Second, what do good standards look like? How specific should they be? What learning trajectories should they incorporate? Should they include assessment frameworks? Instructional strategies? What research exists on the most effective characteristics of standards? Have any states benchmarked their standards against international standards and, if so, with what effect on teaching and student learning? Do we (and how do we) know if one state's standards are superior to another's? How can research on how students' learning typically proceeds over time in specific content areas inform the design of standards?

Third, who should develop national standards? Should this be the purview of federal organizations, such as the National Assessment Governing Board; national bodies, such as the National Academy of Sciences; professional organizations in the disciplines, such as NCTM or AAAS; or consortia of states, such as the American Diploma Project? What should be the relative roles and contributions of academics, practitioners, parents, business, and the public in the development of standards? As discussed earlier in this chapter, these decisions have both normative and political implications.

Fourth, what are the incentives for states to adopt new standards? Is it politically feasible for the federal government to require states to benchmark their standards against national, international, or multistate standards as a condition of receiving Title I funds? Previous attempts to do so have failed. The Goals 2000 Act of 1994 created a federal agency, the National Education Standards and Improvement Council (NESIC), with the responsibility of certifying voluntary national content and performance standards and certifying that state standards "are comparable to or higher in rigor and quality than national standards."[46] The new Republican majority in congress repealed this provision of Goals 2000 the following year and the federal government now approves each state's standard-setting process, not the content of its standards. It is also unlikely that federal legislation will include monetary incentives for change. An early version of the NCLB Act considered monetary sanctions for states that did not close the achievement gap among student subgroups. This idea was dropped, however, and the law requires only that all states participate in NAEP. The publication of NAEP scores is intended to serve as a check on state assessments, enabling the public to compare state proficiency standards and confirm changes in student performance. We do not know, however, whether publicizing discrepancies between performance on states' own assessments and NAEP has led any states to consider raising their standards, particularly because the validity of the NAEP proficiency levels has been questioned.[47]

Fifth, what kinds of support do states, districts, schools, and teachers need to improve failing schools and raise student performance? Who will provide the needed resources and support? Is it fair to hold students and schools accountable for meeting more rigorous academic standards if they are not given the opportunity to learn the tested content? Because a high school diploma is a property right, courts require states to ensure that high school students have sufficient opportunity to learn the skills assessed on a test required for graduation. These include teaching the tested skills ("curricular validity") and evidence of successful remediation attempts. This principle does not apply, however, to other education accountability policies. The Clinton Administration and Congressional Democrats tried unsuccessfully to include school delivery, or opportunity-to-learn (OTL) standards, in Goals 2000 and the 1994 reauthorization of the Elementary and Secondary Education Act. The National Governors Association was a leading critic of these proposals, fearing that even voluntary national OTL standards would be used in state courts to determine the adequacy of their states' school funding systems. Although the concept of OTL standards remains controversial (and not well defined), NCLB's requirement that all schools have "highly qualified" teachers is intended to address one inequity in the delivery of educational services. Yet, large disparities in education spending across as well as within states remain a major barrier to ensuring equal access to a quality education.

In conclusion, adoption of national standards would appear to address concerns about the quality and equity of elementary and secondary education in the United States. Frameworks for national standards exist in several disciplines already. Based on experience with current standards, national standards could make some difference in what is taught and in what students learn. Yet, they are not a panacea for what ails American education. As with most public policy, the devil is in the details of the design and implementation of national standards. And the proposals raise the ever present issue of who controls our educational system. While the federal government expanded its role significantly under NCLB, states remain constitutionally, fiscally, and substantively responsible for education, and schools and their staff ultimately determine how standards are enacted in the classroom. Can national standards alone bring coherence to our highly decentralized and fragmented educational system?

NOTES

1. The Commission on No Child Left Behind, *Beyond NCLB: Fulfilling the Promise to Our Nation's Children* (Washington, DC: Aspen Institute, 2007), www.nclbcommission.org. Accessed on April 1, 2007; Chester E. Finn, Jr., Liam Julian, and Michael J. Petrilli, *To Dream the Impossible Dream: Four Approaches to National Standards and Tests for American Schools* (Washington, DC: Fordham Foundation 2006), www.edexcellence.net. Accessed on May 15, 2007; Education Trust, *Education Trust Recommendations for the No Child Left Behind Reauthorization* (Washington, DC: Education Trust, 2007), www2.edtrust.org. Accessed on May 12, 2007; Council of Chief State School Officers, *ESEA Reauthorization Policy Statement* (Washington, DC: Council of Chief State School Officers, 2006), www.ccsso.org. Accessed on May 12, 2007; Council of Chief State School Officers, *Recommendations to Reauthorize the Elementary and Secondary Education Act* (Washington, DC: Council of Chief State School Officers, 2007), www.ccsso.org. Accessed on May 12, 2007; Forum on Educational Accountability, *Redefining Accountability: Improving Student Learning by Building Capacity* (Cambridge, MA: National Center for Fair & Open Testing, 2007), www.edaccountability.org. Accessed on June 1, 2007; National Conference of State Legislators, *Joint Statement of the National Conference of State Legislatures and the American Association of School Administrators on ESEA Reauthorization* (Washington, DC: National Conference of State Legislatures, 2007), www.ncsl.org. Accessed on May 15, 2007; National Education Association, *Joint Statement on the Reauthorization of the Elementary and Secondary Education Act* (Washington, DC: National Education Association, 2007), www.nea.org. Accessed on June 1, 2007.
2. *Content* standards are descriptions of knowledge and skills that students should acquire in a particular subject area at different grades or grade spans. *Performance* standards identify different levels of student attainment or mastery of the content, or how good is good enough? *Input* standards are the human, programmatic, and fiscal resources required for a school's operation.
3. New Hampshire Constitution. www.nh.gov/constitution/lit.html. Accessed on June 1, 2007.
4. Diane Ravitch, *National Education Standards in American Education: A Citizen's Guide* (Washington, DC: Brookings Institution Press, 1995).
5. Ibid.
6. Marshall S. Smith and Jennifer O'Day, "Systemic School Reform." In Susan H. Fuhrman and Betty Malen (Eds.). *The Politics of Curriculum and Testing* (London: Falmer Press, 1991): 233–267.
7. National Governors Association, *Time for Results.* Executive Summary (Washington, DC: National Governors Association, 1986); National Education Goals Panel, *National Education Goals Report: Building a Nation of Learners, 1994* (Washington, DC: National Education Goals Panel, 1994).
8. Smith and O'Day, "Systemic School Reform."
9. Margaret E. Goertz and Mark C. Duffy, *Assessment and Accountability Systems in the 50 States: 1999–2000.* RR-046. (Philadelphia, PA: University of Pennsylvania, Consortium for Policy Research in Education, 2001).
10. Susan H. Fuhrman, "Less Than Meets the Eye: Standards, Testing and Fear of Federal Control." In Noel Epstein (Ed.). *Who's in Charge Here? The Tangled Web of School Governance and Policy* (Washington, DC: Brookings Institution Press, 2004): 131–163.
11. Lowell C. Rose and Alec M. Gallup, "The 39th Annual Phi Delta Kappa/Gallup Poll of the Public's Attitudes Toward the Public Schools." *Phi Delta Kappan* 89(1), September 2007: 33–48.
12. Public Agenda, *Reality Check 2006: Issue No. 3: Is Support for Standards and Testing Fading?* (New York: Public Agenda, 2006). www.publicagenda.org/specials/realitycheck06/realitycheck06_main.htm. Accessed on August 25, 2006.

13. Diane Massell, Margaret E. Goertz, Gayle Christensen, and Matthew Goldwasser, "The Press From Above, the Pull From Below: High School Responses to External Accountability. In Bethany Gross and Margaret E. Goertz (Eds.). *Holding High Hopes: How High Schools Respond to State Accountability Policies* (Philadelphia, PA: University of Pennsylvania, Consortium for Policy Research in Education, 2005): 17–41; Laura S. Hamilton, Brian M. Stecher, Julie A. Marsh, Jennifer Sloan McCombs, Abby Robyn, Jennifer Russell, Scott Naftel, and Heather Barney, *Standards-Based Accountability under No Child Left Behind: Experiences of Teachers and Administrators in Three States.* MG-589-NSF (Santa Monica, CA: RAND, 2007); Patricia J. Kannapel, Lola Aagaard, Pamelia Coe, and Cynthia A. Reeves, "The Impact of Standards and Accountability on Teaching and Learning in Kentucky." In Susan H. Fuhrman (Ed.). *One Hundredth Yearbook of the National Society for the Study of Education. Part II: From the Capitol to the Classroom: Standards-Based Reform in the States* (Chicago: University of Chicago Press, 2001): 242–262; Public Agenda, *Reality Check 2006.*

14. Goertz and Massell, *Holding High Hopes*; Hamilton et al., *Standards-Based Accountability.*

15. Center on Education Policy. *From the Capitol to the Classroom: Year 3 of the No Child Left Behind Act* (Washington, DC: Author, 2005); Hamilton et al., *Standards-Based Accountability*; Diane Massell, "The Theory and Practice of Using Data to Build Capacity: State and Local Strategies and Their Effects." In Susan H. Fuhrman (Ed.). *One Hundredth Yearbook of the National Society for the Study of Education. Part II: From the Capitol to the Classroom: Standards-Based Reform in the States* (Chicago: University of Chicago Press, 2001): 148–169; Donna M. Harris, Melissa Prosky, Amy Bach, Julian Vasquez Heilig, and Karen Hussar, "Overview of Actions Taken by High Schools to Improve Instruction." In Bethany Gross and Margaret E. Goertz (Eds.). *Holding High Hopes: How High Schools Respond to State Accountability Policies* (Philadelphia, PA: University of Pennsylvania, Consortium for Policy Research in Education, 2005): 81–93; Christine Padilla, Heidi Skolnik, Alejandra Lopez-Torkos, Katrina Woodworth, Andrea Lash, Patrick M. Shields, Katrina G. Laguarda, and Jane L. David, *Title I Accountability and School Improvement From 2001 to 2004* (Washington, DC: U.S. Department of Education, Office of Planning, Evaluation and Policy Development, Policy and Program Studies Service, 2006).

16. Public Agenda, *Reality Check 2006.*

17. Diane Massell and Margaret E. Goertz, "District Strategies for Building Instructional Capacity." In Amy M. Hightower, Michael S. Knapp, Julie A. Marsh, & Milbrey W. McLaughlin (Eds.). *School Districts and Instructional Renewal* (New York: Teachers College Press, 2002): 43–60.

18. Margaret E. Goertz, "Standards-based Accountability: Horse Trade or Horse Whip?" In Susan H. Fuhrman (Ed.). *One Hundredth Yearbook of the National Society for the Study of Education. Part II: From the Capitol to the Classroom: Standards-Based Reform in the States* (Chicago: University of Chicago Press, 2001): 39–59; Hamilton et al., *Standards-Based Accountability*; Carolyn Kelley, Allan Odden, Anthony Milanowski, and Herbert Heneman III, *The Motivational Effects of School-Based Performance Awards.* CPRE Policy Brief RB-29 (Philadelphia, PA: University of Pennsylvania, Consortium for Policy Research in Education, 2000); Massell et al., "The Press from Above."

19. Goertz and Massell, *Holding High Hopes*; Hamilton et al., *Standards-Based Accountability*; Kannapel et al., "The Impact of Standards and Accountability"; Brian M. Stecher, Sheila Barron, Tessa Kaganoff, and Joy Goodwin, *The Effects of Standards-Based Assessment on Classroom Practices: Results of the 1996–97 RAND Survey of Kentucky Teachers of Mathematics and Writing* (Los Angeles: CA: Center for Research on Evaluation, Standards and Student Testing, 1998).

20. Center on Education Policy, *Moving Beyond Identification: Assisting Schools in Improvement* (Washington, DC: Author, 2007); Hamilton et al., *Standards-Based Accountability*; Padilla et al., *Title I Accountability.*

21. Goertz and Massell, *Holding High Hopes.*

22. Jennifer Booher-Jennings, "Below the Bubble: 'Educational Triage' and the Texas Accountability System." *American Educational Research Journal* 42(2), 2005:231–268; Jennifer McMurrer, *Choices, Changes, and Challenges: Curriculum and Instruction in the NCLB Era* (Washington, DC: Center on Education Policy, 2007); William A. Firestone, Roberta Y. Schorr, and Lois Monfils, *The Ambiguity of Teaching to the Test* (Mahwah, NJ: Lawrence Erlbaum & Associates, 2004); Lorrie A. Shepard and K.C. Dougherty, *Effects of High-Stakes Testing on Instruction* (Chicago, IL: Spencer Foundation, 1991); Hamilton et al., *Standards-Based Accountability*.

23. McMurrer, *Choices, Changes, and Challenges*.

24. Susan H. Fuhrman, Margaret E. Goertz, and Mark C. Duffy, "'Slow Down, You Move Too Fast': The Politics of Making Changes in High Stakes Accountability Policies for Students." In Susan H. Fuhrman and Richard F. Elmore (Eds.). *Redesigning Accountability Systems for Education* (New York: Teachers College Press, 2004): 245–273.

25. Diane Massell, "Achieving Consensus: Setting the Agenda for State Curriculum Reform." In Richard F. Elmore and Susan H. Fuhrman (Eds.). *The Governance of Curriculum* (Alexandria, VA: Association for Supervision and Curriculum Development, 2001): 84–108; Goertz, "Standards-Based Accountability."

26. Massell et al., "The Press from Above."

27. James S. Kim, "Research and the Reading Wars." In Frederick M. Hess (Ed.). *When Research Matters: How Scholarship Influences Education Policy* (Cambridge, MA: Harvard Education Press, 2008).

28. Lisa Carlos and Michael W. Kirst, *California Curriculum Policy in the 1990s: "We Don't Have to be in Front to Lead"* (San Francisco: WestEd, 1997); Mary Lee Smith, Walter Heinecke, and Audrey Nobel, "Assessment Policy and Political Spectacle." *Teachers College Record.* 101(2), 1999:157–191; Suzanne M. Wilson, *California Dreaming: Reforming Mathematics Education* (New Haven, CT: Yale University Press, 2003).

29. Margaret E. Goertz, "Implementing the No Child Left Behind Act: Challenges for the States." *The Peabody Journal of Education* 80(2), 2005:73–89.

30. Alan Schoenfeld, "The Math Wars," *Educational Policy* 18(1), 2004:253–286.

31. Kim, *Research and the Reading Wars*.

32. Margaret E. Goertz, Robert E. Floden, and Jennifer O'Day, *The Bumpy Road to Education Reform*. CPRE Policy Brief RB-20 (New Brunswick, NJ: Rutgers University, Consortium for Policy Research in Education, 1996); Massell and Goertz, "District Strategies"; Padilla et al., *Title I Accountability*.

33. Center on Education Policy, *Moving Beyond Identification*; Padilla et al., *Title I Accountability*.

34. Center on Education Policy, *Moving Beyond Identification*; Padilla et al., *Title I Accountability*.

35. Patrick M. Shields, Camille Esch, Andrea Lash, Christine Padilla, Katrina Woodworth, Katrina G. Laguarda, and Nicholas Winter, *Evaluation of Title I Accountability Systems and School Improvement Efforts (TASSIE): First-Year Findings* (Washington, DC: U.S. Department of Education, Policy and Program Studies Service, 2004); Padilla et al., *Title I Accountability*.

36. Padilla et al., *Title I Accountability*.

37. Jane Hannaway and Kristi Kimball, "Big Isn't Always Bad: School District Size, Poverty, and Standards-based Reform." In Susan H. Fuhrman (Ed.). *One Hundredth Yearbook of the National Society for the Study of Education. Part II: From the Capitol to the Classroom: Standards-Based Reform in the States* (Chicago: University of Chicago Press, 2001): 99–123; Eliot Weinbaum, "Stuck in the Middle With You: District Response to State Accountability." In Bethany Gross and Margaret E. Goertz (Eds.). *Holding High Hopes: How High Schools Respond to State Accountability Policies*

(Philadelphia, PA: University of Pennsylvania, Consortium for Policy Research in Education, 2005): 95–121.

38. Center on Education Policy, *From the Capitol to the Classroom*.
39. Center on Education Policy, *Moving Beyond Identification*.
40. Padilla et al., *Title I Accountability*; Shields et al., *Evaluation of Title I Accountability Systems*.
41. Angela Minnici and Deanna D. Hill, *Education Architects: Do State Education Agencies Have the Tools Necessary to Implement NCLB?* (Washington, DC: Center on Education Policy, 2007).
42. "House 'Discussion Draft' Opens NCLB Reauthorization Debate," *Title I Monitor* 12(10), October 2007:1.
43. Achieve, Inc., *Closing the Expectations Gap 2008* (Washington, DC: Achieve Inc., February 2008), www.achieve.org/ClosingtheExpectationsGap2008. Accessed on May 10, 2008; *Tough Choices or Tough Times: The Report of the new Commission on the Skills of the American Workforce* (Washington, DC: National Center on Education and the Economy, 2007).
44. William H. Schmidt, Curtis McKnight, and Senta Raizen, *A Splintered Vision: An Investigation of U.S. Science and Mathematics Education* (Dordrecht: Kluwer, 1997); Robert Rothman, "Benchmarking and Alignment of State Standards and Assessments." In Susan H. Fuhrman and Richard F. Elmore (Eds.). *Redesigning Accountability Systems for Education* (New York: Teachers College Press, 2004): 96–137.
45. Stephanie Stullich, Elizabeth Eisner, Joseph McCrary, and Collette Roney, *National Assessment of Title I: Interim Report to Congress* (Washington, DC: U.S. Department of Education, Institute of Education Sciences, 2006).
46. Ravitch, *National Standards*.
47. James W. Pellegrino, Lee R. Jones, and Karen J. Mitchell, eds. *Grading the Nation's Report Card: Evaluating NAEP and Transforming the Assessment of Educational Progress* (Washington, DC: National Academy Press, 1999).

CHAPTER ELEVEN

No Child Left Behind AND Highly Qualified U.S. History Teachers

Some Historical AND Policy Perspectives

MARIS A. VINOVSKIS

For the past 25 years, federal K-12 education reforms have been packaged as part of America 2000, Goals 2000, and No Child Left Behind (NCLB). Most of them included requirements for drafting challenging state academic content standards, aligning them with the related curriculum, and developing rigorous student assessments. While acknowledging the importance of excellent classroom teachers, they usually devoted less attention and effort to improving teacher quality than to drafting and implementing the state content standards. Under NCLB, however, the legislation specifically mandated that states employ only highly qualified K-12 teachers and paraprofessionals.[1]

Analysts in the past have frequently complained about the poor quality of elementary and secondary school teachers. For example, critics have argued that the best students have not gone into teaching, those who have entered the profession have not been well prepared by teacher education programs, and state teacher certification programs often hindered rather than attracted highly qualified teachers.[2]

During the past decade, several academic committees have published thoughtful overviews of the nature of student learning, the characteristics of effective K-12 teachers, and teacher preparation programs. These panels have explored common themes and made some general recommendations; but they have also concluded that how students learn and how instructors should teach depends on the subject matter being taught. So far, most of the research cited by these panels has been based upon studies of elementary and secondary education subjects such as mathematics, reading, and science. Subjects such as history, geography, or social studies have attracted less attention and rigorous analysis.[3]

This chapter will focus on the teaching of U.S. history in high schools (including the eighth grade, as many students are taught colonial and antebellum history at that level). Building upon the recent studies of student learning and teacher preparation, this analysis will explore the experiences of high school students studying U.S. history today as well as the preparation of future high school history teachers.

A SCHEMA FOR PREPARING TEACHERS FOR A CHANGING WORLD

The National Academy of Education (NAE) in 2001 created a Committee on Teacher Education to undertake a two-year study of teacher education. The Committee, chaired by John Bransford and Linda Darling-Hammond, developed a useful organizing framework for analyzing teacher education, which included three overlapping components: (1) knowledge of learners and their development in a social context; (2) knowledge of subject matter and curriculum goals, and (3) knowledge of teaching.[4]

The concept of the knowledge of learners includes four important components of the learning process: (1) the learner and her/his background; (2) the knowledge and skills to be acquired; (3) the assessment of that learning; and (4) the community within which that learning takes place. In addition, teachers need to be aware of the learner's general development and language use, as well as any individual differences.[5]

Subject matter includes the disciplinary knowledge and skills that students need to master. At the same time, students are expected to meet state and national curriculum goals that have been developed since the 1990s. Thus, instructors should take into consideration not only the nature of the disciplines being taught, but the social purposes of schooling.[6]

The third major component is pedagogical knowledge. It is not enough for teachers just to master disciplinary subject matter and skills; they must also know how to present subject matter to diverse learners, assess the impact of their own teaching, and manage their classrooms. Moreover, they must collaborate with other teachers, school administrators, and parents to develop an effective school-wide learning community.[7]

At the intersection of these three sets of overlapping knowledge is a vision of professional practice. This includes a curricular vision, which takes into consideration student learning, subject matter mastery, and the ability to teach effectively. It also takes into account broader goals such as the academic, vocational, and civic purposes of education.[8]

ADOLESCENT DEVELOPMENT OF HIGH SCHOOL STUDENTS AND THEIR KNOWLEDGE OF U.S. HISTORY

Exploring high school students' learning of history is important for at least three major reasons. First, it provides us with an understanding of what experiences and knowledge potential future high school history teachers may acquire during their secondary school years. Second, it gives us information about what challenges high school history teachers will face in dealing with their students. Finally, it provides us with an opportunity to consider what knowledge and skills future citizens receive about U.S. history as part of their general secondary school training.

Adolescent Development and Learning

As noted in the previous section, all teachers are now encouraged to take into account the developmental aspects of their students. The recent advances in understanding young children's development and learning have been dramatic and relatively easy to convey. Interpreting adolescents' development, however, has been more challenging and harder to understand and communicate to educators.

The NAE's Committee on Teacher Education calls for a broader and more dynamic concept of child development. Yet their essay on child development is not clearly formulated, and their suggestions would be difficult to implement by high school teachers who face the challenge of seeing an average of 130 different students daily in five different classes.[9] The panel urges teachers to understand the "stages of development"—without adequately explaining what it meant by stages or which ones they think adolescents experience. The committee lists several developmental pathways and advised teachers to take into consideration simultaneously cultural, socioeconomic, ethnic, institutional, environmental, and other factors.[10]

Faced with the multitude of ways that one might define and use the concept of adolescent development, U.S. analysts of high school history teaching have not made much use of these perspectives in their analyses. A few British scholars are now exploring child development and historical reasoning. Also, there are some useful studies on how to improve students' understanding of the past. Much of this pioneering work, however, consists of stimulating, but limited, teaching vignettes and case studies (usually with no control groups involved). Though these studies are a necessary and useful first step, we still need broader and more rigorous investigations of adolescents and their varied understandings of historical thinking.[11]

High School History Courses

At the same time that we study the general development of high school students, we should also consider how many of them are taking history courses. In the past, there have been substantial changes in how much and what kinds of history courses are taken in high school. Since only a minority of children attended high schools in the early twentieth century, most of their formal history or social studies training occurred in the elementary grades. Initially a broad menu of history courses were offered in both elementary and secondary schools, including ancient and European history courses. By the 1930s and 1940s, however, social studies courses replaced many of the more traditional history offerings in the primary grades.[12]

Today, graduating high school students take approximately four social studies courses. There still is disagreement about the merits of social studies versus history courses in K-12 education, but almost 95 percent of high school graduates have had a U.S. history course, and another three-fourths have taken world history.[13]

The quality of high school history teaching varies considerably. While there is no simple and reliable index for teacher quality, one commonly used measure is whether the teacher has a major or minor in the subject matter being taught. Analysts also consider whether a teacher is certified by the state to teach that subject. Teaching "out-of-field" (on subjects for which they have little training or education) usually is regarded as inappropriate, even though the teacher may have a major or minor as well as a teaching certificate in another area. Subjects such as history are harder to assess because someone may be certified to teach social studies in general, but not specifically trained for history instruction.[14]

More than half of history teachers in 1993–94 lacked a major or minor degree in those subjects.[15] Fewer than half (45 percent) of students in history courses in 1999–2000 were taught by someone with a postsecondary history major or minor.[16]

Advanced Placement Courses

In the 1950s and 1960s critics complained about low high school academic standards and poor classroom instruction. The College Board in 1955 accepted an invitation to take over the development and administration of the new Advanced Placement (AP) program. The AP high school courses provided rigorous academic training using AP examinations which included multiple-choice items as well as written essays. The AP courses and tests provided talented and highly motivated students an opportunity possibly to earn college-level credits prior to entering a college or university.[17]

Only a total of 2,199 AP examinations were taken in 1955–56, including 207 in U.S. history and 242 in European history. But the program grew rapidly, providing eight times as many tests five years later.[18] On the fiftieth anniversary of the AP program in 2005, nearly 15,000 U.S. secondary schools participated in AP examinations. The U.S. public high school graduating class of 2005 took about a million and a half AP examinations (almost a quarter of that graduating class took at least one AP examination); history examinations were almost a fifth of all AP tests taken by the 2005 graduating cohort. Minority and economically disadvantaged high school students, however, were less likely to take AP courses and examinations than others.[19]

High School Students' Knowledge of History

What do we expect students should be learning in history courses? Many different reasons are offered for studying high school history. One of the most frequently cited reasons, especially by policymakers, is that historical knowledge and skills are essential for preparing future citizens.[20] The assumed causal relationship between historical training and good citizenship, however, has not been rigorously established. Nor do we have a good understanding of what particular aspects of historical knowledge and skills are the most important for future citizens.[21]

How knowledgeable are young people about American history? It is difficult to measure historical knowledge and skills as well as to make meaningful comparisons over time. Nevertheless, there are some interesting indicators that have been used over the past few decades by numerous analysts and policymakers as reasonably valid portrayals of history knowledge.

In the early 1900s, for example, the few students taking the CEEB college entrance examinations in history did not fare well—especially compared to the eight other subjects being tested.[22] During World War II, the *New York Times* commissioned a survey of 7,000 first-year college students in 36 institutions on their knowledge of American history and concluded that "college freshman throughout the nation reveal a striking ignorance of even most elementary aspects of United States history, and know almost nothing about many important phases of this country's growth and development."[23]

Almost immediately after the *New York Times* study, another survey interviewed high school history students, military students, social studies teachers, members of *Who's Who*, and selected others on their knowledge of the past. While the subsequent analysis also showed that student and public knowledge of historical facts was limited, it argued that Americans had an "understanding of trends and movements, the appreciation of past events and persons, and the ability to see a connection between the experience of the country and the experience of the individual. ... [Thus] Americans in general do know a reasonable amount of American history."[24]

Concerns about the inadequate academic training of high school students—including their limited historical knowledge and skills—continued after World War II. As the federal government in the mid-1960s became more involved in K-12 education, an effort was made to develop a national education assessment system, the National Assessment for Educational Progress (NAEP). Most of the initial attention was on developing tests in mathematics, reading, and science, but citizenship and social studies were included as well. Subjects such as U.S. history were not assessed under NAEP until 1988; two years earlier, however, an important national assessment of high school students' U.S. history knowledge, funded by the National Endowment for the Humanities (NEH), was undertaken.[25] The NAEP U.S. history tests were repeated in 1994, 2001, and 2006.[26]

The NAEP history tests indicated a limited knowledge of U.S. history by fourth-, eighth-, and twelfth-graders. For example, the NAEP 1994 U.S. History Report Card commented that "many students found the assessment difficult. For the nation as a whole, few students reached the *Proficient* achievement level—defined as signifying solid grade-level performance—and only 1 or 2 percent reached the Advanced achievement level. This revealed a much lower level of attainment than has been seen in other subjects assessed by NAEP."[27] While there were some slight improvements in the fourth- and eighth-grade scores in 2001, the earlier weak performance of twelfth-graders continued.[28]

At the news conference releasing the 2001 NAEP U.S. history results, U.S. Education Secretary Rod Paige expressed his disappointment with the results: "what this report card is telling us is that too many of our public school children are still struggling in this critical core subject area—history. And the higher the grade in school, the lower their understanding in history." At the same news conference, Diane Ravitch characterized the NAEP high school history scores as "truly abysmal."[29]

Five years later, the 2006 NAEP U.S. history assessments were released. There was a small overall improvement, but "a closer look at the results for students performing at different achievement levels also shows increases over the past five years in percentages of students performing at the Basic level or above, but no significant change in the percentages performing at the Proficient level or above."[30] For example, among twelfth-graders, almost nine out of ten students are not performing at the proficient level (e.g., have not achieved "solid academic performance" and "demonstrated competency over challenging subject matter")."[31]

Unlike her predecessor Paige (and his predecessor, Richard Riley, who bemoaned the 1994 results), Secretary Margaret Spellings hailed the 2006 NAEP findings: "The release today by the Nation's Report Card on U.S. History and Civics proves NCLB is working and preparing our children to succeed. ... The U.S. History report reveals increased scores in all three grade levels and a narrowing achievement gap between both black and white students and white and Hispanic students in the 4th grade since 1994." Spellings pointed out that the small increases in fourth-graders' U.S. history knowledge results from "students' skills in reading fluency and comprehension." Others, however, were less persuaded by the limited gains in the history scores and felt that they should have been much higher.[32]

HISTORY TRAINING IN COLLEGE

Nineteenth-century elementary school teachers usually did not obtain any education or special teacher training beyond their own common schooling. By the early twentieth century, however, increasingly elementary and secondary school teachers were expected to earn a high school diploma as well as attend a college, university, or normal school. Today, a bachelor of arts (BA) degree or its equivalent is required of all regular K-12 teachers as well as a state teaching certificate.[33] Although there is considerable debate among scholars about the impact and value of a college education, most agree that higher education provides an opportunity for high school graduates to develop intellectually, socially, and emotionally.[34]

In addition to any possible general contributions of a college education, some analysts argue that a broad, liberal arts education in particular is useful for future teachers. While intuitively this seems plausible, no systematic research is available on the impact of liberal arts courses outside a teacher's field of specialization.[35]

Subject-specific expertise is seen as a key component of high quality teaching. Many of the studies that have looked at the link between the two provide only simple correlations between teachers' knowledge and their effectiveness (as measured by ratings of those teachers or their students' achievement scores). There are few rigorous studies of the relationship between teacher knowledge and student achievement. Most of these are in the area of mathematics education, but analysts suspect there may be similar, though not necessarily as large, effects for other subjects.[36]

Most professional historians and educators simply assume that teachers' historical knowledge and skills are essential for effective student instruction. This is certainly a reasonable hypothesis and consistent with our general understanding of importance of teacher knowledge and skills. It also reflects the findings from some suggestive qualitative case studies of high school history teaching. Unfortunately, we lack the systematic studies of history teaching necessary to establish that relationship more conclusively.[37]

A small minority of high school students, especially those who have taken AP history courses and examinations, arrive at college with relatively strong backgrounds in historical knowledge and thinking. Yet overall, according to the NAEP and other assessments, most twelfth-graders did not excel in the study of history in high school. Therefore, additional history courses in college may help compensate for any high school shortcomings in this subject area.

Unlike high school students, college undergraduates usually are not required to take any history courses (but often enroll in some social science or humanities courses as part of their general college distribution requirements). While the percentage of undergraduate history BA degrees also increased slightly to 2.13 percent in 2003–04, it is still less than half of what the proportion was in 1970–71.[38] At the same time, however, most college and university students take few if any history courses; and probably those who did not excel in high school history are less likely to enroll in college history courses.

While colleges and universities pride themselves on preparing future voters through courses such as history and political science, critics question the impact and effectiveness of higher education institutions in providing citizenship training. A widely publicized 1999 Roper survey of 556 graduating college seniors, for example, reported that "four out of five—81 percent—of seniors from the top 55 colleges and universities in the United States received a grade of D or F. They could not identify Valley Forge, or words from the Gettysburg Address, or even the basic principles of the U.S. Constitution." The report complained that only one out of eight colleges and universities required U.S. history for graduation.[39]

In the late nineteenth and early twentieth century, the American Historical Association (AHA) and many professional historians tried to improve K-12 education as well as help undergraduates prepare for elementary or secondary school teaching careers. By the 1930s and 1940s, however, the AHA and most college or university history professors paid little attention to grade school or high school history teaching.[40] A recent AHA study of graduate history training found "little interest in the broader liberal arts mission of American undergraduate education or in the preparation of K-12 teachers."[41] The AHA report recommended that "college history faculties be locally engaged in the education of teachers, perhaps in collaboration with schools or departments of education, to ensure that certified social studies teachers have a solid education in history."[42]

At the same time, few undergraduate history majors or minors probably acquire a basic understanding of adolescent development or the pedagogical techniques useful for teaching history.[43] History majors or minors usually do not take child development or psychology courses. And only a few history students take advantage, if offered, of education courses or the opportunity to work toward a teaching certificate as an undergraduate.

Many undergraduate preservice teachers enroll in education programs rather than pursuing subject content majors such as mathematics, history, or geography. Among future high school teachers, for example, some students choose to pursue their history major or minor as part of education major. Sometimes they take these courses through the regular history departments, which are staffed by professional historians; other times, education majors receive training from social studies specialists in education programs who may not have a major or minor in history.[44]

QUALITY OF UNDERGRADUATES ENTERING
HIGH SCHOOL HISTORY TEACHING

Critics frequently complain about the low academic quality of individuals going into elementary and high school teaching. While the quality and training of K-12 teachers in the nineteenth and early twentieth centuries was weak, gradually states and local school boards raised teacher salaries and enacted more demanding teacher licensing standards.[45] More career opportunities for talented women became available after the 1960s while the overall demand for K-12 teachers temporarily fell, so that the relative attraction of a teaching career diminished. One out of three college graduates in the late 1960s taught in either a public or private school within five years of their graduation; by the early 1980s only one in ten new graduates taught.[46]

Overall, a substantial portion of high school teachers earn an undergraduate education degree, which sometimes include a major or minor in the proposed area of teaching. Most prospective teachers are recruited from less competitive colleges and universities in terms of selection. While these candidates are stronger than in the past, they usually are not among the top students in their fields. As a result, the overall quality of undergraduates going into public school teaching is somewhat similar to the broader student body, but without equal representation from the top quartile.[47]

While the quality and training of students going into teaching in the past 25 years has improved, teaching remains a relatively low-status, low-paying occupation which still loses some of the most talented and accomplished college graduates to other fields. Moreover, there are significant racial/ethnic differences in teacher recruitment—reflecting in part the smaller proportion of economically-disadvantaged students and minorities graduating from college and passing the state teacher licensing examinations.[48]

Intuitively educators and policymakers have assumed that recruiting higher quality undergraduates into teaching, as measured by SAT or ACT scores as well as high school or college GPAs, leads to improved academic achievement scores for their high school students. Unfortunately, we do not have much rigorous evidence to that effect, though some studies of math and reading education suggest such a relationship.[49]

We do not have in-depth studies of the pipeline for high school history teachers to compare the quality of students going into teaching rather than other occupations. Instead, most studies analyze the recruitment of K-12 teachers in general; but a few do consider the quality of high school social studies instructors. In 1999–2000 there were approximately 147,000 full-time social science secondary teachers in the public schools (about a third more than in 1991). Most were females and more than half had taught over ten years. In terms of their highest degree, half had earned a bachelor's degree, more than four out of ten had a master's degree, and fewer than 2 percent had a doctorate.[50]

Although the focus of this discussion has been the quality of undergraduates going into high school teaching, one might also explore further the impact of post-BA courses. While some students have acquired a strong substantive background in history during their high school and/or college training, others still would benefit by additional historical training (though often they do not receive rigorous historical training as part of a Master of Arts in Teaching degree). Additional graduate work in the pedagogy of history teaching can be valuable—though in practice often the quality of that instruction may not be rigorous and helpful given the limited number of faculty currently expert in this area.[51]

Another issue that needs further analysis is whether state teacher licensing requirements are helping or hindering recruitment of highly qualified high school history teachers. Educators and policymakers continue to debate the current teacher licensing requirements—especially whether there is persuasive evidence that having a social studies teaching certificate ensures a teacher's ability to provide adequate history instruction. Are there effective alternative programs, perhaps such as Teach for America, which can recruit more talented applicants than the regular schools of education?[52]

PROPOSALS TO IMPROVE HISTORY EDUCATION

During the past century, there have been periodic attempts to improve K-12 history instruction. As these initiatives often involve questions of defining our nation's identity and mission, they sometimes become highly publicized and divisive. Some reforms separate educators who favor a history discipline-oriented curriculum from those who prefer a broader, less history-oriented social studies program. Other disagreements feature teachers and policymakers advocating a traditional, historical heritage approach rather than a critical reanalysis of the past. And decision makers as well as the general public sometimes complain about the generally low quality of elementary and secondary teachers as well as inadequate student performance.[53]

Starting in the 1980s, there were a series of national reform initiatives to improve American K-12 schooling. Most of these efforts focused more on developing higher national and state curriculum standards than on improving the recruitment and training of high quality teachers.[54] During the Reagan administration, for example, Education Secretary Terrel H. Bell appointed the National Commission on Excellence in Education (NCEE) to investigate the condition of U.S. education. The NCEE panel issued its widely distributed and highly influential *A Nation at Risk: The Imperative for Educational Reform*, which warned about the mediocre state of U.S. elementary and secondary schools and called for higher curriculum standards, more-academically oriented courses, better student assessments, and strengthening high graduation requirements.[55]

A Nation at Risk did complain that "too many teachers are being drawn from the bottom quarter of graduating high school and college teachers" and that "teacher preparation is weighed heavily with courses in 'educational methods' at the expense of courses in subjects taught."[56] It also mentioned the importance of schooling for future citizens, though the emphasis was on developing economically prepared and competitive workers in the new global economy. And while the importance of history classes was noted, when the report complained about the lack of qualifications of newly employed teachers it mentioned mathematics, science, physics, and English, but not history or social studies. The NCEE panel recommended three years of high school social studies courses (but did not specifically say history courses).[57]

The NCEE report helped stimulate, but did not cause, the longest, sustained effort to improve K-12 education in the United States.[58] There was considerable support, as well as some challenges, to the report's interpretation of the condition of American education and its recommendations. The National Endowment for the Humanities (NEH), for example, had sponsored four academic conferences at that time to analyze the state of the humanities in education. While many of the essays produced for those conferences applauded many recommendations of *A Nation at Risk*, the authors also felt that the importance of the humanities, including history, had been slighted and misunderstood by the NCEE panel.[59]

A few concerns about the quality and limited number of K-12 history courses had been voiced earlier.[60] But in the wake of *A Nation at Risk* and subsequent reform efforts, historians and history educators began to raise their voices in more organized ways. In the late-1980s the Bradley Commission on History in Schools was created to investigate the quantity and quality of history education in elementary and secondary classrooms.[61] The Commission concluded "that the knowledge and habits of mind to be gained from the study of history are indispensable to the education of citizens in a democracy. The study of history should, therefore be required of all students." The panel recommended a social studies curriculum "requiring no fewer than four years of history among the six years spanning grades seven through twelve." This was to include American history, the history of Western civilization, and world history. The Commission also recommended "that the completion of a substantial program in history (preferably a major, minimally a minor) at the college or university level be required for the certification of teachers of social studies in the middle and high schools." Moreover, college and university departments of history were urged to "review the structure and content of major programs for their suitability to the needs of prospective teachers, with special attention to the quality and liveliness of those survey courses whose counterparts are most often taught in the schools: world history, Western civilization, and American history." Indeed, the Commission recommended "the establishment of special chairs for distinguished professors of survey history."[62]

The teaching of history in elementary and secondary schools received a boost after President George H.W. Bush met with the nation's governors at the 1989 historic Charlottesville Education Summit, where they agreed to develop national education goals that would be reached by the year 2000.[63] In early 1990, President Bush and the nation's governors announced the six national education goals, including goal three which specifically mentioned history, but not social studies:

> By the year 2000, American students will leave grades four, eight and twelve having demonstrated competency in challenging subject matter including English, mathematics, science, history, and geography; and every school in America will ensure that all students learn to use their minds well, so they may be prepared for responsible citizenship, further learning, and productive employment in our modern economy.[64]

The six national education goals were incorporated into the Bush administration's proposed education reform programs, America 2000. While congress did not pass the entire America 2000 package, the Bush administration implemented selected components of the program, including providing financial support for groups of scholars and teachers to draft the national curriculum standards in science, history, geography, civics, the arts, English, and foreign languages.[65]

The history standards were developed by the National Center for History in the Schools (NCHS) at the University of California, Los Angeles (UCLA), which was created in 1988 with a $1.5 million three-year NEH grant. The History Center, under the direction of Charlotte Crabtree, was to analyze history instruction in elementary and secondary schools as well as develop exemplary history teaching models.[66]

Under a $1.5 million contract from the Office of Educational Research and Improvement (OERI) and NEH in 1992, the NCHS and its partners began trying to forge a consensus on developing U.S. and world national history standards. After considerable unanticipated conceptual and ideological difficulties among the participants, a draft of the history standards was released in late 1994.[67]

From the very beginning NCHS involved elementary and secondary school teachers in developing the national history standards. In order to facilitate the use of the standards in classrooms, a large number teaching examples were added. Unlike the standards themselves, however, the teaching examples were not as thoroughly vetted by NCHS and its advisors. The standards came under heavy attack by policymakers and conservatives, but most of the criticism was leveled at the teaching examples. Nevertheless, the U.S. Senate, by a vote of 99 to 1, denounced the history standards. Indeed, the sharp attacks upon the history standards by policymakers and conservatives was heavily focused on the teaching examples which the critics claimed were too one-sided ideologically and underrepresented more traditional historical interpretations of the past. Another independent panel of scholars and teachers was assembled by the Council on Basic Education in 1995 to reexamine the NCHS history standards; their critical, but sympathetic, report, noted that most of the controversy centered on the teaching examples and recommended that NCHS abandon them. Subsequently the NCHS in April 1996 issued a revised version of the history standards, which omitted those teaching examples.[68]

Although the Bush administration tried to develop national standards within the context of their America 2000 proposals, the Democratic Congresses had not endorsed that legislation. With the election of Bill Clinton, however, the White House and the Democratic Congress enacted Goals 2000 in March 1994. Goals 2000, which drew heavily upon many of the America 2000 proposals, emphasized systemic reform, which called for states to develop challenging K-12 content standards, align curricula to them, and develop rigorous student assessments.[69]

Goals 2000 also codified the six national education goals as well as the National Education Goals Panel (NEGP), which had been created by the Bush administration and the nation's governors to monitor progress toward the goals. Despite strong objections from the Clinton administration, NEGP, and many other supporters of the national education goals, however, Congress added two more goals (as well as added additional subjects to be covered under the original six education goals), including one on teaching.[70]

The Clinton administration spent considerable time and energy in developing and expanding policies aimed at improving teachers, especially through the Eisenhower Professional Development Program, an Education Department initiative that provided funds to support teacher learning, and the Statewide Systemic Initiative, a program sponsored by the National Science Foundation. Most of those monies, however, went to helping mathematics and science teachers, without much attention to history or social studies instructors. Moreover, while history remained one of the core subjects under Goals 2000, by the mid-1990s the focus in Washington narrowed mainly to science, mathematics, and reading instruction; subjects such as history and geography received little attention in the U.S. Department of Education.[71]

NO CHILD LEFT BEHIND AND ITS IMPACT
ON HIGH QUALITY HISTORY TEACHING

Almost immediately after his inauguration in 2001, President George W. Bush unveiled his 28-page education program, *No Child Left Behind*. In that document he focused on improving mathematics and reading, including recommending annual student assessments for those subjects in grades three through eight. Almost entirely forgotten today is that Bush also briefly mentioned the importance of creating rigorous history standards as well. "Most states have established standards for what students should know in reading and math. This proposal requires that states also set challenging content standards in history and science."[72] After extensive, bipartisan deliberations, the No Child Left Behind (NCLB) Act of 2001 was passed and then signed on January 8, 2002.[73] While the provision for setting science standards and assessing student knowledge in that subject survived the NCLB legislative process, the earlier history recommendation was quietly dropped.

HIGHLY QUALIFIED HIGH SCHOOL TEACHERS

The federal government supported a variety of K-12 teacher training programs since the late 1960's, but these initiatives did not involve mandating the nature of teacher quality at the state or local levels.[74] Under NCLB, however, for the first time the federal government set minimum professional qualifications for all teachers and paraprofessionals, and required schools and school systems to inform parents about the qualifications of the instructors educating their child. Under the law, all Title I teachers hired after the first day of the 2002–03 school year teaching core academic subjects had to be "highly qualified." This meant that a new middle or high school teacher had to have at least a state teaching certificate (in any field), at least a bachelor's degree, and subject matter competence in each academic subject taught. Subject matter competence could be demonstrated by passing a rigorous state academic test in each academic subject taught or possessing a state certification/license in each academic subject taught. Subject matter competency also could be demonstrated by an undergraduate major (or equivalent course work), a graduate degree, or advanced certification in each subject taught. An undergraduate minor in the academic subject taught was not sufficient. Current middle or high school teachers had the same requirements, but these teachers could demonstrate subject matter competency by passing a high, objective, uniform state standard of evaluation (HOUSSE). By the last day of the 2005–06 school year, all public school teachers (not just Title I teachers) who taught core academic subjects had to be highly qualified.[75]

According to the initial returns from states and local school districts in the school- year 2004–05, most current teachers were already qualified. School districts with large numbers of at-risk children, however, were less likely to have highly qualified teachers.[76]

Based on other data, history teachers might be considered much less likely than teachers in other subjects to be highly qualified under NCLB. According to a 1999–2000 survey, only 37 percent of high school history teachers possessed an undergraduate major in history.[77] Thus, on the eve of the passage of NCLB, only a sizable minority of current high school teachers possessed the historical knowledge many parents and policymakers thought was necessary to teach history courses. In fact, though, most states reported that almost all of their high school history teachers were highly qualified.

There is considerable skepticism among outside experts about whether "highly qualified teachers" are, in fact, well-prepared to teach. Many states set teaching quality standards quite low, including accepting classroom observations and/or a portfolio of a teacher's classroom work as evidence of subject matter competency. Rather than defining precisely how all teachers should demonstrate subject-mat-ter competency, NCLB left it up to the states to certify that veteran teachers were "highly qualified." Some states used that opportunity to give teachers credit for serving on curriculum committees or helping student-teachers. Michael J. Petrilli, who served in the U.S. Department of Education from 2001 to 2005, described the quality provisions for teachers as "a joke." Petrilli stated that, "in hindsight, we would have been better off with *no* new requirements for veteran teachers than *these* requirements."[78] By the end of the school year 2006–07, most observers were disappointed with the results and were looking for new ways to improve the legislation.[79]

The Department of Education generally tried to enforce more rigorous standards for states; however, pressure from the teacher unions and states led the department to back off and await further congressional instructions during the upcoming reauthorization. Moreover, the department in essence allowed states another year in which to document that all of their teachers are highly qualified.[80]

There is another, less well-known provision in NCLB's highly qualified teacher provisions. Until a state meets its "highly qualified" teacher standard, the state education agency must ensure that children from minority and low-income families are not more likely to be taught by inexperienced, unqualified, or out-of-field teachers. Civil rights advocates have complained that the Bush administration and the states have done little to enforce this provision of the law.[81]

TEACHING AMERICAN HISTORY PROGRAM

Although much of the federal action to improve education in the 1990s focused on mathematics and literacy, Congress did aim at improving history education. In 2000, Senator Joseph I. Lieberman (D-CT) and six other cosponsors introduced a bipartisan resolution, named "Expressing the Sense of Congress Regarding the Importance and Value of Education in United States History" (S. Con. Res. 129).

The Resolution passed the Senate on June 30, 2000, and the House agreed on a voice vote on July 10, 2000 (H Con Res 366).

On the same day that the Senate passed its resolution, Senator Robert Byrd (D-WV) offered a one-sentence, handwritten amendment to the FY2001 Labor, Health, Human Services, and Labor Appropriations Bill (H.R. 4577) earmarking $50 million to the U.S. Department of Education to award grants to states "to develop, implement, and strengthen programs that teach American history (not social studies) as a separate subject within the school curricula." The Senate passed the Byrd amendment unanimously and the House-Senate appropriation conferees accepted that provision in mid-December.[82] Later, when the 106th Congress considered the NCLB bill (S. 1), Senator Byrd successfully added his $100 million "Teaching of American History (TAH)" program as an amendment (U.S. Congress 2001, S4619).

The law enabled local education agencies, in partnership with one or more institutions of higher education, history organizations, libraries, or museums, to apply for a three-year TAH grant. The TAH grant "supports programs to raise student achievement by improving teachers' knowledge, understanding, and appreciation of American history." TAH grantees were to use research-proven strategies and/or develop, assess, and disseminate their own innovative programs. Most projects created their own teacher professional development programs, though one out of four relied upon existing models. All grantee activities "must result, however, in systemic information about the effectiveness of the program to strengthen American history instruction and improve student achievement."[83]

From FY2001 to FY2007, the TAH program spent a total of $727 million—more than any other initiative to improve the teaching of K-12 American history. The U.S. Department of Education commissioned an evaluation of the first two years of the TAH program. The assessment noted that "TAH projects exposed participants to a wide variety of historical periods, themes, and thinking skills that were consistent with NAEP standards. In addition, the projects provided opportunities for participants to use historical methods, promoted active learning, and encouraged professional conversations about subject matter and instructional strategies." At the same time, the evaluators argued that the "project emphases, however, did not always correspond to what researchers have identified as key characteristics of effective professional development. In particular, most TAH projects offered little in the way of intensive classroom-based follow-up."[84]

One of the four TAH priorities is to "encourage projects that propose an evaluation plan that is based on rigorous scientifically based research methods to assess the effectiveness of a particular intervention." For the first two TAH project cohorts, however, the evaluators found that "internal evaluations lacked the rigor to measure projects' effectiveness accurately. Almost all of the projects relied on teacher self-reports as part of their assessments. Students' work (25 percent) or achievement (46 percent) was less apt to be analyzed.[85] Moreover, while No Child Left Behind mentioned more than 100 times the need to use scientifically based programs and practices, the U.S. Department of Education has not tried to define or apply such standards to the TAH program; if such criteria were applied, it is unlikely that most TAH projects would meet them.[86]

CONCLUSION

One of the most important components of good high schools is a well-trained and highly qualified teaching staff. Yet there is often considerable disagreement on what constitutes a highly qualified teacher as well as a reluctance to provide the salaries necessary to attract such individuals. In the past, local school district committees with parental input usually made decisions about whom to hire and what compensation should be offered. Over time, however, states and other institutions became more involved in establishing and gradually raising minimum teacher qualifications. And whereas the federal government played only a minor role in elementary and secondary schooling prior to the mid-1960s, today it has become increasingly involved.

While parents usually have been happy with their own child's high school and teachers, critics have often deplored the relatively low quality of individuals entering the teaching profession as well as the training provided for them. As a result, there are periodic calls for attracting better students into teaching and providing them with a more rigorous and appropriate professional education. At the same time, citizens continue to hesitate raising the taxes necessary to support well-qualified high school teachers.

Coinciding with the publication of *A Nation at Risk*, an ambitious and well-publicized elementary and secondary education reform movement started and has lasted for more than a quarter of a century, spanning both Republican and Democratic administrations in the White House. The federal government has played a major role in developing and implementing large-scale reform packages such as America 2000, Goals 2000, and No Child Left Behind (NCLB), even though the federal financial contribution remains less than one-tenth of overall K-12 public school expenditures.

Most of the emphasis under these reform packages has been on systemic, or standards-based, reform. This meant creating ambitious state academic content standards, aligning them with a challenging curriculum, and developing related rigorous student assessments. Although some monies were set aside for teacher professional development, the focus was more on student outcomes than on specifically improving teacher quality. Nevertheless, one of the eight National Education Goals legislated in 1994 emphasized improving teacher quality. And several nongovernmental groups also explored ways of improving teacher recruitment and training.

Under NCLB, the issue of teacher quality was addressed and states and school districts were mandated to have highly qualified teachers and paraprofessionals in the classroom. Yet by allowing states to determine how to define "highly qualified," it appears that little progress has been made to improve the actual quality of the teaching force. In addition, a large portion of the children studying history who are being taught by someone not trained in that area suggests that the ways schools schedule their classes needs improvement.

As NCLB is being reauthorized, various suggestions are being made to improve the highly qualified teacher provisions of that act. The bipartisan, 15-member Commission on No Child Left Behind, for example, recommends employing a value-added teacher effectiveness measure (using three years of student achievement data) as well as principal or teacher peer reviews as part of the teacher quality assessment. Teachers who fail to demonstrate their ability to raise student achievement scores would receive additional professional training; if those teachers have not improved sufficiently, they would not be allowed to teach students who are in most need of help.[87]

The Citizens' Commission on Civil Rights also endorses ensuring highly qualified teachers, and recommended that "the Department should begin to impose sanctions—including the withholding of funds or other legal action—against states that cannot demonstrate full compliance with the teacher equity provisions of the law."[88] Other critics of the present law call for the setting and enforcement of more demanding national standards for highly qualified teachers rather than allowing states to enforce their own, often more lax, provisions.[89]

Yet despite their flaws, NCLB's teacher quality provisions have contributed to the ongoing discussions of what constitutes high quality teachers and what might be done to recruit, train, and maintain them. The calls for teachers to have knowledge of learners and their development in a social context, knowledge of subject matter and curriculum goals, and knowledge of teaching are useful. And the realization that the specific elements of these three components varies by the subject is helpful.

As debates on improving teacher quality under NCLB increase, those at the state level continue as well. There is little agreement on the importance or effectiveness of teacher licensing programs. Do more traditional accreditation programs, such as the National Council for the Accreditation of Teacher Education, improve the quality of teachers in the classroom, as its proponents claim? Or do they prevent highly talented and otherwise qualified individuals from becoming K-12 teachers, as the critics argue? These are important, unresolved issues that are highly politicized and await further rigorous policy analysis.

Compared to other fields such as mathematics, science, or reading, the amount and quality of research on history teaching is underdeveloped. Relatively few professional historians have become involved with these important issues and most of them do not see this as an area for their personal research. Nor have most college or university history departments been particularly interested in hiring and granting tenure to individuals whose careers are focused on researching and improving K-12 history teaching. Some of the best work in this field is done at a few schools of education, but sometimes those individuals have not had strong history training and research experiences. And most historians no longer acquire the type of quantitative, social science training that might be very useful in studying these issues (though many graduate students in schools of education do receive that training).

There is considerable agreement that history should be part of the high school curriculum (though much less agreement on whether history or social studies should be taught in the elementary grades). Most people would also agree that all high school students should receive training in American history. But there is less consensus on how much and what other types of history those students should take. Nor is there much agreement on how and what should be taught in those courses—reflecting conflicting values of the nature and importance of historical training as well as the fact that the research quality of studies on the impact of such courses on students generally is woefully inadequate.

Our understanding and analysis of history training at the college level is even weaker. There is no consensus whether college students should be required to take any history courses or what and how they might be taught most effectively. With notable exceptions, many college and university history departments and their faculty have not been as engaged in the nature of their teaching missions as one might hope and the secondary research literature on college history teaching still is rather limited from a rigorous social science perspective.

In the area of high school history, the new Teaching American History (TAH) Program under NCLB calls for developing and testing rigorously more effective ways of teaching. Despite the three-quarters of a billion dollars spent on TAH in the past seven years, preliminary evaluations of those projects do not indicate many advances in scientifically-rigorous studies that provide reliable information about the teaching American history. As the TAH program is part of the ongoing NCLB reauthorization, it may be necessary to restructure the program in order to meet its various objectives more effectively.

Compared to other fields such as mathematics and science, in-depth "pipeline" studies of the processes by which high school history teachers are recruited, trained, and maintained are nonexistent. Part of the problem is that secondary analyses of secondary school teachers usually only present aggregated information on social studies teachers (including history teachers). Often this difficulty can be readily overcome as the original data in those inquiries did separate out these categories in more detail. At the same time, historians who might be interested in pursuing such issues may have difficulty reanalyzing such data sets, but there are others who could be recruited to collaborate.

In addition, we also need more in-depth analyses of students at various types of colleges and universities who go into teaching high school history, and then longitudinal studies that track their subsequent careers and experiences. What motivates students to consider teaching high school history; what undergraduate training do they receive; what encouragement or support do they receive from faculty members; and how useful is that early training for their later work? How useful are additional professional teacher training and the teacher certification processes? What might be done to improve those experiences and facilitate the transition of these students into the teaching profession?

We need to explore how to recruit some of our best and brightest college history students for teaching in high schools. Some faculty members forget that many of our undergraduates are interested in elementary and secondary teaching careers. For the past five years, for example, I have surveyed my students at the University of Michigan in our introductory U.S. history course about their career goals. About 40 percent of these students say that they are considering teaching in K-12 schools. As faculty, many of us focus more of our attention on undergraduates who want to become professors and researchers like ourselves. We also need to communicate to our undergraduates how important K-12 teaching is for our nation and why many of them might finding teaching a rewarding career choice.

Fortunately, the School of Education at the University of Michigan provides undergraduates an opportunity to receive a teaching certificate. And the School of Education is working closely with the College of Literature, Science, and the Arts faculty in order to recruit high quality student teachers to work in nearby communities. These types of programs and partnerships exist on other campuses and should receive more support and encouragement from history faculty.

NOTES

1. Elizabeth H. DeBray, *Politics, Ideology, and Education: Federal Policy During the Clinton and Bush Administrations* (New York: Teachers College Press, 2006); Kevin R. Kosar, *Failing Grades: The Federal Politics of Education Standards* (Boulder, CO: Lynne Rienner, 2005); Patrick J. McGuinn, *No Child Left Behind and the Transformation of Federal Education Policy, 1965–2005* (Lawrence, KS: University Press of Kansas, 2006).

2. Arthur Bestor, *Educational Wastelands: The Retreat from Learning in Our Public Schools* (Urbana, IL: University of Illinois Press, 1953); James Conant, *The Education of American Teachers* (New York: McGraw-Hill, 1963); James Koerner, *The Miseducation of American Teachers* (Boston: Houghton Mifflin, 1963).

3. John Bransford, Ann L. Brown, and Rodney R. Cocking, eds. *How People Learn: Brain, Mind, Experience, and School* (Washington, DC: National Academies Press, 1999); Marilyn Cochran-

Smith and Kenneth M. Zeichner, *Studying Teacher Education: The Report of the AERA Panel on Research and Teacher Education* (Mahwah, NJ: Lawrence Erlbaum, 2005); Linda Darling-Hammond, and John Bransford, eds. *Preparing Teachers for a Changing World: What Teachers Should Learn and Be Able to Do* (San Francisco: Jossey-Bass, 2005); M. Suzanne Donovan and John D. Bransford, eds. *How Students Learn: History, Mathematics, and Science in the Classroom* (Washington, DC: National Academies Press, 2005).

4. Darling-Hammond and Bransford, *Preparing Teachers for a Changing World.*

5. Ibid, Frances Degen Horowitz, Linda Darling-Hammond, and John Bransford, "Educating Teachers for Developmentally Appropriate Practice." In Darling-Hammond and Bransford, *Preparing Teachers for a Changing World*: 88–125; Guadalupe Valdes, George Bunch, Catherine Snow, and Carol Lee, "Enhancing the Development of Students' Language(s)." In Darling-Hammond and Bransford, *Preparing Teachers for a Changing World*: 126–168.

6. Linda Darling-Hammond, James Banks, Karen Zumwalt, Louis Gomez, Miriam Gamoran Sherin, Jacqueline Griesdorn, and Lou-Ellen Finn. "Educational Goals and Purposes: Developing a Curricular Vision for Teaching." In Darling-Hammond and Bransford, *Preparing Teachers for a Changing World*: 169–200; Pamela Grossman and Alan Schoenfeld, "Teaching Subject Matter." In Darling-Hammond and Bransford, *Preparing Teachers for a Changing World*: 201–31.

7. James Banks, Marilyn Cochran-Smith, Luis Moll, Anna Richert, Kenneth Zeichner, Pamela LePage, Linda Darling-Hammond, and Helen Duffy, "Teaching Diverse Learners." In Darling-Hammond and Bransford, *Preparing Teachers for a Changing World*: 232–74; Lorrie Shepard, Karen Hammerness, Linda Darling-Hammond, and Frances Rust, "Assessment." In Darling-Hammond and Bransford, *Preparing Teachers for a Changing World*: 275–326; Pamela LePageLinda Darling-Hammond, and Hanife Akar, "Classroom Management." In Darling-Hammond and Bransford, *Preparing Teachers for a Changing World*: 327–57.

8. Karen Hammerness and Linda Darling-Hammond, "The Design of Teacher Education Programs." In Darling-Hammond and Bransford, *Preparing Teachers for a Changing World*: 390–441; Karen Hammerness, Linda Darling-Hammond, and John Bransford, "How Teachers Learn and Develop." In Darling-Hammond and Bransford, *Preparing Teachers for a Changing World*: 358–389.

9. Richard M. Ingersoll, "The Problem of Underqualified Teachers in American Secondary Schools," *Educational Researcher* 28(2), March 1999: 26–37.

10. Horowitz et al., "Educating Teachers for Developmentally Appropriate Practice."

11. Robert Bain and Jeffrey Mirel, "Setting Up Camp at the Great Instructional Divide: Educating Beginning History Teachers." *Journal of Teacher Education* 57(3), May/June, 2006: 212–9; Peter N. Stearns, Peter Seixas, and Sam Wineburg, eds. *Knowing, Teaching, and Learning History: National and International Perspectives* (New York: New York University Press, 2000); Samuel S. Wineburg, *Historical Thinking and Other Unnatural Acts: Charting the Future of Teaching the Past* (Philadelphia: Temple University Press, 2001).

12. Anne-Lise Halvorsen, The Origins and Rise of Elementary Social Studies Education, 1884 to 1941. Unpublished Ph.D. dissertation, University of Michigan, 2006; Maris A. Vinovskis, "History Assessments and Elementary and Secondary Education." In Robert Bain and Robert Orrill, eds. *History Education Policy* (Forthcoming).

13. C. Shettle, S. Roey, J. Mordica, R. Perkins, C. Nord, J. Teodorovic, J. Brown, M. Lyons, C. Averett, and D. Kastberg, *The Nation's Report Card: America's High School Graduates*, NCES 2007–467 (Washington, DC: U.S. Government Printing Office, 2007).

14. Ingersoll, "The Problem of Underqualified Teachers"; Richard M. Ingersoll, "Four Myths about America's Teacher Quality Problem." In Mark A. Smylie and Debra Miretzky, eds. *Developing the*

*Teacher Workforce, 103*rd *Yearbook of the National Society for the Study of Education, Part I* (Chicago: National Society for the Study of Education, 2004); 1–33; Diane Ravitch, "The Educational Backgrounds of History Teachers." In Stearns, Seixas, and Wineburg, *Knowing, Teaching, and Learning History*: 143–55.

15. Ingersoll, "The Problem of Underqualified Teachers."

16. Emily W. Holt, Daniel J. McGrath, and Marilyn M. Seastrom, "Qualifications of Public Secondary School History Teachers, 1999–2000." *NCES Issue Brief* (Washington, DC: U.S. Department of Education, July 2006); Ravitch, "The Educational Backgrounds of History Teachers."

17. Eric Rothschild, "Four Decades of the Advanced Placement Program," *The History Teacher* 32(2), February 1999: 175–206; John A. Valentine, *The College Board and the School Curriculum* (New York: College Entrance Examination Board, 1987); Vinovskis, "History Assessments."

18. Rothchild, "Four Decades of the Advanced Placement Program"; Valentine, *The College Board and the School Curriculum*.

19. College Board, *Advanced Placement Report to the Nation, 2006* (New York: College Board, 2006).

20. Paul Gagnon, ed. *Historical Literacy: The Case for History in American Education* (New York: Macmillan, 1989); Diane Ravitch and Joseph P. Viteritti, eds. *Making Good Citizens: Education and Civil Society* (New Haven: Yale University Press, 2001); Michael Schudson, *The Good Citizen: A History of American Civil Life* (Cambridge, MA: Harvard University Press, 1998); Rogers M. Smith, *Civic Ideals: Conflicting Visions of Citizenship in U.S. History* (New Haven: Yale University Press, 1997).

21. Michael X. Delli Carpini and Scott Ketter, *What Americans Know About Politics and Why it Matters* (New Haven: Yale University Press, 1996); Norman H. Nie, Jane Junn, and Kenneth Stehlik-Barry, *Education and Democratic Citizenship in America* (Chicago: University of Chicago Press, 1996); Richard Niemi and Jane Junn, *Civic Education: What Makes Students Learn* (New Haven: Yale University Press, 1998); Richard Rothstein, "We Are Not Ready to Assess History Performance," *Journal of American History* 90(4), March 2004: 1381–91; Cliff Zukin, Scott Keeter, Molly Andolina, Krista Jenkins, and Michael X. Delli Carpini, *A New Engagement? Political Participation, Civic Life, and the Changing American Citizen* (New York: Oxford University Press, 2006). Also see Halvorson and Mirel, this volume.

22. Claude M. Fuess, *The College Board: Its First Fifty Years* (New York: Columbia University Press, 1950).

23. "American History Survey," *New York Times*, 4 April 1943: E10.

24. Edgar B. Wesley, *American History in Schools and Colleges* (New York: Macmillan, 1944): 1.

25. Diane Ravitch and Chester E. Finn, Jr., *What Do Our 17-Year-Olds Know? A Report on the First National Assessment of History and Literature* (New York: Harper and Row, 1987).

26. Lyle V. Jones and Ingram Olkin, eds. *The Nation's Report Card: Evolution and Perspectives* (Bloomington, IN: Phi Delta Kappa Educational Foundation, 2004); Maris A. Vinovskis, "The Federal Government and the Development of State-Level NAEP Student Assessments." In Michael C. Johanek, ed. *A Faithful Mirror: Reflections on the College Board and Education in America* (New York: College Board, 2001): 271–301.

27. Alexandra S. Beatty, Clyde M. Reese, Hilary R. Persky, and Peggy Carr, *NAEP 1994 U.S. History Report Card: Findings from the National Assessment of Educational Progress* (Washington, DC: U.S. Department of Education, 1996): 75.

28. Michael S. Lapp, Wendy S. Grigg, and Brenda S.-H. Tay-Lim, *The Nation's Report Card: U.S. History 2001* (Washington, DC: U.S. Department of Education, 2002).

29. Rod Paige, "Remarks of Secretary Paige, NAEP History Scores Announcement," U.S. Department of Education Press Release, 9 May 2002, retrieved from http://www.ed.gov; Diane Ravitch, "Statement on NAEP 2001 U.S. History Report" National Assessment Governing Board press release, 9 May 2002, retrieved from http://www.nagb.org.

30. Jihyun Lee and Andrew R. Weiss, *The Nation's Report Card: U.S. History 2006* (Washington, DC: U.S. Department of Education, 2007): 6.

31. Lee and Weiss, *The Nation's Report Card*, 9.

32. Margaret Spellings, "Statement by Spellings on History and Civics Reports Released by the Nation's Report Card," U.S. Department of Education Press Release, 16 May 2007, retrieved from http://www.ed.gov; Sean Cavanagh, "Students' Mastery of NAEP History and Civics Mixed," *Education Week* 26, 23 May 2007: 1, 16.

33. David L. Angus, *Professionalism and the Public Good: A Brief History of Teacher Certification*, Jeffrey Mirel, ed. (Washington, DC: Thomas B. Fordham Foundation, 2001); Gerald Grant and Christine E. Murray, *Teaching in America: The Slow Revolution* (Cambridge, MA: Harvard University Press, 1999); Jurgen Herbst, *And Sadly Teach: Teacher Education and Professionalization in American Culture* (Madison: University of Wisconsin Press, 1989); Donald Warren, ed. *American Teachers: Histories of a Profession at Work* (New York: Macmillan, 1989).

34. Alexander W. Astin, *What Matters in College? Four Critical Years Revisited* (San Francisco: Jossey-Bass, 1993); Ernest T. Pascarella and Patrick T. Terenzini, *How College Affects Students: A Third Decade of Research*, vol. 2. (San Francisco: Jossey-Bass, 1005).

35. Robert Floden and Marco Meniketti, "Research on the Effects of Coursework in the Arts and Sciences and in the Foundations of Education." In Marilyn Cochran-Smith and Kenneth M. Zeichner, eds. *Studying Teacher Education: The Report of the AERA Panel on Research and Teacher Education* (Mahwah, NJ: Lawrence Erlbaum, 2005): 261–308.

36. Floden and Meniketti, "Research on the Effects of Coursework"; Richard J. Murnane and Jennifer L. Steele, "What is the Problem? The Challenge of Providing Effective Teachers for All Children." *The Future of Children* 17(1), Spring 2007: 15–43; Andrew J. Rotherham and Sara Mead, "Back to the Future: The History and Politics of State Teacher Licensure and Certification." In Frederick M. Hess, Andrew J. Rotherham, and Kate Walsh, eds. *A Qualified Teacher in Every Classroom? Appraising Old Answers and New Ideas* (Cambridge, MA: Harvard Education Press, 2004): 11–47.

37. Robert Bain and Jeffrey Mirel, "Setting Up Camp at the Great Instructional Divide: Educating Beginning History Teachers," *Journal of Teacher Education* 57(3), May/June 2006: 212–9; Stearns, Seixas, and Wineburg, *Knowing, Teaching, and Learning History*; Wineburg, *Historical Thinking*.

38. Robert B. Townsend, "History Gains Ground in Majors and Undergraduate Degrees, Graduate Studies Continue to Decline," *Perspectives: Newsmagazine of the American Historical Association* 44(7), October 2006: 12–13.

39. American Council of Trustees and Alumni, *Losing America's Memory: Historical Illiteracy in the 21st Century* (Washington, DC: American Council of Trustees and Alumni, 2000).

40. Halvorson, The Origin and Rise of Elementary Social Studies Education.

41. Thomas Bender, Philip M. Katz, and Colin Palmer, *The Education of Historians for the Twenty-first Century* (Urbana, IL: University of Illinois Press, 2004): 63.

42. Ibid. 64.

43. Bain and Mirel, "Setting up Camp."

44. Ravitch, "The Educational Backgrounds of History Teachers."

45. Angus, *Professionalism and the Public Good.*
46. Ingersoll, "Four Myths about the Teacher Quality Problem"; Christopher J. Lucas, *Teacher Education in America: Reform Agendas for the Twenty-First Century* (New York: St. Martin's Press, 1997); Richard J. Murnane, Judith D. Singer, John B. Willett, James J. Kemple, and Randall J. Olsen, *Who Will Teach? Policies That Matter* (Cambridge, MA: Harvard University Press, 1991).
47. Murnane and Steele, "What is the Problem?"; Karen Zumwalt and Elizabeth Craig, "Teachers' Characteristics of Quality." In Cochran-Smith and Zeichner, *Studying Teacher Education*: 157– 260.
48. Eric A. Hanushek and Richard R. Pace, "Who Chooses to Teach (and Why)?" *Economics of Education Review* 14(2), 1995: 101–17; Ingersoll, "Four Myths about the Teacher Quality Problem"; Murnane et al., *Who Will Teach?*; Emiliana Vegas, Richard J. Murnane, and John B. Willett, "From High School to Teaching: Many Steps, Who Makes It?" *Teachers College Record* 103(3), June 2001: 427–49.
49. Murnane and Steele, "What Is the Problem?"; Zumwalt and Craig, "Teachers' Characteristics of Quality."
50. Snyder and Tan, *Digest of Education Statistics.*
51. Kenneth M. Zeichner and Hilary G. Conklin, "Teacher Education Programs." In Cochran-Smith and Zeichner, *Studying Teacher Education*: 645–735.
52. Karen J. Mitchell, David Z. Robinson, Barbara S. Plake, and Kaeli T. Knowles, eds. *Testing Teacher Candidates: The Role of Licensure Tests in Improving Teacher Quality* (Washington, DC: National Academy Press, 2001); Rotherham and Mead, "Back to the Future"; Suzanne Wilson and Peter Youngs, "Research on Accountability Processes in Teacher Education." In Cochran-Smith and Zeichner, *Studying Teacher Education*: 591–643.
53. Ronald W. Evans, *The Social Studies Wars: What Should We Teach the Children?* (New York: Teachers College Press, 2004); Halvorson, *The Origin and Rise of Elementary Social Studies Education;* Ravitch and Finn, *What Do Our 17-Year-Olds Know?*; Linda Symcox, *Whose History? The Struggle for National Standards in American Classrooms* (New York: Teachers College Press. 2002).
54. Heidi A. Ramirez, "The Shift from Hands-Off: The Federal Role in Supporting and Defining Teacher Quality," In Hess, Rotherham, and Walsh, *A Qualified Teacher in Every Classroom?*: 49–79.
55. National Commission on Excellence in Education, *A Nation at Risk: The Imperative of Educational Reform* (Washington, DC: U.S. Government Printing Office, 1983).
56. Ibid., 15.
57. Ibid., 18.
58. David T. Gordon, ed. *A Nation Reformed: American Education 20 Years after A Nation at Risk* (Cambridge, MA: Harvard Education Press, 2003).
59. Chester E. Finn, Jr., Diane Ravitch, and Robert T. Fancher, eds. *Against Mediocracy: The Humanities in America's High Schools* (New York: Holmes and Meier, 1984); Chester E. Finn, Jr., Diane Ravitch, and P. Holley Roberts, eds. *Challenges to the Humanities* (New York: Holmes and Meier, 1985).
60. Charles G. Sellers, "Is History on the Way Out of the Schools and Do Historians Care?" *Social Education* 33, 1969: 509–16; Richard S. Kirkendall, "The Status of History in the Schools," *Journal of American History* 62(2), September 1975: 557–70.
61. Paul Gagnon, ed. *Historical Literacy: The Case for History in American Education* (New York: Macmillan, 1989).

62. Bradley Commission on History in Schools, "Building a History Curriculum: Guidelines for Teaching History in Schools." In Gagnon, *Historical Literacy*: 16–47.
63. Vinovskis, *The Road to Charlottesville*.
64. White House, "National Goals for Education." Office of the Press Secretary, February, 26 1990.
65. Diane Ravitch, *National Standards in American Education: A Citizen's Guide* (Washington, DC: Brookings Institution Press, 1995).
66. Symcox, *Whose History?*
67. Gary B. Nash, Charlotte Crabtree, and Ross E. Dunn, *History on Trial: Culture Wars and the Teaching of the Past* (New York: Alfred A. Knopf, 1997); Symcox, *Whose History?*
68. Nash, *History on Trial*; Symcox, *Whose History?*
69. John Jennings, *Why National Standards and Tests? Politics and the Quest for Better Schools* (Thousand Oaks, CA: Sage, 1998); Patrick J. McGuinn, *No Child Left Behind and the Transformation of Federal Education Policy, 1965–2005* (Lawrence, KS: University Press of Kansas, 2006).
70. David J. Hoff, "New Education Goal Would Focus on Teacher Training." *Education Daily* 26, 7 May 1993: 2.
71. Margaret Plecki and Hilary Loeb, "Lessons for Policy Design and Implementation: Examining State and Federal Efforts to Improve Teacher Quality," In Mark A. Smylie and Debra Miretzky, eds. *Developing the Teacher Workforce*, 103rd Yearbook of the National Society for the Study of Education, Part I (Chicago: National Society for the Study of Education, 2004): 348–89.
72. George W. Bush, *No Child Left Behind* (Washington DC: U.S. Government Printing Office, 2001): 7.
73. DeBray, *Politics, Ideology, and Education*; Kosar, *Failing Grades*; McGuinn, *No Child Left Behind*.
74. Ramirez, "The Shift from Hands-Off."
75. Kristen Tosh Cowan, *The New Title I: The Changing Landscape of Accountability* (Washington, DC: Thompson Publishing Group, 2005); Plecki and Loeb, "Lessons for Policy Design and Implementation."
76. Center on Education Policy, *From the Capital to the Classroom: Year 3 of the No Child Left Behind Act* (Washington, DC: Center on Education Policy, 2005).
77. Emily W. Holt, Daniel J. McGrath, and Marilyn M. Seastrom, "Qualifications of Public Secondary School History Teachers, 1999–2000." *NCES Issue Brief* (Washington, DC: U.S. Department of Education, July 2006).
78. Michael J. Petrilli, "Improving Teacher Quality: Better Luck Next Time," *Education Week* 25, August 31, 2005: 42, 52.
79. Bess Keller, "NCLB Rules on Quality Fall Short." *Education Week* 26, May 16, 2007: 1, 16.
80. Andrew Brownstein, "ED Backtracks on Restricting HOUSSE Provision for Teachers," *Title I Monitor* 11, October 2006: 1–2.
81. Cowan, *The New Title I*; Phyllis McClure, Diane Piche, and William R. Taylor, *Days of Reckoning: Are States and the Federal Government Up to the Challenge of Ensuring a Qualified Teacher for Every Student?* (Washington, DC: Citizen's Commission on Civil Rights, 2006).
82. Bruce Craig, *NCC Washington Update* 6(45), December 21, 2000; retrieved from http://h-net. msu.edu/cgi-bin/logbrowse.
83. U.S. Department of Education, "Frequently Asked Questions." Teaching American History Program, January 11, 2006, retrieved from http://www.ed.gov/print/programs/teachinghistory; Daniel C. Humphrey, Christopher Chang-Ross, Mary Beth Donnelly, Lauren Hersh, and Heidi Skolnik, *Evaluation of the Teaching American History Program* (Washington, DC: U.S. Department of Education. 2005).

84. Ibid.
85. Ibid.
86. Maris A. Vinovskis, "From Gardner's Education Task Force to the Institute for Education Sciences: Improving the Quality of Federal Education Research, Statistics, and Development." In Pamela Barnhouse Walters, Sheri Ranis and Annette Lareau, eds. *Education Research on Trial: The Search for Rigor and the Promotion of Randomized Studies* (New York: Routledge, forthcoming).
87. Commission on No Child Left Behind, *Beyond NCLB: Fulfilling the Promise to Our Nation's Children* (Washington, DC: Aspen Institute, 2007).
88. McClure, Piche, and Taylor, *Days of Reckoning.*
89. Keller, "Rigor Disputed in Standards for Teachers"; Keller, "NCLB Rules on Quality Fall Short."

V. THE USES AND MISUSES OF HISTORY

CHAPTER TWELVE

Conflicting Questions

Why Historians AND Policymakers Miscommunicate ON Urban Education

JACK DOUGHERTY

In my mind, history and policy tend to go together. Fifteen years ago, while teaching high school history in Newark, New Jersey, I guided my students as we investigated local urban policy issues. From there I enrolled as a graduate student the Department of Educational Policy Studies at the University of Wisconsin-Madison, where I concentrated in educational history and policy, and also studied with professors in the Department of History as well as the La Follette Institute of Public Policy. Currently, as an associate professor at Trinity College, my teaching focuses on the intersection of educational history and policy, through courses such as *Education Reform: Past & Present*. My first book concluded with a chapter titled "Rethinking History and Policy in the Post-*Brown* Era," which argued that in order to move forward on our present-day dilemmas over race and education, we needed to reexamine the past and our stories about how we arrived at our contemporary dilemmas.[1]

Yet while history and policy come together in my work, they do not coexist harmoniously. In recent years, while my students and I have worked on the Cities, Suburbs, and Schools research project and interacted with a broad array of local, regional, and state policymakers, we have occasionally found ourselves in the midst of conflict and miscommunication. On these days, when the history side of my brain is pushed closer to the policy side, it makes me feel somewhat schizophrenic. Historians and policymakers tend to ask different types of questions, and as a result, I sometimes feel as if I'm hearing competing voices inside my head.

This chapter outlines three types of conflicting questions posed by historians and policymakers on the topic of urban education:

1. Conflicting orientations on past, present, and future
2. Conflicting purposes of historical interpretation
3. Conflicting views on historical understanding versus policy action

Furthermore, I will illustrate each topic with examples drawn from historical research and policy discussions in metropolitan Hartford, Connecticut, and will offer reflections on the writings of other scholars who also have addressed similar themes.

CONFLICTING ORIENTATIONS ON PAST, PRESENT, AND FUTURE

The first and most basic difference between historians and policymakers concerns our conflicting orientations with respect to the past, present, and future. Historians stand in the present and look backward to ask: *What happened? How has change or continuity occurred from the past to the present?* By contrast, policymakers also stand in the present, though they look in the opposite direction, oriented toward the future, to ask: *What will happen next?*

This fundamental difference in orientations appears simple, but I wish to offer a concrete example to illustrate how it leads to significant miscommunication between historians and policymakers. Recently, my students and I prepared a report for policy audiences on the progress of the long-running *Sheff v O'Neill* school desegregation case. In 1989, Elizabeth Horton Sheff and other parents filed a lawsuit against then-Governor William O'Neill, charging that Connecticut's system of separate city and suburban school districts led to racially segregated schools, which violated their state constitutional rights to equal educational opportunity. In 1996, after a prolonged trial, Connecticut's Supreme Court split 4–3 in favor of the plaintiffs, ruling that the racial and socioeconomic isolation of Hartford schoolchildren violated the state constitution. However, the Court did not specify a goal, remedy, or timetable to resolve this problem, turning it over to the executive and legislative branches instead. Eventually, in 2003, the Sheff plaintiffs and state defendants agreed on a legal settlement, approved by the Connecticut General Assembly, which relied upon voluntary desegregation efforts and additional funding to meet a specific goal. According to the settlement, by 2007, at least 30 percent of the public school minority students residing in Hartford were to be educated in a reduced-isolation setting, through inter-district magnet schools, city-suburban school transfers, and part-time cooperative exchange programs.[2]

Since the four-year settlement period was coming to a close, we decided to issue a policy report, documenting the racial composition of public schools and the efficacy of desegregation reforms from 1989 to the present. We pulled together nearly two decades of data on local school districts, plus the results of adding 22 inter-district magnet schools and expanding city-suburb transfers, into a coherent package of maps and charts to illustrate what had (and had not) changed over time. In essence, we became unofficial scorekeepers in a numbers-driven legal battle because no one else had risen to fill that role. Our report did not feature in-depth historical analysis, because we were simply trying to put facts into public view, to provide a deeper knowledge base for broader policy discussion.

To ensure that policy audiences understood our report, my students and I gave several preview sessions, where we walked readers through the data from past to present, documenting how little progress had been achieved under the current desegregation plan. Although the settlement had called for a goal of 30 percent of Hartford minority students in reduced-isolation settings, we found that only 17 percent of students were in schools that passed the legal requirement (and only 9 percent were enrolled in schools that met the spirit of the goal, in practice). In our minds, we thought that our longitudinal report, with key data from 1989 to the current school year, had addressed their policy needs. But during the question and answer period, one policymaker turned to us and said, "This is all very interesting. But what I really want to see are the data projections. Can you tell us where we will be in the future?"

The pained expression on my face revealed much about why historians and policymakers speak in different languages. Unwittingly, the policymaker had asked me to step over a line, dividing the past and future, that respectable historians dare not cross. Back in graduate school, our instructors socialized us to adopt what might be called the historians' Hippocratic oath, particularly for those working on topics relevant to contemporary policy issues, such as education. We swore an oath against *presentism*. In the words of our advisor's advisor, the eminent Harvard historian Bernard Bailyn, it sounded like one of the Ten Commandments: Thou shalt not write histories of the past as "simply the present writ small."[3] The classic example of the fallen historian was always Ellwood Cubberley, the Progressive-era Stanford professor of educational administration whose erroneous interpretation of the past was fused with his politics of the present.[4] As a rule, historians of our current generation are very cautious against becoming trapped in the present. Of course, we recognize that our views on the past are inevitably shaped by our present-day circumstances. But our stated mission is to understand the past on its own terms, not solely through the lens of present-day policy debates. When I became trained as an historian, it seemed that presentism itself was a sufficiently serious charge to warrant excommunication from the profession; crossing over into futurism could only be worse.

So, back in Hartford, I turned to the policymaker and mumbled something about our report focusing only on historical data, from past to present. If he wanted future projections on school racial populations and policy forecasts, I recommended that he consult a different specialist, such as a demographer, who could mix together various assumptions and deliver the type of speculation they were looking for. (From my narrow perspective as an historian, it was tempting to add that these future-oriented social scientists practiced something akin to the Dark Arts, but I held my tongue.) But our miscommunication was caused by differing temporal outlooks: policymakers looked forward, while historians like me looked back.

CONFLICTING PURPOSES OF HISTORICAL INTERPRETATION

A second area of disagreement concerns how different parties envision the purpose of historical interpretation. Historians tend to explore these questions for their own sake, asking: *Which interpretation best explains how and why change and/ or continuity occurred?* Yet policymakers tend to use history for more instrumental purposes, asking: *Which interpretation helps to advance our broader policy goals?* In drawing this distinction, I do not wish to perpetuate the false dichotomy that policymakers crassly seek their own interests while historians nobly pursue the dream of "objectivity."[5] Historians are self-interested people, too. Instead, my intention is to illuminate how the different contexts surrounding each group's work shapes our conceptualization and use of history.

Historians are not foreigners to educational policy disputes, particularly those involving the judicial branch of government. Several prominent U.S. historians have authored important legal briefs or served as expert witnesses on school deseg-regation cases. For instance, in 1953, when the U.S. Supreme Court instructed the attorneys in *Brown v Board of Education* to reargue their case, they asked for historical evidence on whether members of the Reconstruction-era Congress and state legislatures intended that the Fourteenth Amendment would abolish public school segregation. Thurgood Marshall and the NAACP turned to three promi-nent Southern historians—Horace Mann Bond, C. Vann Woodward, and John Hope Franklin—to research their case and formulate interpretations to be used in court.[6] More recently, historians have submitted legal briefs on whether the framers of the Fourteenth Amendment were "color-blind" or race-conscious, in an effort to influence the Justices' opinions in the 2007 Louisville and Seattle desegregation cases.[7] Policymakers (at least those involved in judicial cases) call upon the services of historians when they seek evidence on the decades-old intent behind a law or the historical facts on a case.

In Connecticut, the *Sheff v O'Neill* desegregation trial illustrates how historical interpretations can change during the litigation process, particularly as historians and lawyers use them with different ends in mind. History played an important role in this case because both the plaintiffs and defendants sought to persuade the court about the root cause of educational inequality between Hartford and its suburbs. When the Sheff plaintiffs filed their lawsuit in 1989, they initially constructed a two-prong historical argument: the state was culpable for public school inequalities due to the governmental role in creating and maintaining segregated education as well as segregated housing. Specifically, the original lawsuit claimed that the State "also failed to take action to afford meaningful racial and economic integration of housing within school zones and school districts in the Hartford metropolitan region."[8]

But later, when the plaintiffs went to trial in 1992, they amended their legal argument and therefore their historical interpretation. The plaintiffs requested the court's permission to drop the second half of their original two-prong argument, by deleting their claim about the state's role in segregated housing. According to their motion, the plaintiffs sought to "eliminate any ambiguity in the pleadings that may be relied on by the defendants to divert the court's attention from the important educational issues that are at the core of this case."[9] But this significant change in interpreting the root historical cause of the problem was shaped largely by legal strategy. The Sheff case depended entirely upon the guarantees defined by the equal protection and free public education clauses of Connecticut's state constitution. In other words, the law guaranteed the equal educational opportunity, but did not make as strong a statement about housing, so the historical interpretation shifted to fit better with the law.

Once the trial was underway, all sides devoted great attention to a historical question: did state actions play a role in creating educational inequality? The plaintiffs called the State Historian, University of Connecticut Professor Christopher Collier, to the witness stand and questioned him on this issue. Collier was careful with the facts. Connecticut never had a state policy of de jure segregation, he explained. Regarding state policies on racial matters, Connecticut was relatively progressive, compared to other Northern states. But the one specific piece of historical evidence that Collier did provide in support of the plaintiffs' case was Connecticut's policy on designating school district boundaries. In 1909, the state legislature consolidated the existing patchwork system so that each school district boundary would be identical with its municipal boundary. This meant that Hartford students would attend Hartford city schools, and suburban students would attend their own suburban schools. In Collier's view, the 1909 district boundary law was the most important factor contributing to "present segregated conditions" in urban schools.[10]

The Sheff defendants sharply challenged Collier's testimony. In cross-examination, the State Historian conceded that when the school district boundary consolidation law passed in 1909, the act was viewed as an exercise in governmental efficiency. It had "nothing to do with race whatsoever," because at that time, both the city and suburbs were predominantly white.[11] In the defendants' legal briefs, they forcefully argued that the plaintiffs had failed to prove any state action causing segregated schooling, since the 1909 law was adopted long before its racial consequences in the 1950s and '60s could have been foreseen.[12] Furthermore, the defendants reminded the Court that "this is in no way a housing or zoning case, the plaintiffs having expressly disavowed such a claim."[13]

Which historical interpretation about state action was most persuasive? Hypothetically, if the Sheff case had been tried before a court of historians, it would have been very difficult for the plaintiffs to argue persuasively that a 1909 state action on school district boundaries alone (with no reference to housing) was the primary culprit. Historian Kenneth Jackson and others have documented the role that governmental housing policies have played in intensifying city-suburban inequalities during the post-war era. For example, exclusive suburban zoning policies (backed by state governmental approval) designated minimum building lot sizes and single-family housing construction requirements which essentially guaranteed that only higher-income families could afford to purchase new homes in heavily zoned suburbs.[14] But given that the Sheff plaintiffs had to frame their historical interpretation around their constitutional legal argument, this broader analysis of the problem was not discussed in court.

The Sheff plaintiffs narrowly won their case in 1996. The Court's four-vote majority ruling underscored Collier's historical interpretation, by finding that "the state has nonetheless played a significant role. ... Although intended to improve the quality of education and not racially or ethnically motivated, the districting statute that the legislature enacted in 1909 ... is the *single most important factor* contributing to the present concentration of racial and ethnic minorities in the Hartford public school system."[15] But in a strong dissent, the other three justices held to the defendant's historical interpretation, that no evidence of state action in segregating schools had been proven. Framing the inequality case entirely around schools, rather than schools and housing, also had other consequences. To date, the Sheff remedies have focused entirely on educational policy, not housing policy, even though most historians would agree that a combination of the two would be a more compelling explanation for city-suburban inequality over time.

Today in metropolitan Hartford, school desegregation advocates and affordable housing advocates operate largely in separate spheres, working on separate policy agendas, despite their common history and potential for common ground.

CONFLICTING VIEWS ON HISTORICAL UNDERSTANDING VERSUS POLICY ACTION

At the core, there is a third fundamental difference between the roles of these two groups. On one hand, historians *seek a deeper understanding* of how and why change and continuity occurred over time, while on the other hand, policymakers *take actions to govern*. Both groups give serious thought to the problems at hand, but with very different intentions in mind. My recent experience in Connecticut shows how this division has led to some interesting examples where the two sides meet on a topic of mutual interest, yet fail to communicate fully in each other's terms.

At Trinity College, economics professor Diane Zannoni and our students and I worked with officials from a large suburb to study the relationship between home prices and school test scores over time. We framed our inquiry around these questions: Inside this suburban school district, how much more did homebuyers pay to purchase a house on the higher-scoring side of an elementary school attendance boundary, holding constant the characteristics of the home and the neighborhood? Furthermore, how did this economic relationship change over a decade (1996–2005), amid the expanding politics of school accountability and the Internet?

On the academic side, we worked together as economists and historians to understand this complex relationship between homes and schools. Our study found that in this particular suburb, for comparable homes located in geographically similar neighborhoods, a 12 percentage point increase (or one standard deviation) in the number of fourth-graders meeting the state-approved goal on the Connecticut Mastery Test was associated with a 2.8 percent (or $5,065) increase in the price of an average $200,000 home, in year 2000 dollars. Furthermore, we found that this test-price relationship became stronger over time, from the first half of our time period (1996–2000, a 1.2 percent gain) to the second half (2001–05, a 4.2 percent gain), in year 2000 dollars.

Our interpretation of this quantitative result emerged from our historical understanding of politics, markets, and schools in suburbia. Connecticut established a statewide achievement test in 1985, and required uniform reporting of scores in 1992, but these data typically appeared only once a year, in the local newspaper, and were not easily accessible to prospective homeowners. But after 2000, school test scores became more widely available on websites operated by the state government, as well as those by advocacy groups and real estate interests. More important, these data became instantaneously accessible to consumers, rather than appearing only once a year, and became a larger part of public policy discourse with the federal No Child Left Behind Act of 2002. Whether or not Connecticut's standardized test scores actually measured educational quality did not matter; the point is that homebuyers *believed* that these numbers had value, and our study proved that they paid more to buy private homes on the higher-scoring side of attendance boundary lines, to gain access to those public schools.[16]

We returned to the suburb to present our findings to local officials, and to discuss their implications. From my perspective as a historian, I emphasized how public schools and private real estate markets were deeply connected, and had become even more so in recent years. To their ears, my presentation sounded very much like a professor advancing another "big idea," which seemed like common sense to them. Of course their suburban public schools attracted homebuyers; that had been one of the town's implicit development strategies for decades. Our data simply confirmed what they instinctively knew. The local policymakers responded to our research by asking a question arising from their most pressing policy issue of that moment: "How will this help us to get our school budget approved by the voters?" The pressure to maintain the quality of the town's public school system, with limited state funding, had once again created a political standoff between elected officials and a local organization calling for reduced property taxes. My students and I could not provide a meaningful answer to this question, since our research was framed around a "deep question," which failed to translate into a clear policy directive.

Yet other audiences did make effective use of related test-price research produced by other scholars. In 2005, the National Association of Realtors published a resource "toolkit" on public schools for its extensive membership of real estate agents across the nation. In its introduction, the booklet summarized the latest scholarship by leading economists, emphasizing that "the link between public schools and neighborhood quality is not just intuitive to REALTORS®; there is solid academic research to back it up." After reviewing findings from key studies, it encouraged real estate agents to "forge better working relationships with local school boards." After all, "REALTORS® shouldn't be shy about getting involved ... "because what's good for neighborhood schools is also good for real estate markets."[17] In sum, three different constituents each had a different relationship to the schools and housing phenomenon: historians researched how it changed over time, policymakers sought to transform it for their political advantage, business interests asked, "How can we profit from this?" All of us were working for very different goals.

CAN EDUCATIONAL HISTORIANS AND
POLICYMAKERS WORK TOGETHER?

By our nature, historians would be the first to point out that this very question has its own literature. Carl Kaestle, Ellen Condliffe Lagemann, and Bill Reese all have chronicled the weak relationship between educational research, policy, and practice during the nation's past century.[18] Yet many historians seem to hold onto the hope that history can be relevant for policymaking. In their introduction to *Learning from the Past*, Diane Ravitch and Maris Vinovskis, both historians with significant experience in federal policymaking, make a compelling case for significance. School reform and other contemporary policy issues "have historical antecedents," they claim. "Unfortunately, many policy makers and analysts believe that current problems are new and unprecedented. Implicit in many current writings and actions is the unexamined belief that knowledge of history is not necessary or particularly helpful. This is regrettable because so often in retrospect a broader historical appreciation of the earlier efforts to promote educational change might have provided some useful guidance for those previous school reformers."[19]

In a more recent volume, Vinovskis argues that during the earlier years of the nation's history, policy leaders were greatly influenced by historians. Prior to the twentieth century, policymakers "frequently turned to history for guidance and inspiration," he argues, though mostly for "moral instruction rather than specific policy guidance."[20] Yet in recent decades, the influence of history on policy has sharply declined, for two reasons. First, Vinovskis contends that historians have professionalized and many became cautious about preserving their "objective" stance as separate from political activity. Second, observed the policy historian Hugh Graham, when policymakers of the late twentieth century sought advice, they increasingly turned to their "experienced line staff, to lawyers and 'hard' social scientists, or to policy analysts trained in systems analysis and operations research" who were "trained in problem solving" through cost-benefit analysis. By contrast, Graham noted, "historians are quickest to see what's wrong with politically tempting analogies" by arguing how historical contexts differ from setting to setting.[21]

Despite this general decline, Vinovskis points to a rising generation of scholarly historians who have become more interested in policy, the growth of academic presses publishing books with historical analysis of policy issues, and the creation of the *Journal of Policy History* in 1989. Indeed, as Peter Stearns has observed, history and policy have become so deeply intertwined, as policymakers "inevitably use history either to help explicate policy or at least to justify it after the fact," particularly through historical analogies to present-day issues, whether accurate or misleading.[22]

To be sure, conflicts between the worldviews of academics and policymakers are not limited to historians. In *Why Sociology Does Not Apply*, Robert Scott and Arnold Shore underscored the challenges of integrating research grounded in a disciplinary perspective with policymaking that is driven by other motivations.[23] In addition, Douglas Ashford has outlined the difficulties faced in comparative public policy research, where researchers expand the domain of knowledge beyond conventional U.S. case studies, forcing even deeper thought about what does (or does not) apply.[24] But compared to other academics, historians face a more daunting challenge because of the temporal gap: our work is expressly devoted to the past, while policymaking looks toward the future.

If historians and policymakers did wish to cooperate more effectively on educational issues (and that's a big "if"), then both parties would need to make important changes. On one hand, historians would need to rethink our institutionalized aversion to presentism. In a published exchange between historians employed in professional schools, Jonathan Zimmerman argued that there are two different types:

> One type of presentism analyzes contemporary issues in historical perspective, asking how knowledge of earlier eras might make us change the way we look at our own. A second type starts with a present-day opinion or perspective, then seeks historical examples or precedents to justify it. I think the second kind of presentism has given the first kind a bad rap. Of course, we should never write or teach history solely as a means of justifying our current-day predilections or opinions. But we should teach history as a way to interrogate the present—that is, to make our current circumstances less certain, less stable, and less taken-for-granted than they already are.[25]

If historians wish to bridge the divide with policymakers, we need to take a step closer to accepting Zimmerman's first type of presentism and recognizing its difference from the second.

On the other hand, if policymakers wish to cooperate more closely with historians, they need to reflect on how and why historical thinking might possibly alter their decision-making process. Consider what the policy historians Richard Neustadt and Ernest May pose in their book, *Thinking in Time*, as an alternative reason for studying the past: its ability to stimulate historical imagination. "Seeing the past can help one envision alternative futures," they write. While history cannot tell policymakers what to do, studying the past can teach us how to ask probing questions, especially about our presumptions about contemporary policies. "The point is to get forward, as soon as possible, the questions that ought to be asked," Neustadt and May argue, "before anyone says, 'This is what we should do' or 'Here's how to do it'."[26]

Putting forward the questions that "ought to be asked" and debunking misleading historical analogies sounds like good advice for historians. But it places the burden on historians to act *before* the policymaking process begins, and to interrupt conventional trains of thought. Is this possible for historians to do, given all of our differences with policymakers cited above? Change is possible only if policymakers desire for it to happen.

Indeed, policymakers and historians tend to operate on very different schedules, the former usually moving much faster than the latter. But the policy formation process does not always operate at full speed. Occasionally, windows of opportunity can arise when policymakers would benefit from stepping back and welcoming historians to engage in some serious reflection on past and present.[27] At the same time, historians would benefit by preparing for these opportunities in our writing and public outreach, and reconsidering our stance on presentism. After all, what appears to be today's "crisis of the moment" is part of a larger crisis over time. Finding our way out of the present situation requires a deeper understanding of how we arrived here in the first place.

NOTES

1. Jack Dougherty, *More Than One Struggle: The Evolution of Black School Reform in Milwaukee* (Chapel Hill: University of North Carolina Press, 2004).
2. Jack Dougherty, Jesse Wanzer, and Christina Ramsey, *Missing the Goal: A Visual Guide to Sheff Vs. O'Neill School Desegregation* (Hartford, CT: Cities, Suburbs, and Schools Research Project at Trinity College, 2007) <http://www.trincoll.edu/depts/educ/css>.
3. Bernard Bailyn, *Education in the Forming of American Society; Needs and Opportunities for Study* (Chapel Hill: University of North Carolina Press, 1960), 9.
4. Lawrence Arthur Cremin, *The Wonderful World of Ellwood Patterson Cubberley: an Essay on the Historiography of American Education* (New York: Bureau of Publications, Teachers College, Columbia University, 1965).
5. Peter Novick, *That Noble Dream : The "Objectivity Question" and the American Historical Profession* (Cambridge [England]: Cambridge University Press, 1988).
6. Richard Kluger, *Simple Justice: The History of Brown V. Board of Education and Black America's Struggle for Equality* (New York: Vintage, 1975), 617–634.
7. James D. Anderson, "Race-Conscious Educational Policies Versus a 'Color-Blind Constitution': A Historical Perspective," *Educational Researcher* 36, no. 5 (2007): 249–57.
8. *Milo Sheff et al. v William O'Neill et al.*, Complaint filed in Connecticut Superior Court, Judicial District of Hartford/New Britain at Hartford, April 26, 1989, section 71.
9. Plaintiff's Request for Leave to Amend Complaint, July 21, 1992, record item 178, cited in Trial Judge Harry Hammer's initial ruling, *Sheff v O'Neill*, June 27, 1995, 1–2.
10. Citation of Collier's trial testimony from Judge Harry Hammer, *Sheff v O'Neill*, Memorandum of Decision, Superior Court, Judicial district of Hartford/New Britain at Hartford, April 12 1995, 64.
11. Ibid., 64.

12. *Sheff v O'Neill*, Defendant's brief, Supreme Court of State of Connecticut, filed 1 September 1, 1995, p. 53, in Supreme Court of the State of Connecticut *Record*, Connecticut State Library.

13. Ibid., 55.

14. Kenneth T. Jackson, *Crabgrass Frontier: The Suburbanization of the United States* (New York: Oxford University Press, 1985), pp. 241–243. See also David L. Kirp, et al., *Our Town: Race, Housing and the Soul of Suburbia* (New Brunswick, NJ: Rutgers University Press, 1995).

15. *Sheff v O'Neill*, Connecticut Supreme Court decision, July 9, 1996 (678 A.2d 1267 Conn. 1996), p. 1274, emphasis in original.

16. Jack Dougherty, Jeffrey Harrelson, Laura Maloney, Drew Murphy, Russell Smith, Michael Snow, and Diane Zannoni, "School Choice in Suburbia: Public School Testing and Private Real Estate Markets." Conference paper delivered at the American Educational Research Association, 2007. <http://www.trincoll.edu/depts/educ/css> (Accessed Septemper 8, 2008).

17. Carol Everett, et al., *Public Schools: A Toolkit for Realtors* (National Association of Realtors, 2005). <http://www.realtor.org/smart_growth.nsf/Pages/toolkit_publicschools?OpenDocument> (Accessed Septemper 8, 2008).

18. Carl Kaestle, "The Awful Reputation of Education Research," *Educational Researcher* 22, no. 1 (1993): 23, 26–31; Ellen Condliffe Lagemann, *An Elusive Science: The Troubling History of Education Research* (Chicago: University of Chicago Press, 2000); William J. Reese, "What History Teaches About the Impact of Educational Research on Practice," in *History, Education, and the Schools* (New York: Palgrave Macmillan, 2007).

19. Diane Ravitch, and Maris Vinovskis, eds. *Learning From the Past : What History Teaches Us About School Reform* (Baltimore: Johns Hopkins University Press, 1995),p. x. See also Maris Vinovskis, *History and Educational Policymaking* (New Haven: Yale University Press, 1999).

20. Maris Vinovskis, "Historians and Education Policy Research in the United States," in David N. Plank, et al., eds. *Handbook on Educational Policy Research*, (Washington, DC: American Educational Research Association, forthcoming), 1, 2.

21. Hugh Davis Graham, "The Stunted Career of Policy History: A Critique and an Agenda," *Public Historian* 15 (2) (1993): 15, cited in Vinovskis, "Historians and Education Policy Research, " 12.

22. Peter N. Stearns, "History and Public Policy," in George J. McCall, and George H. Weber, eds. *Social Science and Public Policy: The Roles of Academic Disciplines in Policy Analysis* (Port Washington, NY: Associated Faculty Press, 1984), 106–7.

23. Robert A. Scott and Arnold R. Shore, *Why Sociology Does Not Apply: A Study of the Use of Sociology in Public Policy* (New York: Elsevier, 1979). See also Charles E. Lindblom and David K. Cohen, *Usable Knowledge: Social Science and Social Problem Solving* (New Haven: Yale University Press, 1979), and David L. Featherman, and Maris Vinovskis, eds. *Social Science and Policy-Making: A Search for Relevance in the Twentieth Century* (Ann Arbor, MI: University of Michigan Press, 2001).

24. Douglas E. Ashford, ed. *History and Context in Comparative Public Policy* (Pittsburgh, PA: University of Pittsburgh Press, 1992).

25. Jonathan Zimmerman, "Interchange: History in the Professional Schools," *Journal of American History* 92, no. 2 (2005), paragraph 35.

26. Richard E. Neustadt, and Ernest R. May, *Thinking in Time: The Uses of History for Decision-Makers* (New York: The Free Press, 1986), xv, 240.

27. For this final, more optimistic note, I thank Liz Hollander and Carl Kaestle.

CHAPTER THIRTEEN

Lessons FROM THE Past

A Challenge AND A Caution FOR Policy-Relevant History

TRACY L. STEFFES

In their popular 1986 text, *Thinking in Time: The Uses of History for Decision-Makers,* Richard Neustadt and Ernest May of Harvard University's John F. Kennedy School of Government extolled the virtues of using history in the decision-making process. Writing at a time when history was largely out of favor in policy analysis, Neustadt and May sought to stimulate conversation about the role that history could play in guiding policy. History, they argued, can provide policymakers with analogies and comparisons that can profitably guide action; help them more fully understand people, institutions, and issues in negotiating; and locate decisions in "time streams" that have predictive value. History, they suggested, could help policymakers avoid mistakes, inform their understanding of present options, and anticipate future outcomes.

In advising decision-makers on whom to turn to for historical knowledge, however, Neustadt and May relegated academic historians to a minor role. Officials, they argued, "probably do right to put them last" on the list of authorities to consult, because conversations among policymakers and historians "can resemble those between Chinese speaking different dialects." Scholars "know too much and may well have trouble saying anything without qualification." While Neustadt and May "dream[ed] of a day when officials and historians will talk to each other more easily," they viewed the prospects of this as slim.[1]

Neustadt and May's skepticism about the ability of historians and policymakers to speak the same language came at a time when history and policy seemed to be moving ever farther apart. Although earlier generations of historians had directly engaged questions of politics and policy in their scholarship, the social history revolution that began in the late 1960s began to move the discipline of history away from the kinds of questions and research most clearly useful to policymakers. New scholarship rejected the grand political narratives of the past for new histories written "from the bottom up," a trend that shifted who and what historians studied, how they studied them, and how they conceptualized politics and power. Historians began to ask new kinds of questions and explore new sources, for example, to tell the histories of previously marginalized groups like women and African-Americans and to analyze power and inequality in everyday life. While these trends created important new insights into the past and endowed historians with new theories and methodologies, they also widened the gulf between academic historians on the one hand and policymakers on the other. Relatively few historians continued to ask questions that policymakers cared about. Thus while historians continued to be employed by the federal government and to testify in court cases as experts throughout the 1970s and beyond, there has been a growing sense that the role of historians in advising decision-makers and shaping policy has diminished. No historian with the stature of Arthur Schlesinger Jr. has counseled recent presidents, and historians have taken a backseat to economists, sociologists, political scientists, and other social scientists in government service and in the proliferating think tanks and policy institutes. New graduate schools of public policy created at elite universities such as Harvard, Berkeley, Princeton, and Michigan rarely employ historians or historical analysis in policy studies, while the social sciences, with a few exceptions, have also eschewed historical approaches for behaviorist ones.[2]

Despite these general trends over the past four decades, however, some historians and social scientists have joined Neustadt and May in trying to provoke a larger conversation on history's value for policy.[3] Perhaps the largest group includes historians in law schools, education schools, medical schools, and other professional programs where their institutional position requires them to justify their work by articulating their contributions to the field in the present. Housed in diverse sites and often feeling isolated, many of these historians have existed in an uneasy relationship with their parent discipline as it not only moved away from engagement with policy but even looked with overt skepticism at their efforts.[4]

Two other groups of historians, public historians and policy historians, have organized identifiable subfields within history since the 1970s and worked to create institutional structures and intellectual justifications for their work. Public history emerged as a new field in the 1970s to prepare historians for "applied" work in museums and cultural venues, government service, and business. Created partly in hopes of improving the slim job prospects of Ph.D. candidates in the 1970s, the field of public history in the past three decades has created a journal and a national association and initiated discussions about the value of history outside of the academy.[5] At the same time, a small group of historians interested in politics, policy, and statecraft have defined a new subfield of "policy history" with regular conferences and a professional journal that reaches out to historically minded social scientists.

In the past decade, there have been small signs that this conversation about history's value for policy is starting to gain wider hearing and interest. In 2002, the American Historical Association founded the National History Center to advance the study and teaching of history and to promote "historical knowledge in government, business, and the public at large." Its main goal is to bring historians together "to exchange ideas and to help historians reach out to broader audiences by providing the historical context necessary to better understand today's events" through seminars, conferences, congressional briefings, publications, and other forms of dissemination aimed directly at the public and policymakers.[6] In the last several years, conferences considering the relationship between history and policy (like the one on which this volume is based) have proliferated.[7] Policy historians, after years of lamenting their alienation, even declared in a 2004 issue on the state of the field in *Journal of Policy History* that the "state of policy history is good." The introductory essay noted that this pronouncement marks a "dramatic change from only four years ago" because of recent surges in the "quality and volume of scholarship" coming both from historians working to fuse social and political history in innovative new ways and from the growing interest of social scientists in the value of historical analysis for understanding contemporary politics and policy.[8]

The difficulty and hesitancy with which historians articulate the real and potential contributions of history to policy (and to understanding the present more generally) are rooted deeply in the assumptions and practices of the discipline itself. Neustadt and May's observation that historians have difficulty "saying anything without qualification" points to the same problem that Jack Dougherty identifies in this volume: historians and policymakers share fundamentally different goals and assumptions, a fact that complicates their relationship. The latter are concerned with making concrete decisions under time pressure and want to find workable solutions, articulate clear policy prescriptions, and predict future developments. Historians, on the other hand, are trained to complicate rather that simplify, and they eschew large generalizations and predictive models in favor of limited, empirically based claims rooted in particular contexts.[9] This difference is rooted ultimately in very different epistemological orientations. The disciplinary conventions and the practices of historical thinking, as this chpter will show, run counter to some of the key assumptions of policymakers and social scientists. These differences have made historians themselves reluctant to argue that their work generates "useable" lessons from the past and have also led policymakers and social scientists to undervalue the potential contributions of history to policy.

This essay attempts to further the conversation about the uses of history and policy that has been occurring in fits and starts in different locations for the past few decades. It begins by exploring the historical method and historical thinking in order to explain and analyze some of the unique habits of mind that comprise historical scholarship. These help to explain the differences between historians and social scientists and suggest why many historians are reluctant to articulate "lessons of history." While these differences are real, I will argue that most historians do believe that the past has at least something to say about the present. I will then offer a few suggestions how the "lessons of history" might be reimagined to emphasize the ways in which the past provides *questions* rather than *answers* and puts the present into perspective in unique ways that enhance public policy debates. I will also argue that students of policy could benefit from deeper consideration of change, context, contingency, and complexity, considerations that are at the heart of historical inquiry.

Finally, I will address the legitimate concerns of historians that efforts to write policy-relevant history can pose dangers to the vitality and quality of historical scholarship. These dangers should serve as cautionary, however, and not as a justification for not doing it. If we are careful, we historians can make our work relevant to the present without sacrificing its intellectual integrity—and we have a responsibility to try to do so.

This essay thus offers a challenge and a caution for two different audiences. To policymakers, policy analysts, and social scientists, it is a challenge to take seriously the potential contributions of historical scholarship and historical ways of thinking for approaching the present, like the past, with complexity, perspective, and humility. And it cautions these audiences also to take seriously historians' skepticism about how their work can and should be used. Truly learning from the past requires listening to it on its own terms and appreciating its differentness, not insisting upon simple, straightforward answers or "timeless truths." To my fellow historians, this chapter offers a challenge to engage in fuller conversation about the ways in which history can inform the present and for each of us to work harder to articulate the particular contributions that emerge from our own work. Yet it cautions that we should not be so driven by the desire to be relevant that we confine our scholarship to the narrow channels of the present and limit our historical imaginations. Some of our greatest contributions may not be immediately apparent and may come not by illuminating a particular policy but by destabilizing the received wisdoms and categories of the present and pushing policymakers to ask better questions.

HISTORICAL METHOD AND HISTORICAL THINKING

Although for generations historians have discussed among themselves the philosophy and practice of history, most of them learned the key disciplinary tools and habits of mind through apprenticeships in which they did the work, rather than from explicit discussions of method and theory. While in the past two decades postmodern theories of language and interpretation, including the so-called linguistic turn, sent some historians into epistemological crisis and prompted some disciplinary soul-searching, these theories have not drastically changed the way that history is taught or practiced. Courses for undergraduate majors and graduate students, if they engage in explicit discussions of methods at all, often reach back to mid-century or earlier for philosophizing about the practice of history.[10] Most of these courses, particularly at the graduate level, simply engage students in critiquing secondary sources, analyzing primary sources, and constructing historical narratives to learn the discipline of history.

Despite what other social scientists might see as a remarkable lack of theorizing and self-consciousness about our methods, historians do share sets of practices and assumptions that characterize the discipline. Virtually all professional historians would agree that history is not a straightforward record of "what happened" in the past but an interpretive analysis constructed largely on the basis of surviving evidence. Interpretation is inherent in history, and consequently all narratives of the past are subject always to revision as new evidence and new insights are brought to bear on a problem.

History is both rigorously empirical and highly imaginative: it demands tremendous creativity when looking for and interpreting sources. Most historians employ a method in which they frame questions and then continually reframe them as they encounter the evidence. The eminent global historian William H. McNeill explained this method to a group of social, physical, and biological scientists at a 1994 conference: "I get curious about a problem and start reading up on it. What I read causes me to redefine the problem. Redefining the problem causes me to shift the direction of what I'm reading. That in turn further reshapes the problem, which further directs the reading. I go back and forth like this until it feels right, then I write it up and ship it off to the publisher."[11] As McNeill's explanation demonstrates, historians don't "test" a hypothesis about the past, use the past to support an overarching theory, or mine records to support an argument they already have formulated. Historians frame questions that start their exploration of the past but then let the evidence they find reframe the questions and lead them to new ones. Some of the best historical work is produced when historians get lost in the past for a while and let it guide how they ask the questions and understand its answers. It is at this point that historians can try to break free from the categorizations of the present and encounter the past on its own terms.

This effort to understand the past on its own terms and the assumption that the past is fundamentally different from the present are at the heart of historical thinking. Historians recognize that their engagement with the past is mediated through the present and shaped by the times they live in as well as their own values. Few historians cling to the idea of "value-free" or "neutral" history because few historians believe that history is about neutral recitation of facts; judgment and interpretation are inherent in historical inquiry, and these activities are inescapably subjective. This does not mean however, that all interpretations are equally valid, that historians are permitted to impose political or ideological agendas on their reading of the past, or that history is so subjective that it is little more than fiction. Ultimately, what distinguishes history from fiction, and persuasive historical accounts from dubious ones, is firm, critical, explicit, and rigorous grounding of interpretation in evidence. For many historians, it is the effort to ground historical interpretation in evidence and to understand the past as faithfully as possible with critical reflection on one's own subjectivity, not the pursuit of neutrality or effort to purge all values, which defines historical objectivity.[12] At the end of *In Defense of History*, Richard Evans sums up his own belief and that of most historians when he says that, despite the postmodern challenges and the acknowledged difficulties of historical interpretation, "I will look humbly at the past and say, despite them all: It really happened, and we really can, if we are very scrupulous and careful and self-critical, find out how it did and reach some tenable conclusions about what it all meant."[13] Evans also reflects the humility with which most historians approach the past; they know that they can never get it completely right but are driven to get it as right as they possibly can.

Therefore, historians' relationship to evidence is at the heart of the historical method. Historians think imaginatively and critically about where to find evidence and how to read and interpret it. They reflect critically on the limits of evidence, the silences in the record, and the privileging of particular voices in the evidence that survives. Historians search for new sources with which to understand the past and apply new tools and perspectives to analyzing those sources. They debate, often very vigorously, on how to interpret sources and what one can "know" from them and with how much certainty. In the end, however, most historians attempt to interpret and utilize evidence by embedding it in context, often through deep and broad explorations of other sources; for most historians, a text's meaning can be understood only in context—the social milieu, assumptions, circumstances, and meanings of its time and place and its relationship vis-à-vis others. Thus, many historians believe that in order to try to understand the texts in context and minimize the extent to which they read present meanings back into the past, they must immerse themselves in a wide array of sources to help to shed light on the meanings of the texts. If one gropes long and carefully enough in the language of the past, one will get closer and closer to appreciating it according to the categories of the past rather than one's own presentist assumptions. Consequently, most historians feel compelled to arrive at their own understanding of context, which can be aided by the historical work of others but must also be formed through deep and broad reading of the period under study. This is one thing that often distinguishes a historian from social scientists who turn to history; the latter are often much more comfortable doing focused primary-source work on their particular topic or even relying entirely on secondary literature to make claims about the past. Historians' need for deep and broad reading of texts and engagement with context, to form their own historical understanding, reflect some of the deeply embedded assumptions of the discipline and also help to explain why good historical monographs take such a long time to produce.

Historians are also centrally interested in change over time, even if recent decades of hyperspecialization have produced a multitude of studies more limited in chronological scope. At the heart of historical inquiry, as Peter Stearns has noted, is a fundamental orientation toward change. Stearns argues that no other discipline has tools for analyzing change with the same complexity as history, nor does any other discipline regard change as a norm rather than as a disruption. In this orientation toward change, questions of causality and significance are at the heart of historical inquiry; in other words, historians have the habit of asking how and *why* things change and *why it matters*. Historians use analytical devices like periodization to help them think about and categorize change, and they explore cause and effect in complex, multilayered ways. Historians focus on the *long duree,* a practice that allows them to identify cause and effect over the long run, to trace immediate and long-term causes as well as intended and unintended consequences in multiple realms, including both the realm of high politics and the everyday social experience of individuals.[14] The discipline of history treads into all realms of politics, culture, economy, thought, and social relations, rather than limiting itself to one category, and consequently provides ways to view interconnections that many other disciplines miss. As Otis Graham, Jr., notes, by standing at the intersection of social sciences and humanities, albeit uncomfortably in both groups, historians occupy a unique place that offers benefits for policy and for understanding our world. Historians employ a variety of types of inquiry that combine rigorous empiricism and a variety of social science tools with a firm conviction that not all things worth examining can be measured precisely.[15] In the best sense, history is a grab-bag discipline that borrows tools and theories from a host of other disciplines and employs them selectively and only to the extent to which they help to make sense of a particular issue in a particular time and place.

Underlying this historical method and set of disciplinary conventions are a series of assumptions: that the past is fundamentally different from the present; that real explanation depends upon understanding the past on its own terms; that claims and explanations must be grounded in particularities of time and place. Historical thinking is consequently profoundly contingent and contextual, and historians place great stock in understanding the complexities of particular time and places. In his recent study of historical thinking, psychologist Sam Wineburg described it as a complex and "unnatural act." The "natural" tendency of most people, Wineburg argued, was to collapse the distinction between past and present—to understand the past as fundamentally the same as the present—which makes applying "lessons" from one to the other unproblematic. Historical thinking, in contrast, requires one to recognize and embrace the differentness of the past.[16] Most historians subscribe to the view that the past is a "foreign country" and that one cannot simply ascribe one's present values and understandings to make sense of it; even when the language appears to be similar, its norms are not our own. Wineburg argued that this way of thinking confers important benefits, chief among them the perspective that comes from recognizing and empathizing with differentness.

The habits of historical thinking—of seeing the past and present as different and dependent upon context—make historians profoundly uncomfortable with theories and explanations that operate independently of time and context, tactics that social scientists routinely seek and deploy. The idea that "lessons" from one set of circumstances can be unmoored from context and applied in a straightforward manner to another strikes most historians as profoundly ahistorical and deeply problematic. Even more intellectually suspect, from the standpoint of most historians, are attempts to construct "models" to predict behavior or efforts to elaborate principles that hold true, regardless of time and place. John Lewis Gaddis argues that historians are ecological or constructivist thinkers, in contrast to most social scientists, who are reductionist. The latter, he argues, "seek to understand reality by breaking it into its various parts" and "to find the variable within the equation that determines the value of all others." As ecological thinkers, he argues, historians maintain that to understand reality one must view the whole, which may be more than simply the sum of its parts. Historians are therefore skeptical of trying to identify independent variables or understand issues by simplifying them to their parts and instead take the opposite approach: looking at complex interplay between multiple factors.[17] These orientations have tremendous implications for the use of history to inform policy and help to explain both the reluctance of many historians to engage with the present and the criticism they sometimes level at "useable" histories.

THE "LESSONS" OF HISTORY FOR POLICY

Historians interested in policy, including the education historians writing for this volume, have long struggled to reconcile the conventions of their discipline with a personal desire, and sometimes institutional pressure from colleagues in professional schools, to produce history with obvious relevance for the present. They often argue, in a variety of ways, that history offers "lessons" for the present, and for their pains are sometimes criticized by other historians. Gordon Wood, for example, has recently criticized the attempt to draw out present implications from history by arguing that it can distort historical scholarship. The goal of history, he and many others maintain, is to understand the past on its own terms, for its own sake, and although present concerns will undoubtedly shape us, historians have a duty to exert "critical control." Wood argues that "historians who want to influence politics with their history writing have missed the point of the craft; they ought to run for office." [18]

While the extent to which historians embrace the study of the past for the sake of the past varies (and most are not as critical of present-mindedness as Wood is), most historians remain reticent to engage present controversies and offer "lessons from history." Historians trained to complicate rather than simplify, and to emphasize complex causation, contingency, and the particular find that identifying a "useable past" is difficult and contrary to most of our training. More fundamentally, historians' rootedness in context renders the idea of drawing out "lessons" from the past problematic. The willingness of nonhistorians to simply sever "lessons" from a past context and try to apply them to the present or future, through either analogies or generalizing conclusions, reinforces the reluctance of historians to frame the past as "useable." Historians find the way that this past is "used" too often to be ahistorical. The very act of creating historical analogies, which Neustadt and May argue is the most common way that decisionmakers "use" history, relies on treating two very different times and situations as fundamentally the same, in order to extract the "lessons" of one for the other. However, to simply plop the "lessons" from one time to another or to use them to create generalizations that operate outside of time and space is to collapse the fundamental distinction between past and present at the heart of historical inquiry. This is not what careful historians mean when they suggest ways in which the past may provide lessons for the present, but it appears to be the way that many readers understand and apply their work.

If one looks more closely however, one sees that in their arguments about the "lessons" of the past, historians often suggest that what matters about historical analysis is the variety of ways in which it stimulates critical thinking and imagination about the present; in other words the *questions* it raises rather than the *answers* it generates. Elizabeth Rose makes this point explicitly in her examination of how current prekindergarten advocates misuse the "lessons" of Head Start; as a good historian she recognizes that "strategies, ideas, and structures cannot be imported intact from one historical context to another." She argues that, "perhaps rather than providing *answers* in the shape of 'lessons from history' the best contribution that history can make to those engaged in shaping policy is to draw our attention to the most important *questions* we can ask about the present."[19] As historians, we should all be more careful and explicit about this distinction, for while it may appeal less to policymakers who are searching for "answers," it is both more intellectually honest and ultimately more productive when thinking carefully and critically about how history can contribute broadly to public policy and public debate. We historians should also strive to articulate how and why these questions are valuable.

The chapters in this volume present a number of good examples of how historical analysis can ask crucial questions of the present that may prove productive in policy discussions and public debate and also remain true to historical inquiry. Historical accounts can highlight things we may not see from a snapshot: they can point out long-term changes and consequences, draw our attention to factors, causes, and effects in the past which we might do well to examine in the present, and challenge assumptions about what we "know" about the present. They can highlight "lost alternatives" that cannot be simply resurrected but may bear reexamination, or they can bring to light some other potential ways to think and talk about the array of possible policies. In other words, the past can provide perspective by the very nature of its differentness from the present. It can stimulate us to think in broader and more critical ways about elements of the present which can otherwise appear "natural" and immutable.[20]

Anne-Lise Halvorsen and Jeffrey Mirel's analysis of the Detroit Citizenship Education Study (DCES) in the 1930s and 1940s is a good example of the complicated ways in which the study of history can provide perspective and raise important questions for the present. Halvorsen and Mirel note that the DCES originated from a critique of youths' lack of "real" civic knowledge in the period but ironically came to design a citizenship curriculum that created "the kind of well-meaning, but ignorant citizens whose lack of knowledge about democracy and the challenges to it that had inspired the study in the first place."[21] In analyzing the study and its resultant curriculum recommendations, Halvorsen and Mirel explore how intellectual and pedagogical thought and a variety of social and political factors shaped the assumptions and recommendations of the DCES. As any good history does, this chapter locates the debates and the assumptions that undergirded them in time and place and provides a long enough view to examine a variety of influences on and consequences of the curriculum. In their study, we see that the political, social, and intellectual context was crucial: a host of developments in the period created the perception of a "youth problem" that in turn powerfully shaped the DCES's turn toward concerns about "emotional adjustment" as the crucial aspect of citizenship training.

While DCES citizenship training was a product of its particular time and place, this historical account also stimulates us to ask some questions about our own assumptions and helps to put the present in relief. For one thing, in elaborating with care the chief assumptions of the time, it asks us to examine with more precision our own goals, articulated and unarticulated, in citizenship education, and to think about whether we privilege "emotional" over "intellectual" approaches to civic education. Past deliberations over citizenship training may enrich our attempts to do this by emphasizing some of the possible aims one might articulate, such as goals to instill knowledge about democracy and civic responsibilities, encourage critical thinking and problem-solving skills, or cultivate social responsibility and relationships. It also reveals a road-not-taken or lost alternative in the form of George Counts' discipline-based civics curriculum rooted in knowledge about American institutions and the problems of democracy. Counts advocated an academic and intellectual approach to civic education that the authors suggest is worth reexamining, one that offers a contrast to the civic education that did develop. Finally, the chapter helps us to think critically about the connection between ends and means. Halvorsen and Mirel's account challenges simple critiques of progressive education as watered down education, by showing how the turn away from disciplinary content was a distinct choice rather than inherent in progressive pedagogical practices and suggesting that we think about ways in which the two might be joined in productive ways.

William Reese also helps to put the present in relief by exploring the reforms and debates in nineteenth-century Washington, DC, schools as an expanding, modernizing system confronted issues of class, race, and pedagogy.[22] While some readers might be tempted to see these as "timeless" issues in urban education or to conclude that nineteenth-century schoolmen confronted the "same" problems as their twentieth-century counterparts, Reese's study reveals the past's "differentness," particularly in the assumptions that educators brought to these issues. In contrast to our current conceptions of the challenge of equity in urban education, Reese describes a moment when educators were consumed primarily by the question of access and of overcoming the stigma that equated public schooling with "pauper" schooling by attracting more affluent students into the public schools. Consequently, his study helps us to interrogate our own ways of defining quality and equality and points forcefully to the different assumptions which animate our own time.

Reese also puts into relief the very different conceptions of the goals of schooling in nineteenth-century Washington, DC, as embodied in different modes of pedagogy and assessment; large, semi-graded classrooms taught by low-paid and low-status teachers put a premium on skills like memorization and basic literacy and math skills that were demonstrated to the local community in exhibitions, public examinations, contests, and other displays. Overall, the schools sought to inculcate "discipline, patriotism, respect for authority, basic literacy, and moral values." His study challenges us to ask about our own goals and to reflect on the ways that institutional arrangements, pedagogy, and forms of assessment reflect assumptions about the goals of education. In other words, the study prods us to consider what knowledge is of the most worth, and the extent to which how we talk about it and how we actually organize and evaluate schools to produce it are compatible. Finally, Reese explores change (and continuity) over time to analyze how DC schools expanded and modernized by the end of the nineteenth century, encompassing new groups of students and new rationales, while the persistence of old values and practices profoundly shaped the school and framed the debates over progressive education. His account therefore challenges us to think carefully in our own time about the ways in which old ideas and practices can continue to have sway even after the context has dramatically changed.

In illuminating the complexities of the past and unintended consequences that can emerge from policies, history can point us to things to look for or to ask about in the present. In his study of special education programs in Boston, Adam Nelson demonstrates the ways in which federal aid created unintended incentives for local officials to expand the program beyond its original purposes and the consequences that flowed from these decisions. Nelson's study should provoke us to ask whether and in what ways current fiscal policies shape incentives for local officials and what effects these policies have. In demonstrating the differing impacts on city and suburbs, Nelson's study also makes us ask about the ways in which federal aid, intended to promote "equality of educational opportunity," can actually increase inequality across fractured jurisdictions.[23]

Historical accounts may also help us think critically about the present by unsettling what we "know" and challenging the sometimes narrow ways in which we conceptualize problems and solutions in the present. Elizabeth Rose argues that the contemporary pre-kindergarten movement has shaped its strategy in response to false "lessons" gleaned from Head Start. Pre-kindergarten advocates are attempting to make it a universal program rooted in state systems because of the misapplied "lessons" that supposedly tell us that stand-alone programs and programs for poor children will not succeed.[24] Likewise, John Rury argues that our master narratives of urban school crisis have obscured important gains that African-Americans made in closing the attainment gap in secondary schooling from 1960–80 and suggests that these gains should provoke us to ask more precise questions about the ways we define attainment and its relationship to race and place. Our perception of "crisis" may have caused us to miss important developments that require much greater examination.[25] David Gamson likewise points out that contemporary policy discussions overwhelmingly view the local school district as an "obstacle" to reform, but his more nuanced and longer view of the school district raises important questions about the ways in which school districts can both serve and hamper systematic reform.[26] Each of these chapter shows how historical perspective challenges simple explanations and assumptions about the present and destabilizes what we "know."

Study of the past also helps to enrich our understanding of the present by showing how it came to be and illuminating assumptions, factors, structures, and constraints that shape the present moment. This has been the subject of much of the theorizing about the instrumental ways in which history can inform policy, particularly by nonhistorians. Historically minded social scientists, including sociologists and political scientists, have rediscovered how past structures, decisions, and cultures influence the present and so shape and constrain policy. In his monograph of the development of the administrative state in the early twentieth century, for example, political scientist Stephen Skrownek emphasized the ways in which its development was mediated by existing institutional arrangements, which created a "patchwork" of policies. Likewise sociologist Theda Skcopol has examined how Civil War pensions created a set of policies and experiences that shaped and constrained welfare policy in the twentieth century.[27] In addition, political scientist Paul Pierson has emphasized the analytical benefits of temporal context for policy which he argues is too often framed by "snapshot" views of policy issues and by functional interpretations of cause and effect. He argues that history offers a way to explore cause and effect in broader and more nuanced ways because it explores long-term change and continuity, long-term causes and effects, and unintended consequences, and traces them into all domains of social and cultural life. To that end, these and other scholars have elaborated persuasive rationales about "using" history, including arguments about the importance of examining institutional culture and persistence, "policy feedback loops," "path dependence," and long-term structural factors on politics. These scholars recognize, and articulate, sometimes more clearly than historians themselves, what historians have long known: that the present is situated in time, shaped by the past in innumerable ways, and that to really understand it, we must know how it came to be.

Thus history offers "lessons" for the present not by generalizing about the ways in which education always operates, elaborating "timeless" issues, or arguing that the past provides clear answers for present questions, but by challenging us to look critically at the present and locate it in time. It challenges us to ask better questions, look at a wider array of solutions, search for other types of factors or "causes," and unsettle what we "know" about the present. It prompts us to complicate our understanding of the present by uncovering some of the hidden ways in which the past shapes the present and showing how it came to be.

These "lessons" lie not only in the content of historical narratives—the things we learn about the past, the ways in which it sheds light on and provokes new question about the present—but also in the skills and habits of mind that define history "best practices." The "unnatural" cognitive skills of historical thinking, as Wineburg and others suggest, provide crucial ways to think beyond one's own experience, to grapple with diverse perspectives and experiences, and to formulate wise and empathetic thinking. Furthermore, many policymakers, policy analysts, and social scientists more generally could benefit from thinking more carefully about temporal and spatial contexts, change over time, and long-range cause and effect tracked through all domains of life. They would be wise to take seriously the historian's skepticism, thoroughgoing empiricism, and ecological way of thinking about the whole. In a pointed critique of social scientists' reductionist thinking, John Lewis Gaddis argues that more often than not reductionism misrepresents and distorts social reality in its isolation of complex social phenomenon into discrete parts. He argues that historians' ecological thinking is much closer to the natural sciences—and a more compelling way to view the world. While many social scientists might take issue with his characterization or his claim, Gaddis does point to very different orientations between historians and most social scientists in how they approach and understand social life. While social scientists and policymakers may not be ready to embrace entirely the approach of the historian, they should take seriously the ways it might offer new insights into policy beyond as simply a storehouse of "facts" or "lessons" to be applied and invite it into conversation with their own ways of understanding and explaining the world.

Because of both their knowledge and their unique ways of seeing the world, historians do have important roles to play in conversations about policy and in training and advising decision-makers and policy analysts. Their underrepresentation in these sites is regrettable, to say the least. However, historians have contributed to the problem by failing to grapple in sustained ways with the relationship of past and present and to explain what they have to offer to these other audiences. The final section this chapter looks at some of the problems that policy relevance and engagements with the present pose for historical scholarship and argues that in the end these concerns should not prevent us from engaging in conversations and reflection, but caution us to do it with care.

THE CHALLENGES OF POLICY-RELEVANT HISTORY

When recommending that historians do more to engage with policymakers and explain how history may raise important questions for the present, one must also acknowledge the significant dangers that this engagement poses for historical scholarship. As the last section explored, historians have legitimate reasons to be critical about the ways in which "lessons" of history are often framed and utilized. While I have suggested ways in which we might be more explicit about the difference between past and present and the precise kinds of "lessons" that history can teach, ultimately we cannot control how others perceive and utilize our work. No matter how careful we are, there is a real danger that our work will be misused in ways that run counter to our goals and intentions in producing it.

In addition, the pressure to produce policy relevant history, whether derived from internal or external pressures, can significantly limit the kinds of research questions that historians ask and the ways in which they approach their work. It can create pressures to ask much more limited questions and oversimplify the complexity of the past in order to produce useable nuggets. It also privileges contemporary history and increases the risk that we will miss important long-term developments when we limit our temporal scope. Furthermore, while most historians recognize that historical objectivity does not mean that historians must be free of all values or preferences, they do seek to maintain some distance and perspective on the past, an increasingly difficult practice as the subject gets closer to one's own time and more relevant to one's own experiences. Even when one does deep historical research with critical self-reflection on one's own subjec-tivity, policy-relevant history can potentially undermine the credibility of this research by making it appear to be simply another policy argument supported by cherry-picked "facts" about the past, rather than legitimate and careful historical research. Looking at the past does not itself constitute doing good history if one even appears to approach the past with conclusions already drawn or arguments already made.

Many historians fear that too much concern with engaging the present invites anachronisms by imposing the present on the past and therefore it interferes with historical imagination—imagining the past on its own terms. This raises what I think is the most fundamental and serious concern about the ways in which policy relevance can distort and limit historical scholarship if we are not careful: it can inhibit historical thinking and historical method and privilege the present rather than put it into the proper perspective. If we are driven always to explain the current policy moment, it can place limits on our explorations of sources and context, and therefore on our ability to make the kinds of connections and exercise the kind of historical imagination that will ultimately have the most value. The "best practice" of continually redefining one's questions in conversation with the evidence and the quest to understand the past on its own terms rather than those of the present rely on willingness to get lost in the past and to let the sources lead where they may, even if it is far away from where one first imagined. A drive for policy relevance can place significant limitations on one's willingness to follow the sources and consequently produce history that is more limited. Historians then run the risk of replicating the narrow categories of the present rather than offering an avenue for thinking about them critically.

This is not to say that contemporary concerns and policy issues should not stimulate us to ask questions or guide us to particular areas of inquiry. I suggest, however, that we must exercise extra caution in practicing our discipline well—in making sure that the questions that we pose initially are constantly redefined as we interact with sources and that we allow the sources to guide us into unexpected territory. We must be careful to guard against imposing arguments, conclusions, or preferences on our reading of the past. We must insist on taking the time to do the good, hard work of exploring the past on its own terms, even if it leads us away from where we started and its relevance becomes less clear-cut. The very best works of education and policy history do this well. Their authors are drawn to investigate contemporary issues such as curriculum, equity, urban education, and school reform, but they pose large, open-ended questions and then allow themselves to be drawn to the most important issues that emerge. Often it is only at the end, after the historian is far along in crafting the narrative, that the most important resonances with the present can be seen.

The "lessons" that the best histories draw for the present often emerge out of what they find in the past rather than from the starting point of their inquiries. In an interview about his Pulitzer Prize winning book *What Hath God Wrought*, Daniel Walker Howe explained that as he wrote and rewrote and rethought, "to a large extent, I *discovered* my interpretation as I went along" and it was "only late, when trying to explain my book to some fellow scholars working on the problems of developing countries today, did I realize how much the economic development of the early 19th century United States had in common with the problems of the 21st century Third World."[28] As Howe suggests, history can speak to the present in unexpected ways if we are willing to listen. We should, therefore, not limit our framing of questions and topics to what appears at first glance to be most relevant because ultimately we can never predict how and in what ways our work will bear fruit.

By the same token, in thinking about the "lessons" of history for the present, we should think not only in terms of immediate policy relevance but also about the broader contributions we can make to public debate and discussion of the issues. The ways in which we frame and conceptualize problems and understand the array of choices and solutions exert tremendous power before the "policy process" even begins. History has a valuable role to play, therefore, in helping us to challenge our assumptions, ask good questions, and think contextually. For example, the language of education "crisis" today is pervasive and seems to drive a wide array of reform efforts, many of which accept as "given" a narrative of school declension. Historians are well situated to challenge this notion of "crisis," and particularly to pinpoint what is new and not new about it; the ways in which we define the problem have tremendous implications for how we conceptualize and pursue solutions. As many have suggested, what is new is not that schools are systematically failing some groups of students—they have long done that—but that we now expect them to serve all at high levels. If we understand that we are asking schools to do something new, not that they have suddenly starting failing at something they once did well, we may well approach school reform differently.

Historians can raise other probing questions about the origins of this crisis, disentangle some of the assumptions that animate the discussion, and interrogate it empirically. In other words, historians are accustomed to thinking critically about assumptions and to asking big framing questions about causation and significance that would be useful in a multitude of discrete policy discussions framed by this issue. Consequently, historians' greatest contributions may lie in challenging the narrow conceptions, assumptions, and categories of the present and providing key questions and perspectives to move these conversations forward.

Public debate and discussion are particularly crucial today, when "policy" is not addressed only by isolated elites or decision-makers in the federal government. In education the array of "policymakers" is vast, encompassing not only elected officials and bureaucrats at local, state, and federal levels, but also entrepreneurs in other areas of the public and private sector.[29] Education policy emerges from experimentation in charter schools as well as in the legislative halls of state capitals and is influenced by an ongoing, public discussion. This fragmentation of the policy realm presents both challenges and opportunities for historians to inform policy and enhances the importance of participating more directly in public discussions and debates. The multiplicity of arenas and high demand for expertise may present greater opportunities for historians who are interested in activism to get involved in the process itself and add important dimensions to the debates. This fragmentation, however, while expanding opportunities for access, may also work to dilute impact.

A second path to influencing policy may be to try to gain a stronger foothold in institutions of policy research that increasingly dot the policy landscape. This will require a more deliberate effort to convince other social scientists of the value of historical thinking for policy and a willingness of these groups to listen.

For most historians, however, the primary path to influencing policy probably lies in continuing to produce high quality historical scholarship that provides perspective on our assumptions and on the issues of the present. Historians have contributions to make to the very large ways in which we frame and conceptualize issues and understand the present, and these contributions can extend across the entire policy agenda.

Historians have a responsibility to engage in public debate and discussion and to disseminate our academic work to a broader public that we have often neglected. Our habits of asking big questions, of thinking ecologically, and of locating the present in time have much to offer these discussions and serve as a point of contrast to much education and policy research which is more focused in scope and which usually operates within assumptions of the present. Furthermore our work itself often has more relevance for understanding specific issues and discussions than we articulate. Historians should do more to engage in efforts like those of the National History Center to digest, mediate, and disseminate academic work as well as to place a higher value than we have on producing work aimed at the public, including monographs, newspaper, and periodical articles. We also need to encourage and reward this work within the profession and within universities.

Many of us became historians because we thought history teaches us important things about our world. We should not abdicate our responsibility to engage and articulate those things it teaches, just as we should not sacrifice the integrity of our work in the interests of claiming relevance. We should work harder to articulate the contributions that our work and that history itself offer to public policy and public debate rather than leave this to social scientists. We must also insist on the freedom to explore the past as different, to use it to rethink and challenge the narrow categories of the present. Historians have contributions to make that stem from the ways we see the world and the work that we do in trying to understand it by how it has developed over time. We need to continue to strive to articulate these contributions and engage our work with the world while protecting the integrity of our scholarship by carefully maintaining what makes it "history" in the first place. Of course, the impact that our efforts will have will be determined in large measure by the willingness of policymakers, analysts, and social scientists to take seriously the contributions that history can make and by their ability to be open to new ways of thinking about and seeing the world.

NOTES

I owe tremendous thanks to Luther Spoehr and Lisa Andersen for stimulating conversation on the discipline of history and thoughtful feedback and suggestions on this essay.

1. Richard E. Neustadt and Ernest R. May, *Thinking in Time: The Uses of History for Decision-Makers* (New York: Free Press, 1986), 242.
2. For an overview of these developments and historians' sense of marginalization from policy, see Julian E. Zelizer, "Clio's Lost Tribe: Public Policy History Since 1978," *Journal of Policy History* 12, no. 3 (2000): 369–394; Hugh Davis Graham, "The Stunted Career of Policy History: A Critique and an Agenda" *The Public Historian* 15 (Spring 1993): 15–37; Maris A. Vinovskis, *History and Educational Policymaking* (New Haven: Yale University Press, 1999).
3. There is tremendous disagreement, philosophically and institutionally, about whether history should be classified as part of the social sciences, the humanities, both, or neither. Historians' methodology, however, is clearly very different than most social science disciplines and therefore for the purposes of this chapter, I am distinguishing between historians and social scientists rather than grouping them together.
4. For a thoughtful discussion of the issues of practicing history in a professional school, see "Interchange: History in the Professional Schools," *Journal of American History* 92 (Sept. 2005): 553–576.
5. Robert Kelley, "Public History: Its Origins, Nature, and Prospects," *The Public Historian* 1 (Fall 1978): 16–28.
6. National History Center webpage: http://nationalhistorycenter.org. Accessed 6/14/2008.
7. If my own experience is any indication, in the past year I have participated in four conferences on this subject: "Reforming History Education: New Research on Teaching and Learning" by National History Center for policymakers (June 2007); "Clio at the Table: A Conference on the Uses of History to Inform and Improve Education Policy," Brown University (June 2007); "Politics, Activism, and the History of America's Public Schools," University of Pennsylvania (April 2008); Policy History Conference, St. Louis (May 2008).
8. Julian E. Zelizer, "Introduction: New Directions in Policy History," *The Journal of Policy History* 17, no. 1 (2005): 1–11. American Political Development, historical sociologists, new institutionalists among those groups of social scientists in sociology and political science that have begun to embrace history in new ways.
9. Jack Doughtery, "Conflicting Questions: Why Historians and Policymakers Miscommunicate on Urban Education," this volume.
10. While there has been much high-level discussion of the philosophy and practice of history in light of postmodern theories, discussions of methods, particularly in undergraduate and graduate courses, still often reach back to a few "classic" texts: R.G. Collingwood, *The Idea of History* (New York: Galaxy book, 1956); Edward Hallett Carr, *What Is History?* (New York: Alfred A. Knopf, 1962); Marc Bloch, *The Historian's Craft: Reflections on the Nature and Uses of History and the Techniques and Methods of Those Who Write it* (New York: Vintage Books, 1953). Acknowledging this point, a few recent works have tried to provide an updated overview of historical methods, including Richard J. Evans, *In Defense of History* (New York: W.W. Norton, 1997); John Lewis Gaddis, *The Landscape of History: How Historians Map the Past* (New York: Oxford University Press, 2002).
11. William H. McNeill quoted in Gaddis, *The Landscape of History,* 48.
12. Thomas Haskall makes this point forcefully, maintaining that historians seek objectivity, not neutrality, and that this is a legitimate pursuit in response to Peter Novick's conclusions that the entire pursuit of "objectivity" in history is in crisis. Haskall points out that Novick's definition

of objectivity is grounded in a pursuit of value-free science that has been out of fashion for decades and that Novick himself demonstrates the kind of objectivity to which historians should aspire. Thomas L. Haskall, *Objectivity Is not Neutrality: Explanatory Schemes in History* (Baltimore: Johns Hopkins Press, 1998); Peter Novick, *That Noble Dream: The "Objectivity Question" and the American Historical Profession* (New York: Cambridge University Press, 1988).

13. Evans, *In Defense of History*, 220. Appleby, Hunt, and Jacob reach a similar conclusion in their study of the postmodern challenge to history, Joyce Appleby, Lynn Hunt, and Margaret Jacob, *Telling the Truth About History* (New York: Norton, 1994).

14. Peter N. Stearns, "History and Public Policy" in *Social Science and Public Policy: The Roles of Academic Disciplines in Policy Analysis* (Port Washington, NY: Associated Faculty Press, 1984).

15. Otis L. Graham Jr., "The Uses and Misuses of History: Roles in Policymaking," *The Public Historian* 5 (Spring 1983): 5–19.

16. Sam Wineburg, *Historical Thinking and Other Unnatural Acts: Charting the Future of Teaching the Past* (Philadelphia: Temple University Press, 2001).

17. Gaddis, *The Landscape of History*, 54–56.

18. Gordon S. Wood, *The Purpose of the Past: Reflections on the Uses of History* (New York: Penguin Press, 2008), 308. He borrows the warning to historians to exert "critical control" from Bernard Bailyn.

19. Elizabeth Rose, "Learning from Head Start: Preschool Advocates and the Lessons of History," this volume.

20. Zelizer analyzes some of these and elaborates five "categories" of instrumental arguments bout the use of policy for history made by articles in the *Journal of Policy History*. Zelizer, "Clio's Lost Tribe."

21. Anne-Lise Halvorsen and Jeffrey E. Mirel, "Educating Citizens: Social Problems Meet Progressive Education in Detroit, 1930–1952, this volume.

22. William J. Reese, "When Wisdom Was Better Than Rubies: The Public Schools of Washington D.C. in the Nineteenth Century," this volume.

23. Adam R. Nelson, "Equity and Special Education: Some Historical Lessons from Boston," this volume.

24. Rose, "Learning From Head Start".

25. John L. Rury, "Attainment amidst Adversity: Black High School Students in the Metropolitan North, 1940–1980," this volume.

26. David Gamson, "Democracy Undone: Reforming and Reinventing the American School District, 1945–2005," this volume.

27. Stephen Skowronek, *Building the New American State: The Expansion of National Administrative Capacities, 1877–1920* (New York: Cambridge University Press, 1982); Theda Skocpol, *Protecting Soldiers and Mothers: The Political Origins of Social Policy in the United States* (Cambridge: Belknap Press, 1992); Theda Skcopl, "Why I am an Historical Institutionalist" *Polity* 28 (Autumn 1995): 103–106; Paul Pierson, *Politics in Time: History, Institutions, and Social Analysis* (Princeton: Princeton University Press, 2004); Paul Pierson, "The Study of Policy Development" *Journal of Policy History* 17, no. 1. (2005): 34–51.

28. "An Interview with Daniel Walker Howe" in *Historically Speaking: The Bulletin of the Historical Society*, IX, No. 4 (March/April 2008): 30.

29. Lisa Anderson, *Pursuing Truth, Exercising Power: Social Science and Public Policy in the Twenty-First Century* (New York: Columbia University Press, 2003). Anderson argues that traditional policy domains have been radically transformed in the twenty-first century as international and nongovernmental sites of policy rival and even supersede states.

CHAPTER FOURTEEN

Clio AT THE Table

Historical Perspectives AND Policymaking IN THE Field OF Education

CARL F. KAESTLE

What are the connections between historical analysis and the consideration of policy in the field of education? My interest in the scholarship relevant to that question began with the Advanced Studies Fellowship Program at Brown, which culminated in a book of essays that, among other things, related historical studies to policy questions. For this volume, I have addressed the question more directly.

CLIO, THE MUSE OF HISTORY

Clio, the muse of history, was one of nine daughters of Zeus and Mnemosyne, the goddess of memory. Eventually Greek tradition assigned an area of arts and letters to each. Clio's province was history. The Roman poet Valerius Flaccus expressed her role thus: "Do thou, Clio, now unfold the causes that drove the heroes to affrays unspeakable, since to thee, O Muse, has been vouchsafed the power to know the hearts of the gods and the ways by which things come to be."[1]

There is a long tradition of believing that Clio's knowledge is useful in thinking about the future. Thucydides called history "philosophy learned from examples."[2] Santayana warned, "Those who cannot remember the past are condemned to repeat it." Shakespeare said "What's past is prologue." Winston Churchill opined "The further backward you look, the further forward you can see."[3]

But aphorisms about the value of history don't give us an answer; they present us with a problem. How do we learn from the past? And which competing version of the past should I consult? What claims might we make for the "uses" of history? In this chapter I enumerate some specific ways we can think about time as a way to assess such claims. My first proposal is that historians are the principal custodians of longitudinal analysis. Most of the social sciences are devoted to vertical analysis, using cross-sections—what some call "snapshots"—or short-term longitudinal data that can suggest causality but don't capture historical change. Examples would include causal pathways from stimuli to responses, or studies of various educational interventions and their observable consequences. These studies can inform us about how social structures, relationships, or reforms work at a given time. History's horizontal analysis, in contrast, is devoted to examining precedents, seeking origins, charting the development of traditions, and revealing their legacies. Such survivals are all over the landscape of the present, sometimes buried, sometimes blaring at us. An account of their origins, their transformations, and their embedded commitments can be useful in understanding why people support certain ways of doing things and resist other actions, how they understand their motives, social realities, and the nature of the institutions around them.

THE ORIGINS AND EVOLUTION OF IDEAS IN
EDUCATION POLICY

My first example deals with the history of curriculum ideas. In a startling analysis, David Gamson discovered that the early twentieth-century education reformers justified the shift to different curricula for different high school students as an expansion of equal educational opportunity. Because such tracking proved to be pervasively influenced by students' race, gender, and social class, many educators have come to see it as highly undemocratic, especially since educators of the time frequently displayed their biases by characterizing lower-track students by race or class. Gamson does not argue that the proponents of differentiated curricula were *right* in their judgments, but it seems from his analysis that there is no reason to assume that they were hypocritical in their stated belief that the policy aimed at expanding equal opportunity. He further argues that this legacy was reinforced 40 years later with the National Defense Education Act, in its quest for the identification of talent and grouping by academic ability. Gamson did not extend his arguments to the present, but we may, I think, wonder whether present-day advocates of ability grouping are drawing on this submerged conviction that different programs for different children is a form of equal opportunity.

Is it not an idea with staying power? In education for children with disabilities and for English language learners, equality is defined as providing a different, appropriate curriculum for children with different needs. Could the same rationale be considered a democratic practice for other children, in the so-called regular classrooms, if the testing were less biased and family status was kept out of it?

When I introduced students in teacher education programs at the University of Wisconsin to Theodore Sizer's work, I suggested that he was staking out the philosophical high ground on curriculum, that there should be only one curriculum for all children, and that it should be thoroughly academic. Some of the students found this argument bizarre. One student said something like this: "Kids differ in their abilities and needs. To teach all students the same material is not just inefficient, it's unfair."[4] This defense of curriculum differentiation appears to be a popular-level survival of the position on equal opportunity that Gamson is analyzing historically. Careful historical work like David's can bring different perspectives and submerged meanings to the policy table.

SIMPLE OR HEURISTIC ANALOGIES

The idea of longitudinal analysis may be broken down into different forms of temporal thinking relevant to policy analysis. We can make a distinction, for example, between comparing the present policy issue with similar previous situations, and, on the other hand, developing a "policy history," that is, a history of the policy in question. The comparative approach, arguing from analogies, can be further broken down into the simple or heuristic analogy—which compares the current situation with a single precedent, seeking clues for effective action—and the systematic comparisons of several cases, with a view toward discovering generalizations about the policy process.

To dramatize the simple analogy I turn to a well-known book of case studies about historical thinking in policy debates, *Thinking in Time*, by historian Ernest May and political scientist Richard Neustadt. It emerged from a course they offered at Harvard's John F. Kennedy School of Government in the 1970s. Their first chapter is about the Cuban Missile Crisis of 1962. This episode is exciting partly because a misstep could have been catastrophic and partly because it was a profound and secret decision that was minutely documented. May and Neustadt applaud the way the group involved in the decision discussed historical input, both the simple analogy and the "policy history" of the problem at hand. During the first day's discussions, Kennedy articulated three options: bomb the missiles, bomb the missiles and all the aircraft on the ground, or invade the island. By the end of the day the President said rashly, "We're certainly going to do Number

One," meaning, "We're at least going to bomb the missiles." In the next few days, various analogies were raised for consideration. Although analogies are often used in superficial, unhistorical ways in policy debates, the White House group started to give analogies more scrutiny. What were the similarities and the differences? What were the proper policy implications of the comparison? Was there perhaps more than one meaning?

The similarity to the Japanese attack on Pearl Harbor was raised. The obvious analogy would be that a far-away enemy had created a threat to our mainland that could not be ignored. But by Day Two, Robert Kennedy started to use the analogy in a negative way. "It would be a Pearl Harbor in reverse and would blacken the name of the United States." Here Robert Kennedy asserts a similarity between the potential U.S. bombing of Cuba and Japan's attack on Pearl Harbor, rather than comparing the Japanese and the Soviets as hostile threats. Former Secretary of State Dean Acheson then subjected the analogy to on even more rigorous comparison, concluding that the entire comparison was "thoroughly false."[5] May and Neustadt observed that in this debate "analogies were invoked sparingly and, when invoked, were subjected to scrutiny."

While few policy schools feature training in historical reasoning, policymakers commonly use analogies in a casual, seat-of-the-pants way. Everyone who knows about federal education policy in the 1970s can imagine a congressional policy staffer saying, "Get Jack Jennings in here; he's been through six of these reauthorizations – he'll know what works and what doesn't."[6]

Aside from examining analogies carefully, the Kennedy group also emphasized the development of an adequate policy history. From the start, the young President had included several seasoned diplomats in the crisis group. He also added three senior people from the State Department to provide more background knowledge on the Soviet Union and on Cuba. Ultimately the President decided to implement a naval blockade and negotiate for the withdrawal of the missiles, which succeeded. This option was not among those listed by President Kennedy at the end of the first day's discussion. We cannot measure just how much this successful outcome depended upon wise men reasoning from history, or upon some calculus in the mind of Nikita Khrushchev, or other factors. But the main point of May and Neustadt rings true: the careful use of historical reasoning slowed the process down, and in this case, that was a good thing.

MULTIPLE ANALOGIES: SYSTEMATIC COMPARATIVE ANALYSIS

The Cuban Missile example demonstrates the care that is needed in interpreting a single, analogous precedent. In the field of comparative history, however, multiple cases are analyzed with the aim of developing patterns, predictors, enabling conditions, consequences of dissimilar sequences, and other generalizations. This is hugely ambitious and perilous work, bringing history into alignment with the social sciences. An example of this more elaborate mode is Barrington Moore's study of "the role of the bourgeoisie in transitions to democracy and dictatorship." On the basis of his comparative historical work, Moore argued that the emergence of democracy generally depended upon a weakened landed aristocracy, a turn toward commercial agriculture, and a bourgeois rejection of a coalition with aristocrats against peasants and workers.[7]

Some historians eschew these aspirations to generalization altogether, insisting that the job of the historian is to examine the particular and to recognize each situation as unique. The range of ambitions among historians who *do* pursue such generalizations runs from the merely Olympian to the stratospheric, from comparative historians such as Theda Skocpol, Immanuel Wallerstein, Charles Tilly, and Ira Katznelson, who wish to make mid-level generalizations about political processes, to Karl Marx, who proposed master hypotheses explaining human nature and the causes of social change. I shall not pretend to critique or contribute to that literature; except to note in passing that if one wishes to connect history to policy, one must have an answer to the question "Can historians make generalizations?"

PATH DEPENDENCE

The complexity of temporal analysis can be suggested by defining and illustrating just two types, among many: path dependence and sequence. "Path dependence" is a jargon phrase. When you first hear it defined, you may deem it either dubious or self-evident.[8] The idea is this: once a policy is established, it's more likely that people will continue to follow that policy than to switch to another. This, of course, is not always true; if it were, we would not have discovered the usefulness of fire. The unpredictability of path dependence makes the concept useful and quite complex. It creates these questions: What are the major sources of support for a given policy? How might reformers alter those factors? Under what circumstances and with what timing are major policy innovations likely to occur? How do windows of opportunity open? How does resistance wane? Path dependence has several causes, often called "positive feedback." Once established, policies develop constituencies, beneficiaries, bureaucracies, public expectations, well-disseminated rationales, and ideological underpinnings. Paul Pierson, the concept's most articulate proponent, enunciates some of the complexities. For example, some causal processes are incremental and gradual; others depend on threshold effects and critical mass. Sometimes decisions gain strength because lost alternatives drop off the list of future options."[9]

A nice example of path dependence is found in Elizabeth Rose's analysis of pre-K education and daycare. After President Richard Nixon vetoed a federal bill for child care in the 1970s, making a strong ideological argument against state intervention in the family, a system of private and independent nonprofit providers grew up, and they became strong political advocates for that arrangement. As Rose concludes, "Despite efforts to reframe the issue, the legacy of past decisions shapes current options."[10]

At a meeting of a task force on federal financial aid policies three policy experts each commented on the success or failure of a major innovation about which she or he had intimate knowledge: the Bill Clinton welfare bill (a success), the Hillary Clinton health bill (a failure), and the George W. Bush privatization of Social Security (a failure). The panel framed the question thus: What does it take to get past resistance on major issues when there is a deep ideological divide splitting the electorate? They argued, first, that it helps if not only the public but the professionals administering the present policy think it has seriously broken down. But that alone won't do it. Second, if the population is ideologically fractured on issues relevant to your reform, you have to have a narrative in which people from both sides can hear their story. In the case of the successful Clinton welfare bill, that story was about the value of work. This argument is about more than mere rhetoric. It requires a measure of common ideological ground. These conditions did not exist on the health system or on privatizing Social Security. The metaphor about people "hearing their story in your narrative" is apt; for the purposes of this chapter, it is also important to note that without using the terms, these policy analysts were talking about path dependence and the preconditions for change.[11]

SEQUENCE

The next temporal concept is sequence. Sometimes the *order* of events makes a difference. A fine example from the world of education policy is found in the work of Kathryn McDermott. Massachusetts and Connecticut are similar in politics, education governance, demography, and economy. McDermott watched as these two states reacted in the 1990s to the national movement for accountability of school systems. Since this was not a federal initiative, state variation was a natural feature. Massachusetts passed tough, statewide accountability measures and Connecticut did not. One of the crucial factors was the sequence of events.

In Massachusetts, Proposition 2 ½ had already restricted local control somewhat by setting a maximum tax level for education, providing a constraint on local control that was actually popular with voters. In 1989 a case called *McDuffy* was brought by 20 towns, calling for more equalization of funds across districts. It was settled in 1993 in favor of the plaintiffs, but the judge saw that the legislature was about to begin deliberation on an education reform bill, so he simply left the details to the legislature. This set an expectation that the 1993 Massachusetts Education Reform Act (MERA) would necessarily deal with statewide fiscal equity issues. With the focus on fiscal questions, concerns about state power were muted. With business and bipartisan political support, the MERA bill passed. The districts essentially accepted strong accountability measures in return for more money, and more equitable distribution of money. The reform was state-wide and comprehensive, and it greatly strengthened the state's role in insuring district accountability in Massachusetts.

In Connecticut, the sequence of issues and solutions played out very differently. In 1979, a case called *Horton v. Meskill* was settled, requiring an overhaul of the state's equalization process across richer and poorer districts. This was done. In 1986, another bill provided state money for districts to enhance teachers' salaries to raise quality. Thus the statewide finance-equity issues were more-or-less disposed of by the time the 1990s accountability movement became a force on the national scene. And when it did, voters in Connecticut were more focused than their Massachusetts neighbors on the implications of state power to achieve accountability. In 1990 they rejected a proposal for a statewide high school exit exam, and in 1994 a more general education reform bill foundered on the shoals of anxieties about augmented state power, particularly concerning the proposed initiation of "Outcomes Based Education," which greatly disturbed suburban Christian conservatives. Thereafter the emphasis on education reform in Connecticut migrated toward big city systems, in particular Hartford, where race, poverty, and academic achievement were big issues. In 1996, a decision in the *Sheff v. O'Neill* case supported plaintiffs against the failing city school district, and the legislature in 1997 approved a state takeover of the Hartford system. Connecticut held the line against the expansion of state power over other districts as an accountability tool. Little wonder that down the line, when George W. Bush's education team brought us No Child Left Behind, Massachusetts was a poster-state for compliance, and Connecticut sued the federal government for foisting an unfunded mandate upon the helpless states.

TEXT AND CONTEXT: CONSTITUENT AND CONTIGUOUS MEANINGS

It is often said that historians provide "context" in discussions of policy, which may seem tiresome or vague to a policy analyst. Thus it may be instructive to consider briefly historians' serious analytical interest in how much emphasis we should give to changing contexts versus timeless principles. In a recent book called *Darwin Loves You*, George Levine notes that Darwin's theories are "highly usable in very different ways, responsive to the newer contexts." "This contingency of ideas," Levine writes, "means that old ideas in new contexts will take on ideologically different implications."[12] So in Malthus's hands Darwin is rung in to argue for laissez faire social policy, while in Kropotkin's hands, Darwin is a scientific brief for communitarian anarchism. Levine argues that "the *political* and *ideological* implications of Darwin's ideas are not constitutive but contingent"; that is, not inherent and unalterable from the text but dependent upon later interpreters' intentions and settings. Nor is it a case of charlatans misinterpreting Darwin. It is rather the case of "how flexible Darwin's theory is in cultural interpretation."[13] Levine's point is that all knowledge, including Darwin's, is contingent to a great degree, and that it will be freed up to find new interpreters in new contexts. Nonetheless, he says, "My major responsibility was to honor what Darwin actually wrote." "Any interpretation of Darwin has such a responsibility to Darwin's own words, and to the evidence one can find in his life and work." And Levine actually thinks there are some things that are fundamental and incontrovertible—that is, constitutive—about the text. Darwin "drives toward an explanation of all things, physical and spiritual, by means of natural law," and is thus "radically secular."[14] Whether Levine is absolutely correct on this point or not, we could wish that all policymakers who encounter orators hearkening to authoritative texts would have such a sophisticated analyst on hand when considering the original and derived meanings.

We cannot escape contingency, then, but a good historian can help us manage it, be self-conscious of it, sort out what is more directly and incontrovertibly evident from a study of the text, and then proceed to another level of contextual analysis, seeing how the text comes to be interpreted in different ways in different times for different purposes. Historians, then, at their best, take text and context as equally important. By studying both and reflecting on the contingencies that brought us the ideas in a particular framework, we are better equipped to think about our context.

Contingency does not apply only to text. One can also analyze how various salient events, like Selma, Sputnik, or the Civil War have been interpreted in different contexts. George Levine, then, brings us face to face with one of the most difficult challenges to "using" history to think about policies: important historical events or texts rarely have only one authoritative interpretation. Indeed, ironically, one of the most valuable contributions historians can make to the uses of history in policy analysis is to undermine clichés about listening to history and to urge careful examination of popular arguments from history.

There is often a conflict between professional historical inquiry, which is inherently and continually revisionist, and popular history, which attempts to locate and disseminate timeless, inspiring tales. And the two meet where members of the history profession oversee popular history, often as curators, archivists, or public historians. When John D. Rockefeller supported the creation of colonial Williamsburg in the 1930s, he promulgated the slogan, "That the future may learn from the past." But until the 1980s, there were no African Americans represented at colonial Williamsburg, leading critics to label it "mawkish" and "unreal," "hiding American history's darker aspects."[15] Under the influence of social historians as well as the Civil Rights movement, the museum town moved in the 1970s in a more multiracial direction.

The study of "historical memory" has received considerable attention from professional historians in recent years. David Blight, for example, published five years ago a moving analysis of the how the memory of the Civil War changed for whites in the late nineteenth century. In a quest for sectional reconciliation, historians, journalists, and politicians emphasized that the war was a sectional disagreement, conducted gallantly on both sides by honorable white soldiers. Black Americans faded from view. In one of Blight's most compelling visual illustrations, a Union and a Confederate veteran, arm-in-arm, watch the new gallants storming San Juan in the Spanish American War.[16]

From these examples, we may extract some more general points. Historical events have multiple interpretations; some fit the evidence better than others, so historians can help sort out the bad ones, still leaving plausible, contrasting contenders on many issues. Second, part of the historian's task is to distinguish between text and context. But the contexts can stretch all the way from the settings in which the original text or event took place, all the way down to our present day.

In a final, extended example, we return directly to the connection between historical studies and a current policy debates in education. A lingering debate exists about whether the public, legislators, or the courts could be persuaded to remedy the vast inequities across state lines in per pupil expenditures on education. Could it be done through a constitutional amendment, or a new Supreme Court case that might reverse *San Antonio Independent School District* v. *Rodriguez*, in which the court in 1973 rejected the applicability of the Fourteenth Amendment's equal protection clause to this issue, or should it be approached through a mobilization of the public and the Congress to do what is right, to provide equal educational opportunity? In an important historical article in the *Yale Law Journal*, Goodwin Liu wrote about the traditions upon which we might draw.[17] On the issue of interstate disparities in education, there is a forgotten minority position that displayed considerable political and philosophical strength in the 1870s and 1880s, when Congress proposed various schemes for a radical expansion of federal activity in education, toward guaranteeing equal educational opportunity in the states. One central justification was the Citizenship Clause of the Fourteenth Amendment, which has not been part of recent debates about the federal responsibility in education. The importance of the Citizenship Clause was emphasized by Justice John Harlan, in his ringing dissent against the revocation of the Civil Rights Act of 1875. Harlan argued that the first clause of the Fourteenth Amendment, stating that "All persons born or naturalized in the United States ... are citizens of the United States," combined with the enforcement clause that directs congress to make all laws necessary to implement the amendment, creates a "distinctly affirmative" duty for congress to create equal educational opportunity sufficient for citizenship. This position, and the bills proposed to implement it, came within a whisker of passage at several points in those two decades. Liu proposes that the citizenship clause be resurrected in service of this cause, to renew with urgency a mandate for Congressional intervention on this issue.

Speaking as a friend of the author and a person equally enthusiastic about making some headway on these inequities, I nonetheless invoked the importance of context.[18] My argument was simple. As inspiring as Harlan's dissent was (and still is), and as important as the failed congressional policy efforts were, we have to remember that they failed, and from thence we need to inquire about why. Federalism, since the birth of the republic, has had two alter egos, one wary of federal intervention, devoted to local and state control, and the other, people who look to the federal government for a strong central authority, especially with regard to minority and individual rights. The drift in education governance may seem to go gradually toward centralization of authority in U.S. history, but the local-state tradition has remarkable staying power.

The importance and the power of Liu's position is as follows: the texts and acts he has excavated are not a "lost cause"; they are simply a cause that lost. It is a powerful tradition, both in its rhetorical and intellectual content, and in the fact that it several times came close to enactment. But the historian's reminder about context is also relevant and potentially useful to the cause, not just in understanding those periodic defeats in their own day, but also in understanding the present context, which features a still-powerful anti-central ideology. If we are to mobilize public and congressional opinion around this cause, which involves a radical and controversial expansion of federal involvement in education finance, we shall have to think about the metaphor cited above and develop a narrative in which people on both sides of the ideological divide can "see their story." Perhaps that common story would be about giving every American child the opportunity that some have, to go to their local school and find a good education, good enough to prepare them as competent citizens in a complicated republic and give them a chance at advancement in a complicated global economy. In framing that argument, both text and context would be mutually useful.

CONCLUSION

My diverse examples suggest that historians' value in policy discussions is not like the value of an econometrician in predicting whether a specific intervention will work or not, but rather in understanding policy processes, planning large strategies, and mobilizing support. The past lives with us in the present and shapes our ideas and our actions. History is often invoked in policy debates, whether Clio is there to protect the art or not. Good historians can introduce an element of doubt about overly simple analogies and unexamined historical allusions; they can slow the analysis down by raising a set of questions about comparisons, contingency, and sequence, about the conditions under which path dependency can be overcome and the conditions under which previous policy endeavors have garnered support across ideological lines.

But do you really want a skeptical, slow complexifier at the table when you're trying to sort through important policy dilemmas? Well, yes, you do. Historians tend to move slowly, but not always. Historians are generally wary of fads; at their best they can be life-saving contrarians. Historians are good generalists; they often poach off of other disciplines, so they sometimes understand a big picture with some nuance. Also, if you don't have a historian involved in the policy debate, others will make historical arguments, often without the nuance, the self-consciousness, and the useful skepticism of the trained historian. And finally, I might add, historians are generally charming. This is why Clio deserves a place at the table.

NOTES

1. Valerium Flaccus, *Argonautica* translated J. H. Mozley (Cambridge, MA: Harvard University Press, 1934), Book 3, line 15.
2. Bartlett's, 104: 17.
3. George Santayana, *The Life of Reason* (Amherst, NY: Prometheus Books, 1998, p. 82); William Shakespeare, *The Tempest*, Act II, Scene I, line 253; the Churchill quotation is usually attributed to Churchill, but the source is unknown.
4. See Theodore Sizer, *Horace's Compromise: The Dilemma of the American High School* (Boston: Houghton-Mifflin, 1984).
5. Ernest May and Richard Neustadt, *Thinking in Time: The Uses of History for Decision-Makers* (New York: The Free Press, 1986), pp. 6–7.

6. Jack Jennings was a seventeen-year veteran counsel to the House Committee on Education and Labor. Being an astute observer, he would also know how the context had changed, making some of the old lore irrelevant.

7. Barrington Moore, Jr., *Social Origins of Dictatorship and Democracy: Lord and Peasant in the Making of the Modern World* (Boston: Beacon Press, 1966), pp. 430–431. For an elegant, recent assessment of this sub-field, see Theda Skocpol, "Doubly Engaged Social Science: The Promise of Comparative Historical Analysis," in James Mahoney and Dietrich Reuschemeyer *Comparative Historical Analysis in the Social Sciences* (Cambridge: Cambridge University Press, 2003) pp. 407–425.

8. Paul Pierson declares that "path dependence has become a faddish term, often lacking a clear meaning." Pierson, *Politics in Time: History, Institutions, and Social Analysis* (Princeton, NJ: Princeton University Pres, 2004), 10.

9. Pierson, *Politics in Time*, pp. 13–22.

10. Elizabeth Rose, "Where Does Preschool Belong: Preschool Policy and Public Education, 1965–Present," in Carl F. Kaestle and Alyssa E. Lodewick, eds., *To Educate a Nation: Federal and National Strategies of School Reform* (Lawrence, KS: University Press of Kansas, 2007), p. 300.

11. Meeting of the Task Force on Rethinking Student Aid, The College Board, Washington, D C., August 10, 2006. The experts were Rebecca Blank, Dean (Policy School) and Professor of Public Policy and Economics, University of Michigan; Len Nichols, Director of Health Policy, New America Foundation; and Kenneth Apfel, Professor of Public Policy, University of Maryland.

12. George Levine, *Darwin Loves You: Natural Selection and the Re-enchantment of the World* (Princeton, NJ: Princeton University Press, 2006), p. x.

13. Ibid., p. xi.

14. Ibid., p. 21.

15. Edward Rothstein, "An Upgrade for Ye Olde History Park," *New York Times,* Friday, April 6, 2007, Weekend Arts Section E, p. 31.

16. David Blight, *Race and Reunion: The Civil War in American Memory* (Cambridge, MA: Harvard University Press, 2001), p. XX.

17. Goodwin Liu, "Education, Equality, and National Citizenship," *Yale Law Journal* 116:2 (November, 2006): 330–411.

18. Carl F. Kaestle, "Equal Educational Opportunity and the Federal Government: A Response to Goodwin Liu," *Yale Law Journal Pocket Part* 115 (2006): 152—156 at http://thepocketpart.org/w006/11/21/kaestle.html.

About THE Authors

Elizabeth DeBray-Pelot is interim director of the Education Policy and Evaluation Center at the College of Education at the University of Georgia. Her research interests include educational politics and policy and policy implementation. She is the author of *Politics, Ideology, and Education: Federal Policy during the Clinton and Bush Administrations*. She received her EdD from Harvard University.

Jack A. Dougherty is an associate professor and director of the educational studies program at Trinity College. His teaching and research focuses on the connections between educational history, policy, and practice. With assistance from a National Academy of Education/Spencer Foundation fellowship, Dougherty and his upper-level students have launched the Cities, Suburbs, and Schools research project, which investigates how private real estate markets and public school politics came together to shape metropolitan Hartford during the twentieth century. He received his PhD from the University of Wisconsin-Madison.

David Gamson is an associate professor of education at Pennsylvania State University and the professor-in-charge of the department of educational theory and policy. His areas of expertise include the history of education and education reform, past and present. He received his PhD from Stanford University.

Margaret E. Goertz is a professor of education policy in the Graduate School of Education at the University of Pennsylvania and a codirector of the Consortium for Policy Research in Education, where she specializes in the study of state and federal education finance and governance policy. Dr. Goertz has conducted extensive research on state education reform policies, state teacher policies, and state and federal programs for special-needs students. Her current research activities look at the impact of standards-based reform in elementary schools and high schools, the implementation of the No Child Left Behind Act of 2001, and the interface between NCLB and state accountability policies. She also studies how school districts and schools allocate resources in support of standards-based reform. She received her PhD from the Maxwell School at Syracuse University.

Anne-Lise Halvorsen is an assistant professor of teacher education at Michigan State University, specializing in social studies education. Her scholarship includes research on the history of education, social studies on the elementary level, curriculum policy and early childhood education. Currently, she is doing work on the history of elementary social studies and teacher knowledge and preparation in the social studies. She received her PhD from the University of Michigan.

Carl F. Kaestle is professor emeritus of education, history, and public policy at Brown University. His research falls in two large areas: the history of the federal role in elementary and secondary education since 1950, and the history of books and readers in the United States from 1880 to 1950. He received his PhD from Harvard University in 1971.

Kathryn A. McDermott is an associate professor of education policy and leadership at the University of Massachusetts, Amherst. Her professional interests include state and federal education policy, educational equity, and policy implementation. She received her PhD from Yale University.

Jeffrey E. Mirel is the David L. Angus Collegiate Chair in Education at the University of Michigan School of Education, and a Professor of History at the U-M College of Literature, Science and the Arts. His major areas of interest are the history and politics of urban education and the history of school reform, particularly high school curriculum reform. He is the author of the award-winning *The Rise and Fall of an Urban School System: Detroit 1907–81*, which draws on Detroit's experience to offer a new interpretation of urban educational decline in the twentieth century. He is also co-author with David Angus of *The Failed Promise of the American High School, 1890–1995*. He received his PhD from the University of Michigan.

Adam R. Nelson is an associate professor of educational policy studies and history at the University of Wisconsin-Madison. His research has included projects on the history of higher education, the history of radical and experimental education, the history of federal educational policy (including bilingual education, special education, compensatory education, school funding, and desegregation), and the history of study abroad. He is currently working on a history of nationalism and internationalism in the American research university. He received his PhD from Brown University.

William J. Reese is the Carl Kaestle WARF Professor of Educational Policy Studies and History at the University of Wisconsin-Madison. His academic areas of interest are the history of American and European education; the history of childhood and adolescence; historiography; and social reform movements in the twentieth century. His is the former president of the History of Education Society and the former editor of History of Education Quarterly, and the editor, with John L. Rury, of *Rethinking the History of American Education: Essays on the Post-Revisionist Era and Beyond*. He received his PhD from the University of Wisconsin-Madison.

Elizabeth Rose is project director for History Is Central at Central Connecticut State University, a collaborative project that aims to increase student learning in U.S. history. A historian of women, families, and social policy, Rose is the author of *A Mother's Job: The History of Day Care*, which, in dissertation form, was awarded the Allan Nevins Prize from the Society of American Historians. She is completing a book on the evolution of preschool policy, entitled The Promise of Preschool: From Head Start to Universal Pre-Kindergarten. She received her PhD from Rutgers University.

Robert Rothman is senior editor at the Annenberg Institute for School Reform at Brown University and the editor of its quarterly journal, *Voices in Urban Education*. He was the editor of *City Schools: How Districts and Communities Can Create Smart Education* Systems. He received a BA from Yale University.

John L. Rury is a professor of education at the University of Kansas. His specialization is in the history of American education and education policy studies, especially concerning urban schools. He is the editor of *Urban Education in the United States: A Historical Reader*, and the co-editor, with William J. Reese, of *Rethinking the History of American Education: Essays on the Post-Revisionist Era and Beyond*. He received his PhD from the University of Wisconsin-Madison.

Tracy L. Steffes is an assistant professor of education and history at Brown University. Her research focuses on the history of American education, citizenship and civic inclusion, social and democratic theory and practice, state-building and state authority, politics, law, and social movements. She received her PhD from the University of Chicago.

Gail L. Sunderman is a senior research associate in K–12 Education for the Civil Rights Project at the University of California, Los Angeles. Her research focuses on educational policy and politics, and urban school reform, including the development and implementation of education policy and the impact of policy on the educational opportunities for at-risk students. At the Civil Rights Project, she is project director on a five-year study examining the implementation of the No Child Left Behind Act of 2001 and is coauthor of the book, *NCLB Meets School Realities: Lessons from the Field*. She is a former Fulbright scholar and received her PhD in political science from the University of Chicago.

Maris A. Vinovskis is the Bentley Professor of History, Research Professor at the Institute for Social Research, and Professor of Public Policy at the Gerald R. Ford School of Public Policy at the University of Michigan. He worked in the 1990s in the U.S. Department of Education on questions of educational research and policy, in both Republican and Democratic administrations. He is a member of the congressionally-mandated Independent Review Panel on No Child Left Behind. Vinovskis has published nine books, edited seven books, and written over 100 scholarly essays. His *From a Nation at Risk to No Child Left Behind: National Education Goals and Federal Education Policies from Ronald Reagan to George W. Bush* will be published in 2009. He received his PhD from Harvard University.

Kenneth K. Wong is the first Walter and Leonore Annenberg Professor for Education Policy and Professor of Education at Brown University. He is chairman of the Education Department and Director of the Master's in Urban Education Policy Program and is Professor of Education, Political Science and Public Policy. He received his PhD from the University of Chicago.

Index

THIS SERIES EXPLORES THE HISTORY OF SCHOOLS AND SCHOOLING in the United States and other countries. Books in this series examine the historical development of schools and educational processes, with special emphasis on issues of educational policy, curriculum and pedagogy, as well as issues relating to race, class, gender, and ethnicity. Special emphasis will be placed on the lessons to be learned from the past for contemporary educational reform and policy. Although the series will publish books related to education in the broadest societal and cultural context, it especially seeks books on the history of specific schools and on the lives of educational leaders and school founders.

For additional information about this series or for the submission of manuscripts, please contact the general editors:

Alan R. Sadovnik   Susan F. Semel
Rutgers University-Newark   The City College of New York, CUNY
Education Dept.   138th Street and Convent Avenue
155 Conklin Hall   NAC 5/208
175 University Avenue   New York, NY 10031
Newark, NJ 07102

To order other books in this series, please contact our Customer Service Department:

800-770-LANG (within the U.S.)
212-647-7706 (outside the U.S.)
212-647-7707 FAX

Or browse online by series at:

www.peterlang.com